The Macromolecular Chemistry of Gelatin

Molecular Biology

An International Series of Monographs and Textbooks

Edited by

BERNARD HORECKER
Albert Einstein College of Medicine
Yeshiva University
New York, New York

NATHAN O. KAPLAN
Graduate Department of Biochemistry
Brandeis University
Waltham, Massachusetts

HAROLD A. SCHERAGA
Department of Chemistry
Cornell University
Ithaca, New York

THE MACROMOLECULAR CHEMISTRY OF GELATIN

by

ARTHUR VEIS

Department of Biochemistry
Northwestern University
Chicago, Illinois

1964

ACADEMIC PRESS · NEW YORK AND LONDON

ACADEMIC PRESS INC.
111 Fifth Avenue
New York 3, N. Y.

United Kingdom Edition
Published by
ACADEMIC PRESS INC. (London) Ltd.
Berkeley Square House
Berkeley Square, London, W.1.

Library of Congress Catalog Card Number 64-15278

PRINTED IN THE UNITED STATES OF AMERICA

To Eve

Preface

Few manufactured items have as long a history of worldwide general use as gelatin. Yet, in spite of its ancient origin and the essential simplicity of both its preparation and use, gelatin is among the most poorly understood manufactured substances of commercial importance. This lack of understanding is not due to trade secrecy, though to be sure the various processors have their trade secrets, but rather is owing to the inherent complexity of the collagen-gelatin system.

The last serious efforts at correlating the vast amount of information about gelatin were made in the early 1920's by Bogue and by Alexander. Their reviews were appropriate because the pioneering researches of Loeb, Donnan, and other colloid and protein chemists had provided a sound basis for the interpretation of the colloidal properties of gelatin in terms of fundamental physical and chemical principles. Indeed, the initial experiments of many of the early protein physical chemists were carried out with gelatin since it was easy to prepare or obtain in supposedly purified form and it was readily soluble in water. However, many complications soon became evident, the most serious being that gelatins were not always the same, though prepared in the same manner, and were obviously different if prepared by different processing techniques. Furthermore, it was found that gelatin was not at all typical of the proteins, such as the enzymes, which seemed to be of more biological significance. Attention was therefore turned to other systems more representative of the globular proteins.

For many years there was no concerted research effort devoted to the gelatin system and even today there is relatively little work on gelatin specifically. Much of the new insight into the properties of gelatin has been gained through problems connected with work on collagen and on proteins and synthetic high polymers in general. There are many excellent books and reviews covering these latter topics, and Gustavson's recent monograph "The Chemistry and Reactivity of Collagen" provides a superb point of departure for this present volume.

Because of the availability of this background material, the properties of collagen have been reviewed in this monograph only insofar as they seem

vii

to have a bearing on the collagen-gelatin transition. The molecular characterization of proteins and polymers is described in detail in one chapter so that needless repetition and side excursions into methodology are not required in the subsequent discussions of the relationships between the preparative methods or properties and the molecular structure of the gelatins.

This monograph has two aims. The first is simply to analyze the outstanding attributes of the gelatins in terms of specific chemical or macromolecular structural features. The second objective is to point out those areas of study concerning the gelatins which may be used to further our understanding of the parent, biologically significant, collagen fiber systems and to indicate the gains that have been made in this area.

After years of neglect by the biochemists because of the supposed inertness of the collagen fibers, the study of collagen and gelatin has suddenly become respectable, and one consequence of this renewed (or new) interest is a flood of recent literature. Both because of this unceasing flow, and the fact that gelatin has been around so long, it is impossible to make the claim that this review is either complete or definitive. On the contrary, an attempt was made to be critical and selective, and only those works are discussed which appeared to be of help in organizing and understanding of the gelatins in terms of the current concepts of protein and polymer structure and behavior. Conclusions and correlations have been drawn from the data wherever it seemed appropriate, but the gaps and conflicts have also been explicitly delineated. In those cases where the author's interpretations differ from, extend, or modify the conclusions drawn by the original investigators it is clearly indicated that this is the case. In any event, the conclusions drawn will undoubtedly be subject to still further modification in future work.

The author is indebted to several people for their critical comments on the manuscript, Drs. Zachary Felsher, Walter Giffie, Thomas Donnelly, and Maurice Drake. Special thanks are due to Miss Joan Anesey for her help with the figures, to Miss Shirley Mussel, and to Mrs. Rosemary Wells who prepared the manuscript.

The author owes a much more than perfunctory note of thanks to his wife, Eve, for her unstinting labors in proofreading the entire text, in addition to her other, multitudinous, chores.

ARTHUR VEIS

February, 1964.

Contents

Chapter IV

The Degradation of Gelatin

Chapter V

The Gelatin ⟶ Collagen Transition

I

COLLAGEN

I. INTRODUCTION

During the course of this discussion the word "gelatin" will be defined and redefined in more and more precise terms as the base of the necessary background information is developed. At the outset the most general statement that can be made is that "the gelatins" are a class of proteinaceous substances that have no existence in nature but are derived from the parent protein, collagen, by any one of a number of procedures involving the destruction of the secondary structure of the collagen and, in most cases, some aspects of the primary and tertiary structures. The gelatins are the only degraded proteins that have excited much scientific interest. Originally this interest stemmed from the fact that the gelatins

1

have physical properties that make them useful materials of commerce. While this is still true, recent attention has been focused on the gelatins in terms of the information which a knowledge of their basic properties can contribute to the understanding of the biologically significant parent protein, collagen. Although one of the principal objectives of this monograph is to utilize data on the gelatins to expand our view of the organization of the collagens, we begin with a review of certain elements of what is known of the collagens. More detailed accounts are given in reviews by Gustavson (1) and Harrington and von Hippel (2).

Collagen is the principal proteinaceous component of the white fibrous connective tissues. These serve as the chief tensile stress-bearing elements for all mammals and fishes. Related proteins are found in many of the lower phyla (3). It has been estimated that collagen comprises about 30% of the total organic matter in mammals and nearly 60% of the protein content (3). Much of the collagen is localized in major tissues such as skin, tendon, and bone but collagen fibers pervade almost every organ and tissue. Because of this widespread distribution and function, fibers in the various tissues are organized macroscopically in different ways, are produced by different types of cell (fibroblasts, odontoblasts, osteoblasts), and are intimately associated with varying types and amounts of other substances. These differences in both "purity" and gross organization and structure are of considerable importance in terms of the nature of the gelatin that can be produced from a particular tissue collagen source, as well as of the behavior of the collagen itself. These effects will be considered in detail later. For the moment, however, these differences will be ignored and we will temporarily assume that the collagen under examination is pure, that is, free from all other proteins and noncollagenous impurities.

II. CHEMICAL COMPOSITION

Collagen is unique among the proteins because of its amino acid composition. It is the only mammalian protein containing large amounts of hydroxyproline and it is extraordinarily rich in glycine and proline. Hydroxylysine is also almost uniquely characteristic of collagen. The sulfur content of collagen is very low. Cysteine is notably absent and methionine is the only sulfur-containing amino acid. Two facts which stem directly from these statements are: first, that because of the high content of the imino (pyrrolidine ring) acids which have no hydrogen atom on the peptide bonds involving these residues, intramolecularly hydrogen-bond stabilized structures such as the α-helix cannot be formed; second, that disulfide bridges are not available to create the tertiary structure of the collagen system. The composition of a purified bovine corium collagen is given in Table I-1, along with the side-chain formulas of the amino acids. These data are expressed in two ways, in terms of the weight % of each residue, and in terms of the number of residues of each amino acid per 1000 total residues. This latter method is the more readily appreciated and will be used in the subsequent discussions. Since the average residue weight is close to 100 gm/mole, the value for residues per 1000 total residues is approximately equal to the number of residues per 10^5 gm collagen.

Although Table I-1 sets forth an explicit chemical composition, there is no guarantee that the corium collagen sample analyzed was uniform throughout. It appears that collagens can have a fairly wide range of compositions and still have the same overall physical structure. Table I-2 lists a number of analyses carried out by Eastoe (4, 5, 6) on collagens of varying origin. These data show, for example, that native collagens may range in glycine from 320 to 340 residues per 1000, and in hydroxyproline from 73 to 103 residues per 1000. On the basis of direct comparison of the compositions of several collagens and the gelatins derived from them, Eastoe (4) made the point that, except for the amide group and arginine residue content, the amino acid compositions of collagens and their gelatins were quite similar. The gelatins had a tendency to contain more of the amino acids present in the parent collagens in greatest amount, e.g. glycine and proline, and less of the amino acids present in the parent collagen in only small quantities (e.g. tyrosine, leucine, phenylalanine.

A. Ionic Functional Groups

The acidic and basic functional groups govern many of the physical properties of the collagen fiber, as well as determine the reactivity of collagen to acids, bases, and ionic reagents in general. In bovine corium collagen there is a total of 82 residues of basic groups per 1000 residues, including arginine, lysine, hydroxylysine, and histidine, and a total of 121 residues per 1000 residues of aspartic and glutamic acids. If the collagen is undegraded, or kept from the action of alkalis, about 44 residues of amide groups are also present. It has been estimated that there are approximately four asparagines to every glutamine residue (7, 8). In the native state, therefore, collagen bears a small excess of basic groups and, hence, should have a basic isoionic pH.

TABLE I-1 [a]

AMINO ACID COMPOSITION OF PURIFIED BOVINE CORIUM COLLAGEN

Amino acid (or other component)	% Weight (grams residue per 100 gm)	Residues (per 1000 total residues)	Structure of functional group
Lysine	3.40	24.8	NH_3^+—CH_2—CH_2—CH_2—CH_2—
Hydroxylysine	0.81	5.2	NH_3^+—CH—CH_2—CH_2—CH_2— OH
Histidine	0.70	4.8	N——CH HC C—CH_2— N
Arginine	7.98	47.9	NH C—NH—CH_2—CH_2—CH_2— NH_2
Aspartic Acid	5.81	47.3	O ‖ HO—C—CH_2—
Glutamic Acid	9.93	72.1	O ‖ HO—C—CH_2—CH_2—
Ammonia	0.74	41.8 [b]	O ‖ C—NH_2
Proline	13.36	129.0	H_2C——CH_2 O H_2C CH—C— N
Hydroxyproline	11.36	94.1	HOCH——CH_2 O H_2C CH—C— N
Serine	3.64	39.2	HO—CH_2—
Threonine	1.79	16.6	CH_3—CH— OH

Glycine	20.51	336.5	H_2-
Alanine	8.09	106.6	CH_3-
Valine	2.06	19.5	$\begin{matrix} CH_3 \\ \diagdown \\ CH- \\ \diagup \\ CH_3 \end{matrix}$
Methionine	0.55	3.9	$CH_3-S-CH_2-CH_2-$
Isoleucine	1.37	11.3	$\begin{matrix} CH_3-CH_2 \\ \diagdown \\ CH- \\ \diagup \\ CH_3 \end{matrix}$
Leucine	2.89	24.0	$\begin{matrix} CH_3 \\ \diagdown \\ CH-CH_2- \\ \diagup \\ CH_3 \end{matrix}$
Tyrosine	0.80	4.6	$HO-\bigcirc-CH_2-$
Phenylalanine	1.97	12.6	$\bigcirc-CH_2-$
Cysteine	0.00	0.0	$HS-CH_2-$
Glucosamine	0.00	0.0	(ring structure)
Hexose [c]	0.39	2.1[b]	(ring structure)
Nitrogen	18.00	—	—

[a] Data of Schlueter (116).
[b] Based on 1000 amino acid residues plus the specific component.
[c] Measured as anthrone glucose units.

TABLE I-2 [a]

COMPARATIVE ANALYSIS OF COLLAGENS FROM DIFFERENT SOURCES

Amino acid	Residues/1000						
	Ox skin	Ox skin soluble collagen	Lungfish skin	Sturgeon swim bladder	Ox bone	Human bone	Wallaby tendon
Lysine	25.7	24.0	24.2	21.8	26 2	28.0	24.6
Hydroxylysine	6.6	7.8	5.3	10.7	6.4	3.5	8.0
Histidine	4.3	1.9	5.1	4.8	5.8	5.8	5.1
Arginine	44.7	47.1	51.0	52.4	49.0	47.1	51.1
Aspartic Acid	49.4	44.6	48.6	47.5	49.8	47.0	49.3
Glutamic Acid	71.5	73.7	78.9	70.5	75.8	72.2	73.0
Ammonia [b]	(44.0)	(36.3)	(46 8)	(41.0)	(41.8)	(37.3)	(44.4)
Proline	118.6	111.3	126.0	102.2	118 8	123.4	119.1
Hydroxyproline	92.6	102.3	73.1	82.0	100.8	100.2	92.8
Serine	38.4	39.7	43 7	50.5	37.8	35.9	39.0
Threonine	18.0	18.2	26.1	29.2	19.7	18.4	20.1
Glycine	335	341	311	337	314	319	320
Alanine	109.7	115.1	128.0	118.9	109.7	113.5	112.5
Valine	19.9	19.0	21.3	18.0	21.2	23.6	23.2
Methionine	6.2	5.1	4.0	8.8	5.1	5.3	6.6
Isoleucine	13.5	10.4	12.2	11.4	12.3	13.3	8.9
Leucine	26.9	24.0	25.2	17.7	27.9	25.5	26.3
Tyrosine	5.1	2.8	1.1	2.4	2.9	4.5	4.1
Phenylalanine	13.4	11.8	15.3	14.1	16.3	13.9	16.0
Nitrogen	18.6	17.7	18.2	18.5	18.3	18.5	18.3

[a] Data of Eastoe and Leach (6).

[b] Based on 1000 amino acid residues plus the specific component.

There has been considerable discussion as to the location and significance of the isoelectric and isoionic pH's of collagen and gelatin. Since these terms will be referred to frequently in subsequent discussions it may be worthwhile to state the definitions of these terms in the sense in which they are to be used. The definitions are operational, that is, they are in terms of the particular experimental procedures used to determine the pH values. Alberty (9) has stated these as follows. The protein obtained from a solution, thoroughly dialyzed, that contains no noncolloidal ions other than hydrogen of hydroxyl is called the *isoionic material*. The isoionic point (pI) is the pH of a solution of the isoionic material in water, or in a solution of another solute which does not produce hydrogen or hydroxyl ions when dissolved in water alone. In contrast to this definition, which specifies nothing with regard to the net charge on the protein, the isoelectric point (IEP) is the pH of a buffer of specified composition in which no net migration of the protein is produced by application of an electric field.

From these definitions it is clear that both pI and IEP depend on the ionic strength of the nonproteinaceous solutes also present and on their specific character, as well as on the protein concentration. The isoelectric and isoionic pH's of a protein seldom coincide even when determined at the same ionic concentrations of the same neutral salt. Furthermore, neither the pI nor IEP necessarily coincides with zero net charge on the protein. The pI, if not too far removed from neutrality and if determined at low ionic strength, provides important information which should be determined for the analysis of titration curves.

By electrophoretic mobility determinations at low buffer concentration, Highberger found that the IEP of native collagen was 7.8 (10, 11). Similar studies at higher ionic strength ($\sim 0.02 \, N$) yielded an IEP value of 7 (12). Collagens exposed to alkalis for very long times have IEP's closer to 5.0, the shift depending on the temperature and duration of the treatment (12, 13). Cassel and McKenna (14) and Cassel, McKenna, and Glime (15) showed that the shift in IEP resulted from the removal of a portion of the amide nitrogen. They found that there were no other significant differences in the amino acid composition of collagen, hide powder (limed collagen), or the corresponding gelatins that could account for the IEP shift. Courts (16), however, has demonstrated that a decided increase in amino-terminal groups, indicating peptide bond cleavage, does accompany the alkaline treatment of collagen.

The location of the pI is difficult to determine in a heterogeneous system, such as collagen fiber plus solvent, and no experimental data are available. However, Janus, Kenchington, and Ward (17) firmly established the pI of acid-precursor gelatins at pH 9.0–9.2. In view of the fact that the acid-precursor gelatins have the same functional group analyses as native collagen (4, 16), the pI of native collagen should also be about 9.0. Electrophoretic mobility studies on acid-soluble collagen (18, 19) indicated an IEP of 5.8, but Veis et al. (20) established that the discrepancy and variation in pI and IEP values were due to the binding of small ions by the collagen. Unfortunately, the role of small ions has never been sufficiently stressed in discussions of the variation in behavior and properties of collagen fibers with pH and solvent composition. Collagen fibers have a pronounced affinity for even monovalent inorganic ions. Since the pI of both acid-precursor gelatins and native collagen is shifted to the acid side by the addition of dilute 1:1 salts to salt-free collagen systems, cations must be bound preferentially. We shall return to this problem in the chapters dealing with the titration and swelling behavior of gelatins.

B. Hydroxyamino Acids

The neutral hydroxyamino acids, hydroxyproline, serine, threonine, and tyrosine, account for a total of 154 residues per 1000 residues in bovine corium collagen, nearly as many as the total of free acidic and basic groups in the native collagen. Tyrosine, which occurs to only a small extent, ~ 5 residues per 1000, in most native collagens, has been the subject of many arguments in the literature. Data such as that of Eastoe (4), which show a depletion of the tyrosine content of gelatins as compared with the parent collagen, have been used as the basis of a claim that there was a tyrosine-rich impurity in the collagen. Russell (21) claimed to have isolated 10–15% of a tyrosine-rich, hydroxyproline-poor fraction from various gelatin preparations by chromatography on Amberlite IRC-50 columns. Leach (22) was unable to confirm this result and, in a very careful study, was able to isolate only a very small fraction, 0.36% of the gelatin, of a mucoprotein by similar chromatography. Hydroxyproline was present in very small amounts in this mucoprotein fraction, but the tyrosine content was only of the order of ~ 15 residues per 1000 amino acid residues and this could not account for the tyrosine content of the purified collagens. Steven and Tristram (23) also claim to have isolated a noncollagenous fraction in an amount corresponding to about 2% of the total protein nitrogen from acid-soluble collagen. Paper chromatographic analyses indicated that this noncollagenous fraction was a mixture of free amino acids and three fairly long polypeptides. Approximately 35% of the free amino acids were serines and the peptides were also relatively rich in serine. Tyrosine was found in the free amino acid fraction but not in the peptide fraction. Again, however, the tyrosine content of these amino acid impurities is not sufficient to account for the tyrosine content of the collagen preparations. From her examination of varied analyses, Deasy (24) concluded that some tyrosine was an integral part of the collagen molecule.

Although the tyrosine content of collagen is low, the question of its presence is more than academic. Bensusan and Hoyt (25) and Hodge et al. (26) have shown convincingly that the tyrosine residues play an important role in the aggregation properties of the soluble collagens. A special role for serine and threonine has not been demonstrated, but it is likely that these residues may have an important effect on the properties of dentine and other hard tissue collagens (27).

Gustavson (*1, 28-34*) has discussed the possible relationship between the hydrothermal stability of collagen and the hydroxyl group content of collagens in great detail. From comparative composition data on collagens of varying origin, particularly that of Takahashi and Tanaka (*35*), Gustavson showed that of the serine, threonine, and hydroxyproline, only the hydroxyproline varied in content in direct relationship to the shrinkage temperature (T_s) of the fibers. From this and other supporting evidence he postulated an interchain hydrogen bond between the hydroxyl group of the hydroxyproline on one peptide chain and the carbonyl group of a peptide linkage on an adjacent chain:

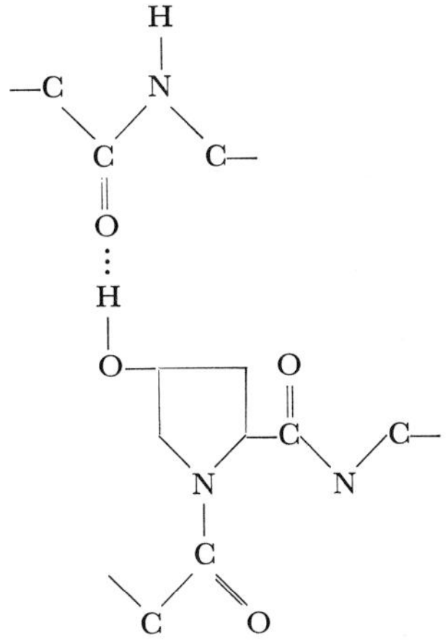

Gustavson then concluded that these hydrogen bonds involving hydroxyproline play the same role in stabilizing the collagen fiber as the disulfide bonds of cystine do in stabilizing keratin. Esipova (*36*) and Doty and Nishihara (*37*) in studies of soluble collagen showed that in acid-soluble collagen in solution, the same connection between hydroxyproline content and denaturation temperature existed as between hydroxyproline content and T_s in the intact fiber. These workers concluded that some of the hydrogen bonds involving hydroxyproline are intramolecular rather than intermolecular. Better correlations between composition and hydrothermal stability of collagen fibers or between composition and denaturation temperature of acid-soluble collagens have been made by considering the total pyrrolidine ring content (*38, 39*). The stabilization of collagen by mechanisms concerning the proline and hydroxyproline residues will be examined in details in Chapter V. The specific role of the hydroxyl group of hydroxyproline in establishing the properties of the collagens is at present unknown. It has not been established that the hydroxyl group of serine, threonine, or hydroxyproline participates in any type of hydrogen bond between peptide chain units.

C. Nonpolar Residues

An examination of composition data such as that given in Tables I-1 and 2 reveals a further interesting point. Nearly 45% of the residues of collagen are either glycine or alanine. This is almost 3 times the proportion found in other proteins, except for silk fibroin and elastin (40). These two amino acids are nonpolar, yet they can contribute little to nonpolar inter-molecular van der Waals interactions or to hydrophobic bonding because of their small size. Ramachandran et al. (41), however, point out that the glycine content is particularly crucial in determining the structure of the peptide strands in collagen. They state that a definite requirement for a protein to be in the collagen class is that glycine must account for close to one-third of all the amino acid residues.

D. Nonprotein Components

In addition to the peptide or amino acid impurities or components indicated by Steven and Tristram (23), very highly purified collagens contain a small amount of simple sugars that cannot be removed by non-degradative extraction. Hörmann (42) has shown that the hexose in acid-soluble collagen is glucose, whereas in insoluble collagen both glucose and galactose were found. Hörmann reported a value of 3.8 glucose units per 1000 amino acid residues in acid-soluble collagen and a total of 3.5 glucose and galactose moieties in collagen fibers. Hörmann (42) and Gallop et al. (43) consider these hexose components as being an integral part of the collagen structure. Highberger et al. (44) also found glucose and galactose to be the principal carbohydrate moieties in acid-soluble collagen. In addition they report that another soluble collagen, the neutral-salt-soluble fraction, contains mannose, fucose, rhamnose, and ribose as essential, or at least as firmly bound, components.

III. THE SHORT-RANGE ORGANIZATION OF COLLAGEN

The configuration of the peptide chains in collagen has been deduced from analyses of the wide-angle x-ray diffraction patterns of collagen fibers. The most characteristic features of the fiber diffraction pattern are a strong meridional arc at 2.86 Å, an equatorial diffuse half-halo at 4.6 Å, and an equatorial spot at 10 Å. The meridional reflection arises from a repeat distance along the fiber axis, while the equatorial spacings relate to distances transverse to the fiber axis. Historical reviews of the interpretation of these fiber diagrams have been given by Bear (3), Low (45), and Harrington and von Hippel (2), along with more general discussions on the significance of x-ray diffraction data. The reader is referred to these reviews for background information.

The generally accepted interpretation of the diffraction pattern of collagen fiber arose from the work of Ramachandran (46-49), who suggested that the 2.86 Å reflection did not refer to a repeat distance along a single polypeptide chain, but described a repeat unit in a system of coiled coils formed by three left-handed chains winding in a right-handed sense around a common axis. The direction of the screw is defined by looking at the screw from the top along a line coinciding with the direction of the screw axis. The sense of the screw is given by the direction in which the screw is coiled from the bottom. Thus, a left-handed screw is one which appears to climb in a clockwise fashion, while a right-handed screw is anticlockwise. Similarly, the direction of a left-handed screw is referred to as "minus" while a right-handed screw proceeds in the "plus" direction.

Ramachandran's views were verified and extended by Cowan et al. (50, 51), Bear (52), and Crick and Rich (53-56). We shall follow the description and nomenclature given by Rich and Crick (56).

Two very similar structures, I and II, appear to be compatible with the x-ray diffraction evidence. Both structures consist of three separate peptide chains, coiled along a left-handed threefold screw axis. That is, each residue takes one $-120°$ around the axis, or three residues complete one turn. The pitch of each coil is such that the three residues complete their turn in about 9 Å. The three chains are put together with their axes parallel and aligned so that a translation perpendicular to the axis of any one chain takes one to a similar site on either of the neighboring chains. Every third peptide group along each chain will be in an identical environment, either near the middle of the group of three chains or near the outside. When the chains are properly oriented, as in native collagen, the third NH group on the backbone of one chain can make a hydrogen bond with every third $C=O$ group on the backbone of a neighboring chain. The difference between the I and II structures is in the positions between which hydrogen bonds can be formed; the same number of hydrogen bonds can be formed in either case. If the peptide bond which is always near the center of the triple-chain group is called position 1 and the next two peptide groups up the chain 2 and 3, respectively, then collagen I is that arrangement of chains in which the hydrogen bonds are between the NH of the residue in position 1 and the C=O of the residue in position 1 on the neighboring chain. Collagen II is the arrangement in which the hydrogen on the peptide nitrogen of the residue in position 1 on each chain is linked to the carbonyl group in position 2 on the neighboring chain. If the two structures are viewed from the carboxyl ends (the top of the helix in the usual convention) the —N—H···O links in collagen I point in a counter-clockwise direction while in collagen II they are directed in a clockwise fashion. Figure I-1 illustrates the chain backbone arrangements viewed

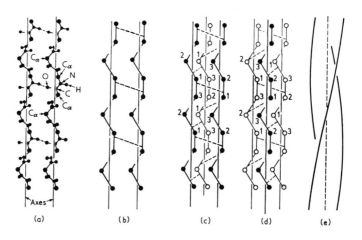

Fig. I-1. Chain backbone arrangements in polyglycine II and related collagen structures based on the single hydrogen-bond model.

(a) Two strands of polyglycine, with black dots representing various atoms and dashed lines as hydrogen bonds. (b) Two chains of the polyglycine II lattice in which only the C_a atoms and hydrogen bonds are shown. (c) The third chain shown with open circles lies behind the two shown in (b) to make a collagen I arrangement. The numbers indicate the phasing of the residues on the polypeptide chains. (d) The third chain is added in front of the two in (b). The chain in front is shown by solid lines. This gives rise to the collagen II model. (e) Solid lines represent the axes around which the polyglycine chains are coiled. These axes are gently coiled around each other in the collagen molecule [Rich and Crick (56)].

parallel to the fiber axis, and Fig. I-2 shows the top view for each structure. In each set of three residues at a similar site in each chain, it is clear that only one-third of the potential hydrogen bonds can be formed. Rich and Crick (56) pointed out that the two structures differ in the way in which the chains are "phased" with respect to each other. Structure II can be created from structure I merely by rotating each individual chain about its own axis by about 60°.

When more than the bare backbone peptide-chain configurations are considered, then it becomes necessary to deform the chains so that they are no longer parallel but, as illustrated in Fig. I-1 e, wind about each other in a gentle right-handed spiral. A rotation of —108° takes one from a residue on one chain to a similar residue on the next chain and a rotation of —324° takes one back to the original chain. The translation in the —108° operation is 2.86 Å and the complete rotation requires a translation of 8.58 Å in the direction of the right-handed composite screw axis.

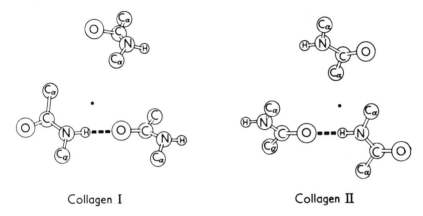

Collagen I   Collagen II

Fig. I-2. An axial projection of a segment of the two single hydrogen-bond collagen models. The dot in the center represents the axis of the molecule. Three peptide groups are shown. The dashed line represents a hydrogen bond [Rich and Crick (56)].

Sequence studies (57, 58) indicate that the collagen structure must be able to accomodate the series Gly·Pro·Hypro·Gly. Both proposed structures can be made to fit this sequence, but position 1, that involving the residue with its peptide bond closest to the helix axis, must be glycine in both structures, and structure I cannot accept hydroxyproline in position 3 without deformation. This restriction is not required in structure II. Table I-3, taken from Rich and Crick (56), lists the possible side-chain positions. Since structure II can be built with the least deformation it is considered to be the most likely structure, but the existence of structure I cannot be ruled out on these grounds. Figure I-3 shows the bond distances and angles in the Gly·Pro·Hypro sequence in the collagen II structure, along with the hydrogen bond and van der Waals contact distances in a pair of chains.

TABLE I-3

REQUIREMENTS FOR THE SIDE-CHAIN POSITIONS
IN THE TWO SINGLE HYDROGEN-BOND STRUCTURES OF RICH AND CRICK [a]

Position	Collagen I		Collagen II
	Undeformed	Deformed	
1	Glycine only	Other residues may be possible; Pro or Hypro impossible	Must be glycine
2	Any residue including Pro and Hypro		Any residue including Pro and Hypro
3	Glycine only	Any residue, including Pro and Hypro, except valine and isoleucine	Any residue including Pro and Hypro
Bonding of the OH of Hypro in position 3	—	*Can* make a hydrogen bond to the neighboring chain within the group of three	Sticks out radially away from the structure and *cannot* make a hydrogen bond *within* the group of three chains

[a] Rich and Crick (56).

In the last row of Table I-3, Rich and Crick emphasize one clear difference between the two structures. In structure I the hydroxyl group of each of the hydroxyproline residues points toward the center of the three-chain unit, whereas these hydroxyl groups point radially outward (see Fig. I-3 b) in structure II. Thus hydrogen bonds can be formed within a chain triad in structure I but only between chain triads in structure II. Another possible stabilizing hydrogen bond might be between a polar side chain and one of the non-hydrogen-bonded backbone peptide groups. Such bonds could not be formed within a chain triad by aspartic acid, asparagine, serine, or threonine side chains, but models showed that such bonds were possible with the side chains of glutamic acid, glutamine, lysine, or arginine. It was also observed (56) that arginine side chains on one triad could form a pair of hydrogen bonds with two adjacent carbonyl groups on the backbone of one of the chains of an adjoining set of three. The arginine residues may thus play an unusually important role in the stabilization of the collagen structure.

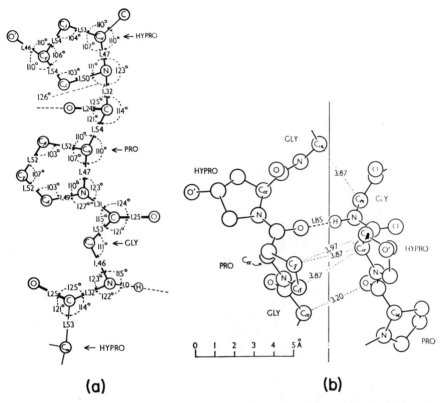

(a)   **(b)**

FIG. I-3. (a) A diagram (*not* to scale) of the bond angles and distances in the Rich and
Crick collagen II structure for the repeating tripeptide sequence Gly·Pro·Hypro.   (b) A
projection of two of the chains of collagen II to show the van der Waals contacts between
chains. In this diagram it can be seen that in this model the proline and hydroxyproline
rings on adjacent chains lie more or less parallel to each other in van der Waals contact
[Rich and Crick (*56*)].

Rich and Crick (*56*) clearly prefer the collagen II structure, of which a
space-filling model is shown in Fig. I-4 for the Gly·Pro·Hypro sequence,
but point out that since the deformations required to form collagen I are
relatively slight, the collagen I structure cannot be ruled out. It is possible
that both collagens I and II may exist within a fiber and Esipova (*36*)
and Doty and Nishihara (*37*) have suggested that acid-soluble collagen
may have the collagen I configuration with intramolecular hydrogen bonding involving the hydroxyl groups on hydroxyproline. The current state of
affairs with regard to the structure of collagen should not, however, be
considered as merely requiring a choice between the I and II structures.

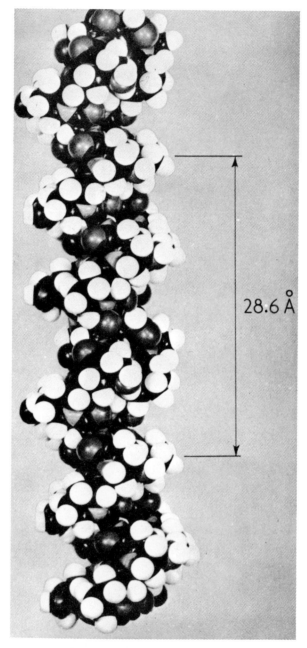

28.6 Å

FIG. I-4. A space-filling model of the sequence Gly·Pro·Hypro according to the single hydrogen-bond collagen II model. Note the helical groove resulting from the lack, of a side chain at every third glycine position [Rich and Crick (56)].

A very detailed reexamination of the diffraction data has lead Ramachandran and his co-workers (*41, 59-61*) to propose a revision of the structure, in which two hydrogen bonds, rather than one, can be established between each set of three amino acid residues. The structure is illustrated schematically in Fig. I-5. This type of doubled hydrogen bonding requires distortion of each peptide chain to a small extent from the ideal bond

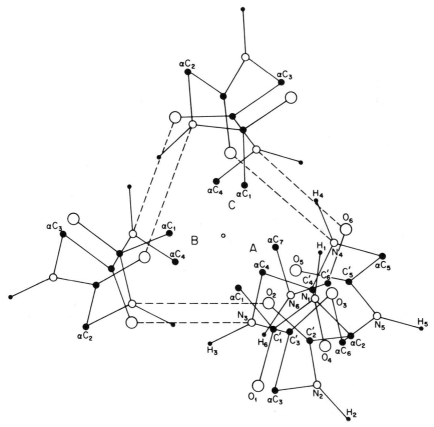

FIG. I-5. A projection of the doubly hydrogen-bonded collagen structure with a residue repeat of 2.95 Å and a twist of 30° for every three residues [Ramachandran *et al.* (*41*)].

distances and angles, but Ramachandran *et al.* (*41*) argue that these distortions are all of permissible magnitude and lead to a unique collagen II type of coiled coil, thus eliminating the I-II structure ambiguity.

The hydrogen bond distances in the doubly hydrogen-bonded structure are about 3.0 Å as compared to the more usually quoted value of ∼ 2.8 Å (*59*). These longer hydrogen bonds must therefore be relatively weak.

This is supported by the fact that the N—H stretching frequency absorption maximum is shifted to lower values in collagen as compared with the frequency absorption maximum in synthetic polypeptides in the α-helical form (62).

A further comment appears to be in order. Consideration of the amino acid compositions of different collagens (as in Table I-2) clearly shows that the amount of proline and hydroxyproline in various collagens, all of which give the characteristic x-ray diffraction pattern with a pronounced 2.86 Å spacing, is not constant. Hence, within certain limits the chain configurations and coiling are independent of the composition. Furthermore, whereas sequence studies indicate that Gly·Pro·Hypro occurs frequently, there are too few proline and hydroxyproline residues to be distributed evenly in this fashion among the three chains or along each chain in the coiled coil (63). Grassmann et al., (64) have isolated large peptide fragments poor in hydroxyproline. This means that certain other chains or chain segments must have more than their share of at least this amino acid. This concept fits naturally into the doubly hydrogen-bonded structure of Ramachandran et al. (41). Since the proline and hydroxyproline residues cannot form hydrogen bonds at their nitrogen positions, the sequence Gly·Pro·Hypro cannot be accommodated in more than one chain of the triad at any particular level of residue repeats. Ramachandran et al. suggest that all of the sequences Gly·Pro·Hypro are in a single peptide chain, though glycine, proline, and hydroxyproline residues may appear in the other chains. An equally likely prospect may be that the Gly·Pro·Hypro sequences occur in different positions in each of the three chains, so that they may differ in overall sequence but not in net content of proline and hydroxyproline. The crucial amino acid is glycine. It must appear at every third peptide site in the doubly hydrogen-bonded system structure.

IV. The Long-Range Organization of Collagen

The wide-angle x-ray diffraction patterns depict collagen in terms of long intertwined filaments. The packing of these filaments is revealed by small-angle x-ray diffraction patterns, characteristic of long repeat dimensions, and by direct electron-optical observations.

The ideal small-angle fiber diagram would be a series of spots centered on the meridian. However, because the macroscopic specimens necessarily used contain many filaments not in perfectly parallel array, the spots broaden to lines or arcs centered on the meridional row line. A typical small-angle collagen diffraction pattern is shown in Fig. I-6. The pattern is that of dried stretched kangaroo tail tendon. Since these small-angle layer lines were found to arise from a single set of diffractions, Bear and his co-workers (3) considered the collagen fibril to correspond to a one-dimensional diffractor. That is, the only periodic regularity extended in the

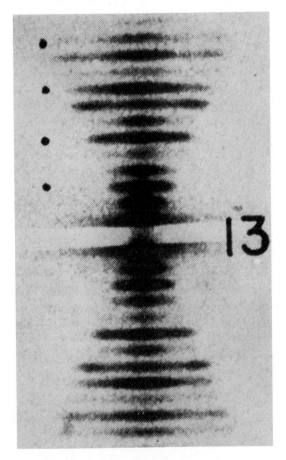

Fɪɢ. I-6. The small-angle x-ray diffraction diagram of dry stretched kangaroo tail tendon. This diagram exhibits the typical "fanned" appearance [Bear (3)].

direction of the fibril axis and there was no ordered distribution of diffracting units normal to the fibril axis. Since each layer line was straight, rather than arced, and extended normal to the pattern meridian, the stretching process must have rendered all of the fibrils into an effectively parallel array. The separation between layer lines, inversely proportional to the axial repeat dimension, was constant and corresponded to an average axial periodicity of 600–660 Å, depending on the pretreatment of the collagen specimen.

A perfect well-organized one-dimensional diffractor, such as a cylindrical fibril, would be expected to yield a diagram with each layer line of constant length. Since the higher order lines lengthen, giving the diagram a "fanned" appearance, a smaller portion of the fibril cross section is able to contribute to each line as smaller structural details are examined. Thus, the line spreading clearly indicates that there is internal distortion within each fibril, but that this is relatively small since there are no large increments in length from line to line. To account for these observations, Bear suggested that the macroscopic fibril was composed on much thinner filaments, or protofibrils, each of which contained along it specifically ordered chemical and structural variations. Within the fibril the protofibrils must be adjusted axially so that equivalent structural details match transversely across the entire fibrillar cross section.

Electron microscopy supplemented these early observations. Collagen fibers shadowed with chromium or other metals showed a very characteristic repeat spacing of about 640 Å, and the fibrils had a banded or striated appearance with the bands apparently being thicker than the interband regions (65-67). A typical shadowed collagen fiber electron micrograph is shown in Fig. I-7.

Bear suggested that the alternations of band and interband regions were the result of periodic alternations in chemical composition along the protofibrillar axis, with the forces of attraction between portions of adjacent

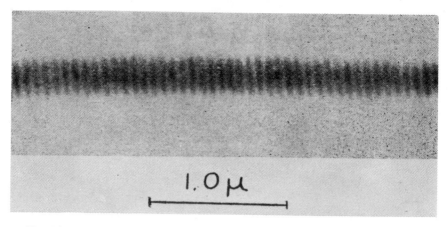

1.0 μ

FIG. I-7. Electron microscopic appearance of a shadowed native collagen fibril demonstrating the major periodicity [Hall *et al.* (67)]

protofibrils varying accordingly, with some regions being more perfectly matched than others. He proposed that the more perfectly matched cross sections of high order give rise to the "interbands" while the less well-matched segments give rise to the distorted and imperfect "band" regions. As electron microscopy techniques and instrumentation improved, more and more detail has been observed in the form of characteristic subperiodic striations in native fibers and in aggregates precipitated from solution (*68-71*). The import of these observations can be more fully appreciated, however, after considering the evidence relating to a basic macromolecular unit common to all collagenous proteins.

V. Basic Macromolecular Unit of Collagen

A. Acid-Soluble Collagen: Tropocollagen

Zachariades (*72*) was the first to observe that some collagen would dissolve in cold dilute acetic acid solutions from acid-swollen collagen fibers. Much later Nageotte (*73-78*) observed that upon dialyzing the acid from such solutions fibers were reformed. After Orekhovitch *et al.* (*79*) demonstrated that soluble collagen could be obtained from any collagen, and in particularly large amounts from tissues of young animals, interest was centered on this soluble collagen as the probable biological precursor of the insoluble collagen fibrils. At about the same time Schmitt, Gross and Highberger began their electron microscope studies of the soluble collagens that led them to outstanding success in elucidating the nature and properties of the macromolecule that is now thought to be the fundamental molecular unit of all collagens (*68-71*).

At sufficiently low concentration, the soluble collagen exists in cold dilute organic acid solutions in the form of long thin rods about 3000 Å in length and 16 Å in diameter (*80-82*). These dimensions were deduced by Boedtker and Doty (*80*) from a physicochemical investigation of solutions of acid-soluble collagen and were then confirmed electron-optically by Hall (*81*) and Hall and Doty (*82*). Hall developed a method of sample preparation in which a dilute solution of the material to be examined is sprayed on a freshly created mica surface. The solution is allowed to dry and the surface is shadowed lightly with platinum at a very low shadowing angle. A layer of collodion is spread over the platinum film. Next, the collodion and its adhering platinum layer is stripped from the mica, deposited on a grid, and viewed in a high resolution electron microscope. In this way direct micrographs of soluble collagen rodlets have been obtained. The rodlets shown in Fig. I-8 have a weight-average length of 2820 Å and diameter of about 15 Å.

These molecular dimensions for the basic macromolecular unit were in excellent agreement with the proposal of Gross et al. (70) that the collagen molecule was a rod 4 times the length of the major repeat distance in the native collagen arrangement. This conclusion was based on the extensive subperiodicity revealed in the native collagen fiber when electron-

Fig. I-8. An electron micrograph of single ichthyocol tropocollagen molecules prepared by the spray technique. The particle widths, obtained from the shadow lengths, are about 15 Å. Magnification × 70,000 [Hall and Doty (82)].

dense stains, such as phosphotungstic acid (PTA) or uranyl nitrate, were used in place of the metal shadowing technique. The wealth of details is indicated in Fig. I-9, which shows a native-type fiber obtained from acid-soluble collagen precipitated by dialysis against tap water and stained with PTA (Hodge and Schmitt, 83). As Bear had anticipated, equivalent basic regions were matched transversely in register throughout the fibril. The negative functional groups, located by use of the cationic uranyl ion, were similarly matched along the fibril axis. Equally important was the observation that the subperiod spacing was not symmetric; the arrangement of basic structure elements was clearly polarized or asymmetric. When the acid-soluble collagen was precipitated from solution by the addition of adenosine triphosphate (ATP), macroscopic fibers did not ap-

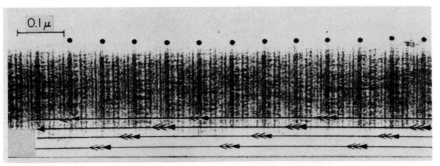

FIG. I-9. Native-type collagen fibers precipitated from solutions of acid-soluble collagen and stained with phosphotungstic acid (PTA) [Hodge and Schmitt (83)].

pear. The precipitate had a spool-like appearance (Fig. I-10). This form of precipitate was called segment-long-spacing (SLS) collagen The SLS spools were 2800–3000 Å in length and were also asymmetric in terms of the subperiodicities. A third form of precipitate, called fibrous-long-spacing (FLS) collagen, was obtained when highly charged negative polyelectrolytes, such as α-1 acid glycoprotein, were added to the acid solutions. The FLS fibers had a major repeat distance of ∼ 2800 Å, but the sub-banding was symmetric within each 2800 Å segment.

Schmitt and his co-workers interpreted these various patterns of organization of collagen as arising from different mechanisms of ordering of a single type of macromolecular monomer unit. Since each of the forms could be reversibly converted from one state to another, and especially to the native state with the 700 Å main spacing, the monomer unit was named tropocollagen (TC) (collagen-former). Since the SLS form is asymmetric in its sub-banding, the TC monomer unit must also be asymmetric or polarized. This polarization arises from the distribution of amino acid residues in the polypeptide chains. It seems evident that the picture drawn by Bear (3) of successive groupings of polar and nonpolar amino acid side chains is reflected even in the monomer unit. Thus, the polypeptide chains themselves are not uniform in average properties along reasonably long sequence sections. According to Schmitt (84), the SLS mode of packing of the TC monomers is most reflective of the properties of the monomer units. In the SLS form the TC monomers are organized so that each TC molecule is polarized in the same direction, and the interband pattern of varying polarity is thus a "fingerprint" of the variations in amino acid residues along the TC backbone.

The arrangement of TC units in the native fiber was deduced by Hodge and Schmitt (83) to be that of a staggered array in which adjacent TC units were shifted, in any particular plane, through a fibril perpendicular to the fiber axis, by one quarter of their length. The heavy staining end

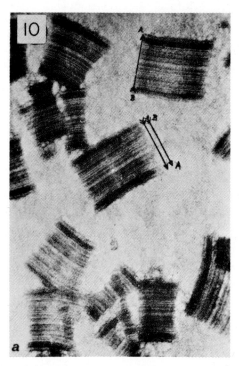

FIG. I-10. The segment-long-spacing form of collagen prepared by precipitation of acid-soluble collagen with ATP and staining with PTA. The direction of the arrows indicates the orientation of the individual TC rods within the SLS spools [Hodge and Schmitt (83)].

regions of each monomer unit were thus aligned at 700 Å intervals to give to the native 700 Å periodicity. The merging of the TC units into the native fiber is beautifully illustrated in Fig. I-11, where SLS segments are shown to be isomorphous with the native arrangement. Recently Petruska and Hodge (85) have reexamined the SLS and nature forms by higher resolution electron microscopy, and concluded that in the native structure the TC units are not linked end-to-end but that holes appear, about 0.6 of a 700 Å repeat distance in length, between ends. The TC units are thought to be 3000 Å in length, so that there is a staggered end-region overlap of ∼ 280 Å which causes the 700 Å spacing to appear.

The physicochemical measurements described earlier (*80*) indicated that the TC unit was composed of three peptide chains. The dimensions of the ordered part of the three chain unit matched those predicted by the electron microscope and x-ray diffraction evidence. However, the weights and hence the lengths of the three chains were not found to be equal, and this suggested to Boedtker and Doty the possibility that the

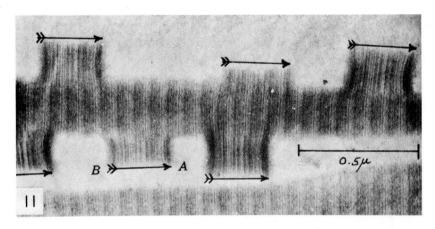

Fig. I-11. A coprecipitate or "dimorphic" ordered aggregate of TC, produced by exposing reconstituted native-type fibrils to a solution containing TC macromolecules and ATP at a pH value favoring the formation of SLS-type aggregates. Most of the segments formed under these conditions occur as outgrowths from the native-type fibrils and always exhibit a characteristic orientation and polarity with respect to the "polarized" band-pattern of the native-type fibrils. Stained with PTA. × 74,000 [Hodge and Schmitt (*83*)].

three-stranded TC unit had freely dangling single chains at one or both ends. Hodge and Schmitt (*86*), following a study of sonic degradation on the ability of collagen fragments to reaggregate in their various forms, concluded that the normal mode of end-to-end polymerization of TC monomers involved the coiling of these free terminal chains about each other to form highly ordered, possibly helical, structures. This thesis must be reevaluated in view of the work of Petruska and Hodge (*85*) but, as will be seen, the end regions of the TC monomer units may be of very special importance in controlling the mode of aggregation of the TC units, and in modifying the properties of the intact fiber.

B. Other Soluble Collagens

Both the wide-angle x-ray diffraction pattern and the appearance of fibers viewed with the aid of the electron microscope are essentially independent of the source of the collagen examined, indicating that the basic peptide-chain configurations and the manner of packing of the TC monomer units into the fiber are identical in all collagens. Yet collagen fibers from different sources have different tensile strengths and melting or denaturation temperatures; even more important, the fibers are of varying solubility and vary in their resistance to conversion to gelatin. These observations suggest that there is an additional type of molecular organization imposed on the basic array of oriented TC macromolecular units within the collagen fibril.

The problem of superorganization is not limited to differences between collagen fibers from different species, from different individuals of the same species, or from different tissues of the same individual. There is a large amount of data clearly showing that all of the monomer units cannot be extracted from a single collagen fibril with equal ease, or with the same solvent. This can be seen most clearly by considering some experiments carried out by Mazurov and Orekhovich (87).

The essential experiment consisted of equilibrating rat tail tendon collagen with successive fresh portions of an acid buffer solution of constant composition. The amount of collagen dissolved was determined at uniform 24-hour intervals. The rate of solubilization in citric acid, pH 3.4, as shown in curve 1 of Fig. I-12, decreased steadily. This behavior is typical of the

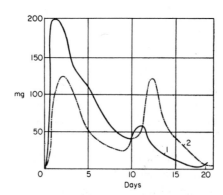

Fig. I-12. The extractability of acid-soluble collagen from rat tail tendons as a function of time. Curve 1: extraction by citrate for 9 days followed by extraction with acetic acid. Curve 2: extraction by acetic acid for 9 days followed by extraction with citric acid [Mazurov and Orekhovich (87)].

extraction of a single component from a mixture of other insoluble substances. When very little more collagen would dissolve in the citrate buffer, Mazurov and Orekhovich began to equilibrate the still insoluble collagen with an acetic acid buffer of the same ionic strength and pH. The amount extracted rose sharply, as indicated by the second maximum in curve 1, and then fell off with successive equilibrations. One could argue from this experiment that the acetate ion merely had a stronger solubilizing effect than the citrate ions and that, if one had started with the acetic acid extractions first, the initial rate of solubilization would have been much higher, while the citrate would not have extracted any additional soluble collagen. This was not the case, however, since such experiments, with the order of esposure of the collagen to the acids reversed, duplicated the original data, as shown in Fig. I-12, curve 2, retaining the two maxima.

These simple but significant experiments lead one inescapably to conclude either that two different molecular species have been extracted from the same fiber, or that similar molecules were bonded differently into the common structure.

Mazurov and Orekhovich (87) found that the two soluble collagens were identical in physicochemical behavior, that is, they had the same sedimentation coefficients, the same intrinsic viscosities and optical rotatory power, and the same denaturation temperature. Amino acid analyses also revealed no significant differences between the overall compositions of these soluble collagens. Furthermore, electron microscope examinations of precipitates showed that both soluble collagens could be reassembled by the same techniques to the native, FLS, or SLS form.

Thus, once freed from the native fiber, the low temperature acid-soluble collagens cannot be distinguished from each other by present methods of examination. This does not rule out the possibility that subtle differences in sequence or in arrangement of the three intertwined peptide chains may occur.

The initial solubility properties, however, clearly show that native collagen fibers are not uniform in terms of the interactions between neighboring, and quite similar, basic molecular units. Indeed, this non-uniformity is made more striking when one considers that the prolonged extractions with both acids left the major part of the tendon collagen still insoluble. Similar conclusions have been reached by Veis and Cohen (88, 89) through solubility studies on bovine corium collagen.

In addition to the acid-soluble collagens, Gross, Highberger and Schmitt (69, 71) and Jackson and Fessler (90) have described another class of soluble collagens. These workers showed that some collagen could be

dissolved from native collagen fibers by extraction with cold, slightly alkaline salt solutions or with cold neutral salts at hypertonic and physiological
ionic strengths. It is of interest to note that the collagen so obtained was
shown to be the probable biological precursor of the insoluble fiber, rather
than the acid-soluble tropocollagen or procollagen as presumed by Orekhovich et al. (79). Jackson (91) fed C^{14}-labeled glycine to actively metabo-
lizing young rats, sacrificed the animals, extracted both the cold neutral-
salt-soluble (NSS) and cold acid-soluble collagens (TC), and measured
the C^{14} activity of each fraction. The activity was concentrated in the NSS
fraction rather than in the TC fraction. Harkness et al. (92) similarly found
incorporation of C^{14}-labeled glycine into pH 9 phosphate-buffer-soluble
collagen extracted from rabbit skin.

The NSS collagen has the interesting property of having a negative
temperature coefficient for solublity, that is, fibrous precipitates form when
NSS collagen solutions are heated to 37°.* Wood and Keech (93) have
suggested that the cold NSS collagen solutions contain polymers of the TC
rodlet type. It has also been shown that the acid TC solutions can be neutralized by dialysis at temperatues below 10° and kept in solution at neutral or slightly basic pH (25). These neutral solutions, once obtained, will
precipitate on heating in a manner quite analogous to the NSS collagen
solutions. The point to be made is that while the acid-solubilized TC can
be kept in solution at neutral pH in the cold, it cannot be dissolved from
the intact fiber under these conditions. The NSS collagen, on the other
hand, can be extracted only at neutrality, illustrating once again the
heterogeneity of intrafibrillar interactions.

These data require one, at this point, to keep an open view with regard
to the question of the identity of the various soluble collagens. Unquestionably these molecules are similar in physical dimensions and gross chemical
properties, but on a more detailed basis the solubility data indicate the
existence of some subtle differences.

VI. Physical Properties of Collagen Fibers

Aside from the solubility properties discussed above, the two most
prominent physical properties of collagen are its swelling behavior and its
ability to undergo very sharp shrinking or contraction under appropriate
conditions.

---

* All temperatures are Centigrade unless specified otherwise.

A. Swelling

Since most mature collagen fibers of mammalian origin do not dissolve without heating, the addition of acids, bases, neutral salts, and other lyotropic agents brings about alterations in fiber length, thickness, and weight that are easily observable. Quantitative measurement of the swelling has been used to explore much of what is known about electrostatic interactions, water binding, and structural integrity in collagen fibers.

Two types of swelling can be readily distinguished, that which takes place as a result of the presence of charged sites along the peptide chains, and that which is induced by certain neutral salts or nonionic reagents. The first type of swelling has frequently been called "osmotic swelling" while the latter has been called "lyotropic swelling."

The osmotic swelling curve has the form shown in Fig. I-13, where the weight uptake of dried purified steer hide corium and limed corium col-

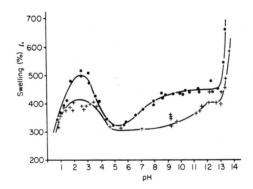

FIG. I-13. The swelling of bovine corium collagen as a function of pH, measured by the percentage increase in weight of dry corium cubes after equilibration; +, native, purified collagen; ●, alkali-pretreated collagen [de la Burde (94)].

lagens is plotted against the equilibrium pH of salt-free solutions (de la Burde, 94). In the neutral pH range the native unlimed hide pieces are white and flaccid. As the pH is raised above 9 or brought below 4.7, the hide pieces take up water, stiffen, and ultimately become firm and translucent. Liming shortens the nonswelling pH range and heightens the swelling maxima in both basic and acidic regions. In general neutral salts at moderate concentration repress the swelling, with the higher salt concentration being the more effective. An exception to this is that sodium chloride is less effective in reducing swelling in the basic region for limed collagen than for purified native collagen.

The gross uptake of water as described above is a function of the fiber weave in hide pieces and varies with the source and pretreatment of the sample examined. A more revealing insight into the effect of swelling reagents on the collagen can be obtained from measurements on single fibers or oriented fiber bundles. Using single fibers, Lloyd, Marriott and Pleass (95) found that, at the acid swelling maximum, the uptake of water was accompanied by net increase in fiber volume of nearly 100%, 400% increase in fiber width but 30% decrease in length. Burge, Cowan and McGavin examined the swelling of fresh native rat tail tendon in salt-free HCl and NaOH by x-ray diffraction techniques (96). They followed the change in position of the first order equatorial diffraction spot, characteristic of the interprotofibrillar spacing, as a function of pH. This dimension increased from about 13 Å at pH 7 to about 15 Å at pH 2 and 12. At the swelling maxima the diffraction diagrams became more diffuse, indicating disorientation of the protofibrils although the fibers appeared to be well oriented macroscopically. Below pH 1.0 and above pH 13 the equatorial reflections were completely diffused and no discrete spots could be observed. These diffraction data did not indicate any reduction in interprotofibrillar spacings at pH's less than or greater than the values corresponding to the swelling maxima. The swelling picture drawn by Bear (3) (Fig. I-14) is generally in accord with these observations. The calculated volume increase resulting from the increased interprotofibrillar distances would correspond, at the swelling maxima, to only about 30%, far below that actually observed. This might indicate that only the ordered interband regions (the regions rich in neutral nonpolar functional groups) are being observed and that the more highly swollen band regions are becoming greatly enlarged, leading to the decrease in length and fiber disorientation. One matter which has not been discussed is the configuration of the individual chains in the protofibrillar units. A more detailed x-ray diffraction analysis will be required to provide insight into the distortion or unwinding of the tropocollagen monomer unit during osmotic swelling.

Lyotropic effects are generally considered under a single heading and as the result of some common mechanism. It is difficult, however, to accept any single mechanism or interaction for lyotropic swelling, since a variety of reagents of quite different properties have the same gross effects on collagen fibers. Gustavson (1), in comparing osmotic and lyotropic swelling, found that lyotropic swelling was generally lower and involved an increase in fiber width initially, accompanied by slight fiber lengthening or relaxation. At the point of maximum lyotropic relaxation the swollen fibers remained flaccid and opaque rather than becoming firm and translucent, as in osmotic swelling. Higher concentrations of some lyotropic reagents, such as urea or potassium thiocyanate, lead to fiber contraction but initially the fibers pass through the relaxed extended stage. Ultimately, the most potent lyotropic reagents gelatinize the collagen at room temperature (97).

Specific ion effects are the rule and anions and cations of the neutral salts act independently, generally following the Hoffmeister series. According to Gustavson (1), the inorganic ions may be ranked in order of decreasing swelling ability as follows:

Cations: Ca > Sr > Ba > Mg > Na, K   Anions: CNS > I > Br > Cl > SO_4, S_2O_3

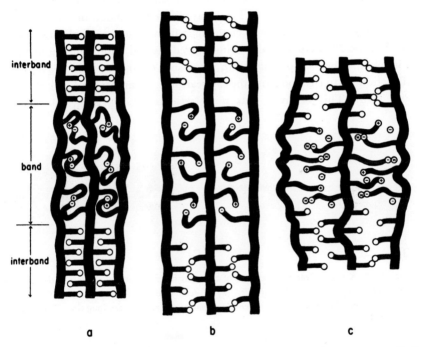

FIG. I-14. Diagrammatic representation of the difference between (a), a dry fibril; (b), a fibril swelling in water at neutrality; and (c), the result of acid swelling. Only polar side chains are shown, with open-circled heads representing uncharged side chains, + and — signs designating correspondingly charged heads or ions, and H indicating hydrogen ions. The long charged side chains at bands normally distort the vertical main chain helices from a straight course. Neutral water (not shown) penetrates bands and interbands, separating main chains to an extent limited by hydrogen bonds between polar heads at interbands, and simultaneously more room becomes available for the charged side chains at bands, which now permit straightening of the main chains. Addition of acid discharges the negative side chains by means of hydrogen ions, and the equal number of free negative ions required to remain at the bands produce local osmotic swellings, which contract the structure axially [Bear (3)].

Salts of the anion-cation combinations at the bottom of the list actually produce fibers less swollen than those in pure water, and the less swollen fibers have a higher melting temperature. The anions and cations have no lyotropic effect in dilute solution; swelling commences for all at about 1.0 M and is strongest in the 2.0–4.0 M range. Ramachandran (98) carried out an x-ray diffraction study of collagen fibers swollen with calcium chloride or with nickel nitrate, which, along with sodium perchlorate, is another powerful lyotropic reagent. Collagen fibers were immersed in concentrated salt solutions and held for a definite period of time during which axial shrinking occurred. At various stages the excess reagent was blotted from the fiber surface. The x-ray diffraction diagram was obtained compared with that of native wet collagen fiber. The principal observation was that the 12 Å equatorial spacing moved inward, indicating an increase in interprotofibrillar spacing. With increasing exposure to the reagent the diffraction patterns took on the appearance of amorphous gelatin gels (Fig. I-15). This behavior was not particularly surprising, but Rama-

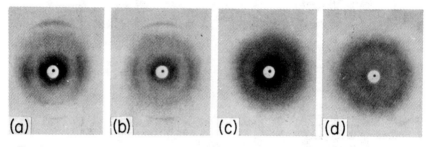

FIG. I-15. X-ray diffraction patterns of collagen fibers during shrinking under the influence of concentrated nickel nitrate. (a) 20-second exposure of fiber to 100% (w/v) salt; (b) 60-second exposure; (c) 65-second exposure; (d) after a very long time [Ramachandran (98)].

chandran then found that when the reagent was washed out with distilled water the normal collagen x-ray diffraction pattern returned. This return of the normal pattern could be achieved with all but the most prolonged neutral salt treatments.

Ramachandran reasoned as follows. In the normal fiber the protofibrils are all arranged in parallel array with short regularly spaced cross-links or interaction sites. When the lyotropic reagent is added these short interprotofibrillar bonds are ruptured and the single protofibrils then fold and twist, leading to disorientation. The regularity along the length of the protofibrils and their parallel orientation are lost, but the triple-chain units remain intact. That is, within the fiber the TC monomer units are not disrupted by the neutral salts, only the inter-TC bonds are severed.

Gustavson (1) compared the binding of various nonionic reagents with native skin collagen pieces and with similar skin pieces treated with lyotropic concentrations of neutral salts and then washed to return them to to the same state as the native pieces. He found that both vegetable tannins and nonionic sulfitochromium complexes were bound by the pretreated collagen to an extent more than 50% greater than by the native collagen. The condensed vegetable tannins are fixed primarily at the peptide (—CO—NH—) links, while the nonionic chromium complexes are bound at hydroxyl groups. Since the hydrogen bonds in which these groups normally participate are not reformed when the lyotropic neutral salts are washed from the fibrous structure, it is evident that the normal protofibrillar arrangement is permanently altered. However, the gross macroscopic fibers are not altered in appearance nor, as Ramachandran demonstrated, is the wide-angle x-ray diffraction pattern, characteristic of short-range order, disturbed. There are, unfortunately, little data from small-angle x-ray diffraction or electron microscopy on the effect of neutral salts. However, Nutting and Borasky (99) and Borasky and Rogers (100) both found that prolonged exposure to 2.0 M potassium thiocyanate did not permanently destroy the collagen fiber periodicity. Even more striking, Veis and Cohen (101) observed that partial solubilization of collagen fibers, swollen in 2.0 M potassium thiocyanate at room temperature and above, did not prevent the residual fibers, when washed free of the salt, from displaying the typical long-range order of native collagen fibers when viewed in the electron microscope.

Urea, in the range above 4.0 M, is a powerful lyotropic swelling agent very similar in effect to 2.0 M potassium thiocyanate. The mechanism of action of urea on proteins is not clear. It does appear, however, that both hydrogen bonds and hydrophobic bonds may be affected by urea at high concentration. Interruption of these bonds leads to structure relaxation and permanent swelling or, in other words, to irreversible disordering.

Phenols, phenol derivatives, and aromatic carboxylic and sulfonic acids comprise another group of swelling agents which operate by binding strongly to the peptide chain backbone. Gustavson's description of these systems (1) summarizes most of the available data. The mechanisms by which these substances swell fibrous collagen are not clear, however, except that their effect is due to their multifunctional character. Their strongly polar groups are bound firmly to the polar or oppositely charged portions of the collagen backbone chains. The nonpolar parts of these large molecules then, probably through micelle formation extending over large areas, disrupt the van der Waals interactions of the nonpolar segments, the interband regions, and cause the disorganization of these segments of the structure. The lower aliphatic carboxylic acids, such as acetic and propionic acids, have somewhat the same effect though to a lesser extent. We will examine the interaction of these classes of molecules with gelatin in more detail in a later chapter.

There is a clear-cut difference in the character of osmotic and of lyotropic swelling. Though the volume changes at maximal swelling are very great in osmotic or electrostatic swelling, the process is entirely reversible. The swelling in this case is interprotofibrillar and the integrity of the trihelical collagen structure is maintained. In lyotropic swelling, the reagents may change the water structure around the collagen fibril, interrupt internal hydrogen bonds, or through direct binding at some sites interact with the internal hydrophobic bonds. These interactions lead to disturbances of the intraprotofibrillar structure and essentially irreversible disruption of the native peptide-chain alignments. More detailed insights into the mechanism of osmotic and lyotropic phenomena will become evident in the discussions on the gelation of gelatin in Chapter V.

B. Thermal Contraction

The skrinkage or abrupt shortening which solvated collagen fibers experience when heated has been widely studied. As Wöhlisch (102-104) suggested, the abrupt change in dimension is very much like an ordinary melting process, a transition from a crystalline to an amorphous state. The "crystalline" collagen consists of extended, practically parallel chains. This extended form cannot be maintained in the melted state where interchain restraints are removed and, hence, the chains assume the more random, less extended form. There have been two approaches to the understanding of this melting process and, since both are pertinent to our subsequent examination of the melting of gelatin gels, they will be examined in some details.

1. The Kinetic Approach

In his study of the thermal shortening of kangaroo tail tendon collagen, Weir (105) noted that the abrupt character of the shortening was more apparent than real and that the contraction temperature depended on the rate of heating. This observation led him to treat the shrinkage as a rate process characterized by an extremely large temperature coefficient. Shrinkage could be measured, at constant fiber load, over a 10–15° temperature range in time periods from less than a minute to more than an hour. The fiber length was found to decrease exponentially with time at any given temperature and from this it was concluded that the shortening could be considered as a first order reaction. Since the initial rate of shrinkage was too rapid to follow accurately, the time required for half-shrinkage was determined. Half-shrinkage was defined as the length, l, at which $l = (l_0 + l_\infty)/2$, where l_0 was the initial fiber length, and l_∞ the fiber length at some time after complete shrinkage. The time for half-shrinkage, $t_{1/2}$, was considered to be proportional to the rate constant and, hence, could be substituted for that constant in the transition state theory. It was then possible to write Eq. 1 in which h is Planck's constant, k Boltzmann's constant, R the gas constant, and T the absolute temperature.

$$2.3 \log \frac{0.693\,h}{k T t_{1/2}} = -\frac{\Delta H^{\ddagger}}{RT} + \frac{\Delta S^{\ddagger}}{R} \tag{1}$$

A plot of the left-hand side of this equation vs. $1/T$ yielded a straight line and the enthalpy of activation, $\Delta H^{\ddagger}$, was evaluated from its slope. From a number of observations on untanned kangaroo tail tendon, Weir calculated the following values for the quasi-thermodynamic activation parameters at 60°: $\Delta F^{\ddagger}_{60} = +24.7$ kcal/mole; $\Delta H^{\ddagger} = +141$ kcal/mole; $\Delta S^{\ddagger}_{60} = +349$ cal/mole degree. Both $\Delta H^{\ddagger}$ and $\Delta S^{\ddagger}$ exhibited a strong dependence on the pH of the aqueous medium in which the rate measurements were carried out. These variations in pH are illustrated in Fig. I-16. Tendons equilibrated at either pH extreme at room temperature for 24 hours showed the greatest decreases in $\Delta H^{\ddagger}$ and $\Delta S^{\ddagger}$ but, when leached with water to pH 7.2–7.3, gave results similar to those quoted above. Hence, as concluded earlier in the discussion of osmotic swelling, the lateral expansion resulting from hydration and electrostatic repulsion effects does not cause permanent alterations in the fiber organization. The lyotropic effect of neutral salt also correlates with the shrinkage rate data (Table I-4). The value of $\Delta H^{\ddagger}$ drops from 141 kcal/mole in pure water to 83 kcal/mole in 2.0 M sodium chloride to 75 kcal/mole in saturated sodium chloride. The values of $\Delta S^{\ddagger}$ vary from 349 e.u. to 176 to 149 in the same solutions. The corresponding $\Delta H^{\ddagger}$ and $\Delta S^{\ddagger}$ values at pH 1.8 in water are 67 kcal/mole and 160 e.u.

The very large $\Delta H^{\ddagger}$ and $\Delta S^{\ddagger}$ values and the apparent abruptness of the shrinkage suggest that whole segments of the structure must be transformed

TABLE I-4 [a]

LYOTROPIC EFFECT OF SODIUM CHLORIDE ON THE ACTIVATION PARAMETERS
FOR THERMAL SHRINKAGE OF TENDON COLLAGEN

Concentration of sodium chloride (moles/liter)	Acidity (pH)	Heat of activation ($\Delta H\ddagger$) (kcal/mole)	Entropy of activation ($\Delta S\ddagger$) (cal/mole degree)	Free energy of activation at 60° ($\Delta F\ddagger_{50}$) (kcal/mole)
0.0	—	141	349	24.7
0.05	6.3	119	285	23.8
0.1	6.2	95	217	23.2
1.0	6.3	93	213	22.4
2.0	6.2	83	176	24.1
4.0	6.1	87	185	25.8
Saturated	6.0	75	149	25.3
0.0	1.8	67	150	17.4

[a] Data of Weir (105).

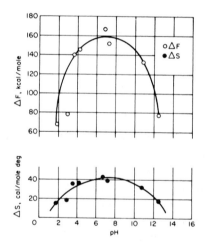

FIG. I-16. The free energy and entropy of activation for the thermal shrinkage of collagen fibers as a function of pH [Weir (105)].

simulatenously to the activated complex, and that the "mole" which forms the basis of the heat and entropy values refers to this large segment that acts as a single kinetic unit. Calorimetric measurements by Küntzel and Doehner (106) gave the value of $\Delta H = +$ 12.5 cal/gm for the transition:

ordered collagen → shrunken collagen.

Weir postulated that the sequence of events was:

$$\text{ordered collagen} \overset{A}{\rightleftharpoons} \text{activated collagen} \overset{B}{\rightarrow} \text{shrunken collagen}$$

in which step B was irreversible and adiabatic. Hence, the kinetic unit had a "molecular weight" of 11,300.

Weir (105) concluded that salt linkages were the primary forces to be disrupted in achieving the activated state but, after analysis of the effects of organic solvents on the rate of shrinkage (107), decided that hydrogen bonds were those principally involved. The reasons cited were (1) the number of salt linkages is probably very small; (2) salt linkages are expected to be labile in aqueous salt solutions; (3) deamination of the collagen did not cause a decrease in the shrinkage temperature; (4) aqueous solutions of organic molecules, such as dioxane, ethanol, and glucose, which decrease the dielectric constant and enhance electrostatic interactions, have the *same* effect on shrinkage temperature as salt solutions; (5) there are about 7 times as many possibilities for hydrogen bonds as salt linkages. Gustavson (1) also concluded that salt linkages were relatively unimportant in collagen stabilization as compared to hydrogen bonding.

Crewther and Dowling (108) carried out a similar investigation on the rate of shrinkage of kangaroo tail tendon collagen in salt solutions. By studying the shrinkage at pH 2 and low temperature, these workers were able to lengthen the shrinkage period and, hence, construct complete percent shrinkage-time curves. Typical data are illustrated in Fig. I-17. The curves representing the data are symmetrical. Crewther and Dowling showed that the conversion of native collagen to the denatured form could not be by a single-step first order reaction. They postulated the reaction to proceed through two consecutive first order reactions, but this resulted in equations that yielded an unsymmetrical shrinkage curve. In a second model, these authors proposed that the observed data were the result of an interaction between rigid collagen and elastomeric denatured collagen. In this model the undenatured rigid units of the structure tend to keep the denatured units in their original form and arrangement. Conversely, the denatured units exert a disorienting force on the native molecular units. The conversion of collagen from the native to the denatured form is again considered to be first order, but the decrease in length is slowed by the resisting force of the undenatured, rigid fiber units. The result, Eq. 2,

$$S = \frac{s(1 - e^{-kt})}{(1 - Me^{-kt})} \tag{2}$$

shows that the structural rigidity modulates the early stages of the shrinkage process. In Eq. 2, S is the percent shrinkage at time t, s is the maximum percent shrinkage, and k is the first order rate constant for the conversion of native collagen to the denatured state. M is a constant which involves the ratio of the elastic moduli of native and denatured collagen. The constants k and M vary with the pH, temperature, and nature of the solvent. In addition M is a function of the applied stress.

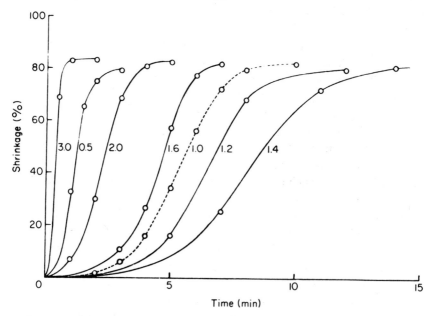

FIG. I-17. Relationship between shrinkage of collagen in solutions of KI at pH 2.0 and time of heating at 50°. Figures refer to molar concentrations. The tendons were presoaked at 2° for 24 hours. The dotted curve compares the equation, $S = 83(1 - e^{-1 \cdot 1t})/(1 + 360\, e^{-1 \cdot 1t})$, with the experimental data for contraction of collagen in 1.0 M KI [Crewther and Dowling (108)].

To arrive at Eq. 2, Crewther and Dowling had to assume that the conversion of native collagen to the denatured form was random and that melted segments were distributed uniformly throughout the fiber structure. This may throw some light on the nature of the kinetic units of $\sim 11,000$ molecular weight that were proposed by Weir (105). Referring back to the tropocollagen hypothesis for the structure of collagen, the collagen fiber is composed of large rodlike units, each $\sim 350,000$ avograms/molecule and 3000 Å in length. Each molecule is composed of three intwined helixes with a gross pitch of about 10 Å and ~ 10 residues per turn. From Weir's data, the kinetic unit would appear to be only a small fraction of this total and to correspond to about three turns of the superhelix. Thus thermal contraction can be considered as resulting from the severance of internal, intra-chain hydrogen bonds, but only a few turns of the helix need be released to initiate shrinkage. In this respect, then, the shrinkage of collagen can be considered as similar to the melting of ordinary polymeric materials. The denaturation is not an all-or-nothing reaction. It does not even appear necessary to assume that all collagens are completely "crystalline" or ordered in their native state and this could explain many of the differences observed.

2. *The Equilibrium Approach*

Weir (*109*) noted that the shrinkage of collagen in aqueous systems was accompanied by a latent volume increase. Similarly Küntzel and Doehner (*106*) and Wöhlisch and his colleagues (*103, 104, 110-112*) found a latent heat for the shrinkage reaction. Garrett and Flory (*113, 114*) compared these observations with the melting behavior of synthetic polymers and concluded that the thermal shrinkage of collagen could be considered as a true first order phase transition, characterized by a well-defined melting point.

Garrett and Flory (*113, 114*) then determined the melting points of various collagen-diluent mixtures by precise dilatometric measurements of the latent volume increase. Ethylene glycol was used as the diluent for most measurements, rather than water, to avoid complications arising from hydrolysis of the collagen and formation of gelatin. Tendon collagen was purified and air-dried to constant weight. Small sections, about 0.01 inch in thickness, were swollen in ethylene glycol vapor to the desired extent, 0.0–0.85 of the weight fraction of collagen. Several grams of the solvated collagen were introduced into special capillary-type dilatometers. Mercury was used as the confining liquid. To study the equilibrium it was necessary to have both melted and crystalline coexisting phases. Therefore the dilatometers were heated quickly to a temperature above the melting point, T_M, to initiate melting, then were quenched to a temperature about $10°$ below T_M. The volume was observed as the dilatometers were reheated slowly to T_M. The evidence for a latent volume increase was readily apparent. A typical dilatometer run is shown in Fig. I-18. In the run illustrated, the latent volume change corresponded to an increase of about 5×10^{-3} ml per gm bovine achilles tendon. Figure I-19 depicts an alternate and more informative method of plotting the dilatometric data. The ordinate, Δy, represents the difference between a calculated scale reading for the com-

pletely melted sample at the indicated temperature, based on the linear
volume, temperature liquidus of Fig. I-18, and observed capillary scale
reading for the partly crystalline sample at the same temperature. Positive
values of Δy indicate a *decrease* in volume, owing to crystallinity. A zero

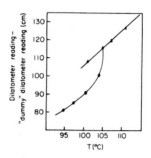

Fig. I-18. The latent volume increase on the melting of bovine achilles tendon collagen
in collagen–ethylene glycol mixture [Flory and Garrett (*114*)].

value for Δy indicates complete melting and the temperature at which Δy
becomes zero is T_M, the equilibrium melting point. As indicated by point
10 in Fig. I-19, a supercooled completely melted collagen can be obtained.
After 63 hours at the temperature of point 10, the volume had decreased

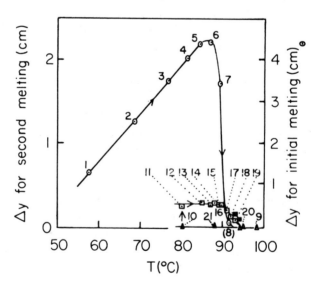

Fig. I-19. The latent volume changes upon first and second meltings of the same collagen fibers. See text for explanation of Δy. Points taken in order as numbered [Flory and
Garrett (*114*)].

to give the Δy value of point 11, showing the slow recrystallization of the completely melted collagen.

As in other polymer systems, the observed melting point is a function of the diluent concentration. This variation in T_M is illustrated in Fig. I-20 and extrapolation of these data gave an extrapolated value of T_M° of 145° when the weight fraction of collagen, v_2, approached 1. With the

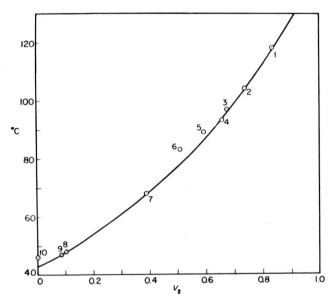

FIG. I-20. Melting temperatures of collagen in collagen–ethylene glycol mixtures as a function of the volume fraction of collagen, v_2, in the mixture [Flory and Garrett (114)].

simplifying assumption that the solvent content of the crystalline portions of the fibrils remains constant, the melting point–composition data can be represented by Eq. 3.

$$1/T_M - 1/T_M^\circ = (R/\varrho_2 \bar{V}_1 \Delta h) \ (v_1 - \chi_1 v_1^2) \tag{3}$$

In this equations Δh is the heat of fusion per gram crystalline polymer, ϱ_2 the density of the amorphous polymer, $\bar{V}_1$ the molar volume of the solvent, v_1 the volume fraction of solvent, and χ_1 a parameter characterizing the interaction between solvent and amorphous polymer. From a plot of the data according to Eq. 3, Flory and Garrett found $\chi_1 = 0.30$, and with $\varrho_2 = 1.35$ gm/ml and $\bar{V}_1 = 56$ ml, a value of $\Delta h = 24$ cal/gm was obtained.

Dilatometric measurements on gelatin-glycol systems showed that both T_M and Δh had the same values as in the collagen-glycol systems. Flory and Garrett concluded from this identity that "the aggregation process responsible for gelation in gelatin is none other than a reversion to the native (collagen) crystalline form." Further, "notwithstanding the low degree of crystallinity in gelatin ... the thermodynamic stability of the crystalline aggregates, indicated by the melting temperature, is quantitatively almost identical with that in native collagen." The implications of these results will be discussed in a later chapter after examining more data on the gelation process.

At this point, it is instructive to compare the above data with that obtained by instantaneous shrinkage measurements. Witnauer and Fee (*115*) measured T_s in bovine corium collagen-glycol systems; using these T_s values and the same method of representation as in Eq. 3, they found Δh to be 17 cal/gm. With an average residue molecular weight of ~ 97, this calculates out to be 1600 cal per peptide unit. On the same basis, Garrett and Flory (*114*) found the heat of fusion to be 2250 cal per peptide unit. This approach also yielded a value of 7200 cal/mole if water was the diluent while, as recorded earlier, Küntzel and Doehner (*106*) found the value of the heat of fusion of collagen in water to be 12.5 cal/gm or 1125 cal per peptide unit. Flory and Garrett ascribe these discrepancies to differences in the solvation of collagen in the various solvents. We shall reserve an interpretation of these results until we have examined the gelation of gelatin in more detail.

VII. THE COLLAGEN-GELATIN TRANSITION

The essential features of the collagen systems about which subsequent discussion will center may be summarized as follows. Collagen owes its distinctive structure to its high content of the imino acids proline and hydroxyproline, combined with its richness in the nonpolar amino acids with short side chains, glycine and alanine. The basic macromolecular unit appears to be a three-chain helical structure in which the individual helical chains are wound in a gentle superhelix about the common molecular axis. Three internal arrangements of the three-chain unit are possible. Two of these are hydrogen-bonded at one of each three residues and cannot be distinguished from each other. Both forms may exist. A more highly hydrogen-bonded form appears to resolve the structural ambiguity, but nevertheless the entire collagen molecule may not have an identical structure. On the molecular level, the basic tropocollagen (TC) units appear to be rods approximately 3000 Å × 14 Å with the end regions having different properties from the body of the rods. There is a distinctly non-uniform distribution of acidic and basic functional groups along the body of each individual rod, so that each is clearly asymmetric.

The basic TC units are packed in a particular staggered side-by-side arrangement within the native fibril. Head-to-tail overlaps occur leaving periodic holes within the fibrillar structure. As solubility studies in particular show, the basic units are either not all identical or interact to varying degrees with their nearest neighbors. Both situations may exist. The interactions leading to insolubilization of the fibers are probably reactions forming covalent cross-linkages.

The gross fibers, which are the forms in which collagen exists and is recognized in living systems, are capable of undergoing considerable mechanical and physical alterations which may vary from entirely reversible swelling, to partial melting, to irreversible dissordering of the entire structure. These changes can occur without solubilization of the fiber. The basic TC units, the fibers, and the various altered forms are all insoluble in pure salt-free water.

Gelatin is the water-soluble product of the dissolution, disorganization, or degradation of these water-insoluble collagen fibers. We may therefore say more specifically that the collagen → gelatin transition is the process whereby the highly organized, quasi-crystalline, water-insoluble collagen fiber is transformed from an infinite, asymmetric network of linked TC units to a system of water-soluble, independent molecules with a much lower degree of internal order. Inasmuch as the original structures are not necessarily identical in chemical composition, macromolecular organization, or crystallinity, and since there are many paths by which the disruption of the structure may be accomplished, we must espect to find equally many varieties of gelatins. Our task is to discover how the molecular properties of a given gelatin depend on the method of its preparation and how these molecular characteristics govern the properties and behavior of gelatin solutions, and to relate these properties back to the structure from which the gelatins were derived to provide new insights into the nature of the collagen fiber systems.

REFERENCES

1. K. H. Gustavson, "The Chemistry and Reactivity of Collagen." Academic Press, New York, 1956.

2. W. F. Harrington and P. H. von Hippel, *Advan. Protein Chem.* **16**, 1 (1962).

3. R. S. Bear, *Advan. Protein Chem.* **7**, 69 (1952).

4. J. E. Eastoe, *Biochem. J.* **61**, 589 (1955).

5. J. E. Eastoe, *Biochem. J.* **65**, 363 (1957).

6. J. E. Eastoe and A. A. Leach *in* "Recent Advances in Gelatin and Glue Research" (G. Stainsby, ed.), p. 173. Pergamon Press, New York, 1958.

7. J. M. Cassel and E. McKenna, *J. Am. Leather Chemists' Assoc.* **48**, 142 (1953).

8. H. Vickery, *Biochem. J.* **29**, 2710 (1935).

9. R. A. Alberty, *in* "The Proteins" (H. Neurath and K. Bailey, eds.), Vol. I, Part A, p. 478. Academic Press, New York, 1953.

10. J. H. Highberger, *J. Am. Chem. Soc.* **61**, 2302 (1939).

11. J. H. Highberger, *J. Am. Leather Chemists' Assoc.* **31**, 345 (1936).

12. J. Beek, Jr., and A. M. Sookne, *J. Res. Natl. Bur. Std.* **23**, 271 (1939).

13. J. Beek, Jr., and A. M. Sookne, *J. Am. Leather Chemists' Assoc.* **34**, 641 (1939).

14. J. M. Cassel and E. McKenna, *J. Am. Leather Chemists' Assoc.* **48**, 142 (1953).

15. J. M. Cassel, E. McKenna, and A. Glime, *J. Am. Leather Chemists' Assoc.* **48**, 277 (1953).

16. A. Courts, *Biochem. J.* **74**, 238 (1960).

17. J. W. Janus, A. W. Kenchington, and A. G. Ward, *Research (London)* **4**, 247 (1951).

18. G. L. Brown and F. C. Kelly, "Nature and Structure of Collagen" (J. T. Randall, ed.), p. 169. Butterworths, London. 1953.

19. D. S. Jackson and A. Neuberger, *Biochim Biophys. Acta* **26**, 638 (1957).

20. A. Veis, J. Anesey, and J. Cohen, *in* "Recent Advances in Gelatin and Glue Research" (G. Stainsby, ed.), p. 155. Pergamon Press, New York, 1958.

21. G. Russell, *Nature* **181**, 102 (1958).

22. A. A. Leach, *Biochem. J.* **74**, 61 (1960).

23. F. S. Steven and G. R. Tristram, *Biochem J.* **83**, 240 (1962).

24. C. Deasy, *J. Am. Leather Chemists' Assoc.* **54**, 246 (1959).

25. H. B. Bensusan and B. L. Hoyt, *J. Am. Chem. Soc.* **78**, 4267 (1956).

26. A. J. Hodge, J. H. Highberger, G. G. S. Deffner, and F. O. Schmitt, *Proc. Natl. Acad. Sci. U.S.* **46**, 197 (1960).

27. A. Veis and R. J. Schlueter, *Nature* **197**, 1204 (1963).

28. K. H. Gustavson, *Svensk Kem. Tidskr.* **54**, 74 (1942).

29. K. H. Gustavson, *Svensk Kem. Tidskr.* **54**, 249 (1942).

30. K. H. Gustavson, *Acta Chem. Scand.* **4**, 1171 (1950).

31. K. H. Gustavson, *J. Am. Leather Chemists' Assoc.* **45**, 789 (1950).

32. K. H. Gustavson, *J. Soc. Leather Trades' Chemists* **33**, 332 (1949).

33. K. H. Gustavson, *Biochem. Z.* **311**, 347 (1942).

34. K. H. Gustavson, *Acta Chem. Scand.* **8**, 1299 (1954).

35. T. Takahashi and T. Tanaka, *Bull. Japan. Soc. Sci. Fisheries* **19**, 603 (1953).

36. N. G. Esipova, *Biofizika* **2**, 455 (1957).

37. P. Doty and T. Nishihara, *in* "Recent Advances in Gelatin and Glue Research" (G. Stainsby, ed.), p. 92. Pergamon Press, New York, 1958.

38. K. A. Piez, *J. Am. Chem. Soc.* **82**, 247 (1960).

39. R. E. Burge and R. D. Hynes, *J. Mol. Biol.* **1**, 155 (1959).

40. G. R. Tristram, *in* "The Proteins" (H. Neurath and K. Bailey, eds.), Vol. 1, Part A, p. 181. Academic Press, New York, 1953.

41. G. N. Ramachandran, V. Sasisekharan, and Y. T. Thathachari, *in* "Collagen" (N. Ramanathan, ed.), p. 81. Wiley (Interscience), New York, 1962.

42. H. Hörmann, *Leder* **11**, 173 (1960).

43. P. M. Gallop, S. Seifter, and E. Meilman, *Nature* **183**, 1659 (1959).

44. J. H. Highberger, T. D. Kroner, and J. J. McGarr, personal communication (1963).

45. B. L. Low, *in* "The Proteins" (H. Neurath and K. Bailey, eds.), Vol. 1, Part A, p. 235. Academic Press, New York 1953.

46. G. N. Ramachandran, *Nature* **177**, 710 (1956).

47. G. N. Ramachandran and G. K. Ambady, *Current Sci. (India)* **23**, 349 (1954).

48. G. N. Ramachandran and G. Kartha, *Nature*, **174** 269 (1954).

49. G. N. Ramachandran and G. Kartha, *Nature* **176**, 593 (1955).

50. P. M. Cowan and S. McGavin, *Nature* **176**, 501 (1955).

51. P. M. Cowan, S. McGavin, and A. C. T. North, *Nature* **176**, 1062 (1955).

52. R. S. Bear, *J. Biophys. Biochem. Cytol.* **2**, 363 (1956).

53. F. H. C. Crick and A. Rich, *Nature* **176**, 780 (1955).

54. A. Rich and F. H. C. Crick, *Nature* **176**, 915 (1955).

55. A. Rich and F. H. C. Crick, *in* "Recent Advances in Gelatine and Glue Research" (G. Stainsby, ed.), p. 20. Pergamon Press, New York, 1958.

56. A. Rich and F. H. C. Crick, *J. Mol. Biol.* **3**, 483 (1961).

57. W. A. Schroeder, L. M. Kay, J. Le Gette, L. Honnen, and F. C. Green, *J. Am. Chem. Soc.* **76**, 3556 (1954).

58. T. D. Kroner, W. Tabroff, and J. J. McGarr, *J. Am. Chem. Soc.* **77**, 3356 (1955).

59. V. Sasisekharan, *in* "Collagen" (N. Ramanathan, ed.), p. 39. Wiley (Interscience), New York, 1962.

60. B. R. Lakshmanan, C. Ramakrishnan, V. Sasiskharan, and Y. T. Thathachari, *in* "Collagen" (N. Ramanathan, ed.), p. 117. Wiley (Interscience), New York, 1962.

61. G. N. Ramachandran, *in* "Collagen" (N. Ramanathan, ed.), p. 1. Wiley (Interscience), New York, 1962.

62. E. J. Ambrose and A. Elliott, *Proc. Roy. Soc.* **A206**, 206 (1951).

63. P. M. Cowan, S. McGavin, A. C. T. North, *Nature* **176**, 1062 (1955).

64. W. Grassmann, K. Hannig, H. Endres, and A. Riedel, *Z. Physiol. Chem.* **306**, 123 (1956).

65. C. Wolpers, *Naturwissenschaften* **28**, 461 (1941).

66. C. Wolpers, *Leder* **1**, 3 (1950).

67. C. E. Hall, M. A. Jakus, and F. O. Schmitt, *J. Am. Chem. Soc.* **64**, 1234 (1942).

68. J. H. Highberger, J. Gross, and F. O. Schmitt, *J. Am. Chem. Soc.* **72**, 3321 (1950).

69. J. H. Highberger, J. Gross, and F. O. Schmitt, *Proc. Natl. Acad. Sci. U.S.* **37**, 286 (1951).

70. J. Gross, J. H. Highberger, and F. O. Schmitt, *Proc. Natl. Acad. Sci. U.S.* **40**, 679 (1954).

71. J. Gross, J. H. Highberger, and F. O. Schmitt, *Proc. Natl. Acad. Sci. U.S.* **41**, 1 (1955).

72. P. A. Zachariades, *Compt. Rend. Soc. Biol.* **52**, 182 (1900).

73. J. Nageotte, *Compt. Rend.* **184**, 115 (1927).

74. J. Nageotte, *Compt. Rend. Soc. Biol.* **96**, 172, 464, 828 (1927).

75. J. Nageotte, *Compt. Rend. Soc. Biol.* **97**, 559 (1927).

76. J. Nageotte, *Compt. Rend. Soc. Biol.* **98**, 15 (1928).

77. J. Nageotte, *Compt. Rend. Soc. Biol.* **104**, 156 (1930).

78. J. Nageotte, *Compt. Rend. Soc. Biol.* **113**, 841 (1933).

79. V. N. Orekhovich, A. A. Tustanovskii, K. D. Orekhovitch, and N. E. Plotnikova, *Biokhimiya* **13**, 55 (1948).

80. H. Boedtker and P. Doty, *J. Am. Chem. Soc.* **78**, 4267 (1956).

81. C. E. Hall, *Proc. Natl. Acad. Sci. U.S.* **42**, 801 (1956).

82. C. E. Hall and P. Doty, *J. Am. Chem. Soc.* **80**, 1269 (1958).

83. A. J. Hodge and F. O. Schmitt, *Proc. Natl. Acad. Sci. U.S.* **46**, 186 (1960).

84. F. O. Schmitt, *in* "Connective Tissue, Thrombosis, and Atherosclerosis" (I. H. Page, ed.), p. 43 Academic Press, New York, 1959.

85. J. A. Petruska and A. J. Hodge, *Abstr. 7th Annual Meeting Biophys. Soc., New York,* 1963, p. TA 12.

86. A. J. Hodge and F. O. Schmitt, *Proc. Natl. Acad. Sci. U.S.* **44**, 418 (1958).

87. V. I. Mazurov and V. N. Orekhovich, *Biokhimiya* **24**, 28 (1959).

88. A. Veis and J. Cohen, *J. Am. Chem. Soc.* **78**, 6238 (1956).

89. A. Veis and J. Cohen, *J. Phys. Chem.* **62**, 459 (1958).

90. D. S. Jackson and J. F. Fessler, *Nature* **176**, 169 (1955).

91. D. S. Jackson, *Biochem. J.* **65**, 277 (1956).

92. R. D. Harkness, A. M. Marko, H. M. Muir, and A. Neuberger, *Biochem. J..* **56**, 558 (1954).

93. G. C. Wood and M. K. Keech, *Biochem. J.* **75**, 588 (1960).

94. R. de la Burde, Ph.D. Dissertation, Technische Hochschule Aachen, 1962.

95. D. J. Lloyd, R. H. Marriott, and W. B. Pleass, *Trans. Faraday Soc.* **29**, 554 (1933).

96. R. E. Burge, P. M. Cowan, and S. McGavin, *in* "Recent Advances in Gelatin and Glue Research" (G. Stainsby, ed.), p. 25. Pergamon Press, New York, 1958.

97. D. J. Lloyd and M. Garrod, *Trans. Faraday Soc.* **44**, 441 (1948).

98. G. N. Ramachandran, *in* "Recent Advances in Gelatin and Glue Research" (G. Stainsby, ed.), p. 32. Pergamon Press, New York, 1958.

99. G. C. Nutting and R. Borasky, *J. Am. Leather Chemists' Assoc.* **43**, 96 (1948).

100. R. Borasky and J. S. Rogers, *J. Am. Leather Chemists' Assoc.* **47**, 312 (1952).

101. A. Veis and J. Cohen, *Abstr. 135th Meeting Am. Chem. Soc., Boston,* 1959. *Massachusetts* p. 25c.

102. E. Wöhlisch, *Ergeb. Physiol., Biol. Chem. Expl. Pharmakol.* **34**, 405 (1932).

103. E. Wöhlisch, *Biochem. Z.* **247**, 329 (1932).

104. E. Wöhlisch and R. D. de Rochemont, *Z. Biol.* **85**, 406 (1927).

105. C. E. Weir, *J. Am. Leather Chemists' Assoc.* **44**, 108 (1949).

106. A. Küntzel and K. Doehner, *Angew. Chem.* **52**, 175 (1939).

107. C. E. Weir and J. Carter, *J. Res. Natl. Bur. Std.* **44**, 599 (1950).

108. W. G. Crewther and L. M. Dowling, *J. Phys. Chem.* **62**, 681 (1958).

109. C. E. Weir, *J. Res. Natl. Bur. Std.* **41**, 279 (1948).

110. E. Wöhlisch, *Kolloid-Z.* **89**, 239 (1939).

111. E. Wöhlisch, *Naturvissenschaften* **28**, 305, 326 (1940).

112. E. Wöhlisch, H. Weitnauer, W. Grüning, and R. Rohrbach, *Kolloid-Z.* **104**, 14 (1943).

113. R. R. Garrett and P. J. Flory, *Nature* **177**, 176 (1956).

114. P. J. Flory and R. R. Garrett, *J. Am. Chem. Soc.* **80**, 4836 (1958).

115. L. P. Witnauer and J. G. Fee, *J. Polymer Sci.* **26**, 141 (1957).

116. R. J. Schlueter, Ph.D. Dissertation, Northwestern University, 1963.

II

THE MOLECULAR
CHARACTERIZATION OF GELATIN

I. INTRODUCTION

Gelatin is a fascinating material to study because it combines in a single substance so many different characteristics. Gelatin is, of course, proteinaceous in nature, being composed of long chains of amino acids joined through peptide linkages. However, gelatin is somewhat unique among proteins owing to the absence of appreciable internal order, so that in aqueous solutions at sufficiently high temperature the peptide chains take up random configurations. This situation is analogous to the behavior of synthetic linear-chain high polymers and allows one to examine the structure and behavior of gelatin from the point of view of the theories developed to treat such high polymeric systems.

Since gelatins are produced by the degradation of a larger structure, a

49

variety of peptide-chain species results. In general, the degradation is not completely random and as a result most gelatin preparations are not homogeneous with respect to molecular weight or weight distribution. Again, this situation is similar to that in systems of synthetic high polymers. The breadth of the molecular weight distribution thus becomes a factor of equal importance with the average molecular weight in specifying the state of a particular gelatin system.

The acidic and basic functional groups of the amino acid side chains confer polyelectrolyte characteristics on the random gelatin chain. These electrically charged sites govern to some extent the interactions between gelatin molecules and between gelatin molecules and the solvent. They affect the viscosity and all other hydrodynamic properties. Hence to understand and characterize a gelatin system one must also take into consideration the net charge of the gelatin molecule, the total charge, the nature of the ionizable groups and their internal distribution.

Finally, in spite of the above emphasis on the typical linear-chain polymeric polyampholyte character of gelatin molecules, their specific peptide composition cannot be neglected. The chain configuration of gelatin is controlled both by the general solvent-peptide backbone interactions and by certain preferred orientations of some of the peptide linkages. In this way the peptide chain sequence imparts to gelatins some of their most interesting and useful properties.

In this chapter we will examine in turn and in some detail the methods which have been used to explore these various properties of the gelatins and the results of these investigations in terms of gelatin characterization. It is important that the characterization techniques be studied in sufficient detail so that the limitations of each method can be appreciated. As will be seen, the results obtained by different techniques are not always in agreement. Reasonable correlations of these data depend on understanding the theoretical and technical limitations of each measurement.

II. Gelatin Considered as a High Polymer

A. Molecular Weight Averages

The concept of a specific, invariant molecular weight for a particular species of molecule loses significance when one considers systems of polymeric molecules. Such systems are invariably heterogeneous with respect to particle weights and particle dimensions. One can consider such systems as composed of homologous molecular species, but the distributions of

weight and dimension may vary from uniform or gaussian to discontinuous
or bimodal. What is required is a means of expressing both the average of
a property and the distribution of that property. Several methods of averaging have become commonly used because they result naturally from specific
methods of experimental examination of high polymer systems.

Lansing and Kraemer (*1*) defined several useful types of molecular
weight averages: the number-average, M_n; the weight-average, M_w; and
the Z-average, M_Z.

1. *The Number-Average*

The number-average molecular weight, M_n, may be defined simply as
that average value obtained by dividing the total weight of a system of
molecules by the total number of molecules in the population or

$$M_n = \frac{\sum_i w_i}{\sum_i n_i} \tag{1}$$

where w_i represents the weight of component i, and n_i the number of molecules of type i. The summations are taken over all components. If M_i is
the molecular weight of component i then

$$M_n = \frac{\sum_i w_i}{\sum_i n_i} = \frac{\sum_i n_i M_i}{\sum_i n_i} \tag{2}$$

If we assume that the distribution of species is a known and continuous
function, $f_n(M)$, then the summations in Eq. 2 may be replaced by the
integral of $f_n(M)$ over all possible weights,

$$\sum_i n_i = \int_{M=0}^{M=\infty} f_n(M)dM \tag{3}$$

and, similarly,

$$\sum_i n_i M_i = \int_{M=0}^{M=\infty} M f_n(M)dM \tag{4}$$

The number of molecules with weights between M_1 and $M_1 + dM$ is
then given by

$$\int_{M_1}^{M_1 + dM} f_n(M)dM \tag{5}$$

It can be seen that a plot of $f_n(M)$ vs. M, appropriately normalized (Fig. II-1), gives the number distribution curve (Williams *et al.*, *2*). Equation 3 represents the total area under the curve and Eq. 4 the first moment of the number distribution curve.

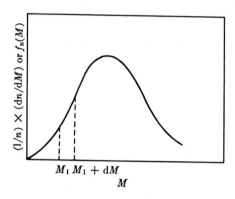

FIG. II-1. Representation of a number distribution function of the molecular weight [Williams *et al.* (*2*)].

2. *The Weight-Average*

The weight-average molecular weight, M_w, is defined by Eq. 6.

$$M_w = \frac{\sum_i w_i M_i}{\sum_i w_i} \qquad (6)$$

As in the preceding discussion, w_i is the total weight of all molecules of species i in the system, and M_i the molecular weight or particle weight characteristic of species i. According to Eq. 2, $w_i = \sum_i n_i M_i$, hence

$$M_w = \frac{\sum_i n_i M_i^2}{\sum_i n_i M_i} \qquad (7)$$

Defining a function $f_w(M)$ to describe the weight distribution, corresponding to $Mf_n(M)$, then

$$M_w = \frac{\int_0^\infty M f_w(M)\,dM}{\int_0^\infty f_w(M)\,dM} = \frac{\int_0^\infty M^2 f_n(M)\,dM}{\int_0^\infty M f_n(M)\,dM} \qquad (8)$$

For polymer systems there will, in general, be a weight distribution curve

$f_w(M)$ having a shape different from that of the number distribution curve, as illustrated in Fig. II-2 (Williams *et al.*, 2). From the relationships in Eq. 8, it can be seen that the numerator of the first ratio is the first moment of the weight distribution curve and that this is equivalent to the numerator of the second ratio, the second moment of the number distribution curve.

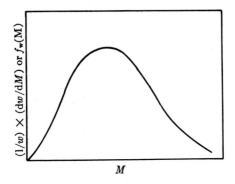

FIG. II-2. Representation of a weight distribution function of the molecular weight [Williams *et al.* (2)].

Both molecular weight averages are sensitive to the form of the distribution function, but in different ways. The number-average is particularly sensitive to low molecular weight components, since the denominator of Eq. 1 increases much more rapidly than the numerator when small molecules are added to a given system. On the other hand, since particle weight appears as the second power in the numerator of Eq. 7, the addition of a relatively few high molecular weight particles will greatly increase M_w. For a homogeneous system $M_n = M_w$, but for any type of particle weight heterogeneity $M_w > M_n$.

3. *Higher-Average Distributions*

It is possible to define any number of higher weight-averages by considering higher and higher moments of the number distribution curve. Of these averages the Z-average molecular weight, M_Z, is of greatest practical interest since it can be determined experimentally. Based on the third moment of the number distribution curve, M_Z is defined by either of the expressions

$$M_Z = \frac{\sum_i n_i M_i^3}{\sum_i n_i M_i^2} = \frac{\sum_i w_i M_i^2}{\sum_i w_i M_i} \tag{9}$$

The next higher average, designated by M_{Z+1}, would be

$$M_{Z+1} = \frac{\sum\limits_{i} n_i M_i^4}{\sum\limits_{i} n_i M_i^3} = \frac{\sum\limits_{i} w_i M_i^3}{\sum\limits_{i} w_i M_i^2} \tag{10}$$

For heterogeneous polymer systems $M_Z > M_u$.

Basically, the number-average provides the mean value of a mole fraction distribution. Similarly the weight-average provides the mean value of a weight fractions distribution. At the same time, the weight-average represents the moment of inertia of the mole fraction distribution and is thus a measure of the standard deviation of the mole fraction distribution about its mean value. In a corresponding fashion, the Z-average is a measure of the standard deviation of a weight fraction distribution about its mean.

4. Molecular Weight Distributions

It is possible to compute the expected molecular weight distributions and, hence, the ratios of M_n, M_w and M_Z for synthetic high polymers if the method of polymerization and degree of polymerization are known. Flory (3) describes such calculations in detail. The situation is much less direct when one is concerned with the distribution of natural high polymers and their degradation products. In this case, the values of the various molecular weight averages must be determined experimentally and then compared with empirical distribution functions, $f_n(M)$, that can be adjusted through two or more parameters to approximate the observed values.

B. Molecular Weight Determinations

1. Osmotic Pressure

According to Raoult's Law the presence of a small amount of solute reduces the activity of the solvent in a binary solution. Osmometry makes use of the fact that the activity, a_i, of each component i is a function of the external pressure P such that

$$\left(\frac{\delta \ln a_i}{\delta P} \right)_{T,\, n_1,\, \ldots} = \bar{V}_i / RT \tag{11}$$

$\bar{V}_i$ is the partial specific volume of component i. A two-phase system is set up in which solution and pure solvent are separated by a barrier permeable only to the solvent components. At osmotic equilibrium the activity of the solvent components must be the same in both phases. In practice, an external pressure is applied to the solution side of the semipermeable membrane to increase a_1, the solvent activity in that compartment, to equal the activity a_1^0 on the other side. The pressure necessary to accomplish this is the osmotic pressure, π. With the provision that $\overline{V}_1$ is independent of the applied pressure and close to the solvent molar volume V_1, then

$$-\ln a_1 = \pi V_1/RT \qquad (12)$$

For ideal solutions at low solute concentration Eq. 12 reduces to

$$\pi/c = RT/M \qquad (13)$$

where c is expressed in terms of grams of solute per unit volume, and M is the solute molecular weight. It can be readily shown that if the solute is a heterogeneous polymer system, then M should be replaced by the number-average molecular weight, M_n. The osmotic pressure method for the evaluation of M is therefore particularly sensitive to low molecular weight contaminants or components and tends to give values which should be considered as lower limits to the molecular weight.

In practice most polymer and protein solutions are not ideal and π/c is not a constant but a function of the concentration. The reduced osmotic pressure is usually expressed in a power series of concentration terms, as in Eq. 14.

$$\pi/c = RT\,[A_1 + A_2 c + A_3 c^2 + ...] \qquad (14)$$

The coefficients, A_1, A_2, ... are called the virial coefficients. A_1, the first virial coefficient, is $1/M_n$, and hence the molecular weight can be obtained from the limiting value of π/c at infinite dilution in a plot of π/c vs. c. The second and higher virial coefficients represent the deviations of the solution from ideality. Usually only A_2 is determined and the higher order concentration terms are neglected. A_2 is related to M_n, to the average effective volume occupied by the molecule, and to solute-solvent interactions. Some interpretations of A_2, can be made theoretically (3, 4) but A_2 cannot be separated into its components on the basis of osmotic pressure measurements alone. If c is expressed in terms of grams/ml then A_2 has dimensions of ml-mole/gm².

Until comparatively recent times, when dynamic osmometers have been adapted to aqueous systems, the osmotic pressure method as applied to aqueous gelatin solutions suffered from the fact that a considerable period of time was required to achieve osmotic equilibrium. In the usual case this was about 24 hours. To avoid gelation and particle aggregation, high temperatures or special solvent environments were required; consequently hydrolytic degradation was an important factor to be contended with. The most extensive investigations of gelatin systems by osmotic pressure measurements have been carried out by Pouradier and Venet (5-7) and Pouradier, Roman and Venet (8). Boedtker and Doty (9) also used osmotic pressure measurements to good advantage in comparing native tropocollagen with the gelatin obtained from it by denaturation.

Typical plots of (π/c) vs. c, taken from the work of Boedtker and Doty (9), are illustrated in Figs. II-3 and 4. The data for both ichthyocol tropo-

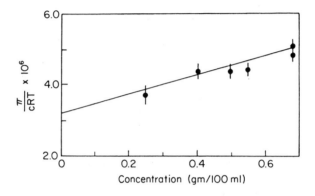

FIG. II-3. Reduced osmotic pressure of ichthyocol collagen: citrate buffer, pH 3.7, at 2° [Boedtker and Doty (9)].

collagen (carp swim bladder) and the gelatin obtained from it show that π/c is a linear function of c over the concentration range examined in each case. Hence, the third and higher virial coefficients are negligibly small. For tropocollagen M_n was 310,000 $\pm$ 50,000 with $A_2 = 2.3 \pm 1.0 \times 10^{-4}$ ml-mole/gm² in pH 3.7 citrate buffer at 2°. The gelatin derived from this collagen had $M_n = 125,000 \pm 10,000$, and $A_2 = 3.0 \times 10^{-4}$ ml-mole/gm² in 2.0 M potassium thiocyanate at 25°. For the gelatin analysis, the 2.0 M potassium thiocyanate had the advantage of eliminating complications resulting from gelation and aggregation permitting the 24-hour equilibration to be carried out at 25° where hydrolytic degradation was minimized. Measurements were made at 36.5° in the pH 3.7 citrate buffer, but the osmotic pressure was found to be constantly decreasing during the equilibration. Extrapolation to zero time yielded results which were consistent with the values obtained at equilibrium in 2.0 M potassium thiocyanate, though the error was large.

Pouradier and Venet (5) measured the osmotic pressure of an alkali-precursor calf skin gelatin (Eastman Kodak F-74) in aqueous solutions containing various reagents. The isoelectric point of this gelatin was determined to be pH 4.75 ± 0.02 by mobility and turbidity measurements.

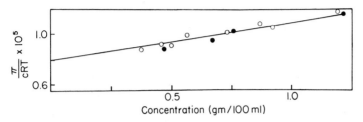

FIG. II-4. Reduced osmotic pressure of ichthyocol gelatin: 2 M KCNS, pH 7, at 25° [Boedker and Doty (9)].

The osmotic pressure data are summarized in Table II-1. It is clear that within a reasonable range of experimental error the gelatin is molecularly dispersed in each of the solvent systems. Although each of the plots of π/c vs. c extrapolated to the same intercept at $c = 0$, distinct differences in

TABLE II-1 [a]

OSMOTIC PRESSURE OF EASTMAN KODAK GELATIN F-74

Solvent	Temperature (°C)	Extrapolated value of π/c at $c = 0$	$\overline{M}_n$
Distilled water	38.2	4.35	60,800
Acetic acid ($M/6$, pH 5.1)	38.2	4.00	66,200
Acetic acid ($M/6$, pH 4.75)	38.2	4.05	65,300
Na$_2$SO$_4$ (0.4 M)	38.2	4.00	65,000
Urea (4.0 M)	25.0	3.80	66,600
Metacresol (pure, nonaqueous)	38.2	4.10	64,500

[a] Data of Pouradier and Venet (5).

solute behavior in each solvent system were evident. Figure II-5 shows the concentration dependence of π/c in each of the solvent systems for which the limiting π/c values are recorded in Table II-1. The value of A_2 for F-74 gelatin in 4.0 M urea at 25° was 1.66×10^{-5} ml-mole/gm², a power of 10 smaller than the value reported by Boedtker and Doty (9) for their denatured tropocollagen in 2.0 M potassium thiocyanate, though concentrated urea and concentrated potassium thiocyanate solutions have very similar effects on the gelatin molecule. This comparison has been made to point out that the second virial coefficient is a function of the molecular weight as well as a function of the polymer-solvent interaction. For this reason, some authors (*3*) prefer to write Eq. 14 in the form

$$\frac{\pi}{c} = \left(\frac{\pi}{c}\right)_{c=0} [1 + \Gamma_2 c + \Gamma_3 c^2 + \ldots] \tag{15}$$

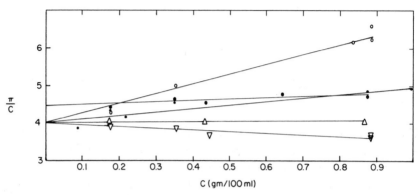

FIG. II-5. The concentration dependence of the reduced osmotic pressure of Kodak F-74 gelatin in various solvents; ●, water; ▽, pH 5.1; ○, pH 4.75; △, 0.4 *M* Na₂SO₄; ○, 4.0 *M* urea. All measurements at 38.2° except for the urea system which was at 25° [Pouradier and Venet (*5*)].

where $\Gamma_2 = A_2/A_1$ and $\Gamma_3 = A_3/A_1$. Since A_2 is a composite of the molecular weight and interaction effects, it is sometimes useful to interpret this quantity as an effective volume. This effective volume relates to the volume, measured from the center of one molecule, that cannot be occupied by the center of a neighboring molecule. For nonrepelling uniform hard spheres this effective or excluded volume is 4 times the volume of each sphere. Large values of the excluded volume indicate interparticle repulsion, negative values indicate interparticle attraction. From the slopes of the π/c vs. *c* plots in Fig. II-5, it would appear that $A_2 = 0$ for the sodium sulfate solutions, $A_2 > 0$ at pH 4.75, and $A_2 < 0$ at pH 5.1. One may interpret these values as indicating that the gelatin molecule is small and noninteracting with its neighbors in 0.4 *M* sodium sulfate, while in dilute acetic acid–acetate systems a net interparticle repulsion exists at pH 4.75 and a small intermolecular attractive force exists at pH 5.1. This interpretation suggests that the value of pH 4.75 reported by Pouradier and Venet (*5*) for the isoelectric point was in error, and that the isoelectric point is closer to pH 5.1 for the F-74 gelatin.

The power of the osmotic pressure method is evident. Osmotic pressure measurements can provide reproducible values for the number-average molecular weight for a given gelatin system. At the same time, the concentration dependence of the osmotic pressure can provide an insight into the gelatin-solvent interaction and gelatin-gelatin intermolecular interaction under a variety of conditions. The principal limitation to the osmotic pressure method is that the precision of measurement drops as the molecular weight increases, since π/c is inversely proportional to M_n. For example, in Pouradier and Venet's measurements for 0.2% F-74 gelatin in 0.4 M sodium sulfate, π was equivalent to a hydrostatic pressure of only 0.80 cm water. If M_n were 180,000 rather than 60,000, then π would have been only 0.26 cm water. Concurrently, as M_n increases, A_2 increases and higher order terms of Eqs. 14 and 15 may be required. Hence, the reliability of the extrapolation to infinite dilution decreases as M_n increases. Degradation during equilibration would drastically reduce M_n if the degraded fragments were nondialyzable, and it is likely that all of the molecular weight data reported by Pouradier and his co-workers (5-8) are subejct to this defect. No zero time corrections were made.

2. Light Scattering

When a plane-polarized light wave impinges upon a small isotropic polarizable particle, the wave will induce an oscillating dipole in the particle. This oscillating dipole will produce a set of secondary waves radiating in all directions from the direction of the incident light beam. The amplitude of the secondary wave in any given direction will depend on the amplitude of the incident plane-polarized wave, the wavelength of the beam, λ, the angle, θ, at which the scattering is observed relative to the direction of the incident wave, and the polarizability of the particle, α. The intensity (energy) of the scattered light is proportional to the square of the amplitude of the scattered wave. In solutions, the polarizability term of interest is the excess polarizability, α, of the particle over that of the solvent and is related to both the number of particles and the difference in dielectric constants of the two substances. The dielectric constant difference is, in turn, equal to the difference of the squares of the refractive indexes of the solute and solvent. All of these factors may be combined in the following expression for unpolarized incident light.

$$\frac{i_\theta}{I_0} = \left(\frac{2\pi^2}{\mathcal{N}\lambda^4 r^2} \right) n_0^2 \left(\frac{dn}{dc} \right)^2 (1 + \cos^2\theta) \, Mc \qquad (16)$$

In Eq. 16 i_θ is the intensity of the scattered wave at angle θ from the direction of the incident beam of intensity I_0. N is Avogadro's number, λ the wavelength of the incident light in vacuum, n_0 the refractive index of the solvent, and r the distance from the scattering particle at which the scattered intensity is measured. M is the particle molecular weight, and c is the particle weight concentration per unit volume, usually expressed in grams/ml.

In practice it is difficult to evaluate r. Measurements are made, therefore, in terms of the function $i_\theta r^2 / I_0$, variously termed the Rayleigh ratio or the reduced intensity of scattering. The symbol R_θ is used to denote the value of this ratio at angle θ. The constant terms of Eq. 16 are combined in a single constant

$$K \equiv \frac{2\pi^2 n_0^2}{N\lambda^4} \left(\frac{dn}{dc} \right)^2$$

Equation 16 may then be rewritten

$$R_\theta = K(1 + \cos^2\theta)\, Mc \tag{17}$$

An alternative approach to light scattering analysis may be made by considering the attenuation of the intensity of the incident beam as it traverses a distance l through the solution. If I_0 is the intensity of the incident light beam, the intensity I at a point l is given by

$$I = I_0 e^{-\tau l} \tag{18}$$

The coefficient τ is called the turbidity of the solution. Since I/I_0 is usually a number very close to 1, the exponent $-\tau l$ is a very small number, so the exponential can be approximated by the first two terms of a series expansion, or

$$\frac{I}{I_0} = 1 - \tau l \tag{19}$$

and

$$\tau l = \frac{I_0 - I}{I_0} \tag{20}$$

The turbidity per cm path is thus seen to be directly related to the energy dissipated, the intensity of light scattered in all directions away from the incident beam. The right-hand side of Eq. 19 can, therefore, be replaced by the integral of Eq. 16, taken over all scattering angles. This integration results in the equation

$$\tau^0 = \left(\frac{32\pi^3}{3\lambda^4 N} \right) n_0^2 \left(\frac{dn}{dc} \right)^2 Mc \equiv H\, Mc \tag{21}$$

or

$$\tau^0 = \left(\frac{16\pi}{3}\right) R_\theta^\circ \, (1 + \cos^2\theta) \tag{22}$$

Equation 22 shows that a measurement of the intensity of scattering at 90° or 0° is equivalent to a measurement of the turbidity and that either quantity can be calculated with the aid of known constants from the other.

The reduced intensity of scattering is proportional to the product Mc. If the polymer is, as usual, heterogeneous, then each molecule i contributes to the scattering according to $M_i c_i$ and $R_\theta = K(1 + \cos^2\theta) \sum_i M_i c_i$. Since

$$c_i = \frac{M_i n_i}{V} \quad \text{and} \quad M_w = \frac{\sum n_i M_i^2}{\sum_i n_i M_i}$$

then

$$R_\theta = K \, (1 + \cos^2\theta) \, \frac{\sum_i n_i M_i}{V} \, M_w$$

and, finally

$$R_\theta = K \, (1 + \cos^2\theta) \, c M_w \tag{23}$$

Thus measurements of the turbidity or light scattering provide the weight-average molecular weight. As pointed out earlier, this makes the scattering particularly sensitive to the presence of a few very large particles, dust or aggregates. For this reason scattering measurements require the experimenter to take the utmost precautions for cleanliness. Molecular weights determined by light scattering should be considered as upper limits to the molecular weight.

The scattering theory outlined above relates to the scattering from a system of noninteracting isotropic particles whose dimensions are small compared to the wavelength of the incident light. To account for the concentration dependence of the scattering, a somewhat different approach is usually taken.

Equation 16 indicates that the scattering phenomenon depends on the creation of refractive index variations in a solution. In pure solvent local fluctuations in density may give rise to a small amount of scattering that can be readily determined. Indeed, pure benzene and carbon disulfide have been used to calibrate light scattering instruments. More important however, solute concentration fluctuations in solutions can produce larger refractive index fluctuations. A local change in concentration decreases the solvent activity in the volume element concerned, giving rise to a local change in the osmotic pressure, so that osmotic work must be expended to effect the concentration of the solute within the volume element. The osmotic work done in changing the concentration from c to $c + \Delta c$ in a volume element V is

$$[\pi_{c+\Delta c} - \pi_c] \frac{V}{c} d(\Delta c) = \frac{d\pi}{dc} \frac{V}{c} d(\Delta c) \tag{24}$$

The corresponding free energy change is

$$\Delta F = \frac{V}{c} \frac{d\pi}{dc} \int_0^{\Delta c} \Delta c \, d(\Delta c) = \frac{V}{2c} \frac{d\pi}{dc} (\Delta c)^2 \tag{25}$$

The probability that a concentration fluctuation of the magnitude of Δc will occur is proportional to $\exp(-\Delta F/RT)$, hence, the average value of Δc^2 is then

$$\overline{\Delta c^2} = \frac{RTc}{V(d\pi/dc)} \tag{26}$$

However, a change in concentration, Δc, causes a change Δn in the refractive index equal to $\Delta c(dn/dc)$, and the amplitude of the wave scattered from the volume element V is proportional to $V\Delta n$. The intensity of the scattered light from V is proportional to $V^2(\Delta n)^2$ so that

$$i = k'V\,RTc \frac{(dn/dc)^2}{(d\pi/dc)} \tag{27}$$

Equation 27 is important because it indicates that the concentration dependence of the scattering intensity can be deduced from the osmotic pressure–concentration relationships, e.g. Eq. 14 or 15, and that the constants are related to the virial coefficients of the osmotic pressure equations. With this relationship in mind Eq. 23 can be rearranged to the form indicated in Eq. 28.

$$\frac{Kc}{R_\theta (1 + \cos^2\theta)} = \frac{1}{M_w} + 2A_2 c + 3A_3 c^2 + \dots \tag{28}$$

A plot of Kc/R vs. c usually yields a straight line with the slope equal to $2A_2$, and the intercept at $c = 0$ is equal to the reciprocal of the weight-average molecular weight. The osmotic pressure and light scattering methods thus provide similar information on molecular interactions while yielding molecular weights averaged in different ways.

When the scattering particles approach the dimensions of the incident light, the light impinging on different parts of the particle may give rise to scattered radiations which are significantly out of phase and lead to destructive interference. The difference in path length traversed by the scattered rays from different parts of the scattering particle will be less for the forward radiation than for the radiation in the backward direction at large angle. Therefore, the destructive interference will be greater at larger values of θ but will approach zero at $\theta = 0$. Thus, the correct value for the molecular weight is obtained from Eq. 28 only for $R_{\theta=0}$. In practice, since it is not possible to measure R_0 directly, one obtains values for R_θ at a series of angles and extrapolates these to $\theta = 0$. The way in which R_θ varies with θ can provide valuable information as to the shape and dimensions of the scattering particles. If R_θ° is the Rayleigh ratio that would be observed in the absence of intraparticle interference, the particle scattering (correction) factor, $P(\theta)$, is defined by $P(\theta) = R_\theta^\circ/R_\theta$. Equations for $P(\theta)$ have been calculated for rods, spheres, and monodisperse and heterodisperse systems of random coils in terms of the major dimensions of the scattering particle. The Z-average radius of gyration of the scattering particle can be determined from the slope of a plot of $(Kc/R_\theta)_{c=0}$ vs. $\sin^2(\theta/2)$. One can then assume a particle shape, calculate $P(\theta)$ as a function of θ, and compare this computed $P(\theta)$ function with that found experimentally. In this way the probable particle shape can be determined. The reader is referred to the excellent review by Doty and Edsall (10) and the monograph by Stacy (11) for the details of these methods. One of the important aspects of the light scattering method for molecular characterization is that the molecular weight and particle dimensions can be obtained independently of each other.

A number of light scattering studies have been made on gelatins but only a few of these, dealing with the characterization of molecularly dispersed gelatins, will be discussed at this point. The remaining studies will be discussed more appropriately in later chapters. An important preliminary requirement of any light scattering investigation is the precise evaluation of the refractive index increment, $(dn/dc)_\lambda$. Representative values of (dn/dc) for gelatin systems at wavelength 4360 Å (blue line of mercury) are listed in Table II-2. In water or dilute salt solutions at neutral pH, $(dn/dc)_{4360}$ is relatively constant and equal to 0.192. In more concentrated solutions, e.g. 1.0 M potassium chloride, 1.0 M potassium thiocyanate, $(dn/dc)_{4360}$ is more dependent on the solvent composition (Gallop, 11 a; M'Ewen and Pratt, 11 b).

The first thorough light scattering investigation of gelatin was reported by Boedtker and Doty (12). They examined an ossein gelatin, Knox P-111-20, prepared in the following manner. Beef bones were heated at 80°

TABLE II-2

REFRACTIVE INDEX INCREMENTS OF GELATIN AND SOLUBLE COLLAGENS [a]

Solvent	Temperature (°C)	Gelatin	dn/dc	Reference
H_2O	25	Knox P-111-20	0.194	(12)
	40	Bovine corium ext.	0.192	(17)
0.1 M NaCl	25	Knox P-111-20	0.1925	(12)
0.25 M NaCl	40	Bovine corium ext.	0.192	(17)
1.0 M NaCl	25	Knox P-111-20	0.186	(12)
0.10 M KCl	40	Bovine corium ext.	0.192	(17)
0.25 M KCl	40	Bovine corium ext.	0.192	(17)
0.20 M KCl	40	Grayslake gelatin (pI 9.0)	0.192	(20)
0.20 M KCl	40	Peter Cooper (pI 5.0)	0.192	(20)
1.0 M KCl	40	Bovine corium ext.	0.176	(18)
1.0 M KCNS	25	Knox P-111-20	0.185	(12)
1.0 M KCNS + 0.1 M KH$_2$PO$_4$ + 0.1 M K$_2$HPO$_4$	30	Knox B-136-1	0.172	(14)
2.0 M KCNS	25	Knox P-111-20	0.173	(12)
2.0 M KCNS	25	Denatured icthyocol	0.173	(9)
pH 3.7 citrate buffer 0.1 M citric acid 0.05 M Na citrate	25	Denatured icthyocol	0.192	(11a)
	25	Native or denatured icthyocol	0.187	(9)
pH 2.99 citrate buffer 0.025 M citrate	25	Rat skin collagen	0.197	(11b)
0.10 M acetic acid	25	Rat tail tendon collagen	0.197	(11b)
0.005 M HCl	25	Rat tail tendon collagen	0.195	(11b)
0.05 M KH$_2$PO$_4$ 0.05 M K$_2$HPO$_4$	30	Knox B-136-1	0.188	(14)

[a] At $\lambda^\circ = 4360$ Å.

for 6 hours, crushed, demineralized with 5% hydrochloric acid for 2 weeks, and washed. The ossein was soaked in saturated lime water at 15° for 4 weeks. The pH was adjusted to 4.5 and the collagen converted to gelatin by heating to 65° for 4 hours. The gelatin was autoclaved at 15-lb pressure at 120° for 20 minutes. The resulting gelatin solution (6%) was dialyzed against distilled water et 4° for 3 days and then electrodialyzed for 2 days at 4°. A partial fractionation was carried out by adding ethanol to make the final solution 50% alcohol by volume. The small amount of precipitate was allowed to settle and after 2 days the clear supernatant solution was decanted. The gelatin was dried by lyophilization. The dried gelatin was readily soluble in water and had an isoelectric point of pH 5.10 ± 0.05.

The gelatin was dissolved in either 1.0 M potassium thiocyanate, pH 5.1 at 25°, or 0.15 M sodium chloride, pH 5.1 at 40°. The solutions were centrifuged at 100,000 × gravity for 90 minutes and then transferred to the light scattering cell under dust-free conditions. The reduced intensity of scattering was measured for various angles between 35° and 135°. These data, in terms of Kc/R_θ, were extrapolated to zero angle and zero concentration by the double extrapolation method described by Zimm (13). A typical Zimm plot is shown in Fig. II-6 for the gelatin in 0.15 M sodium chloride at 40°. The two lines connecting the closed points represent the extrapolated values of Kc/R_θ at $c = 0$ and at $\theta = 0$. The intercept of each line gives the reciprocal of the weight-average molecular weight (Eq. 28). The slope of the $c = 0$ line (the upper line connecting the closed points) provides the Z-average radius of gyration, and the slope of the $\theta = 0$ line (the lowest line on the diagram) provides the value of A_2. The parameters calculated from these data are given in Table II-3. It was evident,

TABLE II-3 [a]

LIGHT SCATTERING RESULTS, KNOX P-111-20 GELATIN IN VARIOUS SOLVENTS

Solvent	M_w	$(\overline{\varrho_Z^2})^{1/2}$ Z-average radius of gyration (Å)	$A_2 \times 10^4$ (ml-mole/gm²)
KCNS (1.0 M, 25°) pH 5.1	90,000	175	2.6
NaCl (0.15 M, 40°) pH 5.1	89,000	165	2.9
pH 3.1	88,000	175	6.0

[a] Data of Boedtker and Doty (12).

as it was in the work of Pouradier and Venet (5), that the gelatin was molecularly dispersed at 40° in dilute salt solutions or in 2.0 M potassium thiocyanate at room temperature. The effect of repulsive intermolecular interactions is strikingly evident at pH 3.1 where A_2 was increased by a factor of 2.

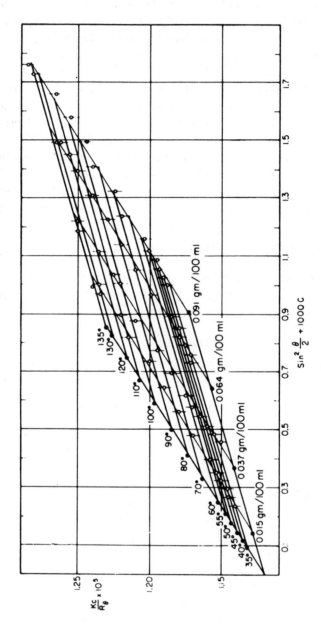

FIG. II-6. Zimm plot of the reciprocal angular envelopes for Knox P-111-20 gelatin in 0.15 M NaCl at the isoelectric point at 40° [Boedtker and Doty (12)].

Since the radius of gyration is a Z-average parameter and the molecular weight is a weight-average weight, ϱ_Z and M_w cannot be used together unless some polydispersity correction is available. Williams, Saunders and and Cicirelli (2), in a report to be discussed later in detail, found from sedimentation analysis that $M_Z/M_w = 2.6$ for P-111-20 gelatin. It was assumed that this gelatin could be represented by a random coil model and, hence, that $\bar{r^2}$, the root mean square end-to-end extension, was proportional to M. With an average value of 170 Å taken for ϱ_Z and the fact that for a random coil $\bar{r^2}$ is related to $\bar{\varrho^2}$ by

$$\bar{r^2} = 6\ \bar{\varrho^2} \tag{29}$$

the weight-average end-to-end chain extension $\bar{r_w^{1/2}}$ was found to be 258 Å.

The values for A_2 are of the same order as that quoted earlier (9) for denatured ichthyocol tropocollagen in 2.0 M potassium thiocyanate at 25°. The denatured TC data were obtained by osmotic pressure measurement.

A similar light scattering investigation on pI 5.0 calf skin gelatin (Knox, type B, lot B-136-1) was carried out by Gouinlock, Flory, and Scheraga (14). In this study the gelatin was fractionated by alcohol precipitation into two subfractions, F-2 and F-3. F-2 was the gelatin precipitated at 37.7° from an aqueous 0.55% solution of gelatin between the alcohol:water ratios of 1.27 and 1.36, and F-3 that precipitated between 1.36 and 1.46 (95% alcohol). F-2 represented 8.3% of the unfractionated gelatin, F-3 amounted to 9.6%. The unfractionated gelatin was designated U.

The scattering measurements were carried out at 30° with U, F-2, and F-3 dissolved in 1.0 M KCNS buffered at pH 6.46–6.49 with 0.1 M KH$_2$PO$_4$ and 0.1 M K$_2$HPO$_4$, or in solutions buffered with 0.05 M KH$_2$PO$_4$ and 0.05 M K$_2$HPO$_4$ at the same pH and temperature but without potassium thiocyanate. The solution turbidities were measured at a series of angles between 40° and 135° at several concentrations. The extrapolations to zero concentration were carried out in a rather unusual fashion by plotting $(c/\tau_\theta)^{1/2}$ vs. c at constant θ. The values $(c/\tau_\theta)_{c=0}$ obtained in this way were then plotted vs. $\sin^2(\theta/2)$ and extrapolated to $\theta = 0$. Representative data are shown in Figs. II-7 and 8. The values of M_w, ϱ_Z, r_Z and A_2 calculated from these data are summarized in Table II-4. The value of r_Z was determined from ϱ_Z, using Eq. 29. The assumption of a random coil configuration is implicit in the use of this equation.

The most striking feature of these results was that the molecular weights of F-2 and F-3 were considerably higher than any previously reported for

TABLE II-4 [a]

LIGHT SCATTERING RESULTS, KNOX B-136-1 GELATIN

Gelatin	Solvent	$M_w \times 10^{-5}$ (gm/mole)	$(\overline{\varrho_Z^2})^{1/2}$ (Å)	$(\overline{R_Z^2})^{1/2}$ (Å)	$A_2 \times 10^4$ (ml-mole/gm²)	$\left(\dfrac{\overline{\varrho_Z^2}}{M_w}\right)^{1/2} \times 10^{11}$
U	Phosphate (0.05 M)	2.70	302	740	2.4	—
U	KCNS (1.0 M)	3.02	302	740	2.6	—
F-2	KCNS (1.0 M)	5.96	280	685	2.4	362
F-3	KCNS (1.0 M)	3.83	242	590	3.3	390
Estimated uncertainty		10%	5–10%	5–10%	10%	—

[a] Data of Gouinlock, Flory, and Scheraga (14).

gelatin. There were no anomalies in the extrapolations to zero concentration, however, and it was concluded that the high molecular weights were not attributable to the presence of dissociable aggregates but actually pertained to molecularly dispersed gelatin. This is especially brought out by the fact that A_2 was 3×10^4 ml-mole/gm², as found by Boedtker and

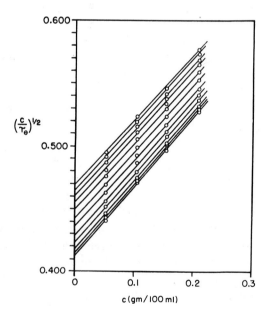

FIG. II-7. Angular scattering plotted as the square root of $[c/\tau(\theta)]$ vs. c for Knox B-136-1, fraction F-2, in 1 M KCNS. Each line represents measurements at constant angle [Gouinlock et al. (14)].

Doty (12). There is one point of discrepancy between the results of Boedtker and Doty (12) and Gouinlock *et al.* (14). If the same model applied in each case then $(\overline{\varrho_Z^2}/M_w)^{1/2}$ should have been the same. For gelatin P-111-20 this ratio was 584×10^{-11} (M in units of gm/mole, ϱ in units of cm), while for gelatin B-136-1 the ratio was 360–390×10^{-11}, the difference being far beyond the experimental error ($\sim 15\%$) inherent in each measurement. This discrepancy may be related to differences in molecular weight distributions in the two gelatin preparations. However, it is more likely that the very high molecular weight gelatins cannot be represented by the random coil model.

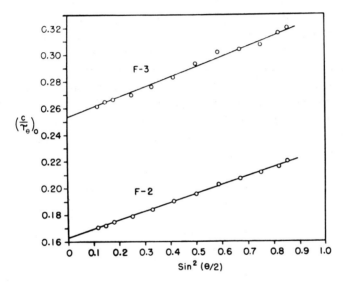

Fig. II-8. The angular dependence of $c/\tau(\theta)$ at zero concentration for two fractions of Knox B-136-1 gelatin. The points were extrapolated as in Fig. II-7 to infinite dilution [Gouinlock *et al.* (14)].

A third light scattering study of an alcohol fractionated pI 4.95 gelatin was carried out by Courts and Stainsby (15). The collagen stock was ox hide limed for 3 months and then extracted under neutral conditions (16). This gelatin was fractionated into five portions, the first containing about 4.5% of the gelatin. The remaining fractions each comprised 20–30% of the gelatin. The fractions were dissolved in 0.5 M sodium chloride, pH 6.5–7.0 at 40°. In contrast to the studies described above, Courts and Stainsby (15) found that at gelatin concentrations below 5×10^{-3} gm/ml the value of c/R_{90} was independent of $c(A_2 = 0)$. Thus a measurement at one concentration only ($c \sim 2.5 \times 10^{-3}$ gm/ml) was used. The dissymmetry, Z ($Z = R_{45}/R_{135}$), was $\leqslant 1.12$ for each fraction; hence, extrapolation to $\theta = 0$ was not used and the particle scattering factor $P(90)$ was determined from Z. The weight-average molecular weights ranged from 320,000 for the first major fraction to 62,000 for the fifth fraction. The unfractionated gelatin yielded a value of $M_w = 190,000$ (16). The dissymmetry data were not reported and no estimates of particle dimension or configuration were made from the scattering data.

Courts and Stainsby also determined M_w for a series of acid-processed ox bone gelatin (pI = 8.8) fractions obtained by alcohol coacervation in the same way. M_w ranged from 1.94×10^5 to 0.25×10^5.

As part of their investigation of the collagen-gelatin transition, Veis, Eggenberger and Cohen (17), Veis and Cohen (18, 19), and Veis, Anesey and Cohen (20, 21) have examined gelatins prepared from unlimed purified steer hide corium collagen by a variety of short neutral or acid extractions. The gelatins were fractionated by an alcohol coacervation technique similar to that described by Pouradier and Venet (5) and Stainsby (22). Particle weights of 8,300,000–200,000 were found in the various factions. Measurements were made in 1.0 M potassium chloride at 40°. Zimm plots were used to extrapolate the data to zero angle and zero concentration, though in 1.0 M potassium chloride at 40° $A_2 \sim 0$. Typical molecular weight and ϱ_z data (18) are shown in Table II-5. As noted in the table, fractions 3-A, 3-B, and 3-C were obtained within the same alcohol:water ratio range from gel-

TABLE II-5 [a]

LIGHT SCATTERING MOLECULAR PARAMETERS OF GELATINS
FROM UNLIMED PURIFIED BOVINE CORIUM COLLAGEN [b]

Fraction	Alcohol:water ratio range	$M_w \times 10^{-5}$	$(\overline{\varrho_z^2})^{1/2}$	$\left(\dfrac{\overline{\varrho_z^2}}{M_w}\right)^{1/2} \times 10^{11}$
2-B	2:1–2.5:1	83.3	2410	835
3-A [c]	2.5:1–3.0:1	7.45	444	514
3-B [d]	2.5:1–3.0:1	3.45	314	535
3-C [e]	2.5:1–3.0:1	2.32	371	770
4-B	3.0:1–3.5:1	2.02	345	769

[a] Data of Veis and Cohen (18).
[b] With pI = 9.0.
[c] A = pH 4 extraction, 60°, 1 hour, 0.1 ionic strength Na acetate, acetic acid, NaCl.
[d] B = pH 6.5 extraction, 60°, 1 hour, salt-free.
[e] C = pH 3 extraction, 60°, 1 hour, 0.1 ionic strength glycine, HCl, NaCl.

atins extracted for the same time period at the same temperature but at different pH. It is perhaps not surprising that M_w varied but, as indicated in the last column of the table, the ratios $(\overline{\varrho_Z^2}/M)^{1/2}$ also varied, indicating basic structural heterogeneity. These data show again that a single model, such as the random coil, cannot be used for all gelatins. It is probable that a single structural model cannot even be used to describe all of the gelatin obtained in a single extract.

The several light scattering investigations discussed above agree only in demonstrating: (1) that gelatins are molecularly dispersed in aqueous solutions at temperatures of 40° and above or in 1.0–2.0 = potassium thiocyanate at temperatures above 25°; (2) that gelatins may range in molecular weight up to values greater than 10^6; (3) that gelatins, even after fractionation, are exceedingly heterogeneous; and (4) that the same configurational model cannot be used for all gelatins. These statements emphasize that serious efforts should be made in any study of gelatin to characterize the molecular weight distribution before relating M_w to other physical properties. It is not adequate to use only M_w or $(\overline{\varrho_Z^2})^{1/2}$ to describe a gelatin system, though these values can be readily obtained from light scattering measurements.

3. *Viscosity*

The hydrodynamic theory underlying the characterization of macromolecules through viscosity data is much less well developed than the theories for the characterization methods already discussed. Nonetheless, because of the simplicity and reproducibility of viscosimetric techniques, viscosity studies have played a prominent role in polymer chemistry. Indeed, in the gelatin field, one of the two principal criteria of gelatin or glue quality is an empirical viscosity scale. At the concentrations ($\sim 6\%$) used in these grading methods, the viscosity appears to be quite sensitive to the molecular weight and weight distribution but such data cannot be interpreted on the molecular level. One, can, however, correlate dilute solution viscosities with molecular properties.

The viscosity, η, of a solution containing a macromolecular solute is greater than the viscosity, η_0, of the solvent alone. A number of ways are available to express this viscosity increase. The relative viscosity, η_{rel}, is the ratio η/η_0; the specific viscosity, η_{sp}, is $\eta_{rel} - 1$; and the reduced viscosity, η_{red}, is defined by equation 30.

$$\eta_{red} = \frac{\eta_{sp}}{c} = \frac{\eta_{rel-1}}{c} = \frac{\eta - \eta_0}{\eta_0 c} \tag{30}$$

The molecular properties of the solute are most readily analyzed in terms of η_{red}. The concentration is usually expressed in grams solute/100 ml and, since η_{rel} is dimensionless, η_{red} has the dimensions 100 ml/gm or deciliters/gm. The reduced viscosity is not a constant but depends on the solute concentration. The limiting value of η_{red} at zero solute concentration is related to the basic hydrodynamic properties of the individual solute molecules and for this reason is called the intrinsic viscosity, $[\eta]$. Specifically,

$$[\eta] = \lim_{c \to 0} \frac{\eta_{sp}}{c} = \lim_{c \to 0} \left[\frac{\ln \eta_{rel}}{c} \right] \tag{31}$$

Huggins (23) showed that a plot of η_{sp}/c vs. c was linear and could be represented by

$$\eta_{sp}/c = [\eta] + k'[\eta]^2 c \tag{32}$$

An alternative method of representing viscosity data is

$$\frac{\ln \eta_{rel}}{c} = [\eta] + k''[\eta]^2 c \tag{33}$$

Equation 33 is based on the observation that a series expansion of $\ln \eta_{rel}$, as η_{rel} approaches unity, shows the equivalence of that term with η_{sp}. The constant k'' is approximately $\frac{1}{2}k'$, hence a plot of $(\ln \eta_{rel})/c$ varies less sharply with c than does a similar plot of η_{sp}/c.

In the absence of an adequate theory, the relationship between molecular weight and intrinsic viscosity has been found, empirically, to be of the form

$$[\eta] = K M^a \tag{34}$$

The parameters K and a both depend on the nature of the solvent and the character of the polymer. For spherical molecules a is ~ 0.5, and approaches 0.8 for molecules with the random coil configuration and is greater than 1 for stiff rods.

Flory (24-26), Debye (27, 28), and Kirkwood (29, 30) and their co-workers have analyzed the hydrodynamic theory for random chain molecules. These works have been summarized by Flory (3). The principal result of interest here is that the intrinsic viscosity depends only on the overall size of the random chain and not particularly on the size of the individual chain elements or on their chemical character. The root-mean-square end-to-end extension $(\overline{r^2})^{1/2}$ and molecular weight M are related by Eq. 35

$$[\eta] = \Phi \frac{(\overline{r^2})^{3/2}}{M} \tag{35}$$

in which Φ is a universal constant equal to 2.1×10^{21} when M is expressed in units of gm/mole, r in cm, and $[\eta]$ in dl/gm. A refinement of this formulation, Eq. 36,

$$[\eta] = \Phi \left(\frac{\overline{r_0^2}}{M} \right)^{3/2} M^{1/2} \alpha^3 \tag{36}$$

introduces two new parameters, r_0 and α. The dimension r_0 is the value of the end-to-end chain extension in the absence of all intramolecular interactions, i.e. the unperturbed dimension calculated directly from a random flight analysis. In the real case, a correction to r_0 must be made to account for the fact that two chain elements cannot simultaneously occupy the same site and that interactions between chain elements may exist. The real dimension r will exceed r_0 by a factor of α. For a given series of polymer homologs $(\overline{r_0^2}/M)$ is a constant as long as M is sufficiently large; hence, one may write

$$[\eta] = K M^{1/2} \alpha^3 \tag{37}$$

where

$$K = \Phi \left(\frac{\overline{r_0^2}}{M} \right)^{3/2} \tag{38}$$

The parameter α has a value somewhat greater than 1 in good solvents but approaches 1 in poor solvents. It is a constant for a particular polymer-solvent system at a given temperature. The similiarity between the theoretical development, Eq. 37, and the empirical relationship, Eq. 34, is striking but, as mentioned earlier, the exponent a varies between 0.5 and 0.8 with 0.5 the lower limit for spherical particles. From this comparison it can be seen that $(\overline{r^2})^{1/2}$ can be considered as the radius of a hydrodynamically equivalent sphere.

In a dilute solution of a heterogeneous polymer mixture the molecules can be considered to contribute to the viscosity independently of each other or

$$\eta_{sp} = \sum_i (\eta_{sp})_i \tag{39}$$

and, assuming extreme dilution

$$(\eta_{sp})_i = K' M_i^a c_i \tag{40}$$

Hence,

$$\eta_{sp} = K' \sum_i M_i^a c_i \tag{41}$$

and

$$[\eta] = \frac{\eta_{sp}}{c} = K' \sum_i M_i^a \frac{c_i}{c} = K' \sum_i M_i^a w_i \tag{42}$$

where $c = \sum_i c_i$, the total polymer concentration, and w_i is the weight fraction of i. The viscosity-average molecular weight $\overline{M}_v$ is therefore defined by

$$\overline{M}_v = \left[\sum w_i M_i^a \right]^{1/a} \tag{43}$$

or

$$\overline{M}_v = \left[\frac{\sum_i w_i M_i^{1+a}}{\sum_i n_i M_i} \right]^{1/a} \tag{44}$$

With the use of Eq. 44, the viscosity–molecular weight relationship of Eq. 34 can be rewritten

$$[\eta] = K' \overline{M}_v^a \tag{45}$$

A comparison of Eqs. 43 and 44 with Eqs. 2 and 7 reveals that the molecular weight average that correctly correlates with viscosity is intermediate between the number- and weight-average molecular weights. Since a is usually > 0.5, M_v is closer to M_w than to M_n.

Pouradier and Venet (5-7) correlated the results of their osmotic pressure measurements on Kodak F-74 gelatin, and alcohol fractions of F-74, with viscosity measurements. For the F-74 fractions at pH 4.75 $\pm$ 0.05, 35°, and in the absence of salt, $[\eta]$ ranged from 0.215 for a number-average molecular weight of 46,000 to 0.83 for $M_n = 207,000$. A plot of these data as log $[\eta]$ vs. log M_n yielded a straight line (Fig. II-9) as predicted by Eq. 45, and resulted in the relationship

$$[\eta]_{\text{F-74}} = 1.66 \times 10^{-5} [M_n]^{0.885} \tag{46}$$

A similar study of alcohol fractions of a pig skin gelatin (7), pI > 9.0, led to a correlation of the same form, but in which the constants were substantially different

$$[\eta]_{\text{pig skin}} = 1.10 \times 10^{-4} [M_n]^{0.74} \tag{47}$$

The nature of the relationship between the two molecular weight–intrinsic viscosity equations is illustrated in Fig. II-10. At any given M_n, the pig skin gelatins have a higher intrinsic viscosity. In addition to these basic observations on the fractionated gelatins, Pouradier and Venet made two further important points.

First, Pouradier and Venet (7) determined M_n and $[\eta]$ for seven gelatins, all with pl 4.7–4.8, but of different manufacture. Their results are listed in

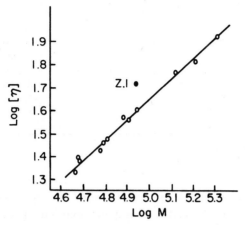

FIG. II-9. The intrinsic viscosity of Kodak F-74 gelatin fractions as a function of the number-average molecular weight. The open circles represent fractions from the same parent gelatin. The point labeled Z.1 is a fraction from a different gelatin preparation [Pouradier and Venet (6)].

Table II-6 in order of increasing molecular weight. It is clear from this list that all gelatins with the same isoionic point do not follow the same empirical molecular weight–viscosity relationship.

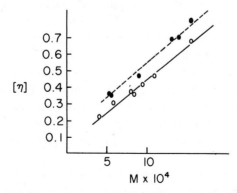

FIG. II-10. The intrinsic viscosity of two series of fractionated gelatins as a function of the number-average molecular weight; O, Kodak F-74, isoelectric point pH 4.8; ●, pig skin gelatin, isoelectric point pH 8.8 [Pouradier and Venet (7)].

TABLE II-6 [a]

COMPARISON OF THE MOLECULAR WEIGHTS AND INTRINSIC
VISCOSITIES OF GELATINS WITH THE SAME ISOIONIC pH

Gelatin	pI	Source	M_n	$[\eta]$ [b]
VIII	4.8	—	18,000	0.260
I	4.8	Bone	46,000	0.505
IV	4.7	Calf skin	50,000	0.590
V	4.75	Rabbit skin	60,000	0.410
F-74	4.75	Calf skin	65,000	0.565
VI	4.8	—	72,000	0.750
VII	4.8	—	86,000	0.615

[a] Data of Pouradier and Venet (7).
[b] At pH 7.0, 0.15 M NaCl, 55°.

Second, Pouradier and Venet (6) followed the hydrolytic degradation of unfractionated F-74 gelatin in isoionic solution. They compared the M_n and $[\eta]$ data at various stages in the degradation with that obtained from analysis of the fractions obtained during alcohol fractionation of undegraded F-74. They found that the same relationship held for all fractions and degraded gelatin mixtures, that is, $[\eta]_{F\text{-}74} = 1.66 \times 10^{-5}$ $[M_n]^{0.885}$ in each instance.

These two apparently conflicting observations led Pouradier and Venet to conclude that either the molecular weight distributions of gelatins were fixed by the method of their manufacture or that the molecular characteristics were different in gelatins of different origin. Nevertheless, neither the nature of the molecule nor the weight distribution was changed during hydrolysis once the basic structure-distribution pattern was set, presumably by the pretreatment of the collagen stock. These conclusions emphasize the difficulty, already noted in the section on light scattering, of using a common structural model and distribution function for all gelatins. As the data of Table II-6 indicate, it would be particularly dangerous to equate intrinsic viscosity with molecular weight in comparing gelatins of different origin, though this has been frequently and sometimes indiscriminately done.

In the course of their investigation of the molecular weight of gelatins by light scattering, Courts and Stainsby (15) had also determined the intrinsic viscosity of each gelatin fraction. They compared an alkali-pretreated bovine hide gelatin and an acid-processed ox bone gelatin. Their data differed from that of Pouradier and Venet (*5-7*) in two important and clear-cut ways. Both sets of data are shown in Fig. II-11 as log $[\eta]$ vs. log M_n (or M_w). The data of Courts and Stainsby relating $[\eta]$ and M_w can be put in the form

$$[\eta]_{\text{hide gelatin}} = 2.97 \times 10^{-3} M_w^{0.45} \tag{48}$$

$$[\eta]_{\text{ossein gelatin}} = 2.21 \times 10^{-3} M_w^{0.45} \tag{49}$$

The great difference in the value of the exponent *a*, as indicated in Eqs. 48 and 49 and in Eqs. 46 and 47, is too large to be explained in terms of differences in the configuration of the gelatins, particularly in comparing

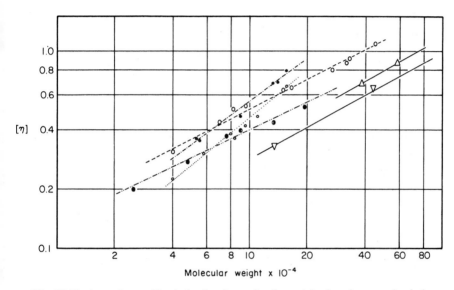

Fig. II-11. A summary of intrinsic viscosity–molecular weight data for several gelatins; o, calf skin, pI 4.8 (*7*); •, pig skin, pI 8.8 (*7*); O, limed ox hide, pI 4.9 (*16*); ●, ossein, pI 8.8 (*15*); △, Knox P-111-20, pI 4.9 (*14*); ▽, unlimed steer hide, pI 9.0 (*21*); ◑, denatured tropocollagen (*9*); ◐, Knox P-111-20, pI 4.9 (*12*).

the two acid-precursor (Eqs. 47, 49) and the two alkali-precursor (Eqs. 46, 48) gelatins. It seems more appropriate to attribute this discrepancy to the non-uniformity of the molecular weight distributions. As noted in Eq. 44, $\overline{M}_v$ is an average intermediate between the number-average and weight-average weights but closer to the weight average. Hence $[\eta]$ will appear to increase more rapidly with M_n than with M_w if $M_w > M_n$ by a relatively large factor. However, this explanation is not entirely adequate since it is evident that the number-average molecular weights reported by Pouradier and Venet (5-7) are not always lower than the weight-average molecular weights of Courts and Stainsby (15) for systems with the same intrinsic viscosity.

A still more serious difficulty lies in the relative positions of the $[\eta]$ vs. M plots for the acid- and alkali-precursor gelatins in the two sets of data. According to Courts and Stainsby, the acid-precursor gelatins have a lower intrinsic viscosity than alkali-precursor gelatins with the same molecular weight. There is no way to resolve this discrepancy at this time. A detailed study of this point is required. The limited evidence available tends to support the molecular weight–viscosity data of Courts and Stainsby rather than that of Pouradier and Venet. Veis and Cohen(19) compared the molecular weights and intrinsic viscosities of two commercial gelatins, unfractionated, but of nearly equal weight-average molecular weight. The alkali-precursor gelatin had the higher intrinsic viscosity (Table II-7).

TABLE II-7 [a]

MOLECULAR WEIGHT-VISCOSITY COMPARISON FOR
TWO UNFRACTIONATED COMMERCIAL GELATINS

Gelatin	$M_w \times 10^{-5}$	$[\eta]$	$(\overline{\varrho_z^2})^{1/2}$ (Å)	pH
Acid-precursor (in 0.2 M KCl)	3 3	0.42	452	7.6
Alkali-precursor (in 0.2 M KCl)	3 3	0 58	447	5.0

[a] Data of Veis and Cohen (19).

Gouinlock et al. (14) and Veis et al. (21) determined weight-average molecular weights and intrinsic viscosities for fractionated gelatins. In each case, for both alkali- and acid-processed gelatins, the exponent a was of the order of 0.5–0.6. However, the alkali-processed gelatins again had higher viscosities for the same molecular weights. The fractions obtained in the two cases were not of similar homogeneity, however. These data are included in Fig. II-11.

Gouinlock, Flory and Scheraga (14) analyzed their light scattering and viscosity data in terms of the parameters of Eqs. 35–38 to determine how closely their gelatin, Knox type B, lot B-136-1, pI 5.0, corresponded to a random chain polymer in configuration. The results of their computations are summarized in Table II-8. In these calculations the unperturbed root-

TABLE II-8 [a]

CONFIGURATIONAL PARAMETERS FOR KNOX TYPE B GELATIN IN 1.0 M KCNS [b]

Parameter	Fraction	
	F-2	F-3
Measured		
M_w	$5\ 96 \times 10^5$	$3\ 83 \times 10^5$
$(\overline{\varrho_z^2})^{1/2}$	280	242
$[\eta]$	0 88	0 69
Derived		
Φ	1.63×10^{21}	1.29×10^{21}
α	1 25	1 25
$\left(\dfrac{\overline{\varrho^2}}{M}\right)^{1/2}$	362×10^{-11}	390×10^{-11}
$\left(\dfrac{\overline{\varrho_0^2}}{M}\right)^{1/2}$	290×10^{-11}	310×10^{-11}
$(\overline{r^2})^{1/2}$	685 Å	590 Å
$\left(\dfrac{\overline{r_{0f}^2}}{M}\right)^{1/2}$	395 Å	395 Å
$\left(\dfrac{\overline{r_0^2}}{\overline{r_{0f}^2}}\right)^{1/2}$	1.8	1.9

[a] Data of Gouinlock, Flory, and Scheraga (*14*).
[b] pI 5.0, lot B-136-1, alcohol fractionated.

mean-square end-to-end chain extension, r_0, was taken as $(6\ \overline{\varrho_0^2})^{1/2}$. The unperturbed radius of gyration ϱ_0 was, in turn, based on estimates of the value of α. The value of r_{0f}, the end-to-end extension for the case of free rotation, was estimated by the method of Benoit (*31*) for polypeptide chains. The value was based on crystallographic data on amino acids and proteins. Gouinlock *et al.* (*14*) state that the value found for the ratio $(\overline{r_0^2}/\overline{r_{0f}^2})^{1/2}$, just under 2, is in close agreement with that found for various synthetic polymers. However, the value of Φ is decidedly lower than the average value, 2.1×10^{21}, found for the same synthetic polymers. A difference of this type, that is, a lower value of Φ, is indicative of chain stiffness and chain branching in cellulose systems (*32*). Nevertheless, it was concluded that the gelatin molecule was very similar to ordinary chain polymers in its configurational character in aqueous solutions.

4. Analytical Ultracentrifugation

Analytical ultracentrifugation techniques are probably those with the greatest potential for the detailed analysis of the molecular weight distributions in heterogeneous gelatin systems. The interpretation of ultracentrifuge data relating to heterogeneous systems is complex, however, and relatively little has been accomplished as yet. The most notable work in this area has been carried out by J. W. Williams and his colleagues (2, 33-37). The treatment which follows is essentially a summary of William's contributions. The further application of these techniques to other gelatin systems will undoubtedly yield information of great value.

a. *Sedimentation equilibrium.* For an ideal two-component system composed of solvent and high molecular weight solute, component 2, at constant temperature, the distribution of solute within a centrifuge cell at equilibrium is described

$$\frac{1}{rc_2}\left(\frac{dc_2}{dr}\right) = \frac{M_2(1 - \bar{v}_2\varrho)\omega^2}{RT} \tag{50}$$

in which c_2 is the solute concentration at a distance r from the center of rotation, M_2 the solute molecular weight, $\bar{v}_2$ the partial specific volume of the solute, ϱ the solution density, and ω the angular velocity if the rotor. Williams (36) has emphasized that this ideal expression cannot be expected to hold for high polymers in general and for gelatin and other systems of high polydispersity in particular. In a heterodisperse polymer system the chemical potential of each component, μ_i, will depend both on the pressure at any particular point in the cell and on the concentrations of all components at that point. Assuming that the density of solution and partial specific volume are both independent of the pressure and composition, then for each component i the equilibrium conditions are described by

$$\sum_{k=2}^{n}\left(\frac{\delta\mu_i}{\delta c_k}\right)_{T, P, c_j \neq c_k}\frac{dc_k}{dr} = \frac{M(1 - \bar{v}_i\varrho)\omega^2}{RT} \tag{51}$$

or, in terms of the activity coefficients, y_i (38)

$$\frac{1}{c_i}dc_i + \sum_{k=2}^{n}\left(\frac{\delta\ln y_i}{\delta c_k}\right)_{T, P, c_j \neq c_k}dc_k = \frac{M_i(1 - \bar{v}_i\varrho)\omega^2 r dr}{RT} \tag{52}$$

It is of interest to note that in an "ideal" heterodisperse system where the term containing the activity coefficients would be zero, Eq. 52 reduces to

$$\frac{M_i c_i (1 - \bar{v}\varrho)\omega^2 r}{RT} = \frac{dc_i}{dr} \tag{53}$$

Rearranging and dividing by the total solute concentration, the equilibrium condition is

$$\frac{\displaystyle\sum_i M_i c_i}{\displaystyle\sum_i c_i} = \frac{RT}{(1 - \bar{v}\varrho)\omega^2} \left(\frac{1}{rc} \frac{dc}{dr} \right) = M_{w,r} \tag{54}$$

showing that the molecular weight derived from equilibrium sedimentation is the weight-average value. $M_{w,r}$ is the weight-average molecular weight at point r within the cell. The overall solute molecular weight, M_w, can be obtained by averaging, $M_{w,r}$ over the entire cell or

$$M_w = \frac{2RT[c_b - c_a]}{(1 - \bar{v}\varrho)\omega^2 c_0 (r_b^2 - r_a^2)} \tag{55}$$

In Eq. 55, the subscripts a and b represent the miniscus and base positions, and c_0 is the initial solute concentration. The heterogeneity of a system may be readily visualized by a plot of $(1/rc)/(dc/dr)$ vs. r. If $M_{w,r}$ is a constant, then the plot is a straight line with zero slope.

There is no completely satisfactory treatment for the evaluation of the activity coefficient terms in Eq. 52 for those cases where the activity coefficient deviates from unity. As a first approximation for a two-component system, the logarithm of the activity coefficient, y, can be expanded as a power series in the solute concentration, c, and from standard thermodynamic analysis the coefficient of the term in c to the first power can be identified as A_2, the second virial coefficient. In polydisperse systems the constants A_{ik} resulting from the differentiation are difficult to evaluate. Recalling that the virial coefficients are functions of the molecular weight, one may write $A_{ik} = B_{ik}M_i$. The practice is to assume that in a homologous series of polymer molecules of uniform chemical composition, all B_{ik} are equal and can be replaced by a constant B.

For a homogeneous non-ideal system, Eq. 52 becomes

$$M = \left(\frac{RT}{(1 - \bar{v}\varrho)\omega^2} \right) \frac{1}{rc} \frac{dc}{dr} \left\{ 1 + c \frac{\delta \ln y}{\delta c} \right\} \tag{56}$$

An apparent molecular weight M^* may be defined such that

$$M^* = \frac{RT}{(1 - \bar{v}\varrho)\omega^2} \left(\frac{1}{rc} \frac{dc}{dr} \right) \tag{57}$$

Hence

$$\frac{1}{M^*} = \frac{1}{M} \left\{ 1 + c \, \frac{\delta \ln y}{\delta c} \right\} \tag{58}$$

and since

$$\ln y = BMc + \dots \tag{59}$$

then

$$\frac{1}{M^*} = \frac{1}{M} + Bc + \dots \tag{60}$$

In analogous fashion the heterodisperse system may be represented as

$$\frac{1}{M_w^*} = \frac{1}{M_w} + Bc + \dots \tag{61}$$

where c is the total solute concentration. Obviously, equilibrium data obtained at several concentrations may be extrapolated linearly to infinite dilution according to Eq. 61, and the intercept at zero concentration will represent the system weight-average molecular weight.

Williams, Saunders and Cicirelli (2) applied Eq. 61 to the analysis of Knox P-111-20 alkali-precursor gelatin, the same lot investigated by Boedtker and Doty (12). The results of a typical plot according to Eq. 61 are shown in curve A of Fig. II-12. The abscissa of Fig. II-12 is the average concentration within the cell during each run and M_{wi} is equivalent to M_w^*, the molecular weight calculated assuming $y = 1$. Line B of the figure is a plot of the same data using the second virial coefficient obtained from osmotic pressure data (33), applied at each concentration. The agreement is excellent and the extrapolated weight-average molecular weight was 95,000. For the same gelatin in the same solvent (2.0 M potassium thiocyanate) Boedtker and Doty (12) found M_w to be 100,000 by light scattering.

The equilibrium centrifugation experiments and calculations are laborious and time-consuming and, if the corroboration of the light scattering data were the only outcome, this method of analysis would not be worthwhile. However, the power of the method lies in the fact that M can be computed at each point in the cell and distribution functions $f_n(M)$, $f_w(M)$, and $f_z(M)$ can be obtained (see Eqs. 4 and 8). From these differential distributions, M_n, M_w, and M_z can be calculated from a single set of measurements.

In the case of Knox P-111-20 gelatin, $M_n = 38,000$, $M_w = 95,000$, and $M_z = 125,000$. The intrinsic viscosity for this gelatin was $[\eta] = 0.36$ and $B = 1.3 \times 10^{-5}$ ml-mole/gm² in 2.0 M potassium thiocyanate. The weight distribution curve can be represented in integral form by plotting a function F_w as a function of M, where F_w is defined by

$$F_w = \int_0^\infty f_w(M)\,dM \qquad (62)$$

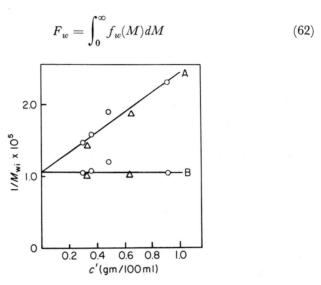

FIG. II-12. The apparent molecular weight as determined from equilibrium sedimentation experiments and plotted according to equation 61. Knox P-111-20 gelatin. Curve A, the actual data. Curve B, the data corrected by the calculated second virial coefficient. $\triangle$, in 0.15 M NaCl; $\bigcirc$, in 2.0 M KCNS [Williams et al. (2)].

The integral distribution curve for P-111-20 is shown in Fig. II-13. An analysis of this curve is shown in Table II-9, which gives the weight % in each molecular weight range. An interesting feature of the results of this distribution analysis is that the distribution is very evidently not gaussian and perhaps is bimodal. It is also remarkable that more than 50% of the gelatin has a molecular weight less than 60,000 whereas more than 20% has a weight greater than 140,000.

b. *Sedimentation velocity.* The thermodynamic treatment of equilibrium sedimentation data provides molecular weight and non-ideality information, but cannot be related to the size, shape, and hydrodynamic properties of the molecular species being examined. Such information can be obtained by observing the rate at which particles sediment under high gravitational fields. Sedimentation data are expressed in terms of the sedimentation

TABLE II-9 [a]

MOLECULAR WEIGHT DISTRIBUTION IN KNOX P-111-20 GELATIN

Molecular weight [b] range	Per cent in range (weight %)
< 10,000	6
10,000– 20,000	11
20,000– 40,000	23
40,000– 60,000	13
60,000– 80,000	9
80,000–100,000	6
100,000–140,000	10
140,000–170,000	6
> 180,000	16

[a] Data of Williams *et al.* (2).

[b] M_w, light scattering, 100,000; M_w, equilibrium ultracentrifuge, 95,000.

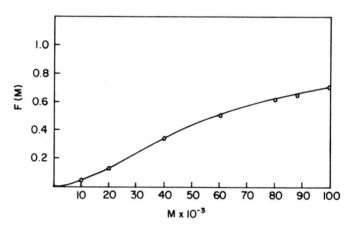

FIG. II-13. The integral weight distribution curve for Knox P-111-20 gelatin [Williams *et al.* (2)].

coefficient, s, which is calculated as the sedimentation rate at unit gravitational field. It can be shown that

$$s = \frac{M}{Nf} (1 - \bar{v}\varrho) \tag{63}$$

where M is the particle molecular weight, f the frictional coefficient, $\bar{v}$ the partial specific volume of the particle, and ϱ the solution density. The principal quantity determining s is thus seen to be f, and f is determined by the intrinsic hydrodynamic properties of the particle. In practice it is common to equate f with the diffusion coefficient D, an experimentally determinable parameter, by

$$D_0 = \frac{RT}{Nf_0} \tag{64}$$

and then substitute D for f in Eq. 63. In Eq. 64 the subscript, 0, is used to indicate that this equation is valid only at infinite dilution. The diffusion coefficient varies with solute concentration both in the way in which f varies with c and in which the solute activity varies with c. Thus in the usual form for determining the value of M from s,

$$M = \frac{RTs}{D(1 - \bar{v}\varrho)} \tag{65}$$

s and D do not vary with c in the same way. If the activity coefficient correction for D is applied in a fashion analogous to that described earlier for the osmotic pressure (Eq. 14), then Eq. 65 can be expanded as

$$D/s = RT \left[\frac{1}{M} + 2A_2c + 3A_3c^2 + \ldots \right] \tag{66}$$

and a plot of D/s vs. c to infinite dilution provides both the particle molecular weight and the same virial coefficients obtainable from osmotic pressure and light scattering data.

The use of independent determinations of s and D for the evaluation of M has not been applied to gelatin systems. Methods for evaluating s/D have recently become available through the application of Archibald's (39) analysis of the boundary conditions during the intermediate period prior to the establishment of equilibrium and at speeds and times sufficiently low so that a solute boundary has not formed. Preliminary studies (40), using the Ehrenberg (41) modification of the Archibald technique, have shown that s/D, measured in the region of the meniscus, varies with time for unfractionated gelatins. In a homogeneous system, s/D is a constant at any particular solute concentration. With the unfractionated gelatin, s/D gave molecular weights that were too low and that decreased with time. These results may be interpreted as signifying that the apparent diffusion coefficient D is much too large, because the molecular heterogeneity leads to a distribution of sedimentation constants.

Bello *et al.* (42) used the Archibald technique to study the molecular weight of an acid-precursor pig skin gelatin and variously degraded preparations. They used only the meniscus values in each case and obtained apparently satisfactory values for the weight-average molecular weight. A good Staundinger-type correlation was established between M_w and $[\eta]$, that is, a plot of log M_w vs. log $[\eta]$ was linear. Further use of this technique will undoubtedly prove to be of great value.

Baldwin and Williams (43) and Williams (44) developed methods to sort out the contributions of heterogeneity and diffusion in the spreading of boundaries in sedimentation experiments. They showed that the second moments of independent distributions were additive to give the second moment of the combined distribution curve. If s_m is the mean sedimentation coefficient, and D the weight-average diffusion coefficient, then at time t the second moment of the concentration gradient boundary curve is

$$\sigma_D^2 = \frac{2 D t}{(1 - \omega^2 s_m t)} + \sigma_0^2 \tag{67}$$

The second moment due to the distribution of sedimentation coefficients is

$$\sigma_s^2 = \bar{x}^2 \left[\varrho \omega^2 t + \frac{(\varrho \omega^2 t)^3}{3!} + \frac{(\varrho \omega^2 t)^5}{5!} + ... \right]^2 \tag{68}$$

In Eq. 68, ϱ is the standard deviation of the sedimentation coefficient distribution and $\bar{x}$ is the average position of the boundary in the cell. Accordingly the observed second moment of the gradient curve is the sum of these contributions,

$$\sigma^2 = \sigma_0^2 + \frac{2Dt}{1 - \omega^2 st} + \bar{x}^2 \left[\varrho \omega^2 t + \frac{(\varrho \omega^2 t)^3}{3!} + ... \right]^2 \tag{69}$$

Since ϱ is less than 1, all terms in ϱ with exponents greater than 2 can usually be neglected. An apparent diffusion coefficient, D^*, can the be defined as

$$D^* = D + \frac{\varrho^2 \omega^4 t}{2} \bar{x}^2 t = \frac{(1 - \omega^2 st)}{2t} (\sigma^2 - \sigma_0^2) \tag{70}$$

D^* can thus be calculated from the standard deviations of the sedimentation concentration gradient curves.

Williams, Saunders, and Cicirelli (2) used these relationships to examine the heterogeneity of Knox P-111-20 alkali-precursor calf skin gelatin. Their objective was to determine a function $g(s)$ defined by

$$g(s) = \frac{dn}{dx} \left(\frac{\omega^2 xt}{n_1 - n_0} \right) \tag{71}$$

which would describe the relative number of molecules with sedimentation coefficient s in the given system when diffusion was negligible. In Eq. 71, n_1 and n_0 are the refractive indexes of the solution ahead of the boundary and of pure solvent, respectively, and dn/dx is the height of the gradient curve at x'. In the actual case diffusion could not be neglected. A gaussian distribution of s was assumed and an apparent distribution of sedimentation coefficients, $g^*(s_e)$, calculated from the formula

$$g^*(s_e) = x' \left(\frac{dn}{dx} \right) \frac{w^2 t}{(A)_{t \to 0}} \exp (2 s_e w^2 t) \tag{72}$$

in which s_e is the experimentally determined sedimentation coefficient, x' the position in the cell of that material with sedimentation coefficient s_e at time t, and $(A)_{t \to 0}$ the limiting area under the gradient curve obtained by plotting the area at various times and extrapolating to zero time.

In diffusion, the boundary spreading is proportional to $t^{1/2}$ while boundary spreading due to differences in s is proportional to $\bar{x}t$. Hence by plotting $g^*(s_e)$ vs. $1/xt$ and extrapolating to infinite time the effects of diffusion may be eliminated, and $g(s)$ is then obtained. Since each s is concentration dependent, the extrapolation must be carried out at several concentrations and the resulting $g(s)$ values extrapolated to infinite dilution to obtain $g(s_0)$. This laborious procedure was carried through for the Knox P-111-20 gelatin in 2.0 M potassium thiocyanate. The values obtained for $g(s)$ at several concentrations are listed in Table II-10 and illustrated graphically

TABLE II-10 [a]

DISTRIBUTION OF SEDIMENTATION COEFFICIENTS, $g(s)$,
AS A FUNCTION OF CONCENTRATION FOR KNOX P-111-20 GELATIN

s, S	$g(s)$ for gelatin concentration (gm/100 ml):			
	0.746	0.524	0.304	0
0.5	0.55	0.50	0.39	0.37
1.0	1.05	1.22	1.18	0.87
1.5	2.24	2.25	2.25	1.81
2.0	5.61	4.25	3.30	2.85
2.4	6.52	5.04	4.00	3.47
2.8	4.55	4.14	3.88	3.50
3.0	2.57	3.46	3.71	3.43
3.5	1.00	1.74	2.43	2.94
4.0	0.31	0.83	1.31	1.75
5.0	0.13	0.37	0.55	0.71

[a] Data of Williams et al. (2).

in Fig. II-14. The several distributions in Fig. II-14 show that the experimentally determined distributions are sharpened and displaced from the true distribution. The distribution is generally broader than indicated by the curves obtained at the experimentally accessible concentrations. One must therefore be very cautious in interpreting single sharp sedimenting boundaries as indicating homogeneity in gelatin systems.

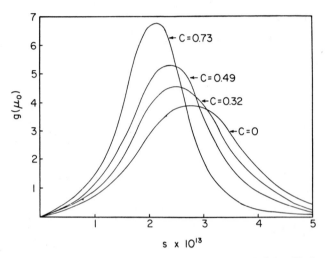

FIG. II-14. $g(s_0)$ vs. s_0 curves at several concentrations and at infinite dilution for Knox P-111-20 gelatin [Williams *et al.* (2)].

Williams and Saunders (34) showed how the distribution of sedimentation coefficients could be combined with the results of sedimentation equilibrium experiments to yield a distribution of molecular weights. The sedimentation equilibrium experiments provide a differential distribution of weights $f_w(M)dM$, and the velocity experiments provide a differential distribution of sedimentation constants $f(s_0)ds_0$. If one assumes that each molecular species present can be described by one, and only one, s_0 and M, then

$$g(s_0)ds_0 = f_w(M)dM \tag{73}$$

Integrating,

$$\int_0^{s_0'} g(s_0)ds_0 = \int_0^{M'} f_w(M)dM \tag{74}$$

or

$$G(s_0') = F_w(M') \tag{75}$$

A double plot can be made of $G(s_0)$ vs. s_0 and $F_w(M)$ vs. M where $G(s_0)$

and $F_w(M)$ are plotted on the same scale on the ordinate. The Knox P-111-20 data are plotted in this fashion in Fig. II-15. From this double plot one can pick out the s value corresponding to each M. Williams, Saunders, and Cicirelli (2) then showed that a plot of s_0 vs. $M^{1/2}$ was linear

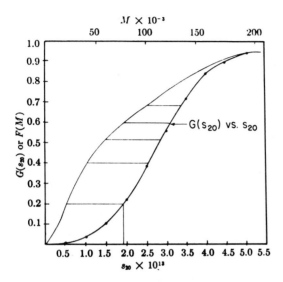

FIG. II-15. Double plot of integral distribution curves of molecular weight, $F(M)$, and of sedimentation constant, $G(s)$, to give relationship between s and M for gelatin P-111-20 [Williams et al. (2)].

(Fig. II-16). This relationship was interpreted as being consistent with the assumption that gelatin exists in 2.0 M potassium thiocyanate in the random coil configuration within which some of the solvent molecules are immobilized. For a free-draining molecule with the random coil configuration s should have been almost independent of M.

The intrinsic viscosities of several Knox P-111-20 fractions were determined in 2.0 M potassium\thiocyanate and combined with the weight-average molecular weights. The resulting Staudinger equation was

$$[\eta] = 2.9 \times 10^{-4} [M_w]^{0.62} \tag{76}$$

A comparison of the constants of Eq. 76 with those of Eqs. 46 and 48 for similar gelatins once again shows the marked dependence of the molecular properties of various gelatins on the particular gelatin preparation.

These detailed studies by Williams and his colleagues point out the very great potential for the ultracentrifugal methods of analysis of gelatin systems. The results are fragmentary as of the moment but undoubtedly the future application of the recent developments in ultracentrifuge theory and technique will provide the most revealing insights into the characterization of gelatin systems.

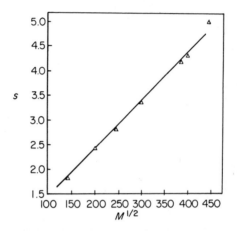

FIG. II-16. Plot of sedimentation constant vs. square root of molecular weight for gelatin P-111-20 [Williams *et al.* (*2*)].

C. Molecular Weight Distributions by Fractional Precipitation

Frequent reference has been made in the preceding sections of this chapter to the results obtained from the analysis of gelatin "fractions." It is important to understand the basis of the principal fractionation procedures and the relationship of the properties of the individual fractions to the initial gelatin mixtures from which they were obtained.

Two procedures have been used successfully to separate gelatin into fractions with obviously different molecular weight distributions and averages. The easiest and most readily reproducible procedure was developed by Pouradier and his colleagues (*5-7*). This method depends on the fact that aqueous gelatin solutions form two-phase coacervate systems in the presence of various simple organic solvents that are miscible with water. The coacervation phenomena are interesting in their own right and gelatin coacervates have been studied extensively. A discussion of the coacervates and coacervation in general is beyond the scope of this monograph; however, a few general remarks are in order. Coacervation systems are reversible two-phase liquid systems, each phase being rich in solvent, but one phase, the coacervate phase, being more concentrated in gelatin (or other polymer) than the other. The concentration and amount of the concentrated coacervate phase depends on solvent composition, polymer molecular weigth, and temperature. In a heterogeneous polymer system the higher weight components are preferentially concentrated in the coacervate phase. Thus careful control of temperature and solvent composition allows one to separate successive fractions of varying molecular weight. The advantages of coacervation over precipitation as a fractionation technique lie in the facts that (1) the coacervates settle out as coherent liquid phases with a sharp phase boundary; (2) the systems are thermodynamically reversible, hence highly reproducible; and (3) the concentrated coacervate phase is usually small in volume and sufficiently more viscous than the equilibrium liquid to permit efficient separation by simple decantation.

Pouradier and Venet (5) used ethanol to produce gelatin coacervates. A 2–3% solution of gelatin was warmed to 38–40° and the pH adjusted to the gelatin isoelectric point. Warm ethanol was added until turbidity developed. The alcohol-water-gelatin mixture was allowed to stand (several hours at least) until the mixture separated into two well-defined phases with a clear equilibrium liquid. This equilibrium liquid was decanted and an additional portion of alcohol was added. The coacervates were collected with successive alcohol additions until no further gelatin precipitates could be obtained. The alcohol was washed from the chilled coacervates with cold water. The gelatin-water gels were diluted and dried by vacuum distillation.

One prime difficulty with this simple technique was that the fractions could not be collected more rapidly than at about 16-hour intervals because the coacervates settled slowly. During this period hydrolytic degradation was liable to occur. Another troublesome point was that some fractions were insoluble after they were dried. Stainsby (45) modified this procedure to eliminate these difficulties. Since Courts (46) had shown that the hydrolytic breakdown of gelatin was slower at pH 6–7 than at either of the isoelectric pH's (4.9 and 9.0) of typical gelatins, Stainsby adjusted all gelatin solutions to pH 7. The temperature was controlled to $40.0 \pm 0.05°$ during the equilibration period following the addition of ethanol. The settling time under these conditions was 4–24 hours. The coacervates were washed free of ethanol, set to gels, and air-dried in thin sections. This method of drying appeared to eliminate the problem of insolubility.

Using this modified procedure, Stainsby (45) fractionated a number of gelatins of diverse origin. The weight in each fraction was determined quantitatively and, subsequently, the viscosity of each fraction was determined. Stainsby reports viscosity data in terms of a "logarithmic viscosity number," abbreviated LVN and defined by Eq. 77

$$\text{LVN} = \frac{1}{c} \ln \eta_{\text{rel}} \qquad (77)$$

in which c is expressed in grams gelatin/ml of solution. The LVN is thus approximately equal to 100 $[\eta]$. It is claimed that at gelatin concentrations of about 0.5% at 35° and in solutions of moderate salt concentration, the LVN is insensitive to small changes in pH, ionic strength, and gelatin concentration (47). The effect of the coacervation, collection, and drying procedures was assessed by determining the LVN of the gelatin before fractionation, the LVN of each fraction, and the LVN of an artificial mixture of the fractions prepared so that each fraction was present in the same relative amount as in the initial gelatin. Typical data are shown in Table II-11. The LVN of each artificial mixture was determined from Eq. 78.

$$\text{LVN (mixture)} = \frac{\sum w_i (\text{LVN})_i}{\sum w_i} \qquad (78)$$

The term w_i is the weight fraction of fraction i. The recoveries, in quantitative experiments in which five fractions were collected, were not less than 97% of the initial gelatin. The very excellent agreement evident in the last two columns of Table II-11 indicates that the only modification in any of the gelatins was a slight amount of thermal hydrolysis.

TABLE II-11 [a]

COMPARISON OF GELATIN VISCOSITIES WITH THE VISCOSITIES
OF MIXTURES OF GELATIN FRACTIONS OBTAINED BY ETHANOL COACERVATION

Gelatin			LVN (initial)	LVN (mixture)
Designation	Source	Isoionic pH		
A-1	Limed bovine hide	4.95	56	55
A-3	Limed bovine hide	4.95	65	64
B	Acid-processed ossein	8.8	34	34
C	Steamed bone	5.5	25	25
D	Alkali-processed ossein	4.9	97	96

[a] Data of Stainsby et al. (47).

The details of the fractionation procedure are illustrated in Table II-12 for the fractionation of gelatin A-1 of Table II-11. Part B of Table II-12 shows the details of the subfractionation of each of the principal fractions of A-1. The quantitative recoveries were excellent and the LVN's of the subfractions agreed well with LVN's of the original fractions. Subfraction 1 of fraction 1 contained the particulate matter and some colored nongel-

TABLE II-12 [a]

FRACTIONATION OF GELATIN A-1

(A) Separation into the principal fractions

Fraction	A-1 (%)	LVN	LVN of mixture of sub-fractions
1	19.9	81	71
2	18.8	64	61
3	24.8	52	50
4	19.8	42	42.5
5	15.5	30	29.5
Residue	1.4	9	—

(B) Subfractionation

Fraction	Subfractions									
	1		2		3		4		5	
	%	LVN	%	LVN	%	LVN	%	LVN	%	LVN
1	4.3	82	11.4	93	42.0	82.5	24.4	62.5	17.4	38.5
2	16.3	76	21.7	72	27.3	63.5	26.2	48.5	7.7	27.5
3	23.9	58	18.5	55	39.8	48	17.0	38	—	—
4	6.9	48	20.2	48	36.3	44	22.7	41	13.0	32
5	38.4	34.5	28.8	32	25.6	21.5	4.0	12	0.9	—

[a] Data of Stainsby et al. (47).

atin impurities present in A-1, hence its LVN was low and it is not representative of the gelatin. The data of part B of Table II-12 may be used to construct viscosity-weight distribution curves. Figures II-17 and 18 show the integral weight distribution corresponding to the integral curve. On the premise that the LVN is proportional to M in the same way throughout the entire range, Stainsby refers to the LVN distributions as molecular weight distribution curves. It is noteworthy that the differential distribution curve of Fig. II-18 suggests a bimodal distribution of weights as did the equilibrium centrifuge results of Williams *et al.* (*2*) (Table II-9).

Veis and Cohen (*18, 48*) used a further modification of the ethanol coacervation fractionation procedure to study and compare the molecular

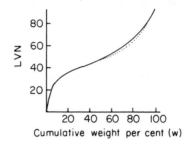

Fig. II-17. Integral weight distribution curves for gelatin A–1. The logarithmic viscosity number (LVN) is taken as a measure of molecular weight [Stainsby (*22*)].

weight distributions of gelatins extracted from a common supply of purified bovine corium collagen under differing conditions. This modification was designed to minimize hydrolytic degradation and to speed the entire fractionation process. It is not suitable for large-scale preparative work. Since comparisons between gelatins were sought rather than the LVN or

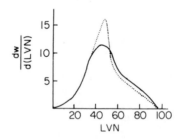

Fig. II-18. The differential weight distribution curves corresponding to the curves in Fig. II-17. The area under a curve between any two LVN's represents the weight of gelatin within that range of molecular weight [Stainsby (*22*)].

other viscosity function distributions, specific ethanol:water ratio cuts were selected and the weight in each cut was determined.

A 2% solution of gelatin was prepared in 0.8 M sodium chloride and the solution was held at 40° for at least one hour to dissociate any aggregates that might have been present. Anhydrous ethanol (formula 3A) was added from a 40° jacketed burette to a measured volume of the gelatin solution in a centrifuge cup, the turbid solution was kept at 40° for 10 minutes, and the suspension was centrifuged for 10 minutes at $\sim$ 3000 rpm in a centrifuge warmed to 40°. The coacervate layer at the bottom of the centrifuge cup was chilled and the supernatant was decanted into another centrifuge cup. The coacervate was dissolved in a small amount of warm water and acetone was added to a final ratio of 2 parts of acetone to 1 of water. Under these conditions the gelatin was precipitated while the salt and ethanol were soluble. The precipitate was washed several times with cold (5–10°) distilled water to remove the acetone, and dissolved in a small amount of warm water. This final gelatin solution was lyophilized and the dried gelatin weighed.

Ethanol was added to the supernatant equilibrium liquid of the first coacervation and a second fraction collected, and so on. Five fractions were collected in the alcohol:water ratio range of 2:1 to 4:1. The sixth fraction was the remainder which proved to be difficult to precipitate even with ethanol:water ratios as high as 20:1.

With this procedure the salt-free dry fractions were all readily soluble in warm water except for fraction 1. As in Stainsby's case this first fraction seemed to contain particulate matter with a very fibrous appearance. However, since Veis and Cohen (18) worked with a highly purified bovine corium collagen, this fraction could not be considered to be rich in non-collagenous material. Hydroxyproline assays verified the fact that this fraction was essentially all gelatin (unpublished results).

An experienced worker can fractionate four or five gelatin samples in a single day by this technique, and the average exposure time to elevated temperature for the gelatins isolated in fractions 5 and 6 is about 4 hours. Fractions 1–4 are exposed to hydrolytic degradation for 2 hours or less. Repeated fractionations of the same gelatin, or gelatin extracted in the same way, showed that the weight fraction in any fraction was readily reproducible to $\pm$ 10%, usually to $\pm$ 5%. The fractionation into only six fractions is sufficiently sensitive to pick up differences in the distributions of gelatins extracted at the same temperature but at different pH (e.g. pH 6.0 or pH 4.0) (18) or at different temperature at constant pH and buffer composition (48). The differential distribution curves for most of the gelatins examined by Veis and Cohen (18, 48) were also bimodal.

Pouradier and Venet (6) made use of the alcohol coacervation procedure in a slightly different way to establish molecular weight ditributions. Kodak F-74 gelatin was separated into several fractions by coacervation. Volumes (100 ml) of solution were prepared, each containing 1 gm isoionic gelatin fraction. The water used in these solutions was thoroughly demineralized. The solutions were warmed to 38° and titrated with 38° ethanol. The volume of ethanol, v, required to cause turbidity in the solution was recorded. Pouradier and Venet found that a direct relationship existed between v and the number-average molecular weight. A plot of $1/v$ vs. $1/M_n$ yielded a straight line (Fig. II-19). Defining an index of precipitation $\gamma = 1/v$, the relationship between γ and M_n can be written

$$\gamma = \alpha + \frac{\beta'}{M_n} \tag{79}$$

For Kodak F-74 gelatin $\alpha = 0.367$ and $\beta' = 1.04 \times 10^4$. Other gelatins were found to fit Eq. 79 but in each case each gelatin preparation required different constants, α and β'. Unfractionated gelatins of different origin did not yield linear plots of $1/v$ vs. $1/M_n$.

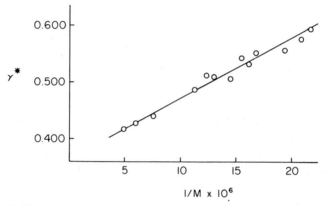

FIG. II-19. The index of precipitation as a function of the molecular weight for Kodak F-74 gelatin; γ^* is the ratio of precipitant (ethanol) to solvent (water). Measurements at pH 4.75, 38° [Pouradier and Venet (5)].

The second fractionation procedure was developed by Stainsby, Saunders and Ward (47). They made use of the fact that detergents form complexes with gelatin in aqueous solution and that the solubility of the complexes depends on pH, ionic strength, and temperature of the solution as well as on the nature of the gelatin (49, 50). As in the ethanol fractionation procedure, the gelatin can be made to settle out as a viscous coacervate phase rather than a solid precipitate. Stainsby et al. (47) chose sodium dodecyl sulfate (SDS) as the complexing detergent and, with a constant ratio of 9.4 mmoles SDS per gm gelatin and constant temperature of 35°, used increasing concentrations of sodium chloride to cause coacervate formation in systems of an alkali-precursor gelatin. Fractions were collected when the supernatants were 0.440, 0.465, 0.500, 0.60, and 1.0 M in sodium chloride. The coacervate droplets settled slowly and 18 hours was required for a clear-cut separation into two layers. The gelatin:SDS ratio remains constant in both phases, hence additional SDS is not required during the fractionation.

The gelatin was recovered from the coacervates by precipitation with acetone with sufficient water present to solubilize the SDS and sodium chloride. The acetone was washed from the coacervate with ice-cold distilled water. The gelatin precipitated slowly upon the addition of the acetone and, if one waited until all the gelatin precipitated, difficulties were encountered upon resolution. Only the gelatin that precipitated immediately was readily soluble in water.

When the fractions were analyzed they were found to contain 0.004–0.4 mmoles SDS per gm gelatin. A second reprecipitation with acetone reduced the SDS content to near the limit of detection, about 3×10^{-5} M. In 1% gelatin solution this corresponded to less than one SDS molecule per seven or eight gelatin molecules. The original SDS concentration in the coacervate corresponded to about 450 SDS molecules per gelatin molecule. Stainsby et al. (47) concluded that the small amount of SDS remaining in the fractions had no detectable effect on the physical properties of the gelatin solutions. It was found that dialysis, electrodialysis, and even ion-exchange resins were less effective than acetone precipitation in removing the SDS from the gelatin.

The one advantage of this SDS fractionation procedure is that it is readily adaptable to large-scale fractionations of gelatin. One does not have to deal with the tremendous volumes required for large-scale ethanol fractionation. In large-scale SDS fractionation it is feasible to collect only the gelatin that settles out rapidly, avoiding the difficulty in dissolving the precipitated gelatin. However, this throws the high molecular weight gelatin that should have settled out into the next lower fraction, so that the fractions obtained in small- and large-scale fractionations at the same salt concentrations are not comparable in composition.

Veis, Eggenberger, and Cohen (17) used the SDS coacervation technique to fractionate some specially prepared pI 9.0 gelatins extracted from purified bovine corium, and a commercial acid-precursor pig skin gelatin. With these gelatins, at an SDS ratio of 9.4 mmoles per gm gelatin and at 40°, a lower sodium chloride concentration was required to bring down the first few fractions than Stainsby et al. (47) required for the fractiona-

TABLE II-13 [a]

COMPARISON OF GELATINS M AND D IN ETHANOL FRACTIONATION AT 40°

Fraction	Alcohol:water ratio	M [b] (%)	D [c] (%)
A-I	1.6	76.7	—
A-II	2.0	9.9	—
A-III	3.0	8.1	9.9
A-IV	4.0	0.6	6.0
A-V	5.0	—	2.3
A-VI	10.0	2.0	2.6
Recovery from final supernatant		—	78.2
Total recovery		97.3	99.0

[a] Data of Veis et al. (17).
[b] Settled out as oily coacervates.
[c] Recovered by centrifugation.

tion of their particular alkali-precursor gelatin. It is interesting to compare the ethanol and SDS fractionation procedures when applied to the same gelatins. Table II-13 shows the recoveries at certain alcohol:water ratios with a high molecular weight gelatin (M) and a lower molecular weight gelatin (D). The fractionation of these same gelatins with SDS is illustrated in Table II-14.

TABLE II-14 [a]

COMPARISON OF GELATINS M AND D IN THE SODIUM DODECYL SULFATE FRACTIONATION METHOD AT 40°

Fraction	Salt concn. (M NaCl)	M (%)	D (%)
B-I	0–0.378	26.9	32.9
B-II	0.378–0.415	15.6	16.1
B-III	0.415–0.440	12.3	7.7
B-IV	0.440–0.650	29.0	32.4
B-V	0.650–1.000	14.7	4.7
Total recovery		98.5	93.8

[a] Data of Veis et al. (17).

The interpretation which Veis *et al.* (*17*) placed on these data was that the ethanol-water-gelatin coacervation equilibria are selective in terms of the molecular properties of the gelatin. That is, gelatins in a certain molecular weight range will form a coacervate at a given ethanol:water ratio. On the other hand, the SDS-gelatin complexes form coacervates depending on the salt concentration and total amount of gelatin in the system. This process is not selective in terms of gelatin molecular weight in the sense that, in a mixture containing gelatins above some minimum molecular weight, the same total amount of gelatin will be precipitated at a given salt concentration regardless of the average molecular weight of the gelatin. It is obvious, however, that in a heterogeneous system the higher molecular weight gelatin enters the SDS-gelatin coacervate phase in preference to the lower weight gelatin in the mixture.

In spite of the fact that the SDS coacervation procedure is more readily adaptable to large-scale work, the ethanol procedure is preferable because the fractionation can be made more critically in terms of the molecular properties of the gelatin, and there is less danger of contamination of the recovered gelatin fractions with the fractionating reagent.

III. Gelatin as a Polyampholyte

In the discussion of the amino acid composition of collagen in Chapter I it was pointed out that collagen, unlike silk or elastin, is rich in both acidic and basic functional groups. These functional groups are retained in gelatin, with the addition of some terminal α-amino and carboxyl groups. Since all gelatins have essentially the same amino acid composition, but different properties as polyampholytes, titration analysis is an important adjunct to gelatin characterization. The titration curves may be used in predicting many aspects of the behavior of gelatin solutions.

A. Titration Curves and Correlation with Chemical Analysis

Several investigators have examined the titration behavior of gelatins of various origin. The most notable studies have been those of Hitchcock (*51*), Ames (*52*), and Kenchington and Ward (*53*). The present state of knowledge depends primarily on the thorough and perceptive work of W. M. Ames (*52*), which established the limits within which the titration curves of all gelatins would fall.

Ames (*54*) had shown in 1944 that all gelatins fit into one of two categories with respect to their isoionic pH. This pH is determined by the pretreatment of the collagen stock and the conditions under which the gelatin extraction is carried out. Alkaline pretreatment followed by neutral or slightly basic extraction yields gelatins with isoionic pH's on the acid side of neutrality and generally close to pH 5.0. Acid pretreatment, even of short duration, followed by acid or neutral extraction yields gelatins with basic isoionic pH's, predominantly near pH 9.0 (54, 55). Using the same batch of dry collagen stock, Ames (52) subjected different portions of the collagen (ox sinews) to exhaustive alkali or acid pretreatment, extracted the gelatin at neutrality, and determined the titration curve of each type of gelatin.

Acid-precursor gelatin was prepared by soaking the equivalent of 50 gm dried tendon in 1 liter of water containing 5 ml concentrated hydrochloric acid. After soaking overnight the acidified tendons were converted to gelatin by heating for 1 hour at 80°. The gelatin solution was neutralized with dilute sodium hydroxide, filtered, gelled, and dried. The dry gelatin sheets were powdered, and washed with cold water to remove the salt. The wet, desalted powder was finally warmed to form a concentrated solution. This solution was set to a gel and dried. The resulting gelatin had an ash content of 0.32% and an apparent isolectric pH of 7.2. The nitrogen content was 18.52%.

Alkali-precursor gelatin was prepared by soaking dry tendons in a calcium hydroxide suspension for 12 weeks. Fresh calcium hydroxide liquors were used each week. At the conclusion of the soaking period the swollen tendons were washed with water, and neutralized with dilute hydrochloric acid until they were close to their isoelectric point. Neutralization was completed with acetic acid to aid in removing the last traces of calcium from the fibers. The surplus water was squeezed from the flaccid isoelectric fibers, which were then soaked in 10% sodium hydroxide for 3 days at room temperature. The highly swollen gelatinous mass was again neutralized with dilute hydrochloric acid to the isoelectric point. The surplus water was expressed and the wet mass of tendon heated to 40°. The tendons dissolved readily to form gelatin. The solutions were filtered, gelled, and dried. The dry sheets were powdered, washed free of salts with cold water, and redried. The gelatin prepared in this way had an isoionic pH of 4.9, an ash content of 0.13%, and a nitrogen content of 18.08%. The original dry tendons contained 18.49% nitrogen and 0.22% ash.

Portions of each gelatin corresponding to 1 gm of dry, ash-free protein were weighed into a series of 100-ml volumetric flasks. Solutions were prepared by adding measured volumes of 0.1 N hydrochloric acid or 0.1 N

sodium hydroxide and then bringing each volume to 100 ml with boiled distilled water. A corresponding series of blanks containing acid or base but no gelatin were also prepared. At the extreme acid end of the series, the solutions were made to contain 2% gelatin and were 0.2 N or 0.5 N in potassium chloride. After a brief equilibration period the pH value of each solution was determined by standard means.

Observations on the acid side of the isoelectric point were translated into titration curves as follows. The blank solution has an acid concentration M_A, and activity coefficient f_A, and a measured pH of pH_A. The corresponding solution containing protein has a free acid concentration M_f with an activity coefficient f_f and pH of pH_f. Assuming that $f_A = f_f$ and that all of the liquid junction potentials involved in the pH measurements are equal in the presence and absence of the gelatin, then

$$\log M_f = pH_A - pH_f + \log M_A \tag{80}$$

Similarly, on the alkaline side

$$\log M_{OH,f} = pH_f - pH_B + \log M_{OH,B} \tag{81}$$

Using these relationships, M_f and $M_{OH,f}$ were computed, and the amount of combined acid or alkali was determined readily from $M_A - M_f$. Ames' titration data (52) are plotted as $(M_A - M_f)$ and $(M_{OH} - M_{OH,f})$ vs. pH in Fig. II-20, expressed as mmoles H^+ or OH^- bound per gm gelatin. The

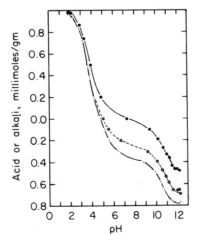

FIG. II-20. The titration curves of gelatins with different isoelectric points; ●, acid-precursor gelatin; ., alkali-precursor gelatin; O, commercial gelatin with intermediate isoelectric point [Ames (52)].

figure also shows the result of the titration of a commercial alkali-precursor gelatin not so exhaustively limed as in the special preparation described above. This commercial gelatin had an ash content of 0.1% and nitrogen analysis of 18.15%.

The interpretation of these titration curves rested on the suggestions of Cannan (56) as to the pH range in which each functional group would be titrated. Cannan's pH ranges are set forth in the second column of Table II-15. Ames' values are listed accordingly in Table II-16. The "analysis" columns in Table II-16 refer to the amino acid compositions of native and exhaustively limed collagen as determined by Bowes and Kenten (57, 58).

TABLE II-15

pH RANGES FOR THE ANALYSIS OF GELATIN TITRATION CURVES

Group	pH range of titration	
	Cannan [a]	Kenchington and Ward [b]
Carboxyl	1.5–6.0	1.5–6.5
α-Amino + imidazole	6.0–8.5	6.5–8.0
ε-Amino (lysine + hydroxylysine)	8.5–11.5	8.0–11.5

[a] Cannan (56).
[b] Kenchington and Ward (53).

The agreement between the analytical and titration data is quite good for the carboxyl, ε-amino, and guanidino groups. The principal difficulties are in rationalizing the values for the imidazole and amido nitrogen groups.

The amide nitrogen value of 0.31 mmole/gm in Table II-16 was determined from the difference in total nitrogen contents of the two gelatins. Bowes and Kenten (57) had determined the amide content of native collagen to be 0.47 mmole/gm, but Ames (52) concluded that the lower value was more nearly correct. His conclusion was based on the fact that native collagen had the same nitrogen content as the acid-precursor gelatin, while limed collagen had the same nitrogen content as alkali-precursor gelatin. Since the loss of nitrogen, as determined by analsyis, agreed with the increase in free carboxyl groups and in base-binding capacity determined from the titration curves, it was evident that the primary change in passing from the native or acid-treated state to the alkali-treated state was the release of amide ammonia.

TABLE II-16 [a]

INTERPRETATION OF THE TITRATION CURVES OF TWO TYPES OF GELATIN

Ionizing group		Acid-precursor		Alkali-precursor	
		Titration	Analysis [b]	Titration	Analysis [b]
(A)	Free carboxyl groups	0.90	0.93	1.22	1.24
(B)	Amide nitrogen (J)	0.31	0.31	—	—
(C)	Total carboxyl (A + B)	1.21	1.24	1.22	1.24
(D)	Imidazole + α-amino	0.12	0.05	0.13	0.05
(E)	ε-Amino	0.43	0.39	0.38	0.36
(F)	Total basic groups	0.98	0.95	0.96	0.87
(G)	Guanidino [F−(D + E)]	0.43	0.51	0.45	0.46
(H)	Maximum acid combined	0.98	—	0.96	—
(I)	Maximum base combined	0.47	—	0.77	—
(J)	Difference in base-combining capacity (= Amide nitrogen)	0.31	—	—	—
(K)	Total nitrogen	13.22	—	12.91	—
(L)	Difference in nitrogen	0.31	—	—	—

[a] Data of Ames (52).
[b] Bowes and Kenten (57, 58).

Since the value of 0.05 mmole/gm for the histidine content, derived from amino acid analysis has been substantiated repeatedly (59), the titration value of 0.12 mmole/gm is obviously far too high and well beyond the range of error noted for the other groups. The same discrepancy was observed for both types of gelatin. Ames noted the same discrepancy in the titration data of Bowes and Kenten (57, 58). The titration of native collagen indicated the presence of only 0.02 mmole/gm of groups titrating in the histidine range, while 0.11 mmoles/gm was titrated in the same range in alkali-pretreated collagen. One possibility was that α-amino groups titrating in the histidine range were set free during the alkali treatment or during the collagen → gelatin conversion. To check this factor Ames conducted formol titrations of each gelatin. Repeated titrations showed that there were more α-amino groups in the alkali-precursor gelatin than in the acid-precursor material. A very careful reexamination was then made of the central region of each gelatin titration curve. These data (Fig. II-21) are summarized in Table II-17, along with similar data from Bowes and Kenten's (57, 58) titration and Van Slyke amino nitrogen analyses of native and limed collagen. Two points are evident. First, the difference in apparent imidazole of the alkali-precursor gelatin over the acid-precursor

TABLE II-17

DETERMINATION OF α-AMINO GROUP CONTENT
FOR COLLAGEN AND GELATIN BY VAN SLYKE AND TITRATION ANALYSIS

Substance examined	Amino N [a] (mmoles/gm)	Imidazole Group titration (mmoles/gm)
Native collagen [b]	0.33	0.02
Limed collagen [b]	0.36	0.11
α-Amino groups by difference	0.03	0.09
Acid-precursor gelatin [c]	0.32	0.10
Alkali-precursor gelatin [c]	0.36	0.13
α-Amino groups by difference	0.04	0.03

[a] Van Slyke determination.
[b] Bowes and Kenten (57).
[c] Ames (52).

gelatin of 0.03 mmole/gm is in good agreement with the 0.04 mmole/gm increase in Van Slyke nitrogen in going from native to limed collagen. Second, the apparent increase in imidazole content of the limed collagen, 0.09 mmole/gm, is so much greater that it is clear that the difference in shape of the titration curves cannot be attributed to an increase in α-amino groups. Ames was not able to resolve this problem.

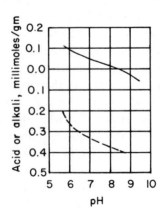

Fig. II-21. An expanded plot of the titration curves of Fig. II-20 in the neutral pH range, emphasizing the difference in shape of the curves for the two extreme types of gelatin. Solid line, acid-precursor gelatin. Dashed line, alkali-precursor gelatin [Ames (52)].

Kenchington and Ward (*53*) attempted a clarification of this point in their study of the titrations of a commercial acid-precursor pig skin gelatin, pI = 9.1, and a commercial alkali-precursor ox hide gelatin, pI = 4.92. Great care was taken in the conduct of the measurements. The titrations were carried out directly by addition of acid or base in gradually increasing amounts to a single gelatin solution held at $40 \pm 0.1°$. A stream of nitrogen was passed through each titration cell to exclude carbon dioxide. A battery of electrodes was used in each titration assembly and readings were recorded from each glass electrode. The pH readings were selected from the electrode which drifted the least from its standardization values during the course of the titration. Blank titrations were run with distilled water. The amount of acid or base combined was computed in the manner already described by Eqs. 80 and 81. The possibility of decomposition of the gelatin at the extreme acid or alkaline pH's was checked by a form of back titration. An amount of acid or base exactly equivalent to the amount of base or acid added during the titration was added at the conclusion of the run. The pH was brought back to within ± 0.02 pH unit of the original value in each case.

The titration curves obtained in this way are illustrated in Fig. II-22. The summaries of these data are given in Table II-18, along with the values obtained by Ames. It is evident from the values listed in the first two lines of the table that the titration measurements of Kenchington and Ward are identical in all respects with those of Ames for the alkali-precursor

TABLE II-18

ANALYSIS OF TITRATION DATA OF KENCHINGTON AND WARD [a]

Titration range of Cannan	Free carboxyl + amide	ε-Amino	Imidazole + α-amino	Guanidino	Total base
Alkali-precursor gelatin					
Kenchington and Ward	1.22	0.39	0.12	0.44	0.95
Ames	1.22	0.38	0.13	0.45	0.96
K-W revised criteria	1.26	0.42	0.06	0.48	0.96
Amino acid analysis	1.30	0.42	0.06	0.48	0.96
Acid-precursor gelatin					
K-W	1.20	—	—	—	—
Ames	1.21	0.43	0.12	0.43	0.98
K-W revised	1.20	0.42	0.06	0.49	0.97

[a] Kenchington and Ward (*53*).

gelatin. In this case, however, an amino acid analysis was carried out on the gelatin titrated. This analysis, included in the table, showed conclusively that the histidine content was of the order of 0.06 mmoles/gm. Kenchington and Ward, therefore, reexamined the titration criteria proposed by Cannan.

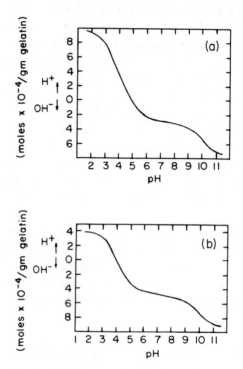

FIG. II-22. Titration curves for gelatins in 0.2 N salt at 40°. (a) Alkali-precursor gelatin, pI 4.92; (b) acid-precursor gelatin, pI 9.1 [Kenchington and Ward (53)].

The first correction was the realization that the upper limit of pH 6.0 for the carboxyl titration left about 3% of the total carboxyl titration to occur above pH 6.0. Revision of the upper limit to pH 6.5 reduced this to less than 1%. This limit, applicable only for proteins low in histidine and α-amino groups, gives a carboxyl titration, in absolute terms, almost equal to the α-amino and histidine titration below pH 6.5.

The second correction was a revision of the ε-amino group titration range. Kenchington and Ward (53) pointed out that 21% of the ε-amino titration involved the ε-amino groups of hydroxylysine. These groups have a pK

of 9.50 compared with pK of 10.3 for the ε-amino group of lysine. Since collagen and gelatin are the only proteins containing significant amounts of hydroxylysine, Cannan's titration range of 8.5–11.5 must be reduced to a lower value, overlapping the histidine range. Moreover, the amino group pK, in contrast to the carboxyl group pK, is temperature dependent. The heat of ionization of the amino group is 10–12 kcal/mole; hence, the pK's are shifted from the above mentioned values to 9.0 and 9.8, respectively, at 40°. At 40°, the appropriate ε-amino titration range is then pH 8.0–11.5. About 1% of the lysine and 10% of the hydroxylysine will still titrate below this range. However, about 15% of the histidine groups will titrate above pH 8.0 and compensate for this error. The revised titration ranges are given in the second column of Table II-15 and the titration analyses with these ranges are recorded in Table II-18. It is clear that these revisions bring the gelatin titrations into accord with the amino acid analysis results. However, if this is the case, then the fact that titrations of native collagen using Cannan's ranges also lead to results in accord with the amino acid analysis data means that Ames was correct in his conclusion that some groups are exposed during the liming of collagen or the conversion of collagen to gelatin, and that these are not α-amino groups created by peptide bond hydrolysis.

B. Isoelectric and Isoionic Points of Gelatin

Since, as Ames (54) so clearly demonstrated, the isoionic pH of gelatins may vary over a range greater than 4 pH units, the determination of the isoionic pH is another important step in gelatin characterization. The isoionic pH has been defined in Chapter I as that pH which is attained by a colloidal polyampholyte in a solution containing no noncolloidal ions other than hydrogen or hydroxyl, or in a solution of another solute which does not produce hydrogen or hydroxyl ions when dissolved in water alone.

The classical procedure for attaining this ion-free state is exhaustive electrodialysis to constant pH and constant conductivity. This method, however, is quite time-consuming and has been replaced by an ion-exchange chromatographic technique which provides substantially the same information. Janus, Kenchington and Ward (60) described a rapid procedure involving the use of a mixed-bed ion-exchange column of 2.5 parts of a strong anion-exchange resin (Amberlite IRA-400) to 1 part of a strong cation-exchange resin (Amberlite IR-120). The ion-exchange column was jacketed and held at 40°. A warm gelatin solution, 1–10%, can be passed through such a column at the rate of 120 gm dry gelatin per hour per liter of resin bed. According to Janus *et al.* (*60*), almost complete removal of micro-ions is attained. For example, the specific resistivity of a 2% solution of deionized gelatin was reduced to the range 50,000–100,000 ohms at 40°. The ash content of the deionized gelatins was less than 0.003% of the gelatin on a dry weight basis.

Janus *et al.* (*60*) obtained pI values on the range pH 4.82–5.10 for a series of alkali-precursor gelatins of varying origin, and a value of pH 9.3 for two samples of acid-precursor pig skin gelatin. Veis and Cohen (*19*) deionized an acid-precursor gelatin by the ion-exchange technique and found values in the range pH 8.9–9.1. Electrodialysis of the same gelatin set the pI at pH 8.86–9.0. Boedtker and Doty (*12*) made a similar comparison of the ion-exchange and electrodialysis procedures with Knox P-111-20 alkali-precursor ossein gelatin. The isoionic point was pH 5.10 ± 0.05 by both methods.

Kraemer (*61*) had observed that salt-free solutions of gelatin showed maximum turbidity in the region of the isoionic point. At the time that his investigation was carried out (1925-26), it was generally believed that all gelatins had isoionic points near pH 5. Kraemer noted that the maximum turbidity of the alkali-precursor gelatins was indeed near pH 5 and quite well defined. However, the acid-pretreated pig skin gelatins showed a much broader turbidity maximum over the pH 6–9 range. Kraemer used this evidence to postulate for the first time the existence of a second type of gelatin. Janus *et al.* (*60*) checked their deionization method with turbidimetric measurements and found excellent agreement in the isoionic points. Measurements of the turbidity in the presence of neutral salts also provided very good values for the isoionic pH (Table II-19). In this case the turbidity maxima were less sharp but not displaced, indicating that either no ions, or equal numbers of anions and cations, were bound by the gelatin. In Table II-19 it is evident that the isoionic pH is shifted by less than 0.02 pH unit in the presence of neutral salts for the alkali-precursor gelatins and that the two procedures check to within ± 0.02 pH unit. Carr and Topol (*62*), in a direct study of the ion binding of alkali-precursor gelatin at the isoionic point, also found no significant binding of sodium chloride. Boedtker and Doty (*12*) supported these observations in two ways. First, they carried out titrations of deionized Knox P-111-20 gelatin in water and in 0.15 *M* sodium chloride. While the curves were shifted slightly due to electrostatic effects away from the isoionic pH, the isoionic pH was not shifted by the addition of salt. Second, measurements of the reduced intensity of scattering of salt-free solutions of the gelatin placed the maximum

TABLE II-19 [a]

COMPARISON OF THE ISOIONIC POINTS OF GELATIN
BY DEIONIZATION AND TURBIDITY MEASUREMENTS

Gelatin	pI		
		Turbidity	
	Deionized	Deionized	Before deionization
Alkali-precursor			
Calf	5.08	5.10	5.09
Hide	4.86	4.86	4.87
Hide	4 84	4.84	4.87
Hide	4.85	4.85	4.85
Ossein	5.05	5.04	5.06
Hide	5.10	5.10	5.12
Tendon	4.85	4.87	4.84
Acid-precursor			
Pig skin	9.3	9.3	—
Pig skin	9.3	9.3	—
Ossein	6.0	6.0	6.1

[a] Data of Janus et al. (60).

turbidity at the titration isoionic point. These experiments are illustrated
in Fig. II-23.

Veis et al. (20) compared the turbidities of deionized acid- and alkali-
precursor gelatins. These data are plotted in Fig. II-24 as the reduced
intensity of scattering. The two gelatins were of equal molecular weight,
and in the manner plotted the minima represent the points of maximum
turbidity. The alkali-precursor gelatin gave a sharp minimum at a pH
agreeing with that determined by deionization. The turbidity maximum
of the acid-precursor gelatin, on the other hand, was broad and did not
coincide with the value obtained by deionization, pH 9.0. This behavior
of the acid-precursor gelatin is indicative of the binding of alkali ions.
Other evidence of the binding of micro-ions by acid-precursor gelatins
has been presented by Bello, Riese and Vinograd (63) and Ghosh and Gyani (64). The specific sites involved in ion binding will be discussed later
in detail.

Because of many inherent difficulties, direct moving-boundary electrophoretic mobility determinations have been rarely attempted. Early in-

vestigators did examine the migration of gelatin-coated particles in electric fields (65, 66) but these studies, in common with most of the early
studies of the gelatins, involved the use of materials of uncertain or poorly
documented origin. These data are therefore of limited use.

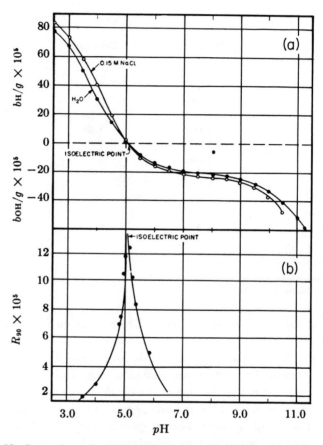

FIG. II-23. Comparison of the potentiometric and turbidimetric titrations of Knox
P-111-20 gelatin. (a) Potentiometric titrations in the presence and absence of supporting
electrolyte. (b) Turbidimetric titration in water at the isoelectric point at 25° [Boedtker
and Doty (12)].

Veis *et al.* (20) measured the mobility of an acid-precursor pig skin gelatin
(pI 9.0 deionization) in a free moving-boundary electrophoresis apparatus
at various pH's in solutions containing sodium chloride and acetate, glycine, phosphate, or barbiturate ions. The ionic strength of each buffer
system was 0.10 and the gelatin concentration, after dialysis, was 0.50–

0.65% protein. The temperature was held at 22° and the formation of solid gels was thereby avoided. The solutions were viscous and turbid, however. Corrections for viscosity and density were made according to the procedures of Johnson and Shooter (67). A plot of the mobility vs. pH,

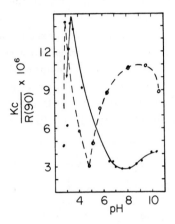

Fig. II-24. The reduced intensity of scattering of salt-free gelatins as a function of pH. Gelatin concentration 0.5 gm/100 ml; temperature 40°; ●, acid-precursor gelatin; ○, alkali-precursor gelatin [Veis et al. (20)].

illustrated in Fig. II-25, showed very clearly that the isoelectric point was markedly displaced, to pH 6.2 from the isoionic pH of 9.0. This pH displacement is again indicative of anion binding in the range pH 6 to > 9.0.

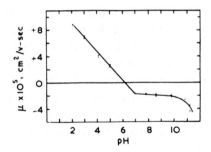

Fig. II-25. The electrophoretic mobility of acid-precursor gelatin from steer corium collagen as a function of pH; at 22° in 0.1 ionic strength buffers [Veis et al. (20)].

The discrepancy in the mobility in the region near neutrality is still more sharply drawn in Fig. II-26, where the mobility vs. the net charge is plotted. In this case the net charge was determined directly from a titration curve of the gelatin in question. The straight line passing through the origin (line *b*) represents the behavior of bovine serum albumin, a typical globular protein (*68*). Line *a* of the figure shows how nonlinear the gelatin mobility-charge relationship is.

Another type of electrophoretic separation of the same acid-precursor gelatin in salt-free solution was carried out (*20*). A 10-cell fractional electrical transport apparatus was used. Each cell, except the two end cells, was connected to the adjacent cells by side arms and a rubber connector that could be clamped shut. The two end cells contained large platinum electrodes. Each cell was filled with conductivity water except one center cell, which was filled with a salt-free deionized gelatin solution. A potential of 7000 volts was applied across the electrodes for 16 hours while the apparatus

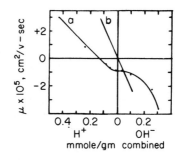

FIG. II-26. The mobility plotted against net charge as computed from titration data obtained at 0.1 ionic strength. (a) Acid-precursor gelatin; (b) bovine serum albumin [Veis *et al.* (*20*)].

was kept at 10°. The protein was distributed according to its mobility in the pH gradient set up within the cells, the cells were clamped off, their pH measured, and the amount of gelatin in each was determined. The results are shown in Fig. II-27. The gelatin was distributed normally about the cell with pH 8.24. The adjacent cells had pH's of 10.45 and 7.32. The results were thus in reasonable accord with the isoionic point as determined by ion-exchange desalting and indicate that in the absence of micro-ions the isoionic and isoelectric points of the acid-precursor gelatins would be in substantial agreement.

The essential fact that emerges from these studies is the contrasting behavior of the two classes of gelatin. The alkali-precursor gelatins have sharply defined isoionic points that agree well with turbidimetric, titration, and ion-binding data. The isoelectric and isoionic points, in 1:1 salts, have the same pH value. The acid-precursor gelatins, on the other hand, have a less well-defined isoionic pH and the gelatin is sensitive to the presence of small ions. The isoelectric pH in the presence of salts may be shifted by several pH units. It is not, therefore, appropriate to use the terms "isoelectric" and "isoionic" interchangeably in these systems, though this is often done. The isoelectric pH can be defined only by direct measurement in any given environment, although such direct measurements are difficult in all gelatin systems. The difference in behavior of the gelatins is important in connection with the elucidation of their molecular structures. This point will be examined more explicitly in the next chapter.

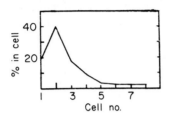

FIG. II-27. The isoelectric point distribution of an acid-precursor gelatin as shown by fractional electrical transport [Veis *et al.* (*20*)].

Cell no.	1	2	3	4	5	6
pH	10.45	8.24	7.32	6.86	5.90	5.89

C. Effect of Charge on the Dilute Solution Properties of the Gelatins

1. *Light Scattering*

We have just seen that gelatin solutions exhibit a maximum in turbidity at, or in the region of, the isoionic pH. The variations in turbidity with pH over a broader range, as shown in Fig. II-24, are also worthy of examination.

Equation 28, reproduced below in slightly modified form to account for internal interference,

$$\frac{Kc}{R(\theta)} = \frac{1}{M_w P(\theta)} + 2A_2 c + \dots \tag{28-A}$$

is the basic equation describing the concentration dependence of light scattering. Each of the terms in Eq. 28-A has been defined in the section on light scattering theory. The second virial coefficient, A_2, is a constant for a particular set of conditions, but it does vary with the net particle charge and the ionic strength. Repulsive electrostatic interactions increase A_2 and, hence, at constant molecular weight and protein concentration reduce the intensity of the scattered light, $R(\theta)$. Thus, as the pH of a gelatin solution is brought to values away from the isoionic pH, the net charge increases, A_2 increases, and the turbidity of the solution drops. A_2 is nearly proportional to the square of the net particle charge.

The turbidity is not a reliable measure of the net charge, however, since dimensional changes may also alter $P(\theta)$, the particle scattering factor. $P(\theta)$ generally assumes values of less than 1 as the particle size or asymmetry increases. Hence, the expansion that accompanies the charging of the gelatin molecule also increases $Kc/R(\theta)$, which is equivalent to reducing the turbidity of a gelatin solution. This internal interference correction could be eliminated by making light scattering measurements at several angles and extrapolating a plot of $Kc/R(\theta)$ vs. $\sin^2(\theta/2)$ to zero angle. The result, $Kc/R(0)$, would be the intercept, $[1/M_w + 2A_2c]$, and it is this term that is required to determine A_2. Unfortunately, such studies have not been carried out. In the more usual case, only the turbidity or $Kc/R(90)$ has been determined as a function of the pH (*61, 20, 12*).

The data of Fig. II-24 have been replotted in Fig. II-28 in terms of the

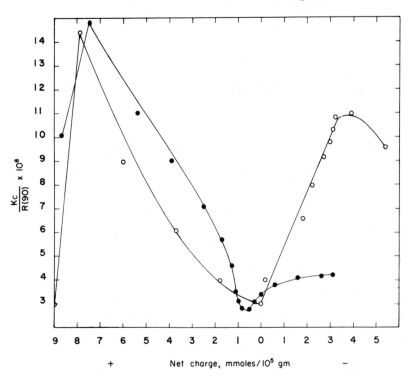

FIG. II-28. The reduced intensity of scattering of acid- and alkali-precursor gelatins as a function of the net charge; ●, acid-precursor gelatin; ○, alkali-precursor gelatin.

reduced intensity of scattering as a function of the net charge. The pH values were related to their net charge values by the use of the titration curves of Kenchington and Ward (53). The interesting feature of this method of presenting these data is that the anomalous behavior of the acid-precursor gelatin is emphasized. The minimum in the curve for the alkali-precursor gelatin coincides with the isoionic pH and zero net charge, while the minimum in the curve of the acid-precursor gelatin occurs at a pH distinctly lower than the pI. At this pH the molecule should have a small positive charge. Electrophoretic mobility data (20) indicate that the iso-electric point of the acid-precursor gelatin is at pH 6.2. This pH corresponds to a net charge of $+10$ per 10^5 gm gelatin. Thus, the anomalous region, $+10$–0 net charge (pH 6.2–9.0), must be a region in which microions are strongly bound to the gelatin or in which strong interactions between different parts of the same molecule must occur. One can also observe that, on the basic side of the isoionic pH, equal net negative charge does not bring about equal decreases in the turbidities of the two types of gelatin.

2. *Viscosity*

The expansion and contraction of the gelatin molecule with varying pH follow the course that one might predict after examining the turbidity data illustrated in the previous section. The viscosity has a minimum value at the isoelectric pH and increases rapidly as the net molecular charge increases. The viscosity approaches a maximum value at about pH 3.5, and a somewhat lower and less distinct maximum in the range alkaline to the isoelectric point. At lower or higher pH the viscosity falls rapidly and may, at the extreme acid end, take on values even less than the viscosity at the isoelectric pH. These effects are shown in Fig. II-29 for an alkali-precursor gelatin, pI 5.08 (69). The addition of neutral salt, curves 2 and 3, swamps out the electrostatic repulsive effect and lowers the viscosity. Moderate salt concentrations, about 0.2 M, also shift the observed maxima to lower and higher pH values on the acid and alkaline sides of the isoelectric point, respectively. Concentrations of salt as high as 1.0 M eliminate the electrostatic effects entirely, and probably bring about changes in solvation of the gelatin paralleling the lyotropic effects of concentrated salt solutions on collagen fibers, as noted in Chapter I. Boedtker and Doty (12) represented similar viscosity-pH data in a more meaningful way. They plotted the intrinsic viscosity vs. the net molecular charge, as in Fig. II-30. In this plot it can be seen that up to a net charge of ± 40

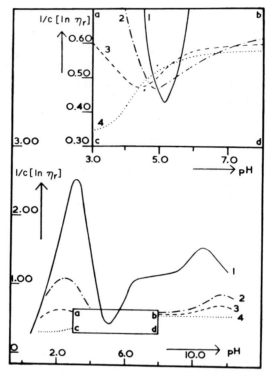

FIG. II-29. The reduced viscosity of an alkali-precursor calf skin collagen as a function of pH at 35°. Curve 1, 0.2% in water; curve 2, in 0.017 N NaCl; curve 3, in 0.10 M NaCl; curve 4, in 1.0 M NaCl. The inset magnifies the detailed shape of each curve in the region near the isoelectric pH [Stainsby (69)].

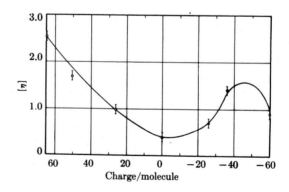

Fig. II-30. The intrinsic viscosity of Knox P-111-20 gelatin as a function of the net molecular charge [Boedtker and Doty (12)].

charges per molecule, the change in viscosity with change in charge is nearly symmetrical about the isoelectric point.

There have been no detailed studies published of the pH-viscosity relationships for pI 9.0 gelatins. One might presume that the viscosity increase would be limited in the alkaline range. Ward and Saunders (70) quote unpublished data of this nature. It would be profitable to carry out such a study because it should be quite revealing in terms of the relative solution configurations of the acid- and alkali-precursor gelatins.

IV. GELATIN AS A DENATURED PROTEIN

The two distinguishing manifestations of native structure in proteins are specific biological activity and specifically ordered peptide chain configurations. So far as our present knowledge is concerned, native collagen does not participate in enzymatic reactions. The collagens serve their essential role, through their ordered fibrous structures, as the principal supporting structural elements of most tissues. The native collagen configuration has been described in Chapter I. In the subsequent discussion of the collagen → gelatin transition, it will be seen that one important aspect of the transition is the loss of this ordered configuration. An equally important feature of the behavior of gelatin solutions is the partial regain of both intramolecular and intermolecular order. These two topics will be discussed at length in the appropriate places. At this point some of the experimental methods by which such order ↔ disorder reactions can be followed will be considered. The significance of these data with respect to the backbone chain properties of the gelatins will be examined in later chapters.

A. Configuration in the Solid State

1. Wide-Angle X-ray Diffraction

As described in Chapter I, ordered collagen fiber bundles give rise to a very characteristic wide-angle x-ray diffraction pattern (Fig. II-31). The most prominent spacings are the meridional arc at 2.86 Å, the equatorial diffuse half-halo at 4.6 Å, and the intense equatorial spots as 11–15 Å. The two smaller dimensions refer to repeat distances within the three-chain collagen helix. When collagen fibers are heated (71), or treated with reagents such as urea or concentrated nickel nitrate (72), the 2.86 Å meridional arc gradually disappears. A diffuse central halo extending out to about 9 Å and a broad ring centered at 4.4 Å are formed. Continued treatment leads to the disappearance of the 9 Å halo, while the ring at 4.4 Å becomes slightly more sharply defined. These changes are shown in Fig. I-15. According to Ramachandran (72), the reagent-induced changes in diffraction pattern can be reversed by washing the fibers with distilled water.

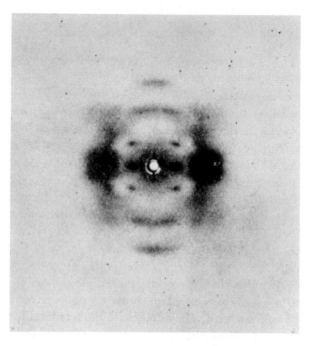

FIG. II-31. The wide-angle x-ray diffraction pattern of stretched rat tail tendon collagen [Randall *et al.* (79)].

Gelatin films prepared by drying warm solutions of gelatins yield a diffraction pattern showing only the 4.4 Å ring (73), while gelatin films prepared by drying cold gelatin gels yield a pattern which also shows the 2.86 Å spacing in the form of a sharp ring (72, 74-76). Treatment of a "cold" gelatin film with concentrated salts or urea transforms the pattern to the "hot" gelatin form exhibiting only the 4.4 Å spacing. This sequence is illustrated in Fig. II-32. The return of the 2.86 Å spacing, which is the spacing most characteristic of the native collagen folding, in a "cold" gelatin along with the absence of the longer-range 10–16 Å spacing indicates the return of randomly oriented local segments with the short-range arrangement of the peptide chains in the native structure. Longer-range ordering could not be detected.

2. Infrared Dichroism

The infrared spectra of polypeptides and proteins in the solid state or in dispersions in nonaqueous media show two strong absorption bands, the C=O stretching at 1650 cm^{-1} and the NH stretching at 3300 cm^{-1}. When a peptide chain is wound in the α-helix arrangement, the NH and C=O groups are linked by hydrogen bonds parallel to the helix axis. If the helixes are oriented, as in a fiber for example, infrared radiation is absorbed preferentially in the vector direction of the oriented hydrogen bonds. Thus the spectra of α-poly-L-alanine show a parallel dichroism

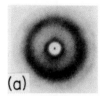 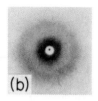

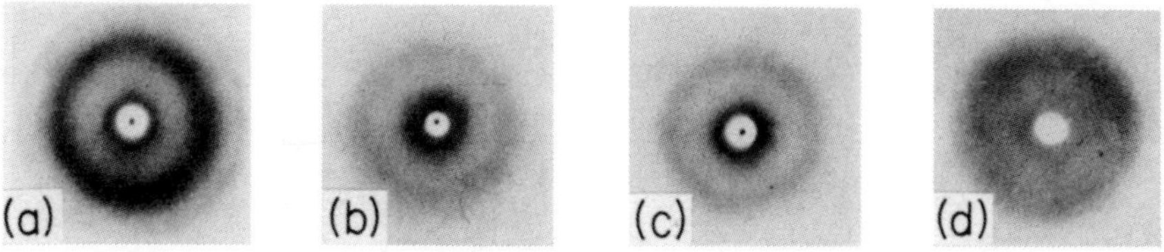

(a) (b) (c) (d)

FIG. II-32. X-ray diffraction patterns of a "cold" gelatin film during exposure to concentrated salt solutions. (a) Normal gelatin; (b) treated with calcium chloride for a short time; (c) treated with nickel nitrate for a short time; (d) treated with nickel nitrate for a long time [Ramachandran (72)].

i.e. an enhanced absorption of the electric vector of the incident radiation when it is parallel to the fiber axis as compared to the case in which the electric vector is perpendicular to the fiber axis (Fig. II-33 a). The β-protein configuration of extended peptide chains in sheet form has the hydrogen bonds perpendicular to the chain axes and, hence, exhibits perpendicular dichroism (Fig. II-33 b).

Ambrose and Elliot (77, 78) studied the infrared dichroism of oriented collagen fibers and "cold" gelatin films. In both cases the materials examined had an NH stretching frequency absorption maximum displaced to 3330 cm^{-1} from the more usual value of 3300 cm^{-1} observed for other proteins. The dichroism was perpendicular (Fig. II-34) (79), indicating that in both native collagen and stretched gelatin films the hydrogen bonds are essentially perpendicular to the peptide backbone chain axis. This is in accord with the collagen I and II structures and the two hydrogen-bond structure derived from the x-ray diffraction data. The perpendicular dichroism of stretched cold gelatin films is surprising, indicating that in addition to the return of the collagen short-range order, as described in the previous paragraphs, the gelation of gelatin involves hydrogen bonds between the small ordered segments.

B. Configuration in Solution by Optical Rotation

In a pioneering investigation of the optical rotation of collagen and gelatin, Carolyn Cohen (*80, 81*) was led to suggest some very fundamental hypotheses concerning the relationship between the optical rotatory power of proteins and their configuration. The first of these was that the

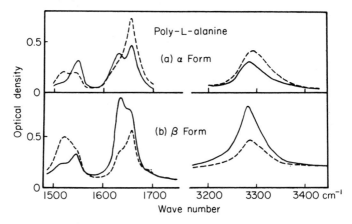

FIG. II-33. Infrared absorption spectra of α- and β-poly-L-alanine. The C=O and NH stretching bonds are situated near 1650 and 3300 cm⁻¹, respectively; solid line, electric vector perpendicular to fiber axis; dashed line, electric vector parallel to fiber axis [Bamford (*93*)].

optical rotations exhibited by randomized or denatured proteins correspond to the sums of the independent contributions of the constituent L-amino acids. The $[\alpha]_D$ values are —80° to —120° for most denatured proteins, including gelatin.

The second postulate was that the changed rotation noted in the native state is the result of effects of specific main-chain configurations superimposed on the independent amino acid contributions. The native globular proteins have $[\alpha]_D$ values of —30° to —60°, while native collagen, in the acid-soluble tropocollagen form, has an $[\alpha]_D$ of —350°. Cohen related the chain configuration contribution to the helical twist of the peptide chains. These views were amply verified and extended by many other workers, particularly Doty and his colleagues (*81-86*). The details of these and other studies have been reviewed by Kauzmann (*87*).

The optical rotation is also a function of the wavelength of the observation, and the consequent rotatory dispersion of polypeptides was found by Moffitt (*88-90*) to fit an equation of the form

$$[\alpha]_\lambda = \frac{100}{M_0} \left(\frac{n^2 + 2}{3} \right) \left[\frac{a_0 \lambda_0^2}{\lambda^2 - \lambda_0^2} + \frac{b_0 \lambda_0^4}{(\lambda^2 - \lambda_0^2)^2} \right] \tag{82}$$

In this equation $[\alpha]_\lambda$ is the specific rotation noted at wavelength λ; M_0 the molecular weight per residue; n the refractive index of the solvent; and a_0, b_0, and λ_0 are constants. λ_0 is called the dispersion constant while a_0

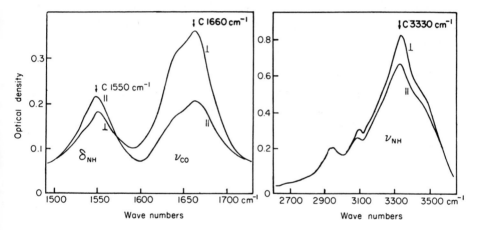

Fig. II-34. The infrared dichroism of fibrous precipitates of acid-soluble collagen. $\perp$: Electric vector perpendicular to fiber axis; $\parallel$: electric vector parallel to fiber axis; C: position of absorption frequency maxima in native collagen [Randall *et al.* (*79*)].

and b_0 are called rotation constants. Moffitt calculated that $b_0 = -580°$ and $\lambda_0 = 2000$ Å for a right-handed α-helix. Mean values of $b_0 = -630°$ and $\lambda_0 = 2120$ Å were obtained for poly-γ-benzyl-L-glutamate and poly-L-glutamic acid in solvents where the helical configuration was the stable form. Most proteins, however, exhibit a simpler rotatory dispersion behavior, which can be represented by a one-term Drude expression, Eq. 83 (*91*)

$$[\alpha]_\lambda = \frac{k}{\lambda^2 - \lambda_c^2} \tag{83}$$

with λ_c having values in the range 250–260 mμ for most proteins in the native state and values of 220–230 mμ in the denatured state. On the basis of these observations Yang and Doty (85) suggested that the dispersion constant could be used as a measure of the helical content in proteins as well as the specific rotation at any given wavelength.

Cohen (81) and Harrington (92) determined λ_c for native collagen and for denatured gelatin. Drude plots of $\lambda^2[\alpha]$ vs. $[\alpha]$ were linear and λ_c was nearly constant at about 210–220 mμ. On the other hand, striking variations were noted in $[\alpha]_D$. For example (92), native rat tail tendon collagen had an $[\alpha]_D$ of —289° compared with —118° for rat tail gelatin in water and —35° for rat tail gelatin in 12 M lithium bromide. In the first two cases λ_c was 217 mμ, while in the latter case λ_c was reduced to 207 mμ. These data indicate that the change in λ_c in gelatin systems is primarily the result of solvent effects rather than configurational effects. Since the variations in λ_c are so small in gelatin systems, optical rotatory dispersion measurements are likely to yield relatively little information unless they are carried out in a very detailed way.

On the other hand, the optical rotatory power of a gelatin solution can be varied very greatly by altering the solvent composition and temperature. The optical rotatory power is, therefore, an extremely sensitive tool for the analysis of configurational changes in gelatin solution.

REFERENCES

1. W. D. Lansing and E. O. Kraemer, *J. Am. Chem. Soc.* **57**, 1369 (1935).

2. J. W. Williams, W. M. Saunders, and J. S. Cicirelli, *J. Phys. Chem.* **58**, 774 (1954).

3. P. J. Flory, "Principles of Polymer Chemistry," pp. 317-398. Cornell Univ. Press, Ithaca, New York, 1953.

4. H. B. Bull, "Physical Biochemistry," 2nd ed., pp. 265-267. Wiley, New York, 1951.

5. J. Pouradier and A. M. Venet, *J. Chim. Phys.* **47**, 11 (1950).

6. J. Pouradier and A. M. Venet, *J. Chim. Phys.* **47**, 391 (1950).

7. J. Pouradier and A. M. Venet, *J. Chim. Phys.* **49**, 85, 239 (1952).

8. J. Pouradier, J. Roman, and A. M. Venet, *J. Chim. Phys.* **47**, 887 (1950).

9. H. Boedtker and P. Doty, *J. Am. Chem. Soc.* **78**, 4267 (1956).

10. P. Doty and J. T. Edsall, *Advan. Protein Chem.* **6**, 35-120 (1951).

11. K. A. Stacy, "Light-Scattering in Physical Chemistry" Academic Press, New York, 1956.

11a. P. M. Gallop, *Arch. Biochem. Biophys.* **54**, 486, 501 (1955).

11b. M. B. M'Ewen and M. I. Pratt, *in* "Nature and Structure of Collagen" (J. T. Randall, ed.), p. 158. Butterworths, London, 1953.

12. H. Boedtker and P. Doty, *J. Phys. Chem.* **58**, 968 (1954).

13. B. H. Zimm, *J. Chem. Phys.* **16**, 1093, 1099 (1948).

14. E. V. Gouinlock, Jr., P. J. Flory, and H. A. Scheraga, *J. Polymer Sci.* **16**, 383 (1955).

15. A. Courts and G. Stainsby, *in* "Recent Advances in Gelatin and Glue Research" (G. Stainsby, ed.), p. 100. Pergamon Press, New York, 1958.

16. P. R. Saunders and A. G. Ward, *in* "Recent Advances in Gelatin and Glue Research" (G. Stainsby, ed.), p. 197. Pergamon Press, New York, 1958.

17. A. Veis, D. N. Eggenberger, and J. Cohen, *J. Am. Chem. Soc.* **77**, 2368 (1955).

18. A. Veis and J. Cohen, *J. Am. Chem. Soc.* **78**, 6238 (1956).

19. A. Veis and J. Cohen, *J. Polymer Sci.* **26**, 113 (1957).

20. A. Veis, J. Anesey, and J. Cohen, *in* "Recent Advances in Gelatin and Glue Research" (G. Stainsby, ed.), p. 155. Pergamon Press, New York, 1958.

21. A. Veis, J. Anesey, and J. Cohen, *J. Am. Leather Chemists' Assoc.* **55**, 548 (1960).

22. G. Stainsby, *Discussions Faraday Soc.* **18**, 288 (1954).

23. M. L. Huggins, *J. Am. Chem. Soc.* **64**, 2716 (1942).

24. P. J. Flory, *J. Chem. Phys.* **17**, 303 (1949).

25. P. J. Flory and T. G. Fox, Jr., *J. Am. Chem. Soc.* **73**, 1904 (1951).

26. P. J. Flory and T. G. Fox, Jr., *J. Polymer Sci.* **5**, 745 (1950).

27. P. Debye, *J. Chem. Phys.* **14**, 636 (1946).

28. P. Debye and A. M. Bueche, *J. Chem. Phys.* **16**, 573 (1948).

29. J. G. Kirkwood and J. Riseman, *J. Chem. Phys.* **16**, 565 (1948).

30. J. G. Kirkwood, *Rec. Trav. Chim.* **68**, 649 (1949).

31. H. Benoit, *J. Polymer Sci.* **11**, 507 (1953).

32. S. Newman and P. J. Flory, *J. Polymer Sci.* **10**, 121 (1953).

33. G. Scatchard, J. L. Oncley, J. W. Williams, and A. Brown, *J. Am. Chem. Soc.* **66**, 1980 (1944).

34. J. W. Williams and W. M. Saunders, *J. Phys. Chem.* **58**, 854 (1954).

35. J. W. Williams, *J. Polymer Sci.* **12**, 351 (1954).

36. J. W. Williams, *in* "Recent Advances in Gelatin and Glue Research" (G. Stainsby, ed.), p. 106. Pergamon Press, New York, 1958.

37. J. W. Williams, K. E. Van Holde, R. L. Baldwin, and H. Fujita, *Chem. Rev.* **58**, 715 (1958).

38. R. J. Goldberg, *J. Phys. Chem.* **57**, 194 (1953).

39. W. J. Archibald, *J. Phys. & Colloid Chem.* **51**, 1204 (1947).

40. A. Veis and J. Anesey, unpublished results, 1962.

41. A. Ehrenberg, *Acta Chem. Scand.* **11**, 1257 (1957).

42. J. Bello, H. R. Bello, and J. R. Vinograd, *Biochim. Biophys. Acta* **57**, 222 (1962).

43. R. L. Baldwin and J. W. Williams, *J. Am. Chem. Soc.* **72**, 4325 (1950).

44. J. W. Williams, *J. Am. Chem. Soc.* **74**, 1542 (1952).

45. G. Stainsby, *Discussions Faraday Soc.* **18**. 288 (1954).

46. A. Courts, *Biochem. J.* **58**, 74 (1954).

47. G. Stainsby, P. R. Saunders, and A. G. Ward, *J. Polymer Sci.* **12**, 325 (1954).

48. A. Veis and J. Cohen, *J. Phys. Chem.* **62**, 459 (1958).

49. K. G. A. Pankhurst and R. C. M. Smith, *Trans. Faraday Soc.* **43**, 6 (1947).

50. K. G. A. Pankhurst, *Research (London) Suppl.* p. 109 (1949).

51. D. I. Hitchcock, *J. Gen. Physiol.* **15**, 125 (1931).

52. W. M. Ames, *J. Sci. Food Agr.* **3**, 579 (1952).

53. A. W. Kenchington and A. G. Ward, *Biochem. J.* **58**, 202 (1954).

54. W. M. Ames, *J. Soc. Chem. Ind. (London)*, **63**, 277 (1944).

55. W. M. Ames, *J. Sci. Food Agr.* **3**, 454 (1952).

56. R. K. Cannan, *Chem. Rev.* **30**, 395 (1942).

57. J. H. Bowes and R. H. Kenten, *Biochem. J.* **43**, 358 (1948).

58. J. H. Bowes and R. H. Kenten, *Biochem. J.* **43**, 365 (1948).

59. J. E. Eastoe and A. A. Leach, *in* "Recent Advances in Gelatin and Glue Research" (G. Stainsby, ed.), p. 173. Pergamon Press, New York, 1958.

60. J. W. Janus, A. W. Kenchington, and A. G. Ward, *Research (London)*, **4**, 247 (1951).

61. E. O. Kraemer, *Colloid Symp. Monograph* **4**, 102 (1926).

62. C. W. Carr and L. Topol, *J. Phys. Chem.* **54**, 176 (1950).

63. J. Bello, H. R. Riese, and J. R. Vinograd, *J. Phys. Chem.* **60**, 1299 (1956).

64. J. C. Ghosh and B. P. Gyani, *J. Indian Chem. Soc.* **30**, 755 (1953).

65. J. Loeb, "Proteins and the Theory of Colloidal Behavior." McGraw-Hill, New York, 1922.

66. H. A. Abramson, "Electrokinetic Phenomena." Reinhold, New York, 1934.

67. P. Johnson and E. M. Shooter, *J. Colloid Sci.* **3**, 539 (1948).

68. R. A. Alberty, *J. Chem. Educ.* **25**, 426 (1948).

69. G. Stainsby, *Nature* **169**, 662 (1952).

70. A. G. Ward and P. R. Saunders, *in* "Rheology" (F. R. Eirich, ed.), Vol. 2, pp. 313-362. Academic Press, New York, 1958.

71. W. T. Astbury, *J. Intern. Soc. Leather Trades' Chemists* **24**, 69 (1940).

72. G. N. Ramachandran, *in* "Recent Advances in Gelatin and Glue Research" (G. Stainsby, ed.), p. 32. Pergamon Press, New York, 1958.

73. J. R. Katz, J. C. Derksen, and W. F. Bon, *Rec. Trav. Chim.* **50**, 725 (1931).

74. J. R. Katz, *Rec. Trav. Chim.* **51**, 385 (1932).

75. C. Robinson and M. J. Bott, *Nature* **168**, 325 (1951).

76. C. Robinson, *in* "Nature and Structure of Collagen" (J. T. Randall, ed.), p. 96. Butterworths, London, 1953.

77. E. J. Ambrose and A. Elliott, *Proc. Roy. Soc.* **A206**, 206 (1951).

78. E. J. Ambrose and A. Elliott, *Proc. Roy. Soc.* **A208**, 75 (1951).

79. J. T. Randall, G. L. Brown, S. Fitton Jackson, F. C. Kelly, A. C. T. North, W. E. Seeds, and G. R. Wilkinson, *in* "Nature and Structure of Collagen" (J. T. Randall, ed.), p. 215. Butterworths, London, 1953.

80. C. Cohen, *Nature*, **175**, 129 (1955).

81. C. Cohen, *J. Biophys. Biochem. Cytol.* **1**, 203 (1955).

82. P. Doty, A. M. Holtzer, J. H. Bradbury, and E. R. Blout, *J. Am. Chem. Soc.* **76**, 4493 (1954).

83. P. Doty, J. H. Bradbury, and A. M. Holtzer, *J. Am. Chem. Soc.* **78**, 947 (1956).

84. P. Doty and J. T. Yang, *J. Am. Chem. Soc.* **78**, 498 (1956).

85. J. T. Yang and P. Doty, *J. Am. Chem. Soc.* **79**, 761 (1957).

86. P. Doty and R. Lundberg, *Proc. Natl. Acad. Sci. U.S.* **43**, 213 (1957).

87. W. Kauzmann, *Advan. Protein Chem.* **14**, 1 (1959).

88. W. Moffitt, *J. Chem. Phys.* **25**, 467 (1956).

89. W. Moffitt and J. T. Yang, *Proc. Natl. Acad. Sci. U.S.* **42**, 596 (1956).

90. W. Moffitt, *Proc. Natl. Acad. Sci. U.S.* **42**, 736 (1956).

91. K. U. Linderstrom-Lang and J. A. Schellman, *Biochim. Biophys. Acta* **15**, 156 (1954).

92. W. F. Harrington, *Nature* **181**, 997 (1958).

93. C. H. Bamford, *in* "Recent Advances in Gelatin and Glue Research" (G. Stainsby, ed.), p. 115 Pergamon Press, New York, 1958.

III

THE CONVERSION OF COLLAGEN TO GELATIN

I. INTRODUCTION

The picture that emerges from the characterization studies discussed in the previous chapter is rather like an early impressionist painting. From a distance the image is clear and the subject distinct, but closer inspection yields confusion—lines blur, subtle shadings become evident, and the precise definition of each object becomes more difficult. In the same way gelatins in the broad view all appear as essentially amorphous structures that can assume in solution many configurations of nearly equal energy. They can expand or contract, depending upon the solvent, pH, or ionic strength. The peptide chains can undergo partial return to the collagen folding and gelation can occur. More detailed examination, however, reveals that the molecular structures may vary from the random coil to three-dimensional multichain networks, the molecular weight distributions are not gaussian, and the ionic or electrical properties vary from one molecule to the next.

In Chapter I some evidence was presented that indicated a basic heterogeneity in the collagen of nature connective tissue. It is reasonable to suppose that some of the variations in the gelatins stem from this heterogeneity. There are also many ways by which collagen can be converted to gelatin and it can be anticipated that these various extraction procedures also contribute to the many differences in the gelatins. In the present chapter an attempt will be made to sort out these various factors and their influence on the course of the collagen-gelatin transition and the properties of the gelatins.

II. AN IDEALIZED CASE: CONVERSION OF ACID-SOLUBLE TROPOCOLLAGEN TO GELATIN

A. Parent Gelatin

The simplest situation that can be realized is the conversion of soluble collagen to gelatin in solutions where the collagen is in the monomer or isolated tropocollagen form. Gallop (1) made the first investigation of this nature.

Gallop extracted carp swim bladder tunics with pH 4.3 citrate buffer. The collagen in the resulting viscous solution was purified by precipitation by dialysis against neutral phosphate buffer, followed by resolution in pH 3.7 citrate buffer, 0.1 M in citric acid and 0.05 M in sodium citrate. The solutions were cleared of large aggregates by centrifugation at 50,000 × G at 5° for several hours. These centrifuged solutions had an intrinsic viscosity of 13 dl/gm and a specific optical rotation, $[\alpha]_D$, of —350°. Upon heating these solutions to 40° Gallop noted that, within a few minutes, the optical rotation dropped to —110°, the value noted as the average value for aqueous gelatin solutions of low ionic strength (2–5). The intrinsic viscosity also dropped precipitously at 40° to a lower limiting value of ∼ 0.3. The same changes could be noted at 30° but in this case it required nearly 2 hours for the specific rotation to drop to —110° and about 3 days for the viscosity to drop to the range 0.3–0.5 dl/gm. The complete, maximal drop in optical rotation was interpreted as indicating that the characteristic helical configuration of the collagen was lost. Similarly, the corresponding drop in viscosity was taken to indicate the collapse of the extended, rodlike configuration of the collagen. Having defined gelatin as the water-soluble product of the denaturation or disordering of collagen, it is evident that this simple heating process was sufficient to have brought about the conversion of acid-soluble collagen to gelatin. Since dialsyis of the gelatin solution against the pH 3.7 buffer at room temperature did not yield dialyzable peptides, Gallop (1) considered that the conversion proceeded without peptide bond hydrolysis. Gallop called the gelatin produced in this fashion "parent gelatin," and concluded that parent gelatin should be the highest molecular weight gelatin obtainable.

Gallop (1) proceeded to carry out a variety of physical measurements, determining sedimentation coefficients, diffusion coefficients, partial specific volume, intrinsic viscosity, and molecular weight by light scattering, all on the parent gelatin in pH 3.7 citric acid sodium citrate buffer. The results of these investigations are given in Table III-1. The sedimentation velocity experiments showed only one fairly sharp sedimenting boundary and Gallop therefore concluded that his parent gelatin preparation was monodisperse. The molecule characterized by the data of Table III-1 can be represented as either a prolate ellipsoid about 20×400 Å or a random coil with a root mean square end-to-end chain extension of 225 Å.

TABLE III-1 [a]

MOLECULAR PARAMETERS OF ICHTHYOCOL PARENT GELATIN

Parameter	Method	Value
s_{20}^{0}	Sedimentation coefficients extrapolated to infinite dilution	3.31 S
D_{20}^{0}	Diffusion coefficients extrapolated to infinite dilution	3.91×10^{-7} cm²/sec
M_w	Weight-average molecular weight by light scattering (90° measurements, dissymmetry = 1.0)	$68,000 \pm 7,000$
M_w	Combination of s, D, $\bar{v}$	$69,700 \pm 4200$
$\bar{v}$	Partial specific volume	0.705 ± 0.005
$[\eta]$	Intrinsic viscosity, capillary viscometer	0.34
(dn/dc) 25°	Refractive index increment, differential refractometer	0.192, 4368 Å mercury line

[a] Data of Gallop (1).

Gallop attempted to ascribe a special significance to the 70,000 molecular weight units in terms of the 640-Å spacing of collagen, but discussion of this will be reserved until after comparison of these results with those of a similar investigation.

After examining Gallop's data (*1*), Boedtker and Doty (*6*) began an investigation of the native and denatured states of soluble collagen that, by virtue of its completeness and clarity, qualifies as the "classical" contribution to this field. The soluble collagen of carp swim bladder tunic was extracted by the procedure of Gallop (*1*) and examined in pH 3.7 citrate buffer of the same 0.10 *M* citric acid 0.05 *M* sodium citrate composition.

The first part of the study was devoted to the preparation of a monodisperse soluble collagen and its thorough characterization. It became apparent, especially in light scattering studies, that soluble collagen aggregated readily at pH 3.7, and that the high viscosity of the collagen solutions prevented their optical clarification by high speed centrifugation. It was found that reproducible minimal turbidity could be obtained only when the collagen solutions were centrifuged at concentrations of less than 0.2% collagen. All measurements of viscosity, flow birefringence, sedimentation coefficient, and light scattering were carried out at concentrations well below this limiting value. Osmotic pressure measurements, in which aggregation is least noticeable, were carried out at concentrations between 0.25 and 0.68%. Typical osmotic pressure, light scattering, sedimentation, and flow birefringence data are illustrated in Fig. II-3 and Fig. III-1, 2, and 3, respectively. The results of these investigations are summarized in Table III-2.

The very excellent agreement between the results for the number- and weight-average molecular weights, and the correspondence of the lengths obtained by various means, showed the monodisperse nature of this acid-soluble ichthyocol preparation. Boedtker and Doty found that the best correlation of these data could be achieved if the collagen molecule were represented as a rodlike structure with an average molecular weight of 345,000, a length of 3000 Å, and a diameter of 13.6 Å.

Gallop's method (*1*) of heating the acid collagen solutions was used to study the conversion of these monodisperse collagen preparations into gelatin. The solution viscosity was used to follow the denaturation. Several solutions were prepared at 14.9° and their viscosities measured. Each solution was heated to a given temperature for 30 minutes and the viscosity measured again. These measurements confirmed Gallop's observation that the complete denaturation of ichthyocol took place over a rather short

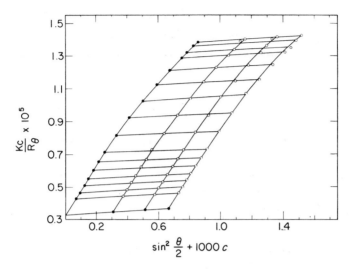

Fig. III-1. Light scattering of monodisperse ichthyocol tropocollagen in pH 3.7 citrate buffer, 15°: O, experimental data; ●, extrapolated points. From the intercept and appropriate slopes: $M_w = 310,000$; $\varrho_Z = 870$ Å; $L = 3000$ Å; $M/L = 103$ [Boedtker and Doty (6)].

temperature interval. The results were plotted as the relative decrease in viscosity ($[\eta]_t/[\eta]_{14.9°}$) vs. the temperature of half-hour heating, (Fig. III-4). The major part of the transition took place between 25° and 32.5°. The denaturation was essentially complete at 33°. The approximation was made that the denaturation was an all-or-nothing process, that is, that it

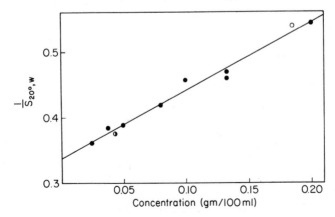

Fig. III-2. Sedimentation coefficients of ichthyocol in pH 3.7 citrate buffer, corrected to water at 20°, as a function of concentration. Data from three preparations [Boedtker and Doty (6)].

TABLE III-2 [a]

MOLECULAR PARAMETERS OF ICHTHYOCOL IN CITRATE BUFFER

Parameter	Method	Value
$s_{20,w}^{0}$	Sedimentation velocity, extrapolation to infinite dilution	2.96 ± 0.10 S
M_w	Light scattering, extrapolation by Zimm plot	$3.45 \pm 0.3 \times 10^5$
M_n	Osmotic pressure, extrapolation to infinite dilution	$3.10 \pm 0.5 \times 10^5$
$[\eta]$	Capillary viscometer	11.5 ± 1.5 dl/gm
$\bar{v}$	Pycnometry	0.695 ± 0.005
L_Z	Length, light scattering data, assumed rod shape	3000 Å
L, major axis minor axis	Viscosity, assumed rod shape	2970 ± 200 Å 13.6 ± 0.4 Å
L	Flow birefringence	2500–3000 Å
A_2	Second virial coefficient, osmotic pressure concentration dependence	$2.3 \pm 1.0 \times 10^{-4}$ ml-mole/gm²

[a] Data of Boedtker and Doty (6).

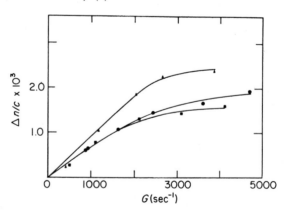

FIG. III-3. Flow birefringence of ichthyocol at pH 3.7 in citrate buffer, 20°, as a function of the shear gradient, G. Upper curve, 0.2 gm/100 ml; middle curve, 0.12 gm/100 ml; lower curve, 0.08 gm/100 ml. The lower curve represents the limiting behavior of the tropocollagen rods [Boedtker and Doty (6)].

involved only an initial and final state. The rate of decrease of viscosity was fitted with the Arrhenius equation. The curve in Fig. III-4 is the theoretical rate of viscosity decrease if the activation energy had the value of 81 kcal. Application of the transition state theory to these data yielded a value of $+ 230$ entropy units (e.u.) for the entropy of activation. This high value of $\Delta S^{\ddagger}$ indicates a high degree of rotational freedom in the transition state, comparable to that found in other cases of protein denaturation. Also, as in other cases of protein denaturation, the addition of reagents such as urea and potassium thiocyanate lowered the denaturation temper-

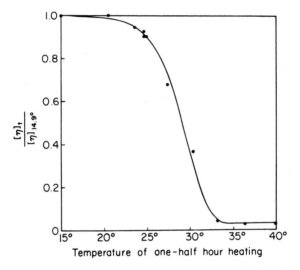

Temperature of one-half hour heating

Fig. III-4. Collagen-gelatin transition, as seen in temperature dependence of the intrinsic viscosity: citrate buffer, pH 3.7; ●, experimental points; solid line, calculated assuming $\Delta H^{\ddagger} = 81$ kcal, $\Delta S^{\ddagger} = 230$ e.u. [Boedtker and Doty (6)].

ature without decreasing the sharpness of the transition. At concentrations of 2.0 M and greater, potassium thiocyanate lowered the denaturation temperature to below 4°.

After making these general observations Boedtker and Doty (6) proceeded to characterize the gelatin in two ways. Light scattering measurements on citrate solutions at 20° and 0.03% collagen concentration were used to establish that the collagen molecular weight was that of a monodisperse preparation. The solutions were then heated for 30 minutes at 36.5° and the angular dependence of scattering was redetermined. The molecular weight of the gelatin was placed in this way at 1.35×10^5. A typical experiment of this type is illustrated in Fig. III-5. Since gelatins normally undergo slow hydrolysis in water, particularly at temperatures above the ambient (7), care had to be taken to assure that the molecular weight determinations were carried out as rapidly as possible. This slow hydrolysis also prevented the use of osmotic pressure measurements at 40° since these required at least 18 hours for equilibration. Another difficulty involved the progressive aggregation (gelation) of gelatin at temperatures below 40° and at concentrations greater than 0.1%.

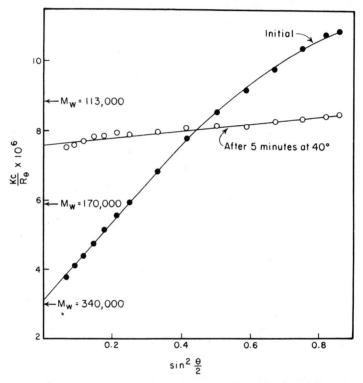

Fig. III-5. Denaturation of collagen solution: citrate buffer, pH 3.7; ●, light scattering of 2.6×10^{-4} gm/ml solution before denaturation; ○, light scattering of identical solution after being heated at 40° for 5 minutes. Arrows indicate the molecular weight of collagen after correcting scattering data to zero concentration, and the expected intercept, if collagen molecule divided into either two or three equal pieces [Boedtker and Doty (6)].

These two difficulties were circumvented by carrying out the measurements at 25° in 2.0 M potassium thiocyanate. As mentioned earlier, the addition of 2.0 M potassium thiocyanate to a solution of collagen in citrate buffer at pH 3.7 brought about the complete denaturation of the collagen. Identical results with respect to the molecular weight of the parent gelatin were obtained regardless of whether the potassium thiocyanate was added to a cool solution of collagen or a solution after heating to 36.5°.

Light scattering measurements (Fig. III-6) in 2.0 M potassium thiocyanate placed the weight-average molecular weight of the parent gelatin at 1.43×10^5. Osmotic pressure measurements in the same solvent, Fig. II-4, placed the number average weight at $1.25 \pm 0.1 \times 10^5$ and the second virial coefficient, A_2, at 3.0×10^{-4} ml-mole/gm². The sedimentation coefficient in 2.0 M potassium thiocyanate was 3.48 S ($s^0_{20,w}$). In the citrate buffer $s^0_{20,w}$ was 3.77 S. The intrinsic viscosity in 2.0 M potassium thiocyanate had the value 0.545 dl/gm and in the citrate buffer at 36.5° was equal to 0.44 dl/gm.

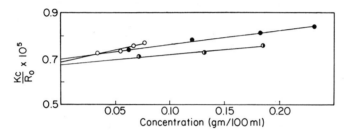

FIG. III-6. Light scattering of parent gelatin solutions: $\bigcirc$, in citrate buffer at 25°; solutions measured immediately after heating to 36.5° for 10 minutes; $\circleddash$, in citrate buffer, at 25°; solutions prepared by denaturing collagen by means of 2 M KCNS at neutral pH, 4°, and then removing KCNS by exhaustive dialysis; $\bullet$, in 2 M KCNS, pH 7, 25° [Boedtker and Doty (6)].

Using this information, a number of runs were made at single low concentrations of collagen; the reduced intensity of scattering was determined at zero angle, and a correction factor based on the concentration and second virial coefficient applied to yield the molecular weight. The solutions were heated and the molecular weights of the parent gelatin was redetermined by the same procedure. This procedure eliminated uncertainties due to clarification of the solutions for the scattering measurements. The results of these investigations are given in Table III-3. From these results and the independent measurements described earlier for each material, Boedtker and Doty concluded that the weight-average molecular weight of the parent gelatin was $(1.38 \pm 0.08) \times 10^5$ and that the ratio of the weight-average molecular weight of the soluble collagen to that of the parent gelatin was 2.5 ± 0.15. The number-average molecular weight of $(1.25 \pm 0.1) \times 10^5$ was almost within the range of experimental error of the weight-average value and indicated that the polydispersity of the parent gelatin was small.

The aim of this study was to determine the number of molecules of gelatin produced by the denaturation of a single soluble collagen molecule. The observed ratio of the molecular weights (M, collagen/M, gelatin $= 2.5$) showed that two or three molecules were produced. However, if two molecules had been formed, then the minimum number- or weight-average molecular weight for the two would have been 1.72×10^5. For three mol-

TABLE III-3 [a]

MOLECULAR WEIGHTS OF MONODISPERSE SOLUBLE ICHTHYOCOL
AND THE PARENT GELATINS DERIVED FROM THEM

Initial collagen concentration (gm/100 ml)	M, collagen $\times 10^{-5}$	M, gelatin $\times 10^{-5}$	$\dfrac{M,\ \text{collagen}}{M,\ \text{gelatin}}$
0.068	3.55	1.30	2.73
0.032	3.40	1.35	2.52
0.026	3.40	1.35	2.52
0.027	3.65	1.48	2.47
Average	3.50	1.37	2.56

[a] Data of Boedtker and Doty (6).

ecules the minimum weight would have been 1.15×10^5. Hence the observed values are compatible only with the three molecule possibility and must be accounted for by polydispersity, that is, by unequal weights for the three peptide strands. These data provide no insight into the nature of the polydispersity. For example, the polydispersity could have arisen from unequal chain weights, because of unequal degrees of polymerization in each chain, or, alternatively, from equal degrees of polymerization but unequal distributions of light and heavy amino acids. Boedtker and Doty favored the first of these alternatives.

In any event, regardless of the source of the heterogeneity, these data do bring one to question the propriety of the term "parent gelatin" which implies the existence of a uniform, homogeneous material. Even in this ideal case where the collagen → gelatin transition had been carried out without apparent rupture of covalent bonds, the gelatin was not of uniform composition.

B. Collagen Subunits

Orekhovich and Shpikiter (*8*) studied the breakdown of citrate-soluble calf skin procollagen in 3 M urea. No attempts were made to assure that procollagen solutions were monodisperse. The conversion to gelatin was accomplished by heating the solutions for 10 minutes at 30°. The gelatin produced in this way (*9*) was examined in an analytical ultracentrifuge in 1–2 M potassium thiocyanate solutions. In this case two components were observed. Similarly, ultracentrifugal observation of the gelatin produced by the denaturation of procollagen, by exposure for 20 minutes to 5 M potassium thiocyanate solution at 70° in pH 8 phosphate buffer, showed the presence of two differently sedimenting components. Orekhovich and Shpitiker (*8*) also noted two components following the denaturation of acid-soluble ichthyocol, acid-soluble cod skin collagen, and acid-soluble rat skin collagen. They therefore concluded that the first stage in the gelatinization of all acid-soluble collagens was the splitting of the collagen molecule into two different fragments.

The slower sedimenting component was designated the α component, the faster sedimenting material the β component. The conventional gelatin fractionation techniques were not able to separate α and β completely, though enrichment of either component could be achieved. A new technique was developed which involved the precipitation of α and β from solutions in 5.0 M urea at 37° by the addition of saturated ammonium sulfate. The component β precipitated first, then at high concentrations of ammonium sulfate the pure α component precipitated. Reprecipitations of the purified components yielded still purer preparations. Artificial mixtures of α and β were prepared and sedimented in varying weight ratios. The sedimentation diagrams were compared with those obtained from the original denatured acid-soluble collagens. These comparisons indicated that the α/β weight ratio was 1:1 in the native acid-soluble collagen molecule. The α and β components were characterized by sedimentation velocity and diffusion measurements. These data are summarized in Table III-4. It is evident that these molecular weights are not consistent with those reported by Boedtker and Doty (*6*).

Subsequent ultracentrifugal examination of denatured acid-soluble ichthyocol by Chun and Doty (*10*) and of denatured acid-soluble calf skin collagen by Doty and Nishihara (*11*) verified the observation (*8*) that two distinct components were obtained upon the denaturation of acid-soluble collagen.

Chun and Doty (*10*) found the slower component of the ichthyocol

TABLE III-4 [a]

MOLECULAR WEIGHTS OF α AND β COMPONENTS OF RAT SKIN ACID-SOLUBLE COLLAGEN

Material	Sedimentation coefficient, S	Diffusion coefficient $\times 10^7$ (cm^2/sec)	M (assuming $\bar{v} = 0.700$)
Native rat skin collagen (in pH 3.7 citrate buffer + 1% CaCl$_2$ or 0.5 M urea)	3.05–3.25	0.35–0.40	700,000
α Component (pH 8 phosphate buffer + 10% KCNS)	4.0	2.6	125,000
β Component (pH 8 phosphate buffer + 10% KCNS)	5.7	1.6	290,000
Rat skin collagen $(2\alpha + \beta)$	—	—	~540,000

[a] Data of Orekhovich and Shpikiter (8).

gelatin to have $s^0_{20,w} = 3.15$ S and a molecular weight of 8×10^4, and the faster component to have $s^0_{20,w} = 4.3$ S and $M_w = 1.6 \times 10^5$. Prolonged heating of the 4.3 S component at 40° or short exposure to 80° or solutions at pH 12 converted this material to the 3.15 S component. After this conversion no further degradative changes were noted in the 3.15 S component under the stated conditions. The activation energy for the thermal conversion of the heavy component to the light component was 24 kcal.

Doty and Nishihara (11) examined the denatured acid-soluble calf skin collagen at pH 3.7 in citrate buffer at 40° and in 2.0 M potassium thiocyanate. Light scattering measurements indicated a weight-average molecular weight of 1.95×10^5, and osmotic pressure measurements yielded a number-average molecular weight of 1.70×10^5. The initial monodisperse soluble collagen had a molecular weight of 3.52×10^5. Thus the ratio of the weight-average molecular weights of the soluble calf skin collagen and the gelatin derived from it (M, collagen/M, gelatin) was 1.85 in contrast to 2.5, previously determined by Boedtker and Doty (6) for the acid-soluble ichthyocol. Doty and Nishihata (11) found the light and heavy components to have sedimentation constants, $s^0_{20,w}$, of 3.85 S and 5.45 S, and molecular weights of 1.2×10^5 and 2.3×10^5, respectively. On the basis of these data they concluded that the acid-soluble calf skin collagen was composed of one molecule each of the light and heavy components, or that the weight fraction of heavy component was 0.64. In this case also, treatment of the gelatin at pH 12 converted the heavy component entirely to a form with the sedimentation constant of the light component (Fig. III-7). The conversion of the heavy component to the light component was not reversible (Fig. III-7 c). Doty and Nishihara suggested that the heavy component was composed of two units comparable in properties to the light component, the two units being held together by a labile bond sensitive to either alkali or heat.

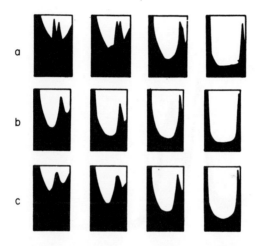

FIG. III-7. Effect of alkali on the α and β components of gelatin. Sedimentation diagrams of denatured calf skin collagen. Time interval: 32 minutes. Speed: 59,780 rpm. (a) Normal sedimentation of α and β components in 0.15 M citrate buffer, pH 3.7, $+$ 1.2 M KCNS. (b) Sedimentation in 0.15 M NaCl $+$ 1.2 M KCNS at pH 12. (c) Solution in (b) dialyzed back to solvent employed in (a) [Doty and Nishihara (11)].

Both Orekhovich and Shpikiter (8) and Chun and Doty (10) fractionated their preparations of denatured acid-soluble collagen by alcohol-salt coacervation procedures, found an enrichment of each component, and determined the hydroxyproline content of each. In each case the heavier component had a substantially lower hydroxyproline content than the original lighter component. Thus, although the heavier component apparently can be converted to two molecules similar to the lighter component, these molecules are not chemically identical. However, in order to simplify terminology it has become the common practice to use the system of Orekhovitch and Shpikiter (8) and to denote the components from the denaturation of acid-soluble collagen as α of β according to their sedimentation coefficients. Those components with an $s^{\circ}_{20,w}$ value near 3.0 S are called α, those with an $s^{\circ}_{20,w}$ value near 4.5 S are called β.

Piez, Weiss and Lewis (*12*) separated the α and β components of acid-soluble calf skin collagen by chromatography on carboxymethylcellulose ion-exchange columns, using a variable ionic strength gradient at pH 4.8. The calf skin collagen was dissolved at pH 4.8 in 0.15 ionic strength acetate buffer and denatured by heating to 40°. Ultracentrifuge patterns of the resulting gelatin (Fig. III-8) were typical in showing the presence of α and β components. This mixture of α and β components was then chroma-

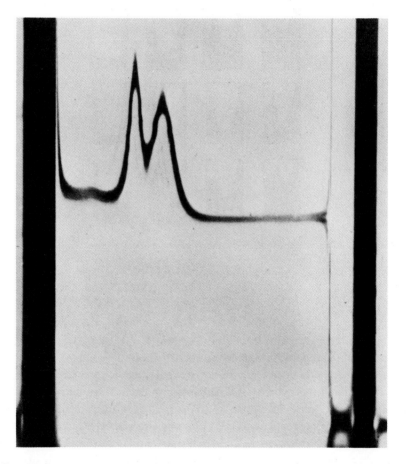

Fig. III-8. A typical ultracentrifuge pattern of parent gelatin from calf skin collagen taken 113 minutes after reaching full speed of 59,780 rpm. The total protein concentration was 0.7% in 0.15 $\Gamma/2$ acetate, pH 4.8. Rotor temperature was 36.7°. Sedimentation was from right to left [Piez *et al.* (*12*)].

tographed. The α component was eluted first (Fig. III-9), but there was considerable overlapping of the peaks. The portions indicated by the arrows in Fig. III-9 were isolated and rechromatographed in the same system. Each component was contaminated with the other; the purest portion of each eluate was used for amino acid analyses. These analyses, together with a similar analysis of the native acid-soluble calf skin collagen, are shown

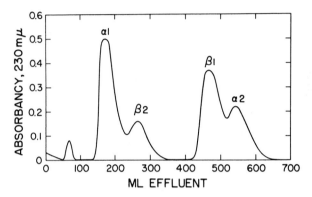

Fig. III-9. Effluent analysis from the chromatography on CM-cellulose of 200 mg of parent gelatin from calf skin collagen. The 2.5×25 cm column was maintained at 37° and eluted with acetate buffer, pH 4.8, varying in concentration from 0.01 $\Gamma/2$ to 0.45 $\Gamma/2$. In the 4-liter, nine-chambered "Varigrad" used to produce the gradient, the concentrations in chambers 1–9 were 0.01, 0.10, 0.12, 0.14, 0.16, 0.18, 0.20, 0.30, and 0.45 $\Gamma/2$, with 225 ml in each chamber. Fractions of 11.3 ml were collected at a rate of 4 ml per minute; 1-ml samples were taken for protein analysis [Piez et al. (12)].

in Table III-5. It is apparent that although the α and β components are similar they are unquestionably not identical. There were no significant differences in the amounts of amide nitrogen, serine, arginine, threonine, phenylalanine, or methionine. The differences between the hydroxyproline, glycine, and tyrosine contents were probably significant. However, the variation in glycine content was small and the amount of tyrosine was near the limit of detection. The hydroxyproline difference was suspect because the assay for hydroxyproline lacks the required precision and reproducibility. Of the remainder of the amino acids, aspartic and glutamic acids, proline, alanine, valine, leucine, isoleucine, lysine, histidine, and hydroxylysine all differed by amounts larger than could reasonably be ascribed to experimental error.

Aside from this very definite evidence that the subunits of tropocollagen are not identical in composition, these data permit one to determine the weight fraction of each component in the intact molecule. Piez et al. (12)

TABLE III-5

AMINO ACID COMPOSITION OF SOME COLLAGENS AND THEIR α AND β COMPONENTS [a]

Amino acid	Calf skin [b]			Rat skin [c]				
	Original	Subuits α	β	Original	α_1	β_2	β_1	α_2
3-Hydroxyproline	85.1	88.0	83.2	0.9	1.0	1.5	0.7	0.0
4-Hydroxyproline				92	96	97	88	86
Aspartic Acid	44.9	43.0	46.0	46	46	45	44	44
Threonine	17.8	16.9	18.1	19.6	19.9	19.8	20.1	19.8
Serine	37.4	38.1	37.5	43	42	41	42	43
Glutamic Acid	71.6	74.4	68.8	71	74	72	70	66
Proline	135.5	140.8	126.9	121	129	128	120	113
Glycine	326.4	322.2	328.6	331	330	333	338	336
Alanine	111.7	118.2	108.5	106	112	111	107	102
Valine	22.5	17.5	27.5	24.0	19.6	19.2	25.6	32.0
Methionine	6.4	6.5	6.2	7.8	8.0	6.6	7.0	6.1
Isoleucine	10.9	9.2	14.0	10.8	6.4	6.5	11.6	16.1
Leucine	24.6	20.5	27.9	23.8	18.1	18.7	25.7	32.4
Tyrosine	3.0	3.4	2.0	2.4	2.1	1.8	2.2	2.4
Phenylalanine	13.4	13.4	14.9	11.3	11.6	12.1	11.0	10.1
Hydroxylysine	7.3	5.5	8.8	5.7	4.3	3.9	6.2	8.0
Lysine	26.5	29.8	22.7	28.1	30.4	30.1	25.8	22.4
Histidine	5.1	2.7	6.0	4.9	1.9	2.0	5.3	8.5
Arginine	50.1	50.1	52.5	51	49	50	50	51
Amide N	(43.7)	(44.3)	(42.2)	(41)	(42)	(41)	(42)	(43)

[a] In residues/1000 total residues.
[b] Data of Piez et al. (12).
[c] Data of Piez et al. (116).

argued that the ratio of the total differences in amino acid residue composition of each component from the composition of the original molecule, without regard to sign, should provide an accurate value for the relative amounts of the two components. In this case, the total differences were 39.3 residues different per 1000 residues for α and 39.0 residues different per 1000 residues for β, indicating a weight ratio close to 1. This agrees with the value obtained by Orekhovich and Shpikiter (8), but not with the value of 2 for the β/α ratio obtained by Doty and Nishihara (11). To be consistent with a tropocollagen weight of 3.5×10^5, Piez, Weiss and Lewis (12) suggested that the weight of the α component must be

8×10^4 and that of the β component 1.6×10^5. Their evidence for these assignments was based entirely on the sedimentation coefficients and was not particularly convincing.

Piez, Lewis, Martin, and Gross (13) examined the chromatographic fractionation of denatured rat skin collagen in still more detail. A slightly different elution system was used than in the earlier work (12) and resolution of the fractions was improved. Both the acid-extractable and neutral-salt-soluble fractions were denatured and chromatographed. In both cases four major peaks were observed (Fig. III-10). Two of these had sedimentation coefficients in the α range and these were labeled α_1 and α_2. Similarly,

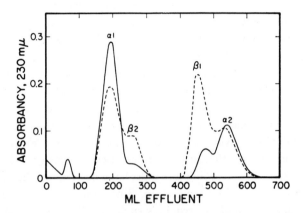

FIG. III-10. Elution patterns of denatured rat skin collagen chromatographed on CM-cellulose at 40°. Solid line, 20 mg salt-extracted collagen; dashed line, 20 mg acid-extracted collagen. A linear gradient between 0.07 and 0.17 $\Gamma/2$ acetate buffer (pH 4.83) was employed. The labels refer to both patterns [Piez et al. (13)].

the other two components had $s^\circ_{20,w}$ values in the β range and were designated β_1 and β_2. Amino acid analyses of these four components revealed that α_1 and α_2 differed in content of hydroxyproline, proline, alanine, valine, isoleucine, leucine, hydroxylysine, lysine, and histidine. The composition values for these amino acids are given in Table III-5. Piez et al. (13) noted that component β_1 had a composition equivalent to a 1:1 mixture of α_1 and α_2, while component β_2 had the same composition as α_1. From these observations, and the previously established fact that β had about twice the molecular weight of α, these workers suggested that the β component was composed of two α chains held together by one or more covalent cross-linkages. It was further supposed, particularly since the chromatograms indicated a 2:1 weight ratio for $\alpha_1:\alpha_2$ in the neutral-salt-soluble fraction where the β components were present in very small amount, that the β components were formed by random cross-linking of the three chains of the basic tropocollagen structure. The observed value of $\beta_1/\beta_2 = 2.7$ rather than 2.0 indicates some preferential cross-linking between the dissimilar α-chains.

In addition to the α and β components, Piez et al. (13) reported some evidence relating to the existence of a third component, γ, that was composed of three cross-linked α chains. Veis, Anesey and Cohen (14, 15) and Altgelt, Hodge and Schmitt (16) had already provided evidence for the existence of such a molecule. Altgelt and colleagues (16) had isolated the γ component from calf skin acid-extractable tropocollagen in low yields. Veis et al. (14) obtained γ from mature insoluble steer corium collagen in larger amounts. Characterization studies (15) showed γ to have a molecular weight of 3.5×10^5 and to be a network of three cross-linked chains, rather than a single-chain random coil. The details of this work will be described in the next section of this chapter. Veis and Cohen (17) and Veis, Anesey and Cohen (14) showed that γ-gelatin could be renatured to the native collagen structure. Rice (18) and Altgelt et al. (16) verified this observation. The renaturation of the three-chain helix of native collagen can most logically be explained on the basis of the presence of cross-linkages holding the chains together in the proper internal register or juxtaposition. If this is the case, the cross-linkages must have been established in the molecule while it was in its native state. Since the cross-linkages in the β- and γ-gelatins are stable in reagents such as 8.0 M urea and 2.0 M potassium thiocyanate, these linkages must be covalent in nature.

C. Summary

In spite of the apparent conflicts in the reports that have just been reviewed, it is possible to draw a single coherent picture that can encompass and account for these varied observations. The situation can be most readily discussed by reference to Fig. III-11. The ordered hydrogen-bonded configuration of the collagen monomer molecule can be melted out readily by heating monodisperse collagen solutions in acid to about 40°. The transition is sharp and complete within a few minutes over a small temperature interval. The activation energy for denaturation is ~ 81 kcal and the entropy of activation is $+ 230$ e.u. The disordered molecule falls apart in one of three ways. If there are no additional restraining bonds between chains (path 1), three randomly coiled single-strand peptide chains result. The three chains are not of identical composition and probably not of equal molecular weight. These chains, each with $s^0_{20, w}$

near 3.0 S, are called α chains. In those cases (path 2) where two chains are joined by one or more covalent cross-linkages, denaturation leads to the appearance of two particles, one an α chain, the other a two-stranded molecule with approximately twice the molecular weight of the α chains. The two-stranded β component has a sedimentation coefficient, $s^{0}_{20,w}$, near 4.5 S. In any particular case, the β component may be composed of two similar or two unlike α chains. The weight distribution will be 67% β and 33% α. In the final case (path 3) it can be imagined that at least two

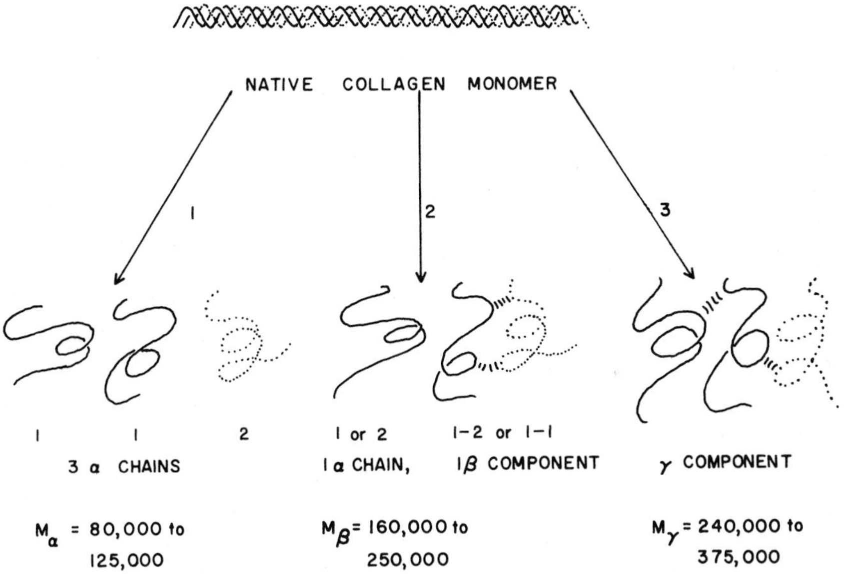

FIG. III-11. A schematic diagram of the modes of conversion of monomeric tropocollagen to various types of gelatins, assuming no rupture of peptide bonds.

covalent cross-linkages hold the three chains together. The disordering process melts out all traces of secondary structure, but the three chains cannot separate and remain as a unit in solution. This three-chain structure is called the γ component. Only small amounts of the γ component have been isolated from acid-extractable tropocollagen preparations. Larger amounts have been obtained from insoluble collagen via another route.

From the variation in α/β ratios determined by the several groups active in this field, one can readily conclude that the distribution of the cross-linkages responsible for the formation of β and γ are not identical in all preparations of acid-extractable tropocollagen. It appears that β and γ are more commonly found in larger quantity, for example, in calf skin or rat skin extracts than in carp swim bladder tunic extracts. The factors which govern the solubility of collagen will be discussed in some detail in the following section of this chapter. One point which will emerge is worth anticipating here. There is no *a priori* reason why one should expect that every molecule of tropocollagen in a particular preparation will have the same number of identically disposed intramolecular cross-linkages. Indeed, it will be shown that the opposite is most likely to be the case. Thus, it is most reasonable to presume that any given preparation is heterogeneous with regard to the degree of intramolecular polymerization, even though one may have a monodisperse preparation in terms of the tropocollagen rodlet structure. The intramolecular heterogeneity will be apparent only on the conversion of the system to gelatin.

From this point of view the "ideal" conversion of the collagen monomer to gelatin should proceed via path 1. The number-average molecular weight of the gelatin system should be one-third the molecular weight of the collagen monomer, and the weight-average molecular weight should be slightly higher due to the nonidentity of the chains. The best values of the collagen monomer molecular weight place this weight substantially above 300,000. Hence the minimum molecular weight of "parent gelatin" must be greater than 100,000. In any real case, where intramolecular polymerization is a factor, both M_n and M_w should be substantially greater than 100,000. The reports of lower molecular weights for the "parent gelatin" mixture (*1, 10, 12*) probably indicate that peptide bond hydrolysis (*1*) was a factor in these studies, or that the sedimentation coefficient–molecular weight relationship used for the calculation of M_w was not appropriate to the molecular weight distribution (*10, 12*). On the same basis, the conclusion that the α component has a molecular weight of 80,000 (*12*) is not consistent with any of the data on the molecular weight of monodisperse acid-soluble collagen. Further work is obviously necessary to clear up these discrepancies.

III. An Idealized Case: Conversion of Purified Insoluble Collagen to Gelatin

Only a small weight fraction of mature mammalian collagenous tissue can be put into solution in the form of acid- or salt-soluble tropocollagen; the major portion of the collagen is insoluble in most aqueous systems. As soon as one turns to the study of the conversion of this insoluble collagen to gelatin, new problems arise in addition to those already encountered in the tropocollagen → gelatin conversion. Chief among these problems is the difficulty in identifying and obtaining a reproducible and well-defined starting material. Almost equally important is the fact that the extraction systems are themselves heterogeneous.

Most of the work on the preparation of gelatin has been carried out in the laboratories of the glue and gelatin manufacturers and has had as its aim the achievement of maximum yields of soluble protein with minimum degradation of the extracted gelatin. Very little of this work is useful for the elucidation of the molecular basis of the collagen → gelatin transition. The most important of the investigations in this vein have been those of Ames (19-24). In summarizing his results, Ames (22) proposed two models for insoluble collagen that merit serious consideration. In one model, Ames proposed that a collagen fiber be considered as consisting of long single chains and that main-chain or backbone ruptures had to occur before randomized chain fragments (gelatin) could be extracted in soluble form. For the second model, Ames suggested that the collagen fiber be considered as a multichain network in which the collagen molecules are of finite length, but are bonded together by covalent linkages between chains in addition to hydrogen bonds and salt bridges. In this case the conversion of the multichain fiber to gelatin is accomplished by the concurrent rupture of main-chain and interchain covalent cross-linkages. Ames was not able to choose between these alternative models and subsequently (23) added the suggestion that collagen should be considered as an intimate mixture of several closely related proteins of differing solubility though of similar, but not identical, composition and nitrogen content. The one feature common to all of Ames' proposals was that each mature collagen fiber was considered as an infinitely large polymeric structure. These ideas served as the starting point for the investigations of the collagen → gelatin transition carried out by Veis and Cohen and their colleagues (14, 16, 25-32).

A. Solubilization of Intact Corium Collagen

Ames (22, 23) and Loeven (33) had shown that alkali pretreatment or extraction of collagen brought about chemical as well as physical changes in the gelatin, whereas acid or neutral extraction gave rise to gelatins that seemed to resemble native collagen in several respects. Veis and Cohen (26), therefore, began their study of the collagen → gelatin transition by examination of the solubilization of purified native bovine corium collagen (25) in the acid range.

In order to obtain a representative insoluble collagen, bovine corium was chosen since considerable quantities could be prepared from a single hide. A typical purification flow diagram is shown in Fig. III-12. The object of this treatment, in addition to removing the noncollagenous components of the corium, was to remove all of the low temperature soluble collagenous components (tropocollagen, neutral-salt-soluble collagen) that would be converted to gelatin according to the paths already described.

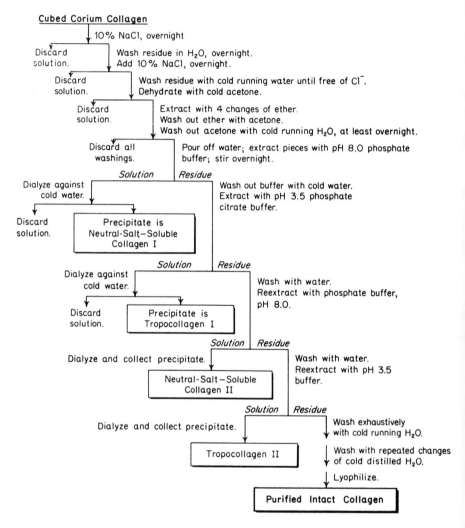

FIG. III-12. Flow diagram for the preparation of purified intact bovine corium collagen [Veis *et al.* (*32*)].

The final residue of the repeated acetate and phosphate extractions has been called "intact collagen." The intact collagen prepared in this fashion was shown to be in the native state (25).

All extractions were performed in essentially the same fashion. Lyophilized intact collagen cubes, about 5 mm on each edge, were thoroughly wetted with the appropriate buffer solution at room temperature. If the extraction pH was to be different from the isoionic pH, hydrochloric acid, in amounts determined from titration data, was added to give the collagen the correct pH. The collagen-buffer slurry, usually 10% collagen by weight, was deaerated and equilibrated overnight at 4°. The slurries were quickly brought to the extraction temperature and extracted for the requisite period of time. At the end of the heating period the slurries were filtered through coarse sintered glass filters. The filtrates were chilled immediately and the insoluble residues were washed on the filter with several portions of distilled water at the extraction temperature. These washings were combined with the filtrates which were dialyzed until salt-free, lyophilized, and weighed. As a check in each instance the insoluble residues were also collected, dialyzed, lyophilized, and weighed. The recoveries were 95–100% of the initial collagen weight. The losses were due to insoluble particles trapped in the filters rather than to dialyzable peptide fragments, except in cases where the most drastic extraction conditions were used.

The most basic observation is shown in Fig. III-13 (26), where the fraction of collagen solubilized, s, is plotted as a function of the duration of extraction, t, at several different pH's. These extractions were all carried

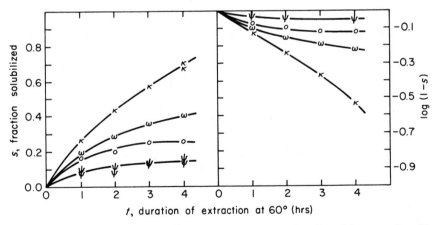

FIG. III-13. Solubilization of bovine corium collagen as a function of the extraction pH and the duration of extraction at 60°: ψ, pH 5.75, 5.0, 4.0; O, pH 3.0; ω, pH 2.5; $\varkappa$, pH 2.0 [Veis and Cohen (26)].

out at 60°, just below the contraction temperature of this corium collagen preparation in neutral aqueous systems. The point of special interest is that at high pH the amount of collagen solubilized did not increase at a constant or accelerating rate. In each case, except at pH ≤ 2.5, s increased rapidly and then leveled off. For example, at pH 4.0, $s = 0.118$ after extraction for 1 hour and increased to only 0.13 after 4 hours. At pH 6.5, $s = 0.07$ after 1 hour and increased to only 0.22 after 16 hours. Titration analyses of both the soluble gelatins and insoluble extraction residues failed to show significant increase (< 1.0 mmole per 100 gm protein) in the number of α-amino groups available as a result of extensive peptide bond hydrolysis. Dye-binding studies also failed to show an increase in the number of free carboxyl groups in any case (25).

These observations led to the hypothesis that solubilization and gelatinization are selective processes if carried out under conditions where peptide bond hydrolysis is minimal. Thus it should be possible to extract discrete units of different molecular character from intact collagen. This hypothesis was tested first (28) by a simple set of extraction experiments. A number of batches of native intact collagen were equilibrated, as outlined above, at various pH values from 6.5 to 2.0, and extracted at 60° or 80°. The ratio of buffer volume to collagen weight was the same in each case. The yield of solubilized collagen was determined.

Another large batch of native collagen was equilibrated at pH 6.5, and extracted for 1 hour. The amount solubilized was determined, and the insoluble residue was dialyzed, lyophilized, and equilibrated with the proper volume of pH 4.0 buffer. The 60°, 1-hour extraction was repeated. The insoluble residue from this step was recovered, equilibrated, and extracted at still lower pH, and so on. The successive extractions were carried out at pH values corresponding to those at which the original single-step extractions were carried out. The amounts of collagen solubilized in the two procedures were compared, as in Table III-6 A. Data from similar successive extractions at 80° are shown in Table III-6 B.

If the solubilization had been a diffusion-controlled extraction of a homogeneous material, then the values of s in columns III and V should have been identical and the s values in column IV should have been larger than these. This behavior was not observed in any case. On the other hand, if hydrolysis of the structure were a random process with the multiple hydrolysis of several bonds being required for solubilization of the chain fragments, then the values of s should have been in the order $s_{IV} > s_{III} > s_V$ for the multiple extractions. The extractions at 80° fit this model rather well. Finally, if the process were selective, and the solubility of various por-

TABLE III-6 [a]

SELECTIVE EXTRACTION OF INTACT BOVINE CORIUM COLLAGEN

Multiple extractions				Single extraction
Extraction pH (I)	Material extracted (II)	s (III) [b]	s_T (IV) [c]	s'_T (V) [d]
(A) Extractions at 60°				
6.5 (1 hr)	Intact native collagen	7.00	7.0	7.0
4.0 (1 hr)	Residue from pH 6.5 extraction	5.17	11.8	11.8
3.0 (1 hr)	Residue from pH 4.0 extraction	9.1	19.9	17.8
2.0 (1 hr)	Residue from pH 3.0 extraction	22.0	37.5	28.8
2.0 (4 hr)	Residue from pH 2.0, 1-hr extraction	80.0	88.0	70.0
(B) Extractions at 80°				
6.5 (1 hr)	Intact native collagen	10.0	10.0	10.0
4.0 (1 hr)	Residue from pH 6.5 extraction	33.3	40.0	22.2
3.0 (1 hr)	Residue from pH 4.0 extraction	87.5	92.5	72.5

[a] Data of Veis and Cohen (28).
[b] Residue dissolved (%).
[c] Original starting weight dissolved (%).
[d] Intact native collagen (%) extracted at this pH in a single step.

tions depended on the extraction pH with more material being soluble at low pH, then s_{III} should have been substantially less than s_{IV} but s_{IV} and s_V should have been equal. This is the behavior seen in the 60° extractions as long as the extraction pH was greater than 2.5. It is important to note the additivity of the successive extractions. Within experimental error, exactly the same amount of intact collagen was solubilized in three 1-hour extractions progressing from pH 6.5 to pH 3.0 as was obtained by a single extraction of intact collagen for 1 hour at pH 3.0.

These extraction data, therefore, supported the hypothesis that within a certain pH and temperature range discrete types of structural elements were being extracted from intact collagen. The solubilized material in each case had all of the usual characteristic of gelatin solutions. The gelatins were soluble in water at 40° and $[\alpha]_D^{40}$ was in the range —110° to —135°. However, under conditions where selectivity was observable, the residue fibers did not irreversibly lose their ordered structure. Residue fibers, teased out from the fiber bundles immediately after extraction, placed on electron microscope grids, and examined, did not appear to have the 700-Å spacing. If, however, the fibers were washed at 40° to remove adhering gelatin, swollen in cold dilute acetic acid, and neutralized in the cold, they had the appearance of native fibers with the 700 Å repeat. The acid swelling and cold neutralization steps thus assisted in returning the slightly disorganized structure to the natural configuration (34). This partial disordering accompanying the extraction of gelatin suggested that the forces involved were of the weak hydrogen bond or van der Waals types and that the different units were not held in place by equivalent numbers of such bonds. The extraction of gelatin from the intact collagen was therefore examined in the presence of collagen denaturants and in relation to the shrinkage temperature of the collagen-solvent system (31).

The direct solubilization-time studies previously discussed indicated that the value of s at 1 hour of extraction was a reasonably good measure of the initial rate of solubilization (26). The parameter $s_{1\,hr}$ was thus equivalent to a rate term and could be related to the activation free energy, $\Delta F^\ddagger$ enthalpy, $\Delta H^\ddagger$, and entropy, $\Delta S^\ddagger$, of the solubilization step. Veis and Cohen (31) determined $s_{1\,hr}$ as a function of extraction temperature, T_e, for intact bovine corium collagen in 2.0 M potassium thiocyanate and in water under isoionic conditions. These measurements were designed to compare the situation in which the intact, organized structure interacted with solvent to yield soluble, solvated, and disorganized fragments (i.e. gelatin), with the situation in which the intact structure was first disorganized and then converted to the soluble, disorganized gelatin form. The terms "organized" and "disorganized" refer to the presence or absence of hydrogen bonds of both inter- and intrachain character. If hydrogen bonds, or van der Waals interactions, were the bonds to be ruptured to bring about solubilization, then extractions carried out below the shrinkage temperature, T_s, in either solvent system should have corresponded to the first case, while extractions carried out above T_s should have corresponded to the second.

The results of the extractions in both solvents (Fig. III-14) did show a parallel behavior with an apparent change in the solubilization reaction occurring at a well-defined temperature. However, these temperatures were significantly above the shrinkage temperature in both solvent systems. Taking s as proportional to the specific rate of solubilization, the transition state theory of reaction rates provides that

$$k's = \frac{kT_e}{h}\, e^{-\frac{\Delta F^{\ddagger}}{RT}} = \frac{kT_e}{h}\, e^{-\frac{\Delta H^{\ddagger}}{RT}}\, e^{+\frac{\Delta S^{\ddagger}}{R}} \tag{1}$$

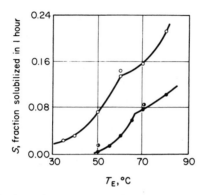

Fɪɢ. III-14. Solubilization of collagen as a function of extraction temperature, T_e, in various solvent systems: ●, H_2O; ○, 2.0 M KCNS; ◑, 2.0 M NaCl [Veis and Cohen (31)].

Accordingly, a plot of $\ln s/T$ vs. $1/T$ should be a straight line whose slope is proportional to $\Delta H^{\ddagger}$. The appropriate plots of these data (Fig. III-15) yielded two straight lines in each case as anticipated for two different types of solubilization reaction. The values obtained for $\Delta H^{\ddagger}$ are given in Table III-7, along with the values of $\Delta F^{\ddagger}$, computed directly from Eq. 1, and $\Delta S^{\ddagger}$, from $\Delta F^{\ddagger} = \Delta H^{\ddagger} - T\Delta S^{\ddagger}$. $\Delta F^{\ddagger}$ and $\Delta S^{\ddagger}$ are shown plotted vs. extraction temperature in Fig. III-16. The shrinkage temperature ranges are also indicated in Fig. III-16.

The two striking features of these results were, first, the negative values found for $\Delta S^{\ddagger}$ and, second, the fact that the temperatures at which the apparent change in reaction type occurred, marked by the discontinuities in the $\Delta S^{\ddagger}$ vs. T_e plots, were substantially different from T_s. Weir and Carter (35) found $\Delta S^{\ddagger}$ to be $+361$ e.u. for the shrinkage of native collagen fibers. It was assumed that the $\Delta S^{\ddagger}$ for the solubilization of the organized structure would have been of this magnitude or greater, and the $\Delta S^{\ddagger}$ for the solubilization of the disorganized structure would have been

TABLE III-7 [a]

THERMODYNAMICS OF THE ACTIVATION STEP IN THE SOLUBILIZATION OF INTACT COLLAGEN

T_e (°C)	Water extraction [b]			2.0 M KCNS extraction [b]		
	$\Delta F_T^{\ddagger}$ (kcal)	$\Delta H^{\ddagger}$ (kcal)	$\Delta S_T^{\ddagger}$ (e.u.)	$\Delta F_T^{\ddagger}$ (kcal)	$\Delta H^{\ddagger}$ (kcal)	$\Delta S_T^{\ddagger}$ (e.u.)
35	—	—	—	25.4	—	—
40	—	—	—	25.6	—	—
50	27.7	42.5	45.6	25.9	13.3	—38.9
55	27.6	42.5	—	— — — — — — — — —
60	27.3	42.5	—	—	—	—
65	— — — — — — — — —	26.3	—	—
70	27.5	5.9	—62.9	27.0	6.7	—59.2
80	28.1	—	—	27.6	—	—

[a] Data of Veis and Cohen (*31*).
[b] Dashed lines indicate a change in the reaction mechanism.

a smaller positive term. The value of only $+45$ e.u. for the $\Delta S^{\ddagger}$ of solubilization of the native, organized collagen was interpreted as indicating that backbone chain hydration, or the accumulation of solvent in the structure, is an essential part of the activation process, outweighing the

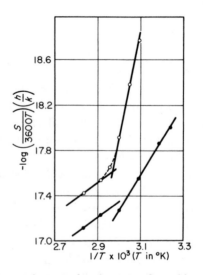

FIG. III-15. Plot of extraction rate data in terms of transition-state-theory parameters for calculation of $\Delta H^{\ddagger}$; ○, H_2O; ●, 2.0 M KCNS [Veis and Cohen (*31*)].

increase in entropy gained on disordering the collagen structure. The solvent ordering must contribute about -300 e.u./mole to the activation step in the solubilization process. On this basis it is not difficult to accept the values of about -60 e.u./mole for $\Delta S^{\ddagger}$ of solubilization of the disordered collagen.

Comparing the values of $\Delta H^{\ddagger}$ in the isoionic and the 2.0 M potassium thiocyanate extractions in the low temperature range, 42 and 13 kcal/mole, respectively, it is obvious that the presence of the thiocyanate ion (or in the equivalent case, urea) made the solubilization easier. The discrepancy between the T_s range and the temperature of the $\Delta S^{\ddagger}$ discontinuity,

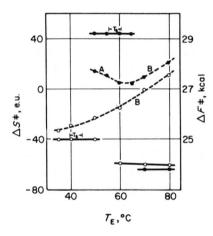

FIG. III-16. Change in free energy and entropy of activation as a function of extraction temperature. Solid lines refer to $\Delta S^{\ddagger}$, dashed lines to $\Delta F^{\ddagger}$; ●, H_2O extraction; ○, 2.0 M KCNS. A and B indicate different reaction mechanisms. [Veis and Cohen (*31*)].

however, indicated that the disruption of the secondary structure of the collagen was not a sufficient condition for solubilization. Veis and Cohen (*31*) therefore proposed that some bonds, stronger than hydrogen bonds and probably covalent in nature, served to interlock the intact collagen structure. Since $\Delta F^{\ddagger}$ in the 2.0 M potassium thiocyanate system increased rather than decreased as more collagen was solubilized, the suggestion was also made that the intact bovine corium collagen was not homogeneous with respect to the distribution of these strong bonds throughout the fibrillar network.

These rate studies thus supported the conclusions of the direct extraction experiments indicating that different structural elements were being selectively extracted. However, the different structural units could not have been the result of differing numbers of hydrogen bonds, but rather must have been the result of varying distributions of strong covalent interchain cross-linkages.

B. Nature of the Gelatins Obtainable from Intact Bovine Corium Collagen

1. Molecular Weight Distributions by Fractionation

The alcohol-coacervation-fractionation methods described in Chapter II were used to characterize the molecular weight distributions of the gelatins extracted from intact bovine corium collagen (28). The two cases of primary interest were the comparisons of the gelatins obtained from the single and multiple extractions at 60° where selectivity was found, and at 80° where progressive degradation was evident. The results of the fractionations are shown in Fig. III-17 and 18. In these figures the weight % of gelatin in each fraction is plotted as a function of the range of alcohol: water ratios between which the fraction was collected. The left-hand set of bar graphs in both figures represents the data on the gelatins obtained by the stepwise extraction of a single portion of intact collagen. The pH of extraction is given at the top of each box. The center set of bar graphs in Fig. III-17 and the right-hand set in Fig. III-18 represent the fraction-ation of the gelatins extracted from fresh portions of intact collagen at the indicated pH. Higher molecular weight material is collected at the lower alcohol:water ratios, so that the molecular weight is decreasing in each graphs as one goes from left to right.

It is evident that the gelatin molecular weight distribution is strongly dependent on the extraction pH, and that different weight distributions were obtained in the successive and single extractions at the same pH. However, as long as the extractions were selective, that is, as long as the sum of the weights obtained in the multiple extractions yielded the same total weight of gelatin as the corresponding single-step extraction, then the molecular weight distributions were also additive. For example, as-suming that the additivity of the weights applied to each fraction and that the single extract obtained at pH 4, 60°, was composed of 59% of the isoionic type gelatin and 41% of the pH 4 multiple extract, then multi-plication and addition of each fraction as indicated in box j, Fig. III-17, should have yielded a net distribution similar to that shown in box c. This additivity was observed. Similarly, the appropriate additions of a, b, and d to yield the distribution noted in k matched the distribution e

of the single extraction at pH 3, 60°. Thus the additivity does apply to the molecular weight distribution as well as to the total gelatin weights, and further strengthens the argument in favor of the selective extraction of specific structural units. When hydrolysis and degradation were proceeding so rapidly that the selectivity was destroyed, as was the case in

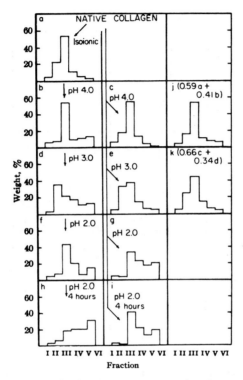

FIG. III-17. Fractionation of 60° isoionic extracts as ethanol coacervates, at 40°, from the following alcohol:water ratios: I, 2:1; II, 2.5:1; III, 3.0:1; IV, 3.5:1; V, 4.0:1; VI, 20:1. The extraction pH is noted in each box. The left-hand column indicates the distribution following successive extractions of the same batch of collagen to the final pH. The data in the center column represents the distributions in each case for extraction of native collagen at the indicated pH. Boxes j and k are the properly weighted sums of $a + b$ and $a + b + d$ distributions, respectively, and are to be compared with c and e [Veis and Cohen (28)].

the 80° extractions, the molecular weight distributions were shifted rapidly to lower average weights and the distributional additivity was lost, as shown in Fig. III-18.

An equally interesting aspect of the fractionation was that, in the selective extraction range, more high molecular weight material was obtained under more drastic (pH 3) extraction conditions than was obtained at higher pH. (Compare *a*, *d*, and *e*, Fig. III-17.) Furthermore, even when the extractions were not highly selective, the serial extractions yielded higher molecular weight gelatins than the single extractions. This can be seen most clearly by comparing the distributions at pH 4 and at pH 3 in Fig. III-18.

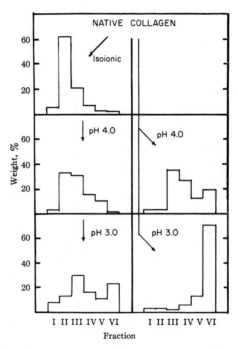

FIG. III-18. Fractionation of 80° extracts as coacervates, at 40°. Alcohol-water ratios as in Fig. III-17. Left-hand column, successive extractions. Right-hand column, single extractions of native collagen [Veis and Cohen (*28*)].

The extractions of intact collagen in 2.0 M potassium thiocyanate were also selective (*31*). Figure III-19 shows a plot of the amounts of gelatin recovered in the two major fractions as a function of the total amount of collagen solubilized. Fractions II and III increased nearly at the same rate until about 15% of the collagen was solubilized. Then the amount of fraction III leveled off while fraction II, the higher molecular weight material, continued to increase. The point where fraction III leveled off in relative amount corresponded to the point of the $\Delta S^{\ddagger}$ discontinuity described above. Hence the apparent change in course of the solubilization reaction may be related to the specific nature of the solubilized units.

2. Molecular Weights and Particle Shape

A number of attempts (26–30) were made to characterize the selectively extracted gelatins, primarily by light scattering and viscosity techniques. These studies suffered from the fact that the distribution of species within each fraction was unknown. Hence, since the light scattering measurements yielded weight-average molecular weights and Z-average radii of gyration, and since the distribution of particle shapes was unknown, these data were subject to considerable potential error in interpretation. In particular, it

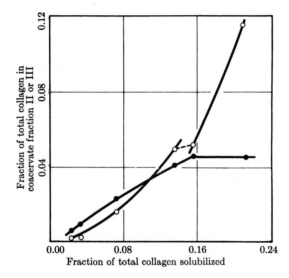

Fig. III-19. Distribution of coacervate fractions as a function of total amount of collagen solubilized in 2.0 M KCNS; ○, fraction II; ●, fraction III [Veis and Cohen (31)].

was observed that each coacervate fraction collected in the same alcohol: water ratio range but from different gelatins had a different molecular weight and intrinsic viscosity.

The ranges of molecular weights and intrinsic viscosities for various coacervate fractions are listed in Table III-8 (28). The gelatins collected in the 2.0–3.0 ethanol:water ratio range comprised the major portion of the extracted gelatin. In this range, depending on the extraction procedure, the molecular weights and intrinsic viscosities did not change regularly but appeared to be of two classes. The gelatins obtained at pH 3.0 or greater had a Staudinger coefficient of about 0.5, whereas the gelatins obtained by extraction at pH 2 had a Staudinger coefficient of about 0.8. Thus the gelatins extracted in the selective range were more compact than

TABLE III-8 [a]

RANGE OF MOLECULAR PARAMETERS FOR VARIOUS ETHANOL-WATER COACERVATE FRACTIONS

Ethanol:water ratio range	M_w range	$[\eta]$ range
2.0–2.5	$\sim 2.0 \times 10^6$	> 1.1
2.5–3.0	2.0×10^6–2.0×10^5	1.1–0.35
3.0–3.5	2.5×10^5–5×10^4	< 0.35
3.5–4.0	$< 5 \times 10^4$	—

[a] Data of Veis and Cohen (28).

would be expected for unperturbed random coils, while the gelatins extracted under more drastic degradative conditions approached the random coil configuration. From these rather tenuous data the suggestion was made that the selectively extracted gelatins could best be represented as multistranded lateral aggregates of peptide chains not in the typical gaussian or random coil configuration (30).

These molecular weight determinations also established that in any given ethanol-water coacervation fractionation the low ethanol:water ratio fractions contained the higher molecular weight gelatins. In turn, this confirmed the earlier conclusion that higher molecular weight gelatins could be extracted later, and under more drastic conditions, than some of the lower molecular weight gelatins.

3. Identification of Specific Molecular Units: Non-Gaussian Particle Weight Distributions

The first clues as to the nature of the molecular weight distributions of the intact collagen structure were obtained by sedimentation velocity studies (14, 32). In the first investigation (32) a relatively large amount of the pH 6.5, 60°, 1-hour extract of intact bovine corium collagen was prepared and fractionated by the ethanol-water coacervation procedure. Seventy-five percent of this gelatin was collected in the two fractions in the ethanol:water ratio range 2.0–3.0. The gelatins were dissolved in 0.1 N potassium chloride at 40° and each fraction examined in the analytical ultracentrifuge at 40°. The first fraction, which represented about 5% of the solubilized collagen, contained some very high molecular weight material and could not be resolubilized. The next two fractions, the major ones, were completely soluble. The sedimentation diagrams of these fractions (Fig. III-20) indicated the presence of several components. The sedimentation coefficient of each component in each fraction was determined at several concentrations and extrapolated to infinite dilution. It was found that the two components of fraction 3 (Fig. III-20 *b*) had the same $s^{\circ}_{40,w}$ values as the slower two components of fraction 2 (Fig. III-20 *a*).

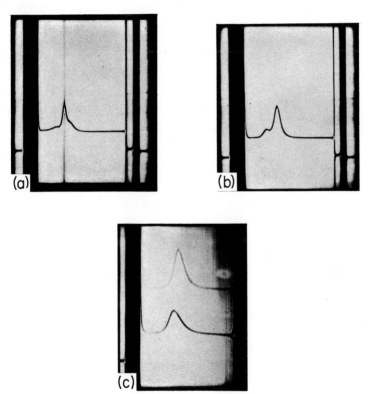

Fig. III-20. Sedimentation patterns for three fractions of corium gelatin obtained by extraction of intact corium collagen at 60° for 1 hour, pH 6.6. (a) Fraction collected between ethanol:water ratio range 2.0–2.5; (b) ratio range 2.5–3.0, (c) ratio range 3.0–3.5; (a) shows α, γ, and δ components from right to left; (b) contains α and γ; (c) illustrates only α, although a very dilute sample was run as well as the standard concentration of (a) and (b). [Veis *et al.* (*14*)].

The next lower fraction, fraction 4, contained only one component, matching the slowest component of the previous two fractions. These three components were therefore considered to be specific molecular entities and designated α, γ, and δ in order of their increasing sedimentation coefficients.

The fractionations did not provide the pure components, but by extrapolations of the sedimentation diagrams to infinite dilution in each case it was possible to determine with reasonable precision the relative composition of each fraction. Light scattering and viscosity data on the component mixtures could then be analyzed as weight-averages derived from the composition analyses, and the component molecular weights and viscosities were deduced. The results of these analyses are shown in Table III-9.

TABLE III-9 [a]

MOLECULAR CHARACTERIZATION OF MAJOR COMPONENTS OF ISOIONIC EXTRACT GELATIN

Fraction	Component	$s_{40,w}^{\circ}$	$M_w \times 10^{-5}$		$[\eta]$ dl/gm		Fractional composition
			Observed	Calculated [b]	Observed	Calculated [b]	
2	—	—	6.6	—	0.76	—	—
	α	4.8	—	1.35	—	0.33	0.18
	γ	7.7	—	4.95	—	0.65	0.47
	δ	9.6	—	13.8	—	1.12	0.35
3	—	—	3.0	—	0.50	—	—
	α	5.0	—	1.35	—	0.33	0.46
	γ	7.0	—	4.95	—	0.65	0.54
4	α	4.9	1.35	—	0.33	—	—

[a] Data of Veis et al. (32).
[b] Weight-average molecular weight.

The relationship between intrinsic viscosity and component molecular weights is shown in Fig. III-21. The linear log-log plot can be represented by

$$[\eta] = 7.04 \times 10^{-4} M_w^{0.52} \qquad (2)$$

These data and calculated values corroborated the previously established high values for the molecular weights of the selectively extracted gelatins. More importantly, the sedimentation experiments gave unequivocal evidence that the gelatins obtained by the partial solubilization of collagen under mild conditions cannot be represented by a gaussian or other single-peaked molecular weight distribution function. The Staudinger viscosity-molecular weight relationship expressed in Eq. 2 indicated that the higher weight components were not single-strand random coils, but were more compact multistranded molecules. Since the procedures by which the high molecular weight gelatins were extracted and fractionated did not seem

likely to have been capable of introducing covalent cross-linkages, Veis
et al. concluded that the specific distributions of the cross-linked gelatins
must have represented the distribution of these polymers in the intact
fiber structure.

Veis and Cohen (*28, 31*) had proposed that the imposition of cross-
linkages in the ordered collagen structure and the maintenance of these
linkages in the extracted gelatins would keep the chains in certain regions
of the cross-linkages in the proper register for renaturation to the native

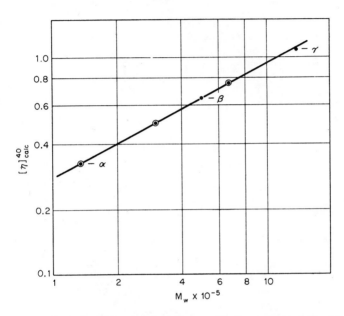

Fig. III-21. Intrinsic viscosity to weight-average molecular weight relationships. Open
circles are the experimental values for fractions 2,3, and 4. Solid points are the calculated
values for components β and γ from Eq. 2; β and γ in this figure represent components
γ and δ respectively as discussed in the text [Veis *et al.* (*32*)].

structure. The renaturation of these gelatins to the collagen structure was
demonstrated (*17*) by the precipitation of native collagen fibers following a
gelation and an annealing procedure. Electron micrographs of the precipitated fibers were typical of native fibers in every respect (Fig. III-22).
The fibers were readily soluble in 6.0 M urea or 2.0 M potassium thiocyanate but could be held indefinitely at 40° in water or dilute salt solutions.
This work was the first demonstration of a completely reversible transformation of gelatin to the collagen structure.

Veis and Cohen (*17*) found that only those gelatins containing the

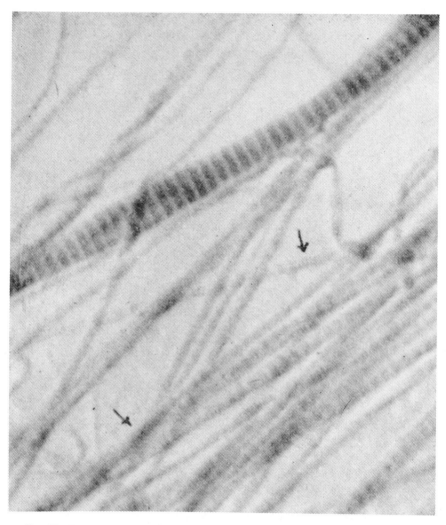

FIG. III-22. Electron micrograph of fibres obtained from fraction III, γ-component-rich gelatin. Chromium shadowed ($\times$ 38,700). The main periodicity is 610 Å, but there is also clearly visible a definite subperiodicity (arrows) of $\sim$ 210 Å in the thinner fibrils [Veis and Cohen (17)].

multichain gelatins could be renatured, and Veis *et al.* (14) showed that only the γ and δ fractions would renature. Fig. III-23 illustrates the sedimentation diagrams of an α, γ mixture before and after renaturation and removal of the collagen fibers. It is quite clear that the γ component was preferentially removed, while the concentration of α was not reduced.

The γ component was identified as an intramolecularly cross-linked tropocollagen molecule because of its molecular weight and behavior after renaturation. The γ and δ components were characterized in a more detailed study of better fractionated preparations (15). These data are

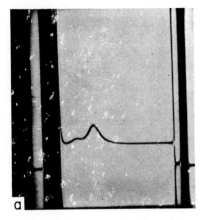 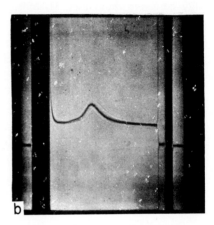

FIG. III-23. Sedimentation patterns of a γ-component-containing gelatin before and after renaturation by the cold nucleation-heat precipitation procedure; (a) a, γ mixture before renaturation; (b) after renaturation, the γ-component content has been preferentially reduced [Veis *et al.* (14)].

summarized in Table III-10 and show that the γ component is indeed equivalent to calf skin tropocollagen in molecular weight, while the δ component appears to be a polymer of four γ units.

One of the more remarkable features of this investigation was that a component comparable to the intermediate β component of tropocollagen

TABLE III-10 [a]

MOLECULAR PARAMETERS [b] OF γ AND δ COMPONENTS OF GELATIN

Component	$M_w \times 10^{-5}$ [b]	$[\eta]$ (dl/gm)	$s^0_{40,w}$ (S)	$(\overline{\varrho_Z^2})^{1/2}$ (Å)
γ	3.5 (ultracentrifuge)	0.50	7.2	360
	3.5 (light scattering)	—	—	—
δ	14.4 (light scattering)	1.12	9.1	360

[a] Data of Veis *et al.* (15).

[b] M_w is weight-average molecular weight; $[\eta]$ is intrinsic viscosity; $s^0_{40,w}$ is sedimentation coefficient; $(\overline{\varrho_Z^2})^{1/2}$ is Z-average radius of gyration.

was never observed in the gelatins extracted from the nature intact bovine corium collagen. This could have been the result of the conversion of any β units that might have been present to α chains because of the prolonged exposure of the extracts to temperatures of 60°. On the other hand, one may consider that since all of the tropocollagen was removed prior to the gelatin extractions, no structural units capable of conversion to an α, β mixture remained in the intact tissue. Equally interesting was the absence of units intermediate in weight between the γ and δ components. That is, there were no dimers or trimers of the γ component even though Drake and Veis (36) could readily produce such dimers and trimers by the cross-linking of tropocollagen preparations prior to denaturation. The absence of both β units and polymers intermediate between the γ and δ components suggests that the gelatin extracts contained molecular units characteristic of the preexisting distribution of cross-linked species in the intact collagen, rather than that such units were all converted to α and γ forms during the extraction.

C. Structure of Intact Collagen

1. Three-Dimensional Network Model

The data reviewed in the two preceding sections enabled Veis and Cohen (29) to choose between the two models proposed by Ames (22) for the structure of mature collagenous tissue. Obviously the existence of the specific polymers of multichain structure lead one qualitatively to prefer the cross-linked model for collagen. The quantitative examination of both of Ames' models, however, gives additional insight into the collagen-gelatin transition. Indeed, in practical terms, both models can be realized by the appropriate pretreatment of the collagen prior to the gelatin extraction.

Consider first the model depicting the collagen fiber as consisting of long single peptide chains and that peptide bonds must be hydrolyzed prior to extraction of the chain fragments. Assume that each peptide chain contains $n + 1$ units connected with n hydrolyzable linkages. It is not necessary that each unit be an amino acid residue; it may also be a larger chain segment between a set of particularly labile bonds. Let

$$s_0 = \text{initial number of insoluble chains}$$
$$s = \text{number of chains intact at time } t$$
$$p_i = \text{number of bonds of type } i \text{ intact at } t$$
$$\chi_i = \text{rate constant for the hydrolysis of } i$$

then if the hydrolysis conditions are such that

$$-\frac{ds}{dt} = \left(\sum_i \chi_i\right) s \tag{3}$$

and

$$-\frac{dp_i}{dt} = \chi_i p_i \tag{4}$$

it can be shown that

$$\frac{dp_i}{ds} = \frac{\chi_i p_i}{\left(\sum_i \chi_i\right) s} \equiv \alpha_i \left(\frac{p_i}{s}\right) \tag{5}$$

and upon integration, that

$$\frac{p_i}{s_0} = \left(\frac{s}{s_0}\right)^{a_i} \equiv R^{a_i} \tag{6}$$

where R is the fraction of chains with no unhydrolyzed bonds. $(1 - R)$ is then the weight fraction of protein solubilized. For the case where all χ_i are equal it can further be demonstrated that the number-average molecular weight of the soluble portion can be given by Eq. (7) and the weight-average molecular weight by Eq. (8)

$$M_n = \frac{n(1 - R) M_0}{(n + 1) - nR^{1/n} - R} \tag{7}$$

$$M_w = \frac{\sum_{i=1}^{n} i^2 R^{(i-1)/n}(1 - R^{1/n}) [2 + (1 - R^{1/n}) (n - i)]}{\sum_{i=1}^{n} i R^{(i-1)/n}(1 - R^{1/n}) [2 + (1 - R^{1/n}) (n - i)]} M_0 \tag{8}$$

In these equations M_0 is the molecular weights of the peptide unit between labile bonds. Equations 7 and 8 are plotted as a function of R in Fig. III-24 for the case of $n = 1000$. In Fig. III-24 it is evident that both the number- and weight-average molecular weights are constantly decreasing functions of $(1 - R)$ and that one could not expect to find increases in the fraction of higher weight materal as $(1 - R)$ increased. The summations inherent in Eq. 8 take into account the situation where there is a distribution in unit weights. If there is such a distribution of weights, then the highest weight species will still have the greatest probability of disappearing in the early stages of the solubilization process. Thus this model clearly cannot account for the observed gelatin molecular weight distributions resulting from the successive neutral and acid extractions in intact bovine corium collagen.

For the quantitative examination of Ames' second model, the multi-chain network, Veis and Cohen (28) proposed a system of parallel rods held together by transverse linkages at random intervals along each chain. It was assumed that there was a distribution of rod lengths such that $M_w/M_n = p > 1$ and that N_i = number of rods which are i-mers, $N = \Sigma_i N_i$ = total number of rods, and α = fraction of monomers which may participate in cross- linkages, the same for each rod or $i\alpha$ cross-linkages per i-mer.

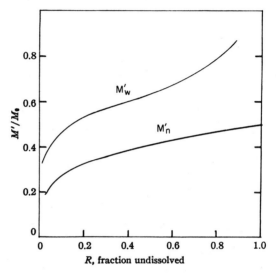

FIG. III-24. Molecular weight distributions of the solubilized fractions, as predicted by Eq. 7 and 8, as a function of the extent of solubilization. M_0 is the assumed particle weight of the original insoluble molecules. R is the fraction of protein still insoluble [Veis and Cohen (28)].

The total number of cross-linkage sites is then $\alpha \Sigma_i i N_i$, and there are one-half this number of cross-linkages possible. Setting p_0 equal to the number of sites bonded in the native protein, and p the number remaining at time t, then there will be $(p_0 - p)$ cross-linkage sites free a t. To solubilize a rod from the macrostructure every cross-link to the structure must be hydrolyzed. Hence, since $(1 - p/p_0)$ will be the probability that a site will be free, the fraction of i-mers solubilized will be

$$\frac{N'_i}{N^o_i} = (1 - p/p_0)^{ai} \tag{9}$$

and the total weight dissolved

$$\sum_i i N_i' M_0 = \sum i N_i^o (1 - p/p_0)^{a_i} M_0 \tag{10}$$

The weight fraction solubilized $(1 - R)$ will then be given by

$$(1 - R) = \frac{M_0}{W} \sum_i i N_i (1 - p/p_0)^{a_i} \tag{11}$$

where W is the initial weight of insoluble protein. To make calculations from Eq. 11 one must know or assume some distribution of the i-mers. However, one can readily see from Eq. 9 that appreciable amounts of the larger i-mers will be solubilized only as the probability of cross-linkage hydrolysis approaches unity. This is illustrated in Fig. III-25 where the ratio $N_{i, \text{soluble}}/N_{i, \text{original}}$ is plotted vs. $(1 - p/p_0)$.

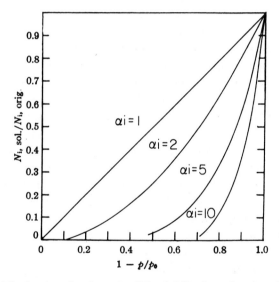

FIG. III-25. The fraction of each species (N_i) solubilized as a function of the fraction of transverse bonds broken, according to Eq. 9 [Veis and Cohen (28)].

It is evident that this cross-linked model may be used to explain the extraction data. That is, in a cross-linked network of filaments of varying length but similar chemical properties, the larger molecules would appear in solution following the more drastic solubilization procedures, provided that the transverse linkages were more labile than the longitudinal bonds. If the transverse and longitudinal bonds were equally labile with regard to hydrolysis, the model would degenerate and become equivalent to the single-strand model, whence constantly decreasing molecular weights would result from the more drastic treatments.

This analysis of the cross-linked model tells one nothing about the nature of the initial structure units except that they are of varying molecular weights. Knowing, however, that the extracted gelatins are themselves lateral aggregates of chains and that the bonds holding the chains together are quite stable under the milder extraction conditions, it would appear that the *inter*unit bonds are different in character from the *intra*unit bonds. Both types of bond are covalent but the interunit bonds must be more susceptible to hydrolysis, either because of intrinsic differences or as a result of more ready availability to the hydrolytic reagents. It is also pos-sible that there are fewer *inter*unit bonds, but in this case the number of interunit bonds must still be proportional to the weight of the unit.

Having come to regard the intact native collagen structure as a cross-linked network of subunits of varying degrees of polymerization, we are in a position to incorporate the concept of the tropocollagen molecule as the basic structural unit. The native collagen fiber is an ordered array of par-allel tropocollagen rods, staggered by approximately one-quarter of their length. As discussed earlier, each tropocollagen rod is composed of three chains of α character but probably of different chemical composition, and may contain intra-tropocollagen cross-linkages to produce the β subunit of two chains or the γ units with bonds joining each of the three chains. All γ units may not be of the same degree of intramolecular polymerization. The γ unit tropocollagens may, in addition, be bonded together with inter-unit cross-linkages to form γ-polymers. This is the situation in the collagen defined as "intact" collagen. The first stable γ-polymer appears to be a γ-tetramer, δ, with a content of twelve α chains. The bonds between the γ units forming the γ-polymers may be of the same nature as the intra-γ cross-linkages. However, as postulated above, there are also cross-linkages of different chemical character superimposed on the system of γ-polymers and distributed randomly throughout the intact collagen, linking these units together to create a three-dimensional infinite network in each fiber. From this point of view the neutral-salt-soluble collagen and low tempera-ture acid-extractable tropocollagen represent monomer units that have not been incorporated into the intact structure by cross-linkages of the sec-ond type. To simplify the discussion we shall introduce here the notation of I-bond for the intra-γ bonds and N-bond for the weaker inter-γ-polymer bonds. The two types of bond should confer different properties on the col-lagen fibers. The imposition of the intramolecular I-bonds on the structure would not alter the solubility of the fiber in cold dilute acid, for example, but would probably raise the fiber melting temperature. The denaturation of tropocollagen molecules containing enhanced I-bonding would lead to the appearance of larger proportions of the β and γ units in the resulting gelatin. Thus, the difference between calf skin and ichthyocol tropocollagen preparations should be discussed in terms of I-bonding as well as intrinsic chemical composition. The imposition of N-bonds, network-forming bonds, on a tropocollagen aggregate would also lead to an increased melting temperature, but would decrease the aggregate fiber solubility and increase its tensile strength.

One can readily see from this model of the mature mammalian collagen fiber why such a great variety of gelatins has been obtained by various workers, and something of the nature of the heterogeneity of every gelatin preparation. At the conclusion of Chapter I, gelatin was defined as the water-soluble product of the dissolution, disorganization, or degradation of water-insoluble collagen fibers. We can now further consider more specifically the collagen $\rightarrow$ gelatin transition as a process involving the following steps:

1. A first order phase transition, the melting of the trihelical structure to the amorphous form.

2. The hydrolysis of N-bonds.

3. The hydrolysis of I-bonds.

4. The hydrolysis of main-chain peptide bonds.

The nature of the gelatin produced from any particular tissue thus depends on the amino acid composition which determines the thermodynamic parameters of the phase transition, on the number and distribution of N-bonds and I-bonds which set the initial degree of polymerization of the fiber network, and on the order in which steps 2, 3, and 4 are accomplished. All four steps are not required to produce a gelatin, nor does it appear necessary that each step be carried to completion.

2. *Nature of the Covalent Cross-Linkages*

In his review of the internal linking of the collagen molecule, Gustavson (37) suggested that an exceedingly strong interchain bond was likely and that it was most probably of esterlike character. Grassman, Endres and Steber (38) claimed that ester linkages were indeed present, on the basis of the reduction of collagen with lithium borohydride. Konno and

Altman (*39*) repeated the work of Grassman *et al.* with similar results. The number of esterlike bonds was rather small, however, and could readily be accounted for on the basis of carbohydrate impurities in the collagen preparations.

In a similar vein Steigmann (*40*), Pouradier and Venet (*7, 41*), Landucci (*42, 43*), and Landucci, Pouradier and Durante (*44*) demonstrated the presence in all gelatins examined of substantial amounts of material which would react with 2-thiobarbituric acid to give a complex with strong absorption at 450 and 530 mμ. These materials were carbonyl compounds identified as dihydroxyacetone, methyl glyoxal, and pyruvic acid. A portion of these compounds was readily available for reaction and was considered to be free, as an impurity, or bound to the N-terminal amino acid residues. The remaining portion, about 1 equivalent of aldehyde per 2×10^6 gm gelatin, was thought to be firmly bound in the chain at a position other than on the terminal amino acid residue. These internally bound residues appeared to be next to a proline or hydroxyproline residue and the bond involved was quite labile, the activation energy for hydrolysis being 11 kcal/mole as compared with the average 24 kcal/mole activation energy for peptide bond hydrolysis. The aldehyde-protein bonds were also more labile in alkali than were the peptide bonds, but some bound aldehydes were still present even after the collagen stock had been subjected to prolonged exposure to alkali in the conventional liming process. Landucci *et al.* (*44*) proposed that these bound aldehydes served as cross-linking reagents that were particularly sensitive to rupture in basic media. Until recently (*36, 45*), very little attention has been given to these interesting results and hypotheses. The ubiquitous presence of reactive aldehydic metabolic intermediates in almost all tissues (*45*) supports the role which Landucci *et al.* (*44*) have suggested for these compounds. More work is required, however, to discover whether or not aldehyde-mediated cross-linkages do, in fact, play a role in the progressive insolubilization of intact collagen *in vivo*. If aldehyde-mediated cross-linkages do occur, they most probably involve the bonding of an ε-amino group of lysine with either the amide group of an asparagine residue or the guanidino group of arginine (*36*).

A major advance in the elucidation of the nature of the cross-linkages was made by Gallop, Seifter and Meilman (*46*). These workers utilized the fact that hydroxylamine reacts much more rapidly to hydrolyze esters than it does to hydrolyze primary and secondary amide linkages in simple compounds. Gelatins were reacted with 1.0 M hydroxylamine at pH 10 in 6.0 M urea at room temperature or without urea at 40°. After a specified interval the reaction was stopped by adjusting the reaction mixture to pH 4.

After removal of excess hydroxylamine by dialysis the protein-bound hydroxamic acid content was determined. Two reactions to form bound hydroxamic acid were indicated, one of which apparently proceeded rapidly to completion within 4 hours in the systems containing urea. The second slower reaction involved the simultaneous removal of amide groups and cleavage of peptide bonds. The fast reaction produced no detectable free amino groups or amino-terminal proline, but the molecular weight of the gelatin decreased rapidly to a value estimated to be about 20,000. When an ichthyocol gelatin was examined, ultracentrifugal analysis showed the disappearance of both the α and β components and the appearance of a diffuse peak with a sedimentation coefficient of about 1.9 S (Fig. III-26). Acid-precursor gelatin and denatured ichthyocol or calf skin tropocollagen contained about 1 equivalent of bound hydroxamic acid per unit of 20,000 molecular weight (~ 6 equivalents hydroxamic acid per 10^5 gm protein) at the conclusion of the fast reaction. Alkali-precursor gelatins were found to contain only half this amount of bound hydroxamic acid, a not unexpected result since the alkali precursor gelatins usually have a lower amide content, and since esterlike bonds could have been hydrolyzed during the alkaline pretreatment. In spite of the lower content of bound hdyroxamic acid groups, the hydroxylamine-treated alkali-precursor gelatin apparently had the same average molecular weight as the hydroxylamine-treated acid-precursor gelatin. These results led Gallop et al. (46) to conclude that esterlike bonds did exist in collagen. However, they proposed that these esterlike bonds were not to be considered as interchain cross-linking bonds, but rather as being incorporated into the backbone peptide chains joining fundamental peptide subunits of about 20,000 molecular weight. Possible hydroxylamine-sensitive bonds are shown in Table III-11. According to the rate arguments presented above, reactive groupings 1–5, in the table, are unlikely candidates for participation in the fast hydroxamic acid formation reaction. On the basis that the number of hydroxylysine residues in collagen (~ 8 equivalents per 10^5 gm) closely approximated the number of equivalents of bound hydroxamic acid, it was suggested that the hydroxylysine might be serving the unique function of joining the basic subunits along the backbone into single strands. Gallop et al. (46) reported that hydrazine behaved it the same manner as hydroxylamine, forming protein-bound hydrazide groups.

Bello (47) similarly examined the reaction of an acid-precursor gelatin and a bovine corium collagen with hydroxylamine. The gelatin was treated with 1.5 M hydroxylamine at pH 8.6 in water, 5 M or 8 M urea, or 5 M lithium bromide. The reaction was carried out for 4 hours at room temperature or for 1–5 days at 4°. The fibrous corium collagen was treated more drastically. The corium collagen was first denatured by soaking in 4 M sodium perchlorate for 24 hours. The residue fibers were separated from the supernatant and treated at pH 8.65 with 3 M hydroxylamine for 16 hours. Most of the collagen was solubilized by this treatment.

Bello (47) found the hydroxamic acid content of the treated gelatins to be 0.5–1.5 equivalents per 10^5 gm, whereas the solubilized collagen

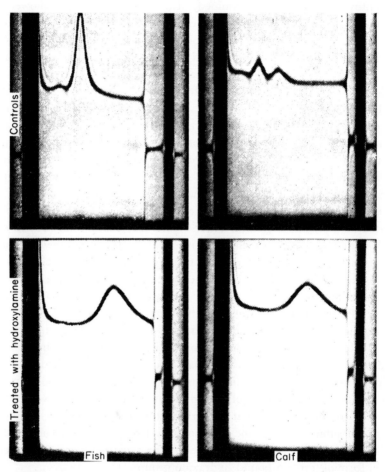

FIG. III-26. Sedimentation patterns of parent gelatins obtained from calf and fish acid-soluble collagens as influenced by treatment with hydroxylamine. The photographs were taken 100 minutes after full rotor speed of 59,780 rpm was attained. The two peaks in each of the upper diagrams represent the α- and β-components. The broad peak in each of the lower diagrams is more slowly sedimenting than α [Gallop et al. (46)].

TABLE III-11[a]

POTENTIAL HYDROXYLAMINE AND HYDRAZINE SENSITIVE BONDS
IN COLLAGEN AND GELATIN

Reactive group	Type linkage	Residues involved
(1) $R-\overset{\overset{O}{\|}}{C}-NH_2$	Side-chain amide	Asp.NH$_2$ or Glu.NH$_2$
(2) $R-\overset{\overset{O}{\|}}{C}-NH-\overset{\overset{O}{\|}}{C}-R'$	Interchain amide	Glu.NH$_2$ or Asp.NH$_2$ with Asp or Glu
(3) $R-NH-\overset{\overset{NH}{\|}}{C}-NH_2$	Side-chain guanidyl	Arg
(4) $R-NH-\overset{\overset{NH}{\|}}{C}-NH-\overset{\overset{O}{\|}}{C}-R'$	Interchain acyl guanidine group	Arg with Asp or Glu
(5) $R-\overset{\overset{O}{\|}}{C}-NH-CH_2R'$	Interchain ε-lysyl amide	Lys with Asp or Glu
(6) $R-\overset{\overset{O}{\|}}{C}-OCH_2R'$	Interchain ester	Ser, Thr, or HO-Lys with Asp or Glu
(6a) $R-\overset{\overset{O}{\|}}{C}-O-CH----CH_2$ with CH_2 and $C-$ joined to N	Interchain ester	HO-Pro with Asp or Glu
(7) $R-C$ with $O-CH-CH_2----$ and $N-CH_2$	Interchain ester with HO-Lys (oxazoline form)	HO-Lys with Asp or Glu
(8) $R-\overset{\overset{O}{\|}}{C}-O-\overset{\overset{C}{\|}}{C}$ with $\overset{\overset{C}{\|}}{C}-O-\overset{\overset{O}{\|}}{C}-R'$ and C	Interchain diester	Carbohydrate with Asp or Glu or both

[a] Data from Gallop *et al.* (*46*).

contained 2 equivalents per 10^5 gm. The hydroxylamine-treated proteins were not reduced to 20,000 molecular weight subunits in Bello's experiments. The gelatin, which originally had a molecular weight of $\sim$ 100,000, was reduced to a heterogeneous mixture with particle weights of 25,000–70,000. Bello (47) was unable to reconcile his lower values for bound hydroxamic acid and higher average molecular weights with the values reported by Gallop et al. (46).

Hörmann (48, 49) and Hörmann et al. (50) also examined the action of hydroxylamine on acid-soluble tropocollagen and ox skin collagen. Bello's (47) results were confirmed in that Hörmann et al. found it necessary to denature the fibrous collagen in order to obtain a significant degree of reaction of the fibers with hydroxylamine, and in that the combined hydroxylamine + denaturant reagent mixture led to the complete solubilization of the insoluble skin collagen. The results of Gallop et al. (46) were also confirmed by the observation that denatured tropocollagen contained intramolecular bonds sensitive to hydroxylamine. The reaction conditions favored by Hörmann et al. (50) were treatment of the collagen at 37° and pH 9.55 with 0.75 M hydroxylamine and 4 M lithium chloride.

Under these conditions it was found (48, 50) that a large number of hydroxamic acids were formed but that a relatively large proportion of these were in dialyzable form. After 12 hours, under the conditions stated above, the hydroxamic acid content of the nondialyzable fraction became constant, and this plateau value was taken as representing the ester-group content of the collagen. These data are illustrated in Fig. III-27 and summarized in Table III-12. Hörmann et al. (50) pointed out that the excess of four bound hydroxamic acids in the intact collagen as compared with the tropocollagen agreed more or less with the hexose content of the col-

TABLE III-12 [a]

HYDROXAMIC ACID CONTENT AND HEXOSE CONTENT OF
NONDYALIZABLE FRACTION OF HYDROXYLAMINE-TREATED COLLAGENS

Sample	Hydroxamic acids (moles/1000 amino acid residues)	Hexoses	
		(moles/1000 amino acid residues)	Type
Tropocollagen	6.4	3.8	glucose
Intact corium collagen	10.4	3.5	glucose + galactose

[a] Data of Hörmann et al. (50).

lagen. They therefore suggested that the intermolecular cross-linkages in collagen were formed from ester linkages between carboxyl groups on the collagen and hydroxyl groups on the hexoses. Since tropocollagen has twice as many hydroxylamine-sensitive linkages as hexose units, Hör-

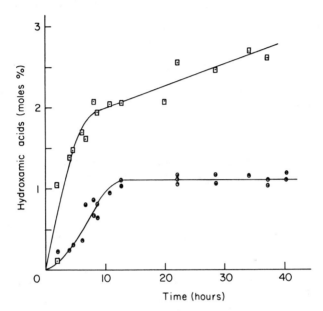

Fɪɢ. III-27. Formation of bound hydroxamic acids upon treatment of corium collagen with 0.75 M hydroxylamine in 4 M lithium chloride at 37° and pH 9.55. Upper curve, total hydroxamate formation. Lower curve, bound hydroxamates which are nondialyzable [Hörmann et al. (50)].

mann (49) pictures the situation as shown in Fig. III-28. In this model, one tropocollagen-hexose bond is on O-glycoside-like linkage and one is an ester. An adjacent tropocollagen unit forms a second ester linkage with another of the hexose hydroxyl groups.

The hydroxylamine-sensitive linkages are also sensitive to liming. Figure III-29 shows the total hydroxamic acid content and the hydroxamic acid content of the nondialyzable fraction of corium collagen at various stages during liming for two corium sections of different thickness. Along with the decrease in hydroxylamine-sensitive linkages, the nondialyzable fraction was reduced in amide nitrogen (Fig. III-30) and increased in number of amino-terminal groups, as indicated by direct reaction with fluorodinitrobenzene (FDNB). The high content of dialyzable hydroxamic acids was attributed (50) to the presence of low molecular weight com-

pounds, such as lipids, that should have been separated before the hydroxylamine reaction was carried out. It is not clear that this explanation is
adequate. Veis and Weiss (51) repeated this analysis, using a purified
ichthyocol tropocollagen preparation, with no evidence of noncollagenous
impurities. Treatment of this collagen with 1.5 M hydrazine at pH 9.0

(a) Tropocollagen intramolecular
carbohydrate bridge

(b) Collagen intra- and intermolecular carbohydrate bridges

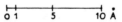

FIG. III-28. Carbohydrate-mediated cross-linkages in collagen: (a) tropocollagen intramolecular carbohydrate bridge; (b) collagen intra- and intermolecular carbohydrate
bridges; as suggested by Hörmann (48).

and 40° for 90 minutes resulted in the formation of approximately 120
moles of bound hydrazide per 10^5 gm collagen, almost equivalent to the
total hydroxamic acid content indicated in Fig. III-29. Subsequent dialysis resulted in a nondialyzable fraction containing approximately 6 moles
of bound hydrazide per 10^5 gm collagen. It would appear, therefore,
that it is possible that small peptides may be broken out from the collagen

during its conversion to the 20,000 molecular weight units, and that these may subsequently be completely hydrazinolyzed to the amino acid hydrazide form. Thus some main peptide chain rupture may be possible during hydroxylamine or hydrazine treatment of collagen. Hörmann *et al.* (*50*)

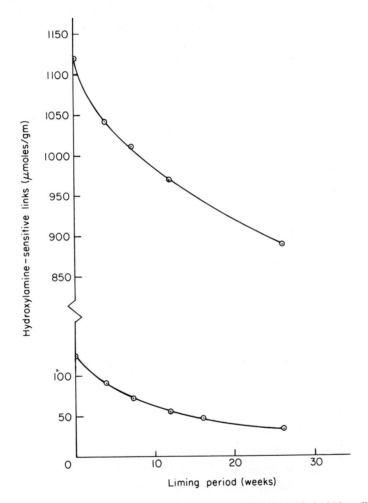

FIG. III-29. Effect of liming on the formation of hydroxamic acids in hide collagen. The upper curve and ordinate refer to the total hydroxamate formation. The lower curve represents the hydroxamate content of the nondialyzable collagen [Hörmann *et al.* (*50*)].

did not believe that the decrease in amide group content was related to the interchain cross-linking of the collagen. Hörmann (*48*) supported his contention that the hexoses were principally involved in interchain cross-

linkages because periodate oxidation in the presence of 8 M urea and 10%
acetic acid markedly enhanced the solubilization of collagen fibers. This
subject is treated more fully in Chapter IV.

De la Burde, Peckham and Veis (*52*) studied the reaction of aqueous
hydrazine with purified native bovine corium collagen at room temperature over a wide range of hydrazine concentrations (1.5–19 M) in the
absence of collagen denaturants. The hydrazine-treated insoluble collagen
was found to contain bound hydrazides and two reactions were proposed

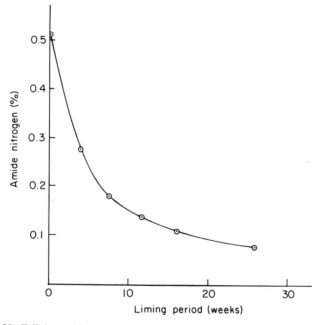

FIG. III-30. Fall in amide nitrogen content of collagen during liming [Hörmann *et
al.* (*50*)].

to account for their formation: deamidation and peptide bond hydrazinolysis. The data are shown in Fig. III-31. The bound hydrazide content
of the collagen gradually increased up to initial hydrazine concentration
> 40% (> 12 M hydrazine), at which point a large increase was noted.
At the same time it was found that the amide group content of the collagen was decreasing throughout this range (Fig. III-32) and, as indicated in
Fig. III-31, the amide group loss was equivalent to the bound hydrazide
content. The sharp rise in bound hydrazide at concentrations > 40%
hydrazine was attributed to peptide bond hydrazinolysis, since FDNB
treatment showed the appearance of new amino-terminal groups at this

point. The collagen did not begin to dissolve until hydrazine concentrations in excess of 50% were utilized (open circles in Fig. III-31), and the solubilization did not correlate with either amide loss or peptide bond hydrolysis. At these concentrations it was found that arginine was deguani-

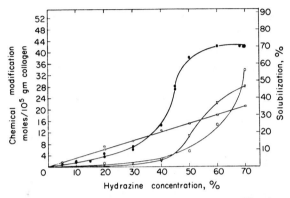

FIG. III-31. Effect of hydrazine on purified corium collagen. All points except the *open circles* refer to the *left-hand ordinate*; ●, moles of bound hydrazide; □, moles of amide removed; ▽, moles of arginine destroyed; ○, dissolution of the collagen [de la Burde *et al.* (*52*)].

dinated and converted to ornithine. This reaction takes place without the incorporation of bound hydrazides into the protein.

A similar examination of limed collagen (*52*) (Fig. III-33) indicated an exact one-to-one equivalence of hydrazide formation and amide group

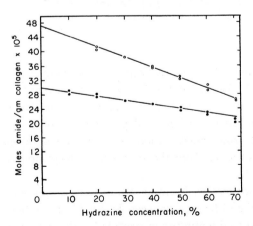

FIG. III-32. Amide group content of hydrazine-treated collagen as a function of hydrazine concentration: ○, native purified collagen; ●, limed collagen [de la Burde *et al.* (*52*)].

removal although, as shown in the lower curve of Fig. III-32, the limed collagen contained less amide initially. The liming process evidently accomplished the hydrolysis of the peptide bonds initially susceptible to hydrazinolysis in the 40–50% hydrazine concentration range. The peptides or amino acids released in this range may correspond to the dialyzable hydroxamic acid-containing species obtained by Hörmann *et al.* (*50*). The reaction conditions utilized by Gallop *et al.* (*46*), Bello (*47*), and Hörmann *et al.* (*50*) were all much more drastic than the conditions under which the hydrazinolysis was carried out by de la Burde *et al.* (*52*).

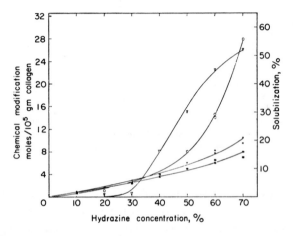

FIG. III-33. A summary of the modification of limed collagen by hydrazine. All points except *open circles* refer to *left-hand ordinate*; ●, moles of bound hydrazide; ■, moles of amide removed; ▽, moles of arginine destroyed; ○, dissolution of the collagen [de la Burde *et al.* (*52*)].

From these data de la Burde *et al.* (*52*) concluded that the possibility of peptide bond cleavage and amide group replacement could not be disregarded in interpreting the hydroxylamine reactivity data. The 2–3 equivalents of amide lost per 10^5 gm collagen, even without denaturation in the 1.5–3.0 M hydrazine concentration range, should be taken as a minimum value to be subtracted from the supposed ester-group content of the collagens.

If one assumes that each amide group lost is replaced by a bound hydrazide, then the difference between hydrazide formation and amide loss should be equal to the number of peptide bonds or ester bonds susceptible to hydrazinolysis at room temperature. A plot of such data is shown in Fig. III-34. These data indicate that 18–19 equivalents of peptide or ester bonds are cleaved per 10^5 gm collagen at hydrazine concentrations of 45–55%. These bonds are also susceptible to alkali in the normal liming process, showing that a particularly alkali-labile set of bonds exists in the native collagen. The native collagen and limed collagens were still insoluble after cleavage of these susceptible bonds, even though osmotic swelling was evident in the 40–60% hydrazine concentration range. On the other hand, the deguanidination reaction was directly paralleled by an increase in solubility of both native and limed collagens without a concomitant increase in hydrazide content.

Bensusan (53) demonstrated the importance of the guanidino group in the ordering of tropocollagen into the native quarter-staggered collagen

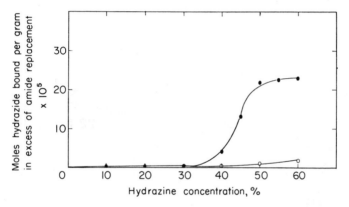

FIG. III-34. Number of peptide bonds cleaved in the residue fibers of hydrazine-treated collagen: ●, native collagen; ○, limed collagen [de la Burde et al. (52)].

structure. Rich and Crick (54) also indicated the structure-stabilizing role of hydrogen bonds involving arginine side chains and neighboring peptide chain backbones. Similarly, Grabar and Morel (55) and Janus (56) have shown that arginine is involved in interchain interactions affecting the setting rate and gelation of gelatin. With this background, de la Burde et al. (52) postulated from the relationship between deguanidination and solubility that the arginine side chains might very well be involved in the cross-linking that stabilizes the mature collagen fibril.

The above argument is not intended to imply that there are no hexose-collagen ester linkages. Blumenfeld and Gallop (57) reacted lithium borohydride with ichthyocol and isolated homoserine and β-aminobutyrolactone from the reaction mixture. Approximately 0.68 residue of homoserine and 0.80 residue of β-aminobutyrolactone per 1000 total amino acid residues were recovered. These two compounds could have resulted only from the reduction of ester groups in which α- and β-aspartyl residues contributed the acyl functions of the hydrazine-sensitive bonds in the ichthyocol. These products could not have arisen from amide groups but only from ester or imide linkages. In the same study kinetic data were reported for the reaction of 1 M hydrazine with ichthyocol at 40°. As indicated in Fig. III-35, the bound hydrazide content leveled off at about 6 residues per 10^5 gm collagen. In the same time period 2–3 residues of new amino-terminal groups per 10^5 gm were created. Combined with the probable amide

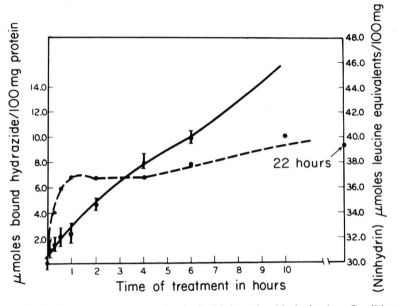

FIG. III-35. Reaction of denatured soluble ichthyocol with hydrazine. Conditions: 1% ichthyocol, 1 M hydrazine, 40°. Dashed line, formation of nondialyzable bound hydrazide. Solid line, increase in free amino groups as reflected by ninhydrin color [Blumenfeld and Gallop (57)].

loss of ~ 2 residues per 10^5 gm, the lithium borohydride reduction data provide a reasonably good estimate of the ester-group content of the ichthyocol. Blumenfeld and Gallop (57) interpret their data differently, however, suggesting instead that the recovery of reduced compounds is low, that the creation of the new amino-terminal groups does not contribute to the hydrazide binding, and that, therefore, the bound hydrazide data provide the correct value for ester-group content, that is, ~ 6 residues per 10^5 gm collagen.

Mechanic and Levy (58) described a quite different type of potential cross-linking bond. They prepared partial acid hydrolyzates of steer corium collagen and isolated and identified the resulting low molecular weight peptides. One of these was a tripeptide with an unusual structure, N^ε-(glycyl-α-glutamyl)lysine. This structure was proved by direct synthesis of the tripeptide. Mechanic and Levy proposed that, since the hydrolysis conditions were unlikely to have led to the appearance of this ε-amino-linked peptide as an artifact, the ε-linked amino acids were part of the original structure and served as branch points between chains. Levy, Cabrera and Fishman (59) further found that although the total yield of this tripeptide following acid hydrolysis of collagen was low, about 30% of the lysine in collagen was resistant to deamination with nitrosyl chloride. Free ε-amino groups should have been deaminated. Thus, these workers (59) suggested that a substantial and significant number of the ε-amino groups of lysine might be involved in this type of interchain linkage. This result is supported by the fact that only one-third to one-half of the ε-amino groups of native fibrous collagen are free to react with fluorodinitrobenzene (60, 61).

It is evident that covalent cross-linkages do stabilize the collagen structure. As we have just seen, there are several classes of linkages that may be implicated: ester bonds involving carbohydrate, covalent bonds involving the participation of aldehydes, and α-glutamyl-ε-aminolysyl interchain amides. Only in the final case has a direct analysis provided a chain fragment containing the cross-linking grouping. The carbohydrate ester linkage receives its strongest support from the work of Hörmann et al. (50) and Blumenfeld and Gallop (57), but the nature of the bond is based on the equivalence of hexose content and hydroxylamine sensitivity. The results of de la Burde et al. (52) dispute the direct relationship of these quantities. Under the conditions in which the hydroxamic acid formation is carried out, ammonia is split out in an amount equivalent to the amount of hydroxamic acid formed. The arginine side chain is implicated because of the close relationship between solubilization and deguanidination of fibrous collagen. If the arginine residues are involved in cross-link formation, it is probable that they are linked via aldehyde-mediated methylene bridges to the ε-amino group of lysine. This conclusion is also inferential, however, since other as yet uncatalogued reactions may also have been involved. Though it is an obviously unwelcome and complicating feature of collagen chemistry, one can only conclude at this point that each of the cross-linking reactions may in fact occur and exist simultaneously in mature collagen. This conclusion is in agreement with the conclusions reached from analysis of the degradation of the three-dimensional network structure. That analysis required the existence of at least two types of intra- and intermolecular cross-linkages. Much more work will be required before any more concrete conclusions can be drawn.

IV. GENERAL PRINCIPLES OF COMMERCIAL MANUFACTURE OF GELATIN

The object of gelatin and glue manufacture is to convert collagen-containing stock of various types into maximum yields of soluble, relatively pure gelatins with a predictable range of commercially desirable properties such as gel strength, viscosity, adhesiveness, tack, color, and clarity. Fundamentally the processing procedure consists of three steps, removal of noncollagenous components from the stock material, conversion of the purified collagen to gelatin, and recovery of the gelatin in dried form. The principal physical properties listed above are related to the intrinsic chemical composition, molecular weight, and molecular configuration of the gelatins. As indicated in the preceding discussions, the resultant molecular properties of the gelatins depend on the number and type of bonds present in the intact collagenous tissue and the relative proportion of each type of bond left unhydrolyzed in the derived product. The collagen converter must arrange his process so as to avoid hydrolysis and solubilization (loss of yield) during the purification and pretreatment stages, to selectively hydrolyze the appropriate structure-stabilizing bonds during extraction, and to minimize random hydrolsyis of the extracted gelatin during the concentration and drying procedures. Unfortunately, the converter does not usually have an entirely free hand. The processing is dictated by the nature and condition of the collagen stock, and this may vary from season to season or even from day to day. There are three processing schemes in general use. These produce gelatins of different chemical character and physical properties.

A. Acid-Precursor Gelatins

1. *General Operating Procedures*

Acid processing is usually applied to pig skins, rabbit skins, and ossein although it is possible to prepare gelatins from any collagenous stock by this means. The most important commercial acid process practiced in the United States is the preparation of edible gelatin from frozen pig skins.

The skins are thawed, washed in cold water, and soaked in fairly concentrated solutions of inorganic acids (up to about 5%) which swell the skin without causing appreciable solubilization. Hydrochloric acid, sulfurous acid, phosphoric acid, and sulfuric acid are most frequently used. The acid soak requires 10–30 hours. The acid supernatant is discharged and cold water is used to wash out the excess acid and raise the pH of the skin pieces to about pH 4. Most of the noncollagenous proteins of the skin have isoelectric points in the range pH 4–5 and are thus least soluble and most readily coagulated during the extraction. The wash water is removed, and the desired amount of water added. This is generally a rather small amount since the collagen pieces contain large amounts of entrapped as well as bound water. At pH 4 native collagen is swollen to about one-half its maximum swelling capacity.

The acid-conditioned skins are subjected to a series of extractions or "cooks." The two variables are time and temperature. The initial extraction is carried out for the longest time at the lowest temperature, usually about 60°. The temperature is raised about 5–10° in each successive extraction. Eight to ten extractions may be made. The gelatin liquors from each cook are processed as rapidly as possible through the drying stages to prevent degradation and bacterial contamination. Each batch of dried gelatin is graded and stored separately. Gel strength and viscosity are the criteria for grading, and these properties usually vary in consistent fashion from one cook to another with a given temperature-time operating cycle and type of raw stock.

2. The Chemistry of the Acid Conversion Process

The acid pretreatment and acid extraction of collagen yield a gelatin which is characterized by an isoelectric point in the alkaline region. This was first noted by Briefer and Cohen (62) and confirmed by Sheppard and Houck (63). These early workers considered gelatins with an isoelectric point in the alkaline range to be anomalous, since most commercial gelatins of that period had isoelectric points in the range pH 5–6. Ames examined this subject in detail (19-24, 64, 65) by preparing gelatins from several typical collagens following various pretreatments. Regardless of the origin of the stock (pig skin, bovine tendon, ossein, rabbit skin), acid pretreatment always yielded a gelatin with an isoelectric point of about pH 8.9 (19). The nitrogen content of gelatin prepared in this way was 18.0–18.6%, very close to that of the collagen stock (19, 22). Loeven (33) obtained similar nitrogen content data in a comparison of pig skin collagen and gelatin.

In addition Loeven compared the titration curve of acid-precursor pig skin gelatin with the titration data obtained by Bowes and Kenten (66) on native ox hide collagen, using their criteria for the titration ranges of the various ionizable groups. The comparative results are shown in Table III-13, along with data computed in the same manner reported later by

TABLE III-13

COMPARISON OF THE TITRATABLE GROUPS OF NATIVE COLLAGEN
AND ACID-PRECURSOR GELATINS

Titratable groups	Titration range or method of computation	mmoles/gm of protein		
		Native collagen [a]	Acid-precursor gelatin	
			A [b]	B [c]
(a) Total basic groups	pH 1.5 to IEP	0.90	1.14	0.98
(b) Imidazole, imino, α-amino	pH 4.9–9.6	0.07	0.04	0.12
(c) ε-Amino	pH 9.6–12.5	0.34	0.62	0.43
(d) Guanidino	a — b — c	0.49	0.48	0.43
(e) Free carboxyl	pH 1.5–4.9	0.87	1.12	0.90
(f) Amide N	Direct analysis	0.47	0.40	0.31 [d]
(g) Total dicarboxylic acid	e + f	1.34	1.62	1.21

[a] Bowes and Kenten (66).
[b] Loeven (33).
[c] Ames (22).
[d] Estimated by Ames from the total nitrogen content.

Ames (23). The conclusion drawn from these comparisons was that the major difference between native collagen and acid-precursor gelatins was an increase in the content of primary amine groups and free carboxyl groups as the result of peptide bond hydrolysis. It appears that Ames' estimate of the amide content of his gelatin was too low. As indicated in the discussion of titration data in Chapter II, the ranges chosen by these workers for the α-amino, imidazole, and ε-amino groups were not appropriate, and the value for the ε-amino group content of the gelatin is probably too high and includes some α-amino groups as well. Loeven (33) and Ames (22, 23) both concluded that the amide group in collagen was not involved in the conversion of collagen to gelatin. Loeven particularly emphasized that peptide bond hydrolysis was the most important event in the preparation of acid-precursor gelatin and that equal numbers of amino and carboxyl groups were produced. There was no evidence that interchain cross-linkages of esterlike nature were severed during the gelatin extraction. The hexosamine contents of pig skin collagen and gelatin were identical within the precision of the measurements (0.11–0.08%). Unfortunately, the hexose content was not measured. Amino acid analyses of acid-precursor gelatins revealed only very slight differences between the compositions of the gelatins and of the native collagens (67) from which they were derived.

Bowes and Moss (60, 68) examined native collagen for amino-terminal group content. They found that there were no groups that would react with fluorodinitrobenzene (FDNB) except the ε-amino groups of lysine. Of those only about 50% were apparently accessible to the FDNB. Sykes (69) confirmed the fact that no amino-terminal groups could be detected in hide collagen by the FDNB reaction. However, he found 75–80% of the ε-amino groups of lysine to be reactive in hide powder. Courts (70) reacted several samples of acid-precursor gelatins, from pig skin, ox tendon, ox bone, and fish swim bladders, with FDNB. Following this reaction the DNP-gelatins were hydrolyzed in acid and the DNP-amino acids separated and isolated by column chromatography. The amino acids were identified both by using standard DNP-amino acid derivatives and by dearylation of the isolated derivatives by the method of Lowther (71), followed by paper chromatography of the regenerated free amino acids. Courts took special precautions to enable the detection of the DNP-derivatives of proline and hydroxyproline if these were present. Table III-14 lists the results of these analyses, along with viscosity and gel strength data that help to characterize the gelatins. Six amino acids were found to be the predominant NH_2-terminal residues: glycine, alanine, aspartic acid, serine, threonine, and glutamic acid. All other amino acids accounted for only 4–15% of the total number of NH_2-terminal residues. Glycine accounted for more than half the NH_2-terminal groups in every case, as might have been expected since glycine is the most abundant amino acid in collagen. However, the next most abundant constituents, proline and hydroxyproline, were not found in significant amounts as NH_2-terminal residues in spite of very careful control to be sure that their DNP-derivatives would not be destroyed during the hydrolysis reaction. Courts (70) did find that 88–97% of the ε-amino groups of the acid-precursor gelatins had become available for reaction with FDNB. If the ε-amino groups are involved in interchain covalent cross-linkage in collagen, as proposed by Mechanic and Levy (58) and Drake and Veis (36), then acid conditioning

TABLE III-14 [a]

AMINO-TERMINAL RESIDUES OF ACID-PRECURSOR GELATINS

Gelatin	Gel strength [b]	Reduced viscosity [c] (dl/gm)	N-Terminal residues (moles/10^5 gm)								Apparent M_n [d]	ε-NH₂ available (%)
			Gly.	Ala.	Asp.	Ser.	Thr.	Glu.	Others	Total		
Pig skin	235	0.43	0.74	0.24	0.13	0.10	0.08	0.07	0.19	1.55	65,000	97
Pig skin	221	0.39	0.59	0.18	0.06	0.05	0.03	0.04	0.19	1.14	87,000	88
Ox tendon	276	—	0.96	0.23	0.02	0.04	0.03	0.04	0.11	1.43	70,000	—
Ox bone	242	0.34	0.72	0.16	0.04	0.06	0.05	0.03	0.05	1.11	88,000	90
Sturgeon swim bladder	—	—	0.25	—	0.03	0.05	0.03	0.04	—	—	250,000	—

[a] Data of Courts (70).

[b] Measured according to British Standards Institution (1944) 757 at 6.6%.

[c] The value of $(\ln \eta_{rel})/c$ at $c = 0.5\%$, pH 7.0 at 35° in 1 M NaCl.

[d] Number-average molecular weight.

and extraction at pH 4 are sufficient to hydrolyze the great majority (but not all) of these bonds.

3. *Molecular Parameters of Acid-Precursor Gelatin*

The molecular weights listed in the next to last column of Table III-14 place the minimum number-average molecular weight of undegraded acid-precursor gelatins in the 70,000–90,000 range, except in the apparently anomalous case of sturgeon swim bladder gelatin. Osmotic pressure measurements of gelatins prepared in a similar fashion by Pouradier and Venet *(72)* gave number-average molecular weights in the same range. Hence Courts *(70)* concluded that the acid-precursor gelatins were single-chain molecules. The reduced viscosities, however, were not consistent with this conclusion or with the values obtained by Pouradier and Venet *(72)*. If one applies the Staudinger relationship derived by Pouradier and Venet for an acid-precursor pig skin gelatin ($[\eta] = 1.1 \times 10^{-5} M_n^{0.74}$), using the number-average molecular weights derived from the end-group analyses, the reduced viscosities obtained by Courts are 30–40% too low.

Veis and Cohen *(29)* examined the behavior of a commercial high molecular weight acid-precursor pig skin gelatin by light scattering and viscosity measurements in dilute aqueous salt solution and under salt-free isoionic conditions. The second virial coefficient was positive for the isoionic gelatin, indicating a slight intermolecular repulsion, and fell to about zero in the presence of salt. The gelatin molecular weight was the same within experimental error in the two solvent systems, and the intrinsic viscosities and viscosity concentration dependencies were quite close. The intrinsic viscosity in either solution was considerably lower than that found for similar molecular weight alkali-precursor gelatins. Since, as indicated above, configurational transitions were small, and since the acid-precursor gelatin did not exhibit the supercontraction noted in solutions of single-chain random coil polyampholytes *(73)*, it was concluded *(29)* that the acid-precursor gelatin could not be represented by a single-chain random coil structure but must have had a more compact structure. It was suggested that the compact structures were formed in such a way as to provide for the proximity of oppositely charged functional groups. Veis *et al.* *(30)* extended this line of investigation. They showed, by light scattering and electrophoretic mobility studies as a function of pH, that the acid-precursor gelatins did not exhibit sharply defined changes in properties in the region of the isoelectric point. Between pH 7 and pH 9, where the net charge was varied from + 10 to — 10 per 10^5 gm, there was no change in either electrophoretic mobility or the second virial coefficient. An alkali-precursor gelatin, on the other hand, did exhibit a very sharply defined turbidity maximum at its isoelectric point and the second virial coefficient was a pronounced function of the pH. Conductivity measurements showed that small ions were bound by the acid-precursor gelatin in the pH 6–9 range, while no salt was bound by the alkali-precursor gelatin in the region of the isoelectric point (pH 5) (*74*). Similarly, Bello, Riese and Vinograd (*75*) showed that many salts shifted the pH of solutions of an acid-precursor gelatin. These workers found evidence that both Cl⁻ and Na⁺ ions were bound at pH 7.3. Veis *et al.* (*30*) interpreted these data as supporting the view that acid-precursor gelatins are network structures in which compensating charged groups are on adjacent segments of laterally aggregated peptide chains. This is a model very similar to that proposed by Bear (*76*) for intact collagen fibrils (see Chapter I). In gelatin, however, the secondary structure is melted out, or disorganized, so in the proposed acid-precursor gelatin models one may consider that only the primary and tertiary structures are intact. This being the case, it followed that some of the covalent cross-linkages present in native collagen must also have been retained intact in the acid-precursor gelatin. For this reason Veis *et al.* (*30*) proposed that the acid-precursor gelatins should be called melted soluble collagen.

Courts and Stainsby (*77*) combined DNP-acid-precursor gelatin end-group studies with molecular weight determinations by light scattering. Their results were not clear-cut. They found that the highest molecular weight gelatin had an M_w of 194,000 and an M_n of 92,000, which would support a multichain model. However, very low molecular weight fractions, M_w 47,000 and 25,000, had M_n values of 74,000 and 44,000, respectively. Courts and Stainsby took these data as indicating that some chains not bearing free terminal α-amino groups were present and that the number-average molecular weights calculated from the end-group content should represent maximum number-average values (or, alternatively, the minimum number of chains). Pouradier (*78*) noted the same anomaly in that low molecular weight acid-precursor gelatins did not show an increase in number of free carboxyl groups during titration as compared to the number of such groups in higher molecular weight gelatins. The number of such groups per unit weight actually decreased with decreasing molecular weight.

B. Alkali-Precursor Gelatins

1. *General Operating Procedures*

The alkaline processing of collagen is the most widely used commercial process for the production of gelatins and glues. Any collagenous stock can be converted to gelatin by this means. The raw collagen stock is washed and thoroughly hydrated in cold water in large tanks or pits. The excess water is drained from the stock and lime is added to the stock in sufficient amounts so that when fresh water is added a saturated solution of calcium oxide in formed. A sufficient excess of calcium oxide must be maintained to make up for the base consumed in the conditioning reactions. The hides or other collagenous stock are left in the liming pits for periods of 3–10 months, depending on the nature of the stock, ambient temperature, cleanliness of the operations, alkalinity of the lime liquors, and so on. For example, one of the longer lime soaks is usually required for the preparation of photographic gelatins from calf skins.

Any water-soluble base can be used to condition collagen for conversion to gelatin. Lime is preferred because its solubility acts as a built-in regulator of the alkalinity of the liquors and because calcium hydroxide does not swell collagen as greatly as the alkali hydroxides at equivalent pH. It is possible to decrease the conditioning time by "sharpening" the alkalinity of the soak liquor with sodium hydroxide or sodium carbonate at concentrations of about 0.5%. Calcium chloride with 0.01% methylamine has also been added to the lime solutions. These processes are more difficult to control and may reduce the yields of the highest quality gelatins.

After the liming is complete it is necessary to lower the pH before the thermal conversion to gelatin can be allowed to proceed. The lime is washed from the surface of the stock with running water for a day or so. Hide collagen is still swollen and basic after this wash. This residual base is neutralized by washing with dilute hydrochloric acid until the collagen stock is deplumped or limp and flaccid. The acid is then washed out, and a final wash is made with a dilute solution of aluminum or zinc sulfate. These reagents harden the collagen stock slightly and somehow improve the color of the gelatin. In the glue industry larger quantities of zinc sulfate are used for bactericidal purposes. At this point the collagen stock has a pH of 5–8 and is ready for conversion to gelatin.

The collagen stock is then loaded into extraction kettles and the gelatin is extracted in a series of cooks at successively higher temperatures, as previously described for the acid process. The highest quality gelatins are obtained in the first few extractions. The liquors from each cook are concentrated and dried separately, except that in some glue production units the liquors from the last few cooks are combined before drying. Even with the best operating control there is very large variability in the "test" of gelatins obtained in any given cook. The overall balance of viscosity and gel strength for a particular quality of gelatin is usually achieved by blending gelatins from several different extractions. Therefore the usual commercial gelatin or glue sample is heterogeneous and one would be very hard put to specify its past history. It is for this reason that so much of the research data on gelatin, particularly that obtained prior to about 1940, is nearly useless for the correlation of gelatin properties with molecular parameters. The only way for investigators, interested in acquiring detailed knowledge of the gelatins, to proceed, is for them to begin their work with purified collagen of known history and to prepare such gelatins as they require by completely controlled and thoroughly documented procedures. Unfortunately such studies are still quite rare. The discussion which follows emphasizes information derived from such studies wherever possible.

2. The Chemistry of the Alkaline Conversion Process

In contrast to the acid processing of gelatin where the pretreatment seems to accomplish only a physical reorganization of the collagen structure with minimal hydrolytic changes, the alkaline soak brings about chemical alterations in the collagen, and the subsequent thermal solubilization procedure is required primarily for rupture of the relatively weak physical forces that maintain the fibrillar structure. Ames (65) showed the importance of the duration of the lime soak in his study of the conversion of ox sinew to gelatin. Figure III-36 clearly indicates the improvements in both yield and quality with increasing liming of the stock, all other factors of extraction, concentration, and drying of the liquors being equal. These changes in the stock take place without appreciable solubilization of the collagen.

The highest grade alkali-precursor gelatins have an isoelectric point at about pH 5. Ames (19) showed that the pH of the isoelectric point could be varied between 6.0 and 4.8 by controlling the duration of the lime soak. Earlier investigators (79-83) had observed that ammonia was formed during the alkaline soak, probably due to the splitting of amide nitrogen from the collagen (80, 81). Ames (22, 23) confirmed these results and showed a definite correlation between nitrogen content, amide group loss, duration of the liming, and shift of the isoelectric point to lower pH.

Comparison of the nitrogen contents of collagen, limed collagen, and alkali-precursor gelatins (Table III-15) demonstrated that the nitrogen
loss occurred during the lime soak and not subsequently. The shift in
isoelectric point to lower pH was attributed to the loss of amide nitrogen
and the creation of a corresponding number of free carboxyl groups.
There was also a small but experimentally significant increase in the formol
titration of the gelatins as the pH of the isoelectric point decreased, indicating the release of free basic groups as well. The relationships of these
changes to the duration of the lime soak and the rate at which gelatin

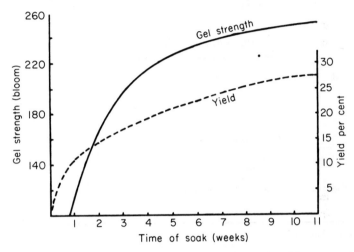

FIG. III-36. Effect of liming on the yield and physical properties of the extracted gelatin
[Ames (65)].

could be extracted from the limed stock are indicated in Table III-16.
Notably, Ames (22) found no correspondence between the change in isoelectric point and the rate at which the stock could be converted into gelatin. From this observation he concluded (23) that the deamidation reaction was not involved in the collagen → gelatin conversion, though, of
course, this reaction resulted in chemical modification of the gelatins obtained by the alkaline process as compared with those obtained by acid processing. A plot of pH of the gelatin isoelectric point vs. duration of the alkaline soak (Fig. III-37) indicated that the deamidation reaction was virtually
complete after 10 days of liming, whereas the conditioning reactions leading to increased yields of higher gel strength gelatins continued at least
throughout the 43-day period examined. Another aspect of Fig. III-37
is that these data suggest that there are two sets of amide groups in colla-

TABLE III-15 [a]

VARIATIONS IN NITROGEN CONTENT OF COLLAGENS AND GELATINS

(A) *Total nitrogen*

Material	Nitrogen content (%)
Ossein, native	18.49
Alkaline-process gelatin	18.08
Acid-precursor gelatin	18.52

(B) *Nitrogen loss during conversion*

Material	Treatment	Nitrogen loss (as % of N in solution)
Ox sinew	No pretreatment, 7 hrs, 80°	0.49
Ox sinew	Limed, then heated at pH 8, 80°:	
	2 hrs	0.010
	4 hrs	0.023
Ox sinew gelatin (4% solution)	Heated at pH 8, 7 hrs, 80°	0.081

[a] Data of Ames (*22, 23*)

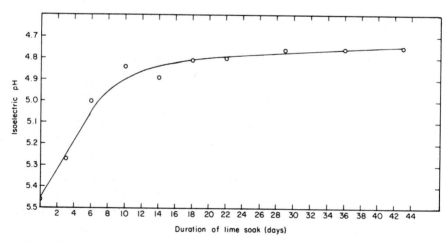

FIG. III-37. Changes in the isoelectric point of the extracted gelatin as a function of the duration of the liming of the collagen stock [Ames (*23*)].

TABLE III-16 [a]

CORRELATION OF THE EASE OF CONVERSION OF LIMED STOCK TO GELATIN WITH VARIOUS PARAMETERS

Duration of lime soak (days)	Isoelectric pH of extracted gelatin	Formol titration of extracted gelatin (eq. NaOH required per 10^5 gm gelatin)	Gel strength of derived gelatin, Bloom (6.66% gelatin)	Rate of conversion (% extracted/hr, 80°)
0	5.46	32.3	86	6.0
3	5.27	32.1	91	8.1
6	5.00	34.6	106	9.7
10	4.84	33.6	110	15.9
14	4.89	34.4	120	18.3
18	4.81	34.1	130	14.8
22	4.80	34.5	141	22.4
29	4.76	34.8	162	18.3
36	4.76	36.0	165	25.0
43	4.75	40.1	182	37.1

[a] Data of Ames (22, 23).

gen, one set being much more susceptible to hydrolysis than the other. Such behavior might correspond to the known difference in the ease of hydrolysis of glutamine and asparagine amide groups (*84*). Titration data (*23, 33*) yield no surprises. The titratable groups of alkali-precursor gelatin are similar in nature and amount to those listed in Table III-13, except for an increase in free carboxyl-group content to ~ 1.2 mmoles per gm gelatin.

The data of Table III-16 and Fig. III-37 compare favorably with the recent amide loss data reported by Hörmann *et al.* (*50*) (Fig. III-30). These workers correlated liming time, nitrogen content, amide content, amino-terminal groups, and hydroxylamine-sensitive linkages with the ease of conversion of the limed collagen to gelatin. Their data are indicated in Table III-17.

TABLE III-17 [a]

CHANGES IN BOVINE SKIN DURING LIMING

Liming time (days)	N (%)	Amide N (%)	Amino-terminal groups (eq/10^5 gm)	Number-average chain weight	Esterlike groups (eq/10^5 gm)	% Converted to gelatin at 60° in 5 hr
0	15.4	0.51	1.00	100,000	12.4	5.3
27	15.1	0.28	1.08	93,000	9.2	34.8
53	14.8	0.18	1.16	86,000	7.3	39.2
83	15.4	0.14	1.39	72,000	5.7	53.2
113	14.2	0.11	1.55	65,000	4.8	73.6
184	13.9	0.08	1.79	55,000	3.5	75.7

[a] Data of Hörmann *et al.* (*50*).

Amino-terminal group analyses made by Courts (*70*), using the FDNB technique (Table III-18), again showed that the bonds most susceptible to hydrolysis during the processing procedure were those involving glycine, serine, threonine, alanine, aspartic acid, and glutamic acid at the amino terminus. In contrast to the acid-precursor gelatins (Table III-14), serine replaced alanine as the most labile bond, excepting glycine. Substantially all of the ε-amino groups of the alkali-precursor gelatins were readily available for reaction with FDNB. The chain number-average molecular weights were significantly lower for the alkali-precursor gelatins, whereas the reduced viscosities were higher than those of the acid-precursor gelatins.

TABLE III-18 [a]

AMINO-TERMINAL RESIDUES OF ALKALI-PRECURSOR GELATINS

Gelatin	Gel strength (Bloom) [c]	Reduced viscosity (dl/gm)	N-Terminal residues (moles/10^5 gm)								Apparent M_n [b]	ε-NH$_2$ available (%)
			Gly.	Ala.	Asp.	Ser.	Thr.	Glu.	Others	Total		
Ox bone	217	0.59	0.95	0.13	0.10	0.24	0.11	0.14	0.01	1.68	60,000	100
Ox bone	186	0.45	0.98	0.17	0.12	0.23	0.10	0.13	0.14	1.87	53,000	97
Calf skin	208	0.60	0.83	0.11	0.11	0.19	0.11	0.10	0.12	1.57	64,000	97
Calf skin	250	—	0.80	0.10	0.08	0.19	0.11	0.10	0.12	1.50	67,000	—
Ox hide	191	0.56	1.27	0.20	0.14	0.24	0.14	0.15	0.20	2.34	43,000	96
Ox tendon	274	—	1.00	0.17	0.15	0.23	0.14	0.12	0.08	1.89	53,000	—

[a] Data of Courts (70).

[b] Number-average molecular weight.

[c] The Bloom unit is a measure of the rigidity of a gel formed from a solution of specified concentration in an explicitly defined manner. It is the weight, in grams, required to depress a standard position into the gel surface to a depth of 4 mm.

Grassmann and Hörmann (85) confirmed these results qualitatively for the amino-terminal groups, and showed in addition that glycine, threonine, and alanine were the predominant carboxy-terminal amino acid residues. Heyns and Wolff (86) substantiated Court's (70) amino-terminal residue data, using similar techniques. With a modification of the FDNB reaction that permitted the determination of the amino-terminal residues directly in the reaction mixture, without separation, Heyns and Legler (87) found almost 30% more amino-terminal residues for an alkali-pretreated ox bone gelatin than did Courts (70). The carboxy-terminal residues were also determined for this same gelatin sample by the Akabori hydrazinolysis reaction (88). The results of these analyses are shown in Table III-19 in terms of both absolute amounts and ratios of the terminal amino acids to their total content in the gelatin. These data very clearly emphasize the lability of the peptide bonds involving phenylalanine, serine, threonine, aspartic acid, and glutamic acid, and the hydrolytic stability of the bonds involving proline and hydroxyproline.

The titration curves obtained by Bowes and Kenten (89) on alkali-pretreated collagen showed an increase of about 9 equivalents per 10^5 gm in the number of total basic groups as compared with native collagen. Bowes (90) was reluctant to ascribe this to peptide bond hydrolysis and proposed instead that, of the increase, 3 moles of amino groups per 10^5 gm collagen were the result of the conversion of some arginine to ornithine. It is likely, however, that the additional basic groups were the consequence of peptide bond hydrolysis during the alkaline soak (52). As mentioned earlier, de la Burde et al. (52) compared the hydrazinolysis of native and limed collagen. As illustrated in Figs. III-31 and 33, native collagen showed a very pronounced reaction with hydrazine to form protein-bound hydrazide at concentrations of about 40% hydrazine, whereas this reaction was absent in the alkali-pretreated collagen. Amino-terminal group analyses demonstrated that peptide bond hydrolysis had occurred in this hydrazine concentration range. As indicated earlier, it appears that 16–18 moles of peptide bonds per 10^5 gm collagen were hydrazinolyzed. Since this reaction did not occur in the alkali-pretreated collagen, it was concluded that these same peptide bonds had already been cleaved during the alkaline soak. Thus it is likely that the major part of the hydrolytic reactions takes place during the soak and not during the gelatin extraction steps of the alkali-processing procedure.

Highberger and Stecker (81) observed that urea was produced during prolonged liming. It was known that arginine could be deguanidinated with alkali to form ornithine and urea (91), and it was postulated that

TABLE III-19 [a]

N- AND C-TERMINAL RESIDUES OF AN ALKALI-PRETREATED OX BONE GELATIN

Amino acid	Total content (moles/10⁵ gm)	N-Terminal [b]		C-Terminal [b]	
		(moles/10⁵ gm)	residues per total residues × 10³	(moles/10⁵ gm)	residues per total residues × 10³
Glycine	363	1.28	3.6	0.68	1.9
Alanine	126	0.18	1.5	0.13	1.1
Valine	23.7	0.05	2.1	0.03	1
Leucine+isoleucine	38	0.14	3.9	0.03	1
Methionine	4.2	—	—	—	—
Phenylalanine	15.1	0.09	6.1	0.04	2
Serine	35.5	0.29	9.9	0.17	4.8
Threonine	19.8	0.13	6.1	0.13	6.5
Aspartic acid	50.5	0.19	4.2	0.39	7.7
Glutamic acid	78.6	0.16	2.1	0.40	5.1
Lysine	29.9	0.06	2.0	—	—
Hydroxylysine	4.7	—	—	—	—
Arginine	51.9	—	—	(—)	(—)
Histidine	4.5	—	—	(—)	(—)
Proline	134	0.07	0.5	0.13	1.0
Hydroxyproline	101	—	—	0.15	1.5
Tyrosine	1.3	—	—	—	—

[a] Data of Heyns and Legler (87)

[b] — Determination made, residue not found; (—) no determination made.

this same reaction was occurring in the collagen. The deguanidination reaction,

$$
\begin{array}{c}
NH_2 \\
| \\
CH-CH_2-CH_2-CH_2-NH-C \overset{NH}{\underset{NH_2}{\diagup}} \overset{H_2O}{\longrightarrow}
\end{array}
\quad
\begin{array}{c}
NH_2 \\
| \\
CH-CH_2-CH_2-CH_2-NH_2 \\
| \\
COOH
\end{array}
+
\begin{array}{c}
NH_2 \\
| \\
C=O \\
| \\
NH_2
\end{array}
$$

arginine   ornithine

$$
\xrightarrow{\;H_2O\;}
\begin{array}{c}
NH_2 \\
| \\
CH-CH_2-CH_2-CH_2-N-C \overset{O}{\diagup} NH_2 \\
| \\
COOH
\end{array}
+ NH_3
$$

citrulline

as indicated, can also yield citrulline and ammonia (*92*). This latter reaction accounted for only a small fraction of the deguanidination (*81*) during prolonged liming. De la Burde *et al.* (*52*) also found that the citrulline content of limed collagen was low, even after the primary deguanidination reaction had removed up to 20% of the total arginine.

The deguanidination reaction is slow and becomes important only in the later stages of a normal alkaline soak. In a sample of collagen limed for only 5 days de la Burde *et al.* (*52*) could not detect a significant difference between the arginine content of the original and limed collagens. Hamilton and Anderson (*93*) examined various gelatins for their content of arginine and ornithine, using the chromatographic system of Moore and Stein (*94*). A gelatin extracted from demineralized ox bone after 5–6-week liming contained only 2% ornithine, a gelatin from 10–20-week limed stock contained 21% ornithine, and a calf skin gelatin from skins limed for 4–8 months averaged 34% ornithine. In no case did Hamilton and Anderson detect more than a trace of citrulline. There was also no evidence for the destruction of other amino acids during the gelatin manufacturing process.

3. *Physical Changes in Collagen Fibers during the Liming Process*

When limed collagen fibers have been neutralized and brought to their isoelectric pH, they are grossly indistinguishable from the native fibers and even at the level of the electron microscope there are no apparent differences in fibrillar organization. There are, however, two striking changes in the properties of the fibers. They are more readily swollen to a greater extent than the native fibers (see Fig. I-13), and the internal cohesion of each fibril is reduced (95).

The difference in shape of the two swelling curves shown in Fig. I-13 can be readily explained in terms of the shift of the isoelectric point of the alkali-treated collagen to lower pH. However, the deamidation reaction alone would not be expected to decrease the cohesion between fibrils and thus account for the elevated swelling of the limed collagen. Bowes (90, 96-99) refers to the resistance of collagen to the osmotic swelling pressure as owing to the cohesion of the fibers. The forces of cohesion are made up of structural components, related to the interweaving of the fibers and to the existence of reticular sheaths around fiber bundles, and of chemical forces which directly stabilize each fibril. Calculations (96) of the swelling expected due to the Donnan equilibrium effects indicated that the principal discrepancy occurred in the alkaline region at pH values greater than 12.0. At a pH of about 11.5 the calculations indicated that the swelling should attain a maximum value and then decrease at higher pH. The swelling should also have been depressed by the addition of neutral salts. In fact, the collagen continued to swell at pH's greater than 11.5 and neutral salts did not inhibit swelling at pH's greater than 13.0. On the other hand, swelling studies on gelatin in alkali (Fig. III-38) showed that while a maximum was attained at about pH 11.5, a definite minimum also occurred at pH 12.7 and swelling then increased rapidly. From these observations Bowes and Kenten (96, 97) concluded that while it was evident that the gross fibrillar organization contributed to the cohesion between fibers, there must also have been a substantial contribution to the cohesive forces from intermolecular links between polypeptide chains in adjacent structure elements.

De la Burde (95) examined the internal fiber cohesion by a penetration test that, in essence, measured the flow characteristics of organized collagen fibrils. The effect of calcium or sodium hydroxide was not measured directly. In this study the collagen was reacted with aqueous hydrazine, the excess hydrazine solution was removed, and the structural integrity of standard-size hide pieces was measured in a type of modified penetrometer. The ease of penetration increased with increasing hydrazine concentration as anticipated, but it also was clear (Fig. III-39), that the mechanical breakdown paralleled the chemical modification of the collagen. The nature of the modification in the 40% hydrazine concentration range, principally formation of new amino-terminal amino acids, has been discussed previously. It was assumed that alkali-pretreated collagen was already partially hydrolyzed and that it should behave quite similarly in this study to the purified native collagen. This proved to be the case; the alkali-pretreated collagen was rendered relatively easier to penetrate at lower hydrazine concentration, and the increased ease of penetration changed sharply in the same hydrazine concentration range as with the

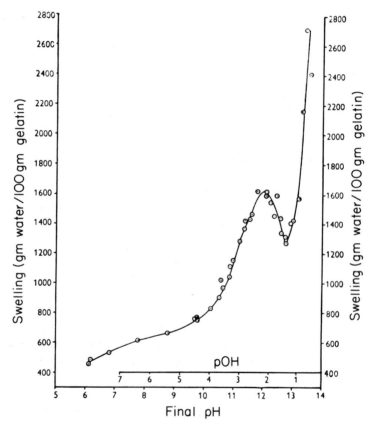

FIG. III-38. Swelling of an alkali-precursor gelatin in salt-free solutions of sodium hydroxide at 0° as a function of pH [Bowes and Kenten (96)].

native collagen (Fig. III-40). The swelling of the collagens paralleled these alterations in mechanical fibril stability. It would therefore appear that the structural integrity or internal cohesiveness of collagen fibrils is destroyed by rupture of certain peptide bonds and the consequent introduction of new ionic groups in the molecules. These changes may be brought about by prolonged liming, and their probable correlation with the increased ease of solubilization and conversion of collagen into gelatin is obvious. It is not, on the other hand, clear how this progressive degradation can lead to increased viscosity and gel strength in the derived gelatins.

In spite of the evident correlation between the chemical modification and/or peptide bond hydrolysis and the intermolecular structure-stabilizing

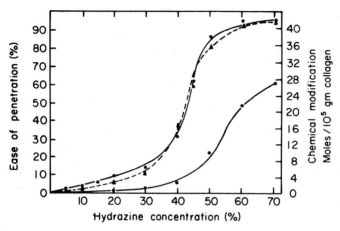

FIG. III-39. Relationship between the ease of penetration of fibrous corium collagen and the chemical modification of collagen by hydrazine. Left-hand ordinate: △, ease of penetration. Right-hand ordinate: ○, moles of bound hydrazide; ●, moles of arginine converted to ornithine [de la Burde (95)].

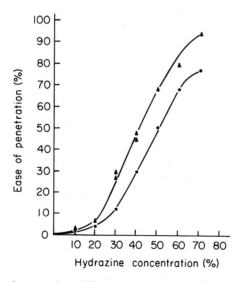

FIG. III-40. Ease of penetration of fibrous limed corium collagen as a function of hydrazine treatment concentration: ▲, limed collagen; ●, native collagen [de la Burde (95)].

forces, alkali by itself is not sufficient to disrupt the trihelical intramolecular order of the basic macromolecular units. This can be readily demonstrated by the fact that limed fibers are entirely normal in appearance in the electron microscope and yield normal x-ray diffraction patterns. Heat or the action of protein denaturants such as urea or potassium thiocyanate is necessary to convert limed fibers to gelatin.

Sequence studies, particularly by Grassmann and his colleagues (*100-103*), have shown that the collagen peptide chains are composed of sequences alternately rich and poor in the imino acids and, correspondingly, rich and poor in polar and apolar residues. The polar regions, containing glutamic and aspartic acids and arginine, histidine, and lysine, comprise the relatively less well-ordered band regions (*76, 101*). It is in these regions that ionic effects are manifested and the swelling phenomena are presumably controlled. Since liming, or the equivalent hydrazinolysis, frees aspartic and glutamic acids as the predominant amino-terminal residues (*52*) (in addition, of course, to glycine), and since the gelatins produced by either acid or alkaline pretreatment contain these amino acids as well as serine and threonine as the major amino-terminal residues (*70, 86, 87*), one may conclude that the alkaline hydrolysis occurs primarily in the polar regions.

The alkaline hydrolysis also disrupts the intermolecular forces and permits very extensive swelling, indicating that the covalent inter-tropocollagen cross-linkages (*N*-bonds) must be located in the polar regions and are also susceptible to alkali. During the entire sequence of hydrolytic events in alkali, those portions of each molecule in the imide-rich interband regions retain their collagen helix configuration. Moreover, as the gelatins produced by the alkali-pretreatment process may have number-average molecular weights of the order of 100,000 or higher, whereas electron micrographs of phosphotungstic acid-stained segment-long-spacing collagen reveal twenty or more polar regions per tropocollagen molecule (*104*), it would appear that only a few of the polar regions are subject to the alkaline hydrolysis and that these same regions are involved in the covalent inter-tropocollagen cross-linkages. The end regions of the tropocollagen molecule, in the segment-long-spacing form, are the most heavily staining regions and it may very well prove to be the case that these chain ends are involved in the structure stabilization by both covalent and weaker physical bonds. Hodge and Schmitt (*104*) and Grassmann (*105*) have also made suggestions of this nature.

In summary, the alkaline pretreatment which prepares collagen for ready conversion to gelatin can be considered as a depolymerizing reaction, in which a few specific peptide-chain regions are affected. The depolymerization results from hydrolysis of intermolecular cross-linkages (N-bonds), which returns a mature and highly polymerized collagen to a form in which ideally only γ-tropocollagen units or lower intramolecularly cross-linked (I-bonded) units exist. These units are readily solubilized in water when the collagen helix is melted out by heat or other denaturants. The hydrolysis reaction apparently proceeds more slowly than the parallel deamidation reaction. As illustrated in Fig. III-37 and Tables III-16 and 17, deamidation is complete within 12 days while the gelatin yield and test may increase over a period of several months. The swelling of the limed stock proceeds in two stages; the initial rapid equilibrium swelling is complete within 3 days, the slower swelling indicative of structural breakdown proceeds during the entire lime soak, as indicated in Fig. III-41.

Courts (*106*) carried out a thorough study of collagen in the condition described above, in which the majority of cross-linkages had been ruptured and gelatinization would occur readily upon heating or upon addition of any of the common protein denaturing reagents. The work was based on an observation made by Ames (*24*) that collagen subjected to a dual pretreatment, first with cold hydrochloric acid and then with a normal alkaline soak, was much more susceptible to the lime soak. Stock treated in this manner could be converted to gelatin of high quality and in good yield following a much shorter period of liming. In addition to this approach, Courts made use of the fact that swelling of the collagen could be inhibited by use of concentrated sodium sulfate (*107*) and, hence, with such control of mechanical factors, the direct chemical effects of various reagents could be determined. Following various combinations of acid and alkali pretreatments, Courts (*106*) determined the yield of gelatin, amino-terminal groups of the treated collagen stock before conversion to gelatin, and amino-terminal groups of the gelatins produced. All of the experiments were carried out with ossein obtained from sun-dried Indian ox bones by hydrochloric acid demineralization. The end-group analyses were made with the FDNB reagent. The results are summarized in Tables III-19 and 20. The ossein collagen had a number-average chain weight, C_n, $> 350,000$, and a negligible solubility when exposed to water at 60° for 2 hours. Inspection of Table III-20 shows first of all that each of the pretreatments reduced the value of C_n in the fibrous collagen before conversion to gelatin. Except in the case of the sulfuric acid pretreatment the residue fibers after extraction had nearly the same C_n value as before, indicating that the mild conditions of extraction of the gelatin did not bring about any hydrolytic degradation in addition to that of the pretreatment

TABLE III-20[a]

EFFECT OF PRETREATMENT ON PARAMETERS RELATED TO THE CONVERSION OF COLLAGEN TO GELATIN

Parameter	Saturated Ca(OH)$_2$ (2 weeks)			Saturated Ca(OH)$_2$ (6 months)			5% NaOH (10 days)		
	Collagen		Gelatin	Collagen		Gelatin	Collagen		Gelatin
	Treated	60° Extracted		Treated	60° Extracted		Treated	60° Extracted	
Yield gelatin (%)[b]	12			53			97		
Swelling factor for treated collagen	2.0			5.0			2.7		
N-Terminal residues[c]									
Glycine	0.40	0.46	1.40	0.66	—	1.00	0.75	0.78	1.13
Serine	0.22	0.26	0.31	0.19	—	0.20	0.19	0.20	0.30
Threonine	0.10	0.10	0.21	0.18	—	0.15	0.16	0.10	0.22
Alanine	0.05	0.07	0.13	0.12	—	0.12	0.12	0.14	0.18
Aspartic acid	0.06	0.08	0.11	0.15	—	0.19	0.12	0.19	0.16
Glutamic acid	0.06	0.06	0.30	0.09	—	0.21	0.07	0.06	0.16
Others	0.04	0.04	0.10	0.05	—	0.13	0.10	0.10	0.15
Total	0.93	1.07	2.56	1.44	—	2.00	1.51	1.57	2.30
Number-average chain weight	107,000	93,000	39,000	69,000		50,000	66,000	64,000	44,000

[a] Data of Courts (106).
[b] At 60°, 2 hours,
[c] In moles/10⁵ gm.

TABLE III-20 [a]

EFFECT OF PRETREATMENT ON PARAMETERS RELATED TO THE CONVERSION OF COLLAGEN TO GELATIN

| Parameter | 2.5 N HCl (3 days), sat. Ca(OH)$_2$ (9 days) | | | 2.5 N HCl (7 days), sat. Ca(OH)$_2$ (9 days) | | | 1% H$_2$SO$_4$ in 20% Na$_2$SO$_4$ (24 hr) | | |
| | Collagen | | Gelatin | Collagen | | Gelatin | Collagen | | Gelatin |
	After acid	After acid + Ca(OH)$_2$		After acid	After acid + Ca(OH)$_2$		Treated	60° Extracted	
Yield gelatin (%) [b]		48	—		95	—		35	
Swelling factor for treated collagen		5.1	—		10	—		1.8	
N-Terminal residues [c]									
Glycine	0.39	0.64	—	0.48	0.80	—	0.35	0.96	0.96
Serine	0.10	0.24	—	0.15	0.27	—	0.05	0.08	0.11
Threonine	0.18	0.17	—	0.34	0.25	—	0.08	0.12	0.07
Alanine	0.13	0.10	—	0.18	0.12	—	0.10	0.08	0.16
Aspartic acid	0.08	0.14	—	0.16	0.26	—	0.05	0.06	0.07
Glutamic acid	0.05	0.09	—	0.08	0.08	—	0.08	0.13	0.11
Others	0.10	0.07	—	0.17	0.08	—	0.05	0.11	0.10
Total	1.03	1.45	—	1.56	1.86	—	0.76	1.54	1.58
Number-average chain weight	98,000	69,000	—	64,000	54,000	—	132,000	65,000	64,000

[a] Data of Courts (106).
[b] At 60°, 2 hours.
[c] In moles/10^5 gm.

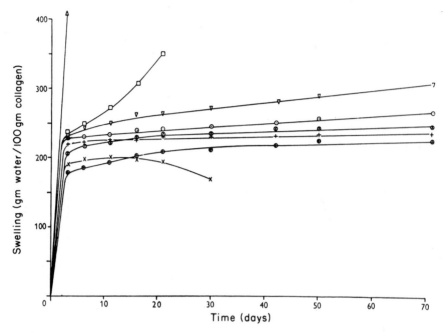

FIG. III-41. Effect of duration of exposure to alkali on the swelling of collagen [Bowes and Kenten (*96*)].

		pH at 3 days	pH at 18 days
×,	NaOH	11.34	10.80
⊙,	NaOH	12.84	12.83
▽,	NaOH	13.05	13.02
□,	NaOH	13.32	13.21
+,	NaOH + 0.1% Na₂S	12.72	12.67
⊕,	Saturated Ca(OH)₂	12.66	12.66
⊗,	Saturated Ca(OH)₂ + 0.1% Na₂S	12.72	12.69

process. The same types of amino-terminal residues were found in all of the treated collagens and gelatins. On a quantitative basis, however, the pretreatments were definitely selective and in almost every case the gelatins had lower C_n values than the residues from which they had been extracted. The amino-terminal glycine content of the gelatins was substantially enhanced over that in the residues following alkaline pretreatment. Amino-terminal glutamic acid was also markedly enhanced in each of the gelatins. Serine and threonine appeared at the amino-terminus in relatively large amounts in the gelatins after alkaline pretreatment. On the other hand, acid pretreatment alone did not create substantially more amino-terminal glutamic acid, serine, or threonine in the gelatin than in the collagen, but did lead to a clear enrichment of amino-terminal alanine.

The flow diagrams in Table III-21 show the relationships between number-average chain weights in the fibers and in the gelatins. The acid pretreatment was apparently much less affective in hydrolyzing peptide bonds without heat than was the alkaline soak. Courts (106) confirmed Ames' (24) observation that an acid soak followed by a calcium hydroxide soak was an extremely effective and rapid procedure for the preparation of gelatin. A 7-day exposure of ossein collagen to 2.5 N hydrochloric acid followed by only a 9-day exposure to calcium hydroxide was more effective than either a 6-month exposure to calcium hydroxide alone of a 10-day exposure to 5% sodium hydroxide. The gelatin yield from the dual processing was almost double that of the calcium hydroxide treatment, and the gelatin had a higher number-average chain weight. The yields were comparable between the dual and sodium hydroxide processes, but in the first instance C_n was 54,000 whereas it was only 44,000 in the latter case. When the acid-base treatment was reversed so that the 7-day calcium hydroxide soak preceded the 3-day hydrochloric acid soak, the gelatin yield on extraction for 2 hours at 60° dropped precipitously from 95% to only 5%. Courts interpreted these data as suggesting that two types of insolubilizing bond were present. One set of bonds was presumably labile in acid or in very strong base (5% NaOH $\approx$ pH 14) and the other set was labile only in base (Ca(OH)$_2$ $\approx$ pH 12.6). As a result of the failure of the reversed dual soak to produce high yields of gelatin, Courts postulated that the acid-labile bonds, when intact, protected some of the alkali-labile bonds from alkaline hydrolysis at pH 12.6.

In addition to the above experiments, Courts (106) found that the dual-soak process rendered the collagen fibers susceptible to solution in dilute organic acids to give viscous solutions very similar to those of tropocollagen. Ward et al. (108) found that bovine corium collagen could be solubilized by the dual-soak process in similar fashion to the ossein. The tropocollagen-like organic-acid-soluble material could be denatured at elevated temperature or could be precipitated to yield fibers upon addition of salt or dialysis to higher pH. However, the fibers produced in this way did not have the characteristic banding so readily apparent upon electron microscope examination of similar tropocollagen precipitates. Courts (106) coined the term "eucollagen" (readily converted into gelatin) to describe the altered mature collagen rendered soluble in dilute organic acids. The lack of phosphotungstic acid-staining regions in the eucollagen suggests that the arginine content of the eucollagen had been reduced, or that some specific sites of interchain interaction were blocked or modified.

There are a number of difficulties in applying Court's data, as epitomized

TABLE III-21 [a]

NUMBER-AVERAGE CHAIN WEIGHTS OF INSOLUBLE COLLAGEN AND
THE DERIVED GELATINS AT VARIOUS STAGES DURING CONVERSION PROCESS

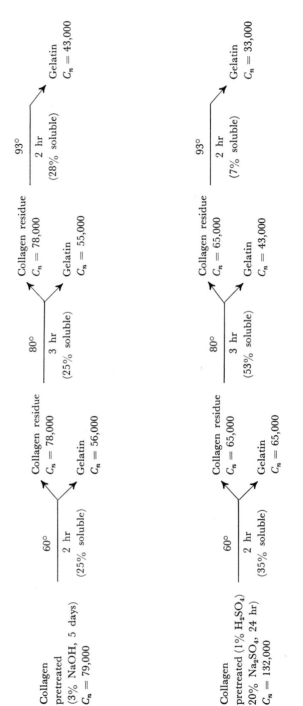

[a] Data of Courts (106).

in Tables III-20 and 21, to the model system postulated earlier in which it was proposed that alkaline pretreatment solubilized collagen because interchain cross-linkages were hydrolyzed. The major difficulty is emphasized in the data of Table III-21. In the first comparison of the extraction of sulfuric acid- and sodium hydroxide-treated collagens at 60° for 2 hours, it is evident that the collagen with the higher initial average number-average chain weight gave the higher yield of gelatin, 35% as compared with 25% and that the acid-precursor gelatin was also of higher average chain weight than the alkali-precursor gelatin, 65,000 as compared with 56,000. The swelling factors listed in Table III-20 also showed no correlation with the yields of gelatin. Finally, there was no correlation between the C_n of the treated stock and the gelatin yield, although the C_n's tended to approach a minimum value of about 60,000 in the fibrous residues. Any lower weight fragments supposedly were in the soluble gelatin extracts. It would appear therefore that the appearance of the amino-terminal residues is not an adequate measure of cross-linkage rupture, and that a substantial number of peptide bonds can be cleaved without complete destruction of the infinite three-dimensional network of covalent cross-linkages. One may also conclude that the cross-linkages are as stable to hydrolysis as the stronger bonds in the collagen backbone peptides. From this view of the collagen network structure, one would expect that single straight-chain gelatins would be the exception rather than the rule when extracted from mature, cross-linked collagens, and that the gelatin molecular weights measured by physical means would be substantially higher than the number-average chain weights. This is indeed the case.

4. *Molecular Parameters of Alkali-Precursor Gelatin*

In spite of the numerous studies on the characterization of alkali-precursor gelatins there are only five which are sufficiently informative to merit serious consideration. These are the works of Pouradier and his colleagues (*7, 22, 109, 110*), Williams and his collaborators (*111, 112*), Boedtker and Doty (*113*), Gouinlock, Flory and Scheraga (*114*), and Courts and Stainsby (*77*). Various aspects of each of these investigations have been discussed in Chapter II in terms of the methods by which the characterization analyses were carried out. Substantial areas of disagreement were noted and it is not possible to present an entirely coherent and self-consistent summary of these data. It is instructive, however, to consider the alternative structures which have been proposed.

Williams *et al.* (*111, 112*) established two significant relationships for an alkali-precursor gelatin (Knox P-111-20): the sedimentation coefficient was nearly proportional to the square root of the molecular weight; and the intrinsic viscosity was similarly nearly proportional to the square root of the molecular weight. In both cases the exponent of the molecular weight was thus that expected for random coil molecules that were swollen and contained immobilized solvent, rather than that for free-draining linear randomly coiled molecules. Boedtker and Doty (*113*), on the other hand, concluded that Knox P-111-20 was similar in behavior to a typical synthetic aliphatic straight-chain polymer, polyisobutylene, of equal weight-average molecular weight. This conclusion was based on the close correspondence of the weight-average dimension obtained from light scattering data, $(\overline{r_z^2})^{1/2}$, and intrinsic viscosity (258 Å, 0.38) of the gelatin with the same parameters (231 Å, 0.31) for a polyisobutylene in a good solvent and having 3,000 carbon atoms in its backbone chain. Boedtker and Doty did note, however, that the rotation about the C^α—N bond in the polypeptide backbone should have been strongly restricted because of the partial double bond character of the peptide linkage, and that rotation about 20–25% of the C^β—N bonds, those involving the proline or hydroxyproline imino ring, was not possible. Thus, if the alkali-precursor gelatins were free-draining random coils, the kinetic units would have been relatively larger and the end-to-end extension should have been greater.

In a more searching examination of the configuration of the alkali-precursor gelatins, Gouinlock et al. (*114*) took the peptide chain character into account and concluded that the experimentally estimated chain dimension was nearly twice that calculated for free rotations, a result in agreement with corresponding ratios for synthetic polymers (*115*). All other parameters, as tabulated in Chapter II, were also within the range of those expected for randomly coiled linear-chain polymers, though the range of uncertainty was of the order of 25% for the major parameters compared. The deviations from random coil behavior were all in the direction corresponding to chain stiffness and chain branching.

As in their study of the acid-precursor gelatins, Courts and Stainsby (*77*) combined both light scattering weight-average molecular weight determinations and amino end-group number-average chain weight determinations to examine the question of the possible chain branching of the alkali-precursor gelatins. The essential results are shown in Table III-22 and apply to a gelatin extracted at neutral pH from ox hide limed 3 months. The gelatin was fractionated by ethanol coacervation. Fraction X-2-2 was a subfraction of refractionated X-2. These data very convincingly demonstrate that the high molecular weight alkali-precursor gelatins are

TABLE III-22 [a]

COMPARISON OF THE WEIGHT-AVERAGE AND CHAIN-AVERAGE
MOLECULAR WEIGHTS OF AN ALKALI-PRECURSOR GELATIN

Gelatin fraction	Initial Material (%)	Reduced viscosity (dl/gm)	M_w [b]	C_n [c]
X-2	31.2	0.88	320,000	55,000
X-3	25.3	0.655	165,000	70,000
X-4	21.0	0.51	81,000	70,000
X-5	18.0	0.40	62,000	63,000
X-2-2	—	0.92	330,000	60,000

[a] Data of Courts and Stainsby (77).
[b] Weight-average molecular weight, from light scattering data.
[c] Number-average chain weight, from FDNB end-group analysis.

multichain structures, and that the single chains average about 65,000 in chain weight. There was no evidence for the breaking of weak bonds within gelatin chains by the FDNB reaction. It is not clear whether these particular gelatin samples could be classified as random coils on the same basis as those studied by Gouinlock et al. (114). The doubt arises because of the discrepancy between the values of the intrinsic viscosities obtained in the two studies for gelatins of similar molecular weight. For example, Gouinlock et al. (114) found $[\eta] = 0.69$ for $M_w = 383,000$, whereas Courts and Stainsby (77) reported a value of $[\eta] = 0.88$ for $M_w = 320,000$. In the form of a Staudinger equation, $[\eta] = KM^a$, the two sets of data may be represented by

$$[\eta] = 6 \times 10^{-4} M^{0.55} \quad \text{(Gouinlock et al.)}$$

and

$$[\eta] = 3 \times 10^{-3} M^{0.45} \quad \text{(Courts and Stainsby).}$$

Evidently the branched-chain gelatins do not show as marked a molecular weight dependence of the intrinsic viscosity as the linear-chain gelatins, although the former have generally higher intrinsic viscosities.

Once again the danger inherent in generalizations about gelatins, even those preparaed by apparently similar means, is sharply brought into focus. Obviously the gelatins described in the above paragraphs were heterogeneous and undoubtedly had very different molecular weight distributions. The gelatins approach similar behavior as the molecular weight decreases to values below 60,000. Even in this situation Pouradier and Venet (7) feel that the degraded gelatins are not homogeneous from the point of view of molecular weight, but are at least as heterogeneous as the original gelatin. Since the weakest bonds would probably the cleaved first during degradation, Pouradier and Venet (7) further concluded that the most unstable linkages in the peptide backbone could not the spaced equally along the polypeptide chains but must be located in some fairly irregular sequence.

The evidence cited appears to favor the interpretation that the alkali-precursor gelatins are branched-chain molecules. However, since the average molecular dimensions are approximately those of random coil molecules, the degree of branching must be very low, of the order of only one or two cross-linkages per chain. The existence of gelatins with molecular weights greater than the α chain weight of $\sim 100,000$ is a direct verification of the existence of inter-α-chain bonds, and the fact that the molecular weights may exceed 400,000 (114) explicitly demonstrates the existence of inter-α-unit bonds. Since the acid-precursor gelatins have lower intrinsic viscosities than the equivalent molecular weight alkali-precursor gelatins (27–29, 77), the acid-precursor gelatin molecular structures must be more compact and the cross-linkage densities higher.

The heterogeneities noted in gelatins probably result from the preparation of gelatins containing both different numbers and distributions of intact cross-linkages as a result of random hydrolysis of the original cross-linkages. The heterogeneities might also result from the very non-uniform character of the collagen stock. An understanding of the chemical nature, number, and location of the covalent interchain and intermolecular cross-linkages in collagen and gelatin is one of the central themes of current research in collagen and gelatin chemistry.

Another perplexing and currently unresolved problem is the dicrepancy between the molecular weight of an α chain ($\sim 100,000$) and the number-average chain weight ($\sim 65,000$). Two explanations appear to be reasonable. There may be a particularly weak peptide bond or other intrachain linkage within an α chain, as suggested by Gallop et al. (46), which is hydrolyzed at the same rate as the cross-linkages between α chains, or slightly more rapidly. This might lead to the appearance of a peptide chain fragment of about 300–400 residues (molecular weight 30,000–40,000) and a larger chain unit, with a molecular weight of about 60,000, cross-linked into the remaining structure. The integral molecular weight distribution curve obtained by Williams, Saunders and Cicirelli (111) for Knox P-111-20 gelatin (Fig. II-12 and Table II-10) does show a bimodal molecular weight distribution with a substantial fraction of the gelatin averaging a molecular weight of about 30,000. An alternate explanation may be that some chains may be without free terminal α-amino groups, as suggested by Courts and Stainsby (77) and Pouradier (78).

C. High Pressure Steam Extraction

An important commercial procedure for the production of gelatin and glue from bones is the direct extraction of crushed bones with high pressure steam. The advantage of this process is that the extraction can be carried out rapidly without prior pretreatment of the bones. Decalcification and prolonged liming of the resulting ossein is not required. The details of this procedure have not been published and there have been no reports concerning the molecular parameters of the gelatins produced. However, in practice the bone glues and gelatins extracted in this manner have proven to have viscosities and gel strengths equivalent to the hide gelatins and glues.

One of the more interesting features of the high pressure steam extraction is that hydrolysis of the insolubilizing linkages is carried out at high temperature and process control is achieved by keeping the gelatin at high temperature for a limited time. Conversion of the collagen to soluble form apparently takes place while the collagen is surrounded by its sheath of hydroxyapatite crystals. The gelatin is extracted at lower temperature to avoid degradation. It is probable that the high temperature hydrolysis is less specific than the low temperature hydrolysis of pretreated collagenous stock.

REFERENCES

1. P. M. Gallop, *Arch. Biochem. Biophys.* **54**, 486, 501 (1955).

2. R. C. M. Smith, *J. Am. Chem. Soc.* **41**, 135 (1919).

3. J. Thaureaux, *Bull. Soc. Chim. Biol.* **27**, 327 (1945).

4. E. O. Kraemer and J. R. Fanselow, *J. Phys. Chem.* **29**, 1169 (1925).

5. C. Robinson, *in* "Nature and Structure of Collagen "(J. T. Randall, ed.), p. 96. Butterworths, London, 1953.

6. H. Boedtker and P. Doty, *J. Am. Chem. Soc.* **78**, 4267 (1956).

7. J. Pouradier and A. M. Venet, *J. Chim. Phys.* **49**, 238 (1952).

8. V. N. Orekhovich and V. O. Shpikiter, *Dodklady Akad. Nauk S.S.S.R.* **101**, 529 (1955).

9. A. A. Tustanovskii and V. O. Shpikiter, *Vopr. Med. Khim.* **4**, 70 (1952).

10. E. H. L. Chun and P. Doty *in* "Recent Advances in Gelatin and Glue Research" (G. Stainsby, ed.), p. 261. Pergamon Press, New York, 1958.

11. P. Doty and T. Nishihara, *in* "Recent Advances in Gelatin and Glue Research" (G. Stainsby, ed.), p. 92. Pergamon Press, New York, 1958.

12. K. A. Piez, E. Weiss, and M. S. Lewis, *J. Biol. Chem.* **235**, 1987 (1960).

13. K. A. Piez, M. S. Lewis, G. R. Martin, and J. Gross, *Biochim. Biophys. Acta* **53**, 596 (1961).

14. A. Veis, J. Anesey, and J. Cohen, *Arch. Biochem. Biophys.* **94**, 20 (1961).

15. A. Veis, J. Anesey, and J. Cohen, *Arch. Biochem. Biophys.* **98**, 104 (1952).

16. K. Altgelt, A. J. Hodge, and F. O. Schmitt, *Proc. Natl. Acad. Sci. U.S.* **47**, 1914 (1961).

17. A. Veis and J. Cohen, *Nature* **186**, 720 (1960).

18. R. V. Rice, *Proc. Natl. Acad. Sci. U.S.* **46**, 1186 (1960).

19. W. M. Ames, *J. Soc. Chem. Ind. (London)*, **63**, 200, 234, 277, 303 (1944).

20. W. M. Ames, *J. Soc. Chem. Ind. (London)* **64**, 242 (1945).

21. W. M. Ames, *J. Soc. Chem. Ind. (London)* **66**, 279 (1947).

22. W. M. Ames, *J. Sci. Food Agr.* **3**, 454 (1952).

23. W. M. Ames, *J. Sci. Food Agr.* **3**, 579 (1952).

24. W. M. Ames, *J. Sci. Food Agr.* **8**, 169 (1957).

25. A. Veis and J. Cohen, *J. Am. Chem. Soc.* **76**, 2476 (1954).

26. A. Veis and J. Cohen, *J. Am. Chem. Soc.* **77**, 2364 (1955).

27. A. Veis, D. N. Eggenberger, and J. Cohen, *J. Am. Chem. Soc.* **77**, 2368 (1955).

28. A. Veis and J. Cohen, *J. Am. Chem. Soc.* **78**, 6238 (1956).

29. A. Veis and J. Cohen, *J. Polymer Sci.* **26**, 113 (1957).

30. A. Veis, J. Anesey, and J. Cohen, *in* "Recent Advances in Gelatin and Glue Research" (G. Stainsby, ed.), p. 155. Pergamon Press, New York, 1958.

31. A. Veis and J. Cohen, *J. Phys. Chem.* **62**, 459 (1958).

32. A. Veis, J. Anesey and J. Cohen, *J. Am. Leather Chemists Assoc.* **55**, 548 (1960).

33. W. A. Loeven, *J. Soc. Leather Trades' Chemists* **38**, 117 (1954).

34. A. Veis and J. Cohen, *Abstr. 135th Meeting Am. Chem. Soc.*, Boston, 1959 p. 25c.

35. C. E. Weir and J. Carter, *J. Res. Natl. Bur. Std.* **44**, 599 (1950).

36. M. P. Drake and A. Veis, *Federation Proc.* **21**, 405 (1962).

37. K. H. Gustavson, "The Chemistry and Reactivity of Collagen" Academic Press, New York, 1956.

38. W. Grassman, H. Endres, and A. Steber, *Z. Naturforsch* **9b**, 513 (1954).

39. K. Konno and K. I. Altman, *Nature* **181**, 995 (1958).

40. A. Steigmann, *Sci. Ind. Phot.* **21**, 10 (1950).

41. J. Pouradier and A. M. Venet, *Bull. Soc. Chim. France* **19**, 347 (1952).

42. J. M. Landucci, *Bull. Soc. Chim. France* **21**, 120 (1954).

43. J. M. Landucci, *Bull. Soc. Chim. France* **21**, 124 (1954).

44. J. M. Landucci, J. Pouradier, and M. Durante, *in* "Recent Advances in Gelatin and Glue Research" (G. Stainsby, ed.), p. 62, Pergamon Press, New York, 1958.

45. R. A. Milch, *J. Am. Leather Chemists Assoc.* **57**, 581 (1962).

46. P. M. Gallop, S. Seifter, and E. Meilman, *Nature* **183**, 1659 (1959).

47. J. Bello, *Nature* **184**, 241 (1960).

48. H. Hörmann, *Leder* **11**, 173 (1960).

49. H. Hörmann, *Beitr. Silikose-Forsch.*, *Sonderband* **4**, 205 (1960).

50. H. Hörmann, A. Riedel, T. Altenschöpfer, and M. Klenk, *Leder* **12**, 175 (1961).

51. A. Veis and M. Weiss, unpublished results (1963).

52. R. de la Burde, L. Peckham, and A. Veis, *J. Biol. Chem.* **238**, 189 (1963).

53. H. B. Bensusan, *Biochemistry* **1**, 215 (1962).

54. A. Rich and F. H. C. Crick, *J. Mol. Biol.* **3**, 483 (1962).

55. P. Grabar and J. Morel, *Bull. Soc. Chim. Biol.* **32**, 643 (1950).

56. J. W. Janus, *in* "Recent Advances in Gelatin and Glue Research" (G. Stainsby, ed.), p. 214. Pergamon Press, New York, 1958.

57. O. O. Blumenfeld and P. M. Gallop, *Biochemistry* **1**, 947 (1962).

58. J. Mechanic and M. Levy, *J. Am. Chem. Soc.* **81**, 1889 (1959).

59. M. Levy, G. Cabrera and L. Fishman, *Abstr. 5th Intern. Congr. Biochem.*, Moscow, 1961 p. 38.

60. J. H. Bowes and J. A. Moss, *Biochem. J.* **55**, 735 (1953).

61. E. Kulonen, *Ann. Med. Exptl. Biol. Fenniae* (*Helsinki*) **33**, No. 8 (1948).

62. M. Briefer and J. H. Cohen, *Ind. Eng. Chem.* **20**, 408 (1928).

63. S. E. Sheppard and R. C. Houck, *J. Phys. Chem.* **34**, 273 (1930).

64. W. M. Ames, *J. Soc. Chem. Ind.* (*London*), **66**, 270 (1947).

65. W. M. Ames, *J. Soc. Leather Trades Chemists* **33**, 407 (1949).

66. J. H. Bowes and R. H. Kenten, *Biochem. J.* **43**, 358 (1948).

67. J. E. Eastoe and A. A. Leach, *in* "Recent Advances in Gelatin and Glue Research" (G. Stainsby, ed.), p. 173. Pergamon Press, New York, 1958.

68. J. H. Bowes and J. A. Moss, *Nature* **168**, 514 (1951).

69. R. L. Sykes, *J. Soc. Leather Trades Chemists* **36**, 267 (1952).

70. A. Courts, *Biochem. J.* **58**, 70 (1954).

71. A. G. Lowther, *Biochem. J.* **54**, 638 (1953).

72. J. Pouradier and A. M. Venet, *J. Chim. Phys.* **47**, 11 (1950).

73. G. Ehrlich and P. Doty, *J. Am. Chem. Soc.* **76**, 3764 (1954).

74. C. W. Carr and L. Topol, *J. Phys. Chem.* **54**, 176 (1950).

75. J. Bello, H. C. A. Riese, and J. R. Vinograd, *J. Phys. Chem.* **60**, 1299 (1956).

76. R. S. Bear, *Advan. Protein Chem.* **7**, 69 (1952).

77. A. Courts and G. Stainsby, *in* "Recent Advances in Gelatin and Glue Research" (G. Stainsby, ed.), p. 100. Pergamon Press, New York, 1958.

78. J. Pouradier, *in* "Recent Advances in Gelatin and Glue Research" (G. Stainsby, ed.), p. 265. Pergamon Press, New York, 1958.

79. M. Kaye and R. H. Marriott, *J. Intern. Soc. Leather Trades' Chemists* **9**, 591 (1925).

80. R. H. Marriott, *J. Intern. Soc. Leather Trades' Chemists* **15**, 25 (1931).

81. J. H. Highberger and H. C. Stecker, *J. Am. Leather Chemists Assoc.* **36**, 368 (1941).

82. A. Küntzel and J. Phillips, *Collegium* pp. 193, 207, 213 (1933).

83. V. Kubelka and G. Knoedel, *Collegium* p. 49 (1938).

84. H. Vickery, *Biochem. J.* **29**, 2710 (1935).

85. W. Grassmann and H. Hörmann, *Z. Physiol. Chem.* **292**, 24 (1953).

86. K. Heyns and G. Wolff, *Z. Physiol. Chem.* **304**, 200 (1956).

87. K. Heyns and G. Legler, *in* "Recent Advances in Gelatin and Glue Research". (G. Stainsby, ed.), p. 186. Pergamon Press, New York, 1958.

88. S. Akabori, K. Ohno, T. Ikenaka, and A. Nagata, *Proc. Japan Acad.* **29**, 561 (1953).

89. J. H. Bowes and R. H. Kenten, *Biochem. J.* **43**, 358 (1948).

90. J. H. Bowes, *J. Soc. Leather Trades' Chemists* **33**, 176 (1949).

91. R. C. Warner, *J. Biol. Chem.* **142**, 705 (1942).

92. S. W. Fox, *J. Biol. Chem.* **123**, 687 (1938).

93. P. B. Hamilton and R. A. Anderson, *J. Biol. Chem.* **211**, 95 (1954).

94. S. Moore and W. H. Stein, *J. Biol. Chem.* **192**, 663 (1951).

95. R. de la Burde, Ph.D. Dissertation, Technische Hochschule Aachen, 1962.

96. J. H. Bowes and R. H. Kenten, *Biochem. J.* **46**, 1 (1950).

97. J. H. Bowes and R. H. Kenten, *Biochem. J.* **46**, 524 (1950).

98. J. H. Bowes, *Biochem. J.* **46**, 530 (1950).

99. J. H. Bowes and R. H. Kenten, *Biochem. J.* **43**, 365 (1948).

100. W. Grassmann, K. Hannig, H. Endres, and A. Riedel, *Z. Physiol. Chem.* **306**, 123 (1956).

101. W. Grassmann, K. Hannig, and M. Schleyer, *Z. Physiol. Chem.* **322**, 71 (1960).

102. W. Grassmann, A. Nordwig, and H. Hörmann, *Z. Physiol. Chem.* **323**, 48 (1961).

103. A. Nordwig, H. Hörmann, K. Kühn, and W. Grassmann, *Z. Physiol. Chem.* **325,** 242 (1961).

104. A. J. Hodge and F. O. Schmitt, *Proc. Natl. Acad. Sci. U.S.* **44**, 418 (1958).

105. W. Grassmann, *Leder*, **6**, 241 (1955).

106. A. Courts, *Biochem. J.* **74**, 238 (1960).

107. A. Kuntzel, N. Cars, and E. Heidemann, *in* "Recent Advances in Gelatin and Glue Research" (G. Stainsby, ed.), p. 149. Pergamon Press, New York, 1958.

108. A. G. Ward, N. T. Crosby, D. G. Higgs, R. Reed, and G. Stainsby, *Abstr. 8th Congr. Intern. Union Leather Chemists Soc., Washington, D.C., 1961* p. 15.

109. J. Pouradier and A. M. Venet, *J. Chim. Phys.* **47**, 391 (1950).

110. J. Pouradier and A. M. Venet, *J. Chim. Phys.* **49**, 85 (1952).

111. J. W. Williams, W. M. Saunders, and J. S. Cicirelli, *J. Phys. Chem.* **58**, 774 (1954).

112. J. W. Williams, *in* "Recent Advances in Gelatin and Glue Research" (G. Stainsby, ed.), p. 106. Pergamon Press, New York, 1958.

113. H. Boedtker and P. Doty, *J. Phys. Chem.* **58**, 968 (1954).

114. E. V., Jr. Gouinlock, P. J. Flory, and H. A. Scheraga, *J. Polymer Sci.* **16**, 383 (1955).

115. P. J. Flory, "Principles of Polymer Chemistry", p, 618. Cornell Univ. Press, Ithaca New York, 1953.

116. K. A. Piez, E. Eigner, and M. Lewis, *Biochemistry* **2**, 58 (1963).

The Degradation of Gelatin

I. Introduction

Gelatin is not stable when dissolved in aqueous solvent systems. It under-
goes a progressive hydrolytic degradation to lower average molecular
weight with a concomitant decay in many useful physical properties. The
rate of hydrolytic degradation is a function of the temperature and pH of
the system, and to a lesser extent of the pressure on the solution and the
nature of the other solutes which might be present. In attempting to understand the properties of collagen in terms of the gelatins which have been
derived from it, one must take into account the changes occurring in the
gelatin after it has been extracted. The degradative changes are also of
serious technical importance since they set the practical limits of permissible conditions during chemical modification of the gelatins, and, obviously,
affect the shelf-life and quality of gelatin and glue solutions. Many stud-

ies have been carried out to determine the details of the kinetics of the hydrolytic degradation reactions.

The mechanisms of various modes of enzymatic hydrolysis reactions have also been the subjects of considerable research effort. The primary emphasis in these studies has been on the elucidation of the amino acid sequences in collagen and gelatin. The data gained from the sequence analyses have been very useful in the analysis of configurational transitions in the gelatins. In the ensuing discussion both the hydrolytic and enzymatic degradation of gelatin will be approached via consideration of the model systems which have been set up in each case. The results of the several degradation studies will then be correlated in terms of the relative stabilities of the various types of covalent bond in the peptide backbones and in the cross-linked regions of the gelatins.

II. HYDROLYTIC DEGRADATIONS

A. Models of Chain Degradation

The simplest model that can be envisioned for gelatin is that of infinitely long single chains in which every peptide bond can be hydrolytically ruptured with equal probability. The further hydrolytic cleavage of any peptide bond in the smaller chain fragments can also be considered to be equally probable, irrespective of the size of the peptide fragment involved. This model is quite similar to the first model discussed on page 166 in Chapter III and was first examined by Kuhn (1, 2). Following the treatment given by Kuhn, we designate the probability that any particular peptide bond will be broken as α. The probability that this particular bond is unbroken is then $(1 - \alpha)$. In a chain containing $(i - 1)$ bonds or i groups the probability that the particular bond under consideration is the first bond in the chain is then the probability that the bond just before it in the infinite chain is broken, and that the ith bond after it is broken but that the $(i - 1)$ bonds in between are intact. In other words, the probability that a chain contains i units and $(i - 1)$ bonds is

$$P_i = (\alpha_0)(\alpha_i) \prod_{j=1}^{i-1} (1 - \alpha_j) = \alpha^2 (1 - \alpha)^{i-1} \tag{1}$$

If N is the total number of units in the system, in this case the total number of amino acid residues, then the number of i-mers, N_i, is

$$N_i = NP_i = N\alpha^2 (1 - \alpha)^{i-1} \tag{2}$$

while the weight fraction of each i-mer, w_i, is

$$w_i = \frac{iN_i}{N} = i\alpha^2(1 - \alpha)^{i-1} \tag{3}$$

Setting M_0 as the monomer residue weight, the molecular weight of an i-mer, M_i, is then just iM_0, and the molecular weight averages become

$$M_n = \frac{\sum N_i M_i}{\sum N_i} = \frac{\sum iN \alpha^2(1 - \alpha)^{i-1} M_0}{\sum N \alpha^2(1 - \alpha)^{i-1}} \tag{4}$$

$$M_w = \frac{\sum w_i M_i}{\sum w_i} = \frac{\sum i^2 \alpha^2(1 - \alpha)^{i-1} M_0}{\sum i \alpha^2(1 - \alpha)^{i-1}} \tag{5}$$

$$M_z = \frac{\sum N_i M_i^3}{\sum N_i M_i^2} = \frac{\sum i^3 \alpha^2(1 - \alpha)^{i-1} M_0}{\sum i^2 \alpha^2(1 - \alpha)^{i-1}} \tag{6}$$

The summations in Eq. 4, 5, and 6 can be readily reduced to the very simple forms

$$M_n = \frac{M_0}{\alpha} \tag{7}$$

$$M_w = \frac{2 M_0}{\alpha} \tag{8}$$

$$M_z = \frac{3 M_0}{\alpha} \tag{9}$$

Equations 7, 8, and 9 indicate that if one followed the number- and weight-average molecular weights during the hydrolytic degradation of gelatin, these two parameters should maintain a constant ratio, $M_w/M_n = 2$, during the entire depolymerization. Furthermore, these equations specify that M_w/M_n can never exceed a value of 2. As indicated in Chaper II, Williams et al. (3) found that $M_w/M_n = 2.6$ for Knox P-111-20 gelatin, in agreement with the data of Boedtker and Doty (4). The weight fraction distribution function for chain length, given by Eq. 3, is a function with a single maximum, and provides that the maximum number of monomer units must occur in polymers with the number-average chain weight. The infinite chain model with equal probability of chain scission cannot, therefore, accomodate bimodal molecular weight distributions.

Scatchard, Oncley, Williams, and Brown (5) modified the basic model by assuming that collagen contained a number of particularly labile bonds and that each of these was ruptured during the formation of soluble gelatin, yielding a system of peptide chains each containing only the more refractory peptide bonds. With the further assumption that the weaker linkages were distributed in the original collagen in a uniform manner, these workers then proposed that the gelatin going into solution should be an essentially homogeneous system of nearly equal chain-length molecules. The term "parent gelatin" was coined to describe such systems. The degradation of the parent gelatin was then treated in terms of the basic Kuhn hypothesis of equal probability of rupture of all chain bonds. Scatchard et al. (5) set p equal to the number of amino acid residues per parent gelatin molecule, and then considered that any gelatin solution would consist of a mixture of molecules with less than p residues. These degraded molecules could have any number of residues from $(p-1)$ to 1. The fraction of molecules with p residues, c_p, is then

$$c_p = (1-\alpha)^{p-1} \tag{10}$$

and the weight fraction of molecules with i bonds intact, c_i, is given by

$$c_i = [2\alpha + (p-i-1)\,\alpha^2]^i \, \frac{(1-\alpha)^{i-1}}{p} \tag{11}$$

Setting $i = xp$ and $\alpha p = a$, where x is some fraction between 0 and 1, and presuming that p approaches ∞ as an upper limit, then

$$c_p = e^{-a} \tag{12}$$

and

$$c_i \Delta i = \int f(x)\,dx = \int ax[2 + a(1-x)]e^{-ax}\,dx \tag{13}$$

from which one may derive the average molecular weight relationships

$$M_n = \frac{M_p}{1+\alpha} \tag{14}$$

$$M_w = \frac{2\,M_p}{a}\left[1 - \frac{1-e^{-a}}{a}\right] \approx \frac{2\,M_p}{a} \quad \text{when } a \gg 1 \tag{15}$$

and

$$\frac{M_w}{M_n} = 2\left(\frac{1+a}{a}\right)\left(1 - \frac{1-e^{-a}}{a}\right) \tag{16}$$

Scatchard *et al.* (*5*) applied these equations to the analysis of a bone gelatin. The molecular weight was determined by ultracentrifugation, with the result that $M_n = 35,000$, $M_w = 57,000$. Hence $M_w/M_n = 1.6$ and, from Eq. 16, $a = 1.50$ and $p = 1170$, so that $M_p = 110,000$.

Pouradier and Venet (*6*) pointed out that it was difficult to determine the degree of depolymerization, α, of the parent gelatin with any certainty, since the value of α depends on the value assigned to p. They suggested an alternative approach. Since all of the bonds in the parent gelatin are assumed to break with equal probability, then the rate of increase in α depends only on the number of bonds intact at any time, or

$$\frac{d\alpha}{dt} = k(1 - \alpha) \tag{17}$$

Also,

$$\frac{M_0}{M_n} = \alpha + \frac{1 - \alpha}{p} \tag{18}$$

where M_0 is the monomer molecular weight. Hence,

$$d\alpha = -\frac{M_0}{M_n}\left(\frac{1 - \alpha}{M_n - M_0}\right) dM_n \tag{19}$$

and, combining Eqs. 17 and 19, one obtains Eqs. 20

$$\frac{1}{M_n}\left(\frac{dM_n}{dt}\right) = -\frac{k}{M_0}(M_n - M_0) \tag{20}$$

which indicates that a plot of $(1/\overline{M}_n)\ (d\overline{M}_n/dt)$ vs. M_n should be linear. Pouradier and Venet (*6*) tested Eq. 20 by studying the kinetics of the degradation of Kodak F-74 gelatin at its isoelectric point. Figure IV-1 shows the rate data obtained for the 80° hydrolysis of F-74, plotted according to Eq. 20. The molecular weights were determined by osmometry. The nonlinearity of these data indicated that the basic assumptions of the treatment of Scatchard and his co-workers (*5*) could not be accepted without modification.

Pouradier and Venet (*6*) proposed that the proper route to the solution of this problem was to accept two of the basic postulates of Scatchard *et al.* (*5*), specifically that (1) the probability of rupture of a bond does not depend on its position in the macromolecule, and (2) the products of the degradative hydrolysis cannot be recombined; but to reject the third postulate that the probability of rupture of a bond did not depend on the weight of the molecule of which it was a part. Primarily arguing from the fact that the partial hydrolysis of gelatin does not lead to the appearance of any significant number of monomeric amino acids, as predicted by the analysis of Scatchard *et al.* (*5*), they assumed that the probability of the rupture of a peptide bond depended on the weight of the molecule containing that bond.

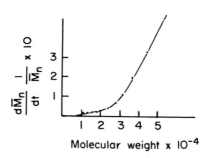

FIG. IV-1. Test of Eq. 20 for the isoelectric degradation of Kodak F-74 gelatin at 80°. According to that equation the plot should have resulted in a straight line [Pouradier and Venet (*6*)].

If M_0 is the monomer residue weight, then a molecule of weight M_x will contain $i = M_x/M_0$ residues and $(i-1)$ intact bonds. Designating the number of molecules of weight M_x at time t by N_{xt}, then the increase in the number of molecules in the system in time dt by the rupture of molecules of weight M_x is

$$dN_{xt} = k_x N_{xt} (i-1) \, dt \qquad (21)$$

where k_x is the probability of rupture of a bond in a molecule of weight M_x. The total increase in the number of molecules during dt is

$$dN_t = \sum_{M_x = M_0}^{M_x \to \infty} k_x N_{xt} (i_x - 1) \, dt \qquad (22)$$

or

$$\frac{dN_t}{dt} = \frac{1}{M_0} \sum_{M_x = M_0}^{M_x \to \infty} k_x N_{xt} (M_x - M_0) \qquad (23)$$

Equation 23 reduces to Eq. 20 if k_x is designated to be a constant independent of x. However, the principal assumption of Pouradier and Venet (*6*) is to propose that $k_x = F(M_x)$. The simplest function would be to set $k_x = k\,M_x$, or to state that the probability of rupturing a bond is directly proportional to the weight of the molecule considered. Equation 23 then becomes

$$\frac{dN_t}{dt} = \frac{k}{M_0} \sum N_{xt} M_x (M_x - M_0) \tag{24}$$

The number-average molecular weight at time t is

$$M_{nt} = \frac{\sum N_{xt} M_x}{\sum N_{xt}} = \frac{\sum N_{xt} M_x}{N_t} \tag{25}$$

whence

$$dN_t = - dM_{nt} \left(\frac{\sum N_{xt} M_x}{M_{nt}^2} \right) \tag{26}$$

Combining Eq. 26 with Eq. 24 Pouradier and Venet found

$$\frac{1}{M_n^2} \frac{dM_n}{dt} = - \frac{k}{M_0} (M_w - M_0) \tag{27}$$

where M_w is the weight-average molecular weight. Equation 27 is the analog of Eq. 20 and states that a plot of $(1/M_n^2)\,(dM_n/dt)$ should be a linear function of M_w. Since Pouradier and Venet were measuring M_n only via osmotic pressure measurements they could not evaluate M_w. However, assuming $M_w = f\,M_n$, Eq. 27 was restated as

$$\frac{1}{M_n^2} \frac{dM_n}{dt} = - \frac{kf}{M_0} \left(M_n - \frac{M_0}{f} \right) \tag{28}$$

justifying a plot of the left-hand side of Eq. 28 vs. M_n. Such a plot of the same data as in Fig. IV-1 is shown in Fig. IV-2. Though not perfect

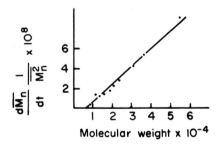

Fig. IV-2. Test of Eq. 28 for the isoelectric degradation of Kodak F-74 gelatin at 80°. The fit of the data is much closer than in the plot illustrated in Fig. IV-1 [Pouradier and Venet (6)].

by any means, the agreement of the data with Eq. 28 is much more satisfactory than the agreement with Eq. 20, indicating that the assumption
of the dependence of the probability of chain rupture on the chain weight
is in the correct direction.

These analyses of Pouradier and Venet (6) have not been tested in
any greater detail than given above. It seems likely that further modi-
fications of the single-chain model would have to concentrate on a more
detailed formulation for the functional relationship $k_x = F(M_x)$. The simplest approach would be to consider that the gelatins contained several
sets of peptide bonds of varying average free energy of hydrolysis. The
more reactive bonds would split first, leaving the chain fragments progressively more and more resistant to subsequent hydrolytic rupture. A
second direction for further kinetic and statistical evaluation would be
the analysis of a cross-linked chain network model. In this case, chain rupture or cross-link rupture could conceivably occur in such a way as initially not to decrease the molecular weight of the system. Indeed, such a
mode of degradation might prevent a fall in viscosity or even lead to an
initial increase in viscosity. [Unpublished studies in the author's labora-
tory (7) with high molecular weight fractions of a cross-linked gelatin
have shown that both the viscosity and dissymmetry of light scattering
of the gelatin solutions first increased about 10% before falling off to lower
values.]

B. Thermal Degradation at the Isoelectric pH

The extent and rate of hydrolytic degradation of gelatin depends on
the pH of the system, temperature of heating, and length of time the hydrolytic reaction is allowed to proceed. Ames (8) established the fact that
the hydrolytic degradation proceeded most slowly at neutral pH, and
demonstrated that, in unbuffered systems, solutions of gelatins acid to
their isoelectric point shifted to higher pH values during degradation,
while the pH of solutions basic to the isoelectric point decreased. The pH
remained constant for degradations carried out at the isoelectric point.
Since there is a very marked pH dependence of the hydrolysis rate, the
isoelectric degradation represents the simplest case.

Pouradier and Venet (6) examined the kinetics of the degradation of
Kodak F-74, alkali-precursor calf skin gelatin, pI = 4.75, at its isoelectric point. They followed the number-average molecular weight, M_n, and
intrinsic viscosity, $[\eta]$, as a function of time and temperature. They first
verified the results of Northrop (9, 10) and Ames (8), who had observed

that the initial rate of the degradation was independent of the gelatin concentration. Pouradier and Venet also found that a variety of bactericidal agents, necessary in order to obtain consistent results, did not affect the rate of hydrolysis at the concentrations used and that oxygen dissolved in the solutions also had no effect. Figures IV-3 and 4 show the changes

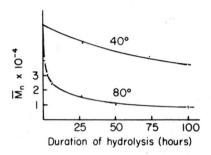

Fig. IV-3. Molecular weight decay during the isoelectric degradation of Kodak F-74 gelatin at the indicated temperature [Pouradier and Venet (6)].

in M_n and η_{red} as a function of time at 40° and 80°. The F-74 gelatin had an initial M_n of 65,000 and $[\eta]$ of 0.450. The use of Eq. 44 of Chapter II led to a value of 102,000 for the viscosity-average molecular weight, M_v, for an initial M_v/M_n ratio of 1.57. The value of M_v/M_n is a measure of the polydispersity of the system.

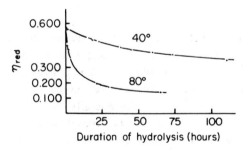

Fig. IV-4. Decrease in reduced viscosity during the isoelectric degradation of Kodak F-74 gelatin at the indicated temperature [Pouradier and Venet (6)].

At 80° both M_n and η_{red} fell rapidly to very low values and then remained constant for more than 50 hours. In this final state M_n was close to 7000, and it was concluded that the gelatin molecule contained segments of average weight 7000 in which the peptide bonds were particularly resistant to hydrolysis. M_v was calculated from $[\eta]$ at small intervals throughout the first 50 hours of the 80° degradation, and M_t/M_n was computed. This ratio remained essentially constant at ~ 1.6 for the first 20 hours during which M_n decreased from 65,000 to 17,500. Pouradier and Venet (6) concluded from this that the polydispersity of the gelatin was not altered by the hydrolytic degradation. A comparison of the times required at 40° and at 80° to reduce η_{red} to the same amount, and the use of the van't Hoff equation in the form

$$\Delta H^\ddagger = \frac{RT_1T_2}{T_2 - T_1} \ln \frac{t_1}{t_2} \tag{29}$$

yielded an activation energy for hydrolysis, $\Delta H^\ddagger$, varying from 18,000 to 22,000 cal, depending on the extent of the reaction. This variable $\Delta H^\ddagger$ suggested that different types of chain linkage were being broken at different stages of the reaction.

C. Effects of pH on the Rate of Hydrolysis

Ames (8) found that both the gel strength and viscosity could be used as measures of the extent of hydrolytic degradation, and he compared the pH dependence of these properties for two gelatins, one an acid-precursor gelatin with an isoelectric point of 7.95, the other an alkali-precursor gelatin with an isoelectric point of 4.76. Both gelatins were heated at 85° for 2 hours in 2% solutions. The viscosities, in centistokes, and the gel strength, as Bloom 6.66%, are shown in Figs. IV-5 and 6. These data led Ames to note that the acid-precursor gelatins were more susceptible to alkaline degradation than to acid degradation, whereas the alkali-precursor gelatins were more stable at alkaline pH and much more readily degraded by acids. These differences were much more apparent in the variations in gel strength than in the viscosity measurements.

Croome (11), therefore, used the gel strength as the principal criterion of degradation in a detailed study of the kinetics of the hydrolysis reactions. He examined a limed ossein gelatin, isoelectric pH 4.75, Bloom gel strength 6.66%, 250 gm, holding samples at 60°, 70°, or 80° and at pH's in the range 2.08–8.9 for varying periods of time. The samples were prepared at 6.66% in standard Bloom jars and were quenched to 10° immediately following the degradation. Each quenched sample was aged for 16–18 hours at 10° before the gel strength was determined. Croome argued that the gel strength was proportional to the content of undegraded gelatin, and that the decrease in gel strength was, therefore, a direct measure of the decomposition of the gellable protein remaining. He discounted the possibility that the low molecular weight, nongellable fractions would have an adverse effect on the gellable protein remaining. Both of these assumptions are subject to considerable question but neither has been examined critically.

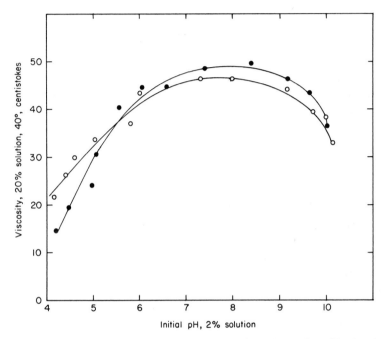

FIG. IV-5. Effect of pH during thermal degradation of gelatin as reflected by the viscosity of the degraded gelatin solutions. Degradation, 2 hours at 85° and the designated pH; O, acid-precursor gelatin, initial viscosity 68.5 centistokes; ●, alkali-precursor gelatin, initial viscosity 74.1 [Ames (8)].

In spite of the interpretational difficulties, the data plotted as logarithm of the concentration of gellable protein vs. degradation time yielded a series of straight lines with slopes varying according to the pH and temperature. This linearity indicated that at constant pH the gelatin hydrolysis was a first order reaction with the rate constant, k, defined by Eq. 30. In Eq. 30,

$$k = \frac{1}{t} \ln \left(\frac{a}{a - x} \right) \tag{30}$$

a is the original gelatin concentration, or gel strength, and x is amount of gelatin decomposed at time t to a nongellable state so that $(a - x)$

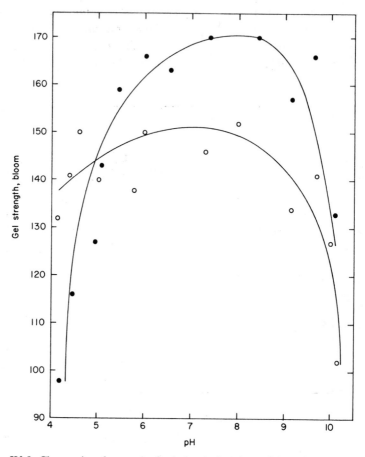

FIG. IV-6. Changes in gel strength of gelatins during thermal degradation as a function of pH. Degradation conditions as in Fig. IV-5; ●, acid-precursor gelatin; ○, alkali-precursor gelatin [Ames (8)].

is just the gel strength at t. Figure IV-7 shows the dependence of the first order rate constant on the pH at 60°. The curve is symmetrical about the minimum point, pH_m, and there is only a slight shift in pH_m towards more alkaline values at elevated temperatures. Croome defined pH_m as the iso-catalytic point at which the catalytic effects of hydrogen and hydroxyl ions on the hydrolysis are equal, implying that the hydrolysis reaction is the sum of two independent simultaneous reactions, so that k may be written

$$k = 55.5\, k_w + k_H[H] + k_{OH}\, \frac{K_w}{[H]} \qquad (31)$$

where K_w is the ion product of water, and k_w is the "uncatalyzed" spontaneous hydrolysis reaction in undissociated water. The values of the various rate constants at 60°, 70°, and 80° are listed in Table IV-1. Plots

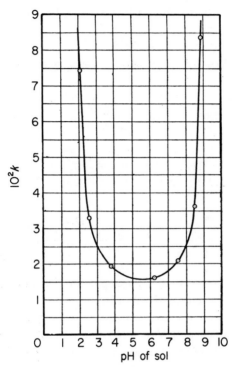

FIG. IV-7. The first order rate constant for decay of gel strength at 60° as a function of pH [Croome (11)].

TABLE IV-1 [a]

FIRST ORDER RATE CONSTANTS[b] FOR GELATIN HYDROLYSIS AS A FUNCTION OF TEMPERATURE

Individual rate constants	Value of k (sec^{-1}) at		
	60°	70°	80°
k_w	2.9×10^{-4}	5.6×10^{-4}	1.14×10^{-3}
k_H	7.0	14.3	23.35
k_{OH}	976.8	2742	8492

[a] Data of Croome (11).
[b] Defined in Eq. 31.

of the logarithms of the overall k's vs. $1/T$ also resulted in straight lines at all pH's (Fig. IV-8), and the activation energies calculated from these data are tabulated in Table IV-2. These activation energies cover the same range as those determined by Pouradier and Venet (6), and their variability suggests that different bonds might be involved at different pH.

TABLE IV-2 [a]

ACTIVATION ENERGIES FOR GELATIN HYDROLYSIS AS A FUNCTION OF pH

	pH						
	3.05	3.60	4.75	7.10	8.50	9.35	9.85
Rate constant							
k_{60}	0.0742	0.0327	0.0197	0.0166	0.0211	0.0369	0.0840
k_{70}/k_{60}	2.8	2.8	2.0	2.0	2.0	2.0	2.8
Activation energy							
E (kcal/mole)	25.63	25.63	17.25	17.25	17.25	17.25	26.00

[a] Data of Croome (11).

It is more likely, however, that the activation energies are varying according to the extent of hydrolysis. At extreme pH the extent of hydrolysis is greater and the average activation energy is higher. This is similar to the finding by Pouradier and Venet (6) that $\Delta H^{\ddagger}$ appeared to increase, at constant pH and temperature, as the extent of degradation increased.

D. Chemical Changes during Hydrolytic Breakdown

Courts (12) analyzed the chemical changes during thermal degradation by quantitative examination of the amino-terminal residues created during hydrolysis. He examined a deionized limed ossein gelatin, isoelectric pH 5.1, Bloom gel strength 6.66%, 217 gm, and viscosity, 6.66%, 40°, 7.05 centipoise. Courts determined the number of amino-terminal residues, the viscosity, and gel rigidity as a function of pH, temperature, and time. The data are shown in Table IV-3 as a function of pH for a series of degradations carried out at 75° for a 24-hour period in sealed tubes. All amino-terminal residue results in the body of the table are in terms of moles per 10^5 gm gelatin. A more striking representation of these data is given in Fig. IV-9, in which the appearance of amino-terminal residues of each kind is plotted as the percent of total residues created as a function of the degradation pH. Peptide bonds involving the amino groups of serine and threonine seem especially labile to both acidic and basic hydrolysis. Aspartic acid peptides are particularly susceptible to acid hydrolysis only, whereas peptide bonds involving the amino group of glutamic acid are stable. Glycine peptides are intermediate in stability.

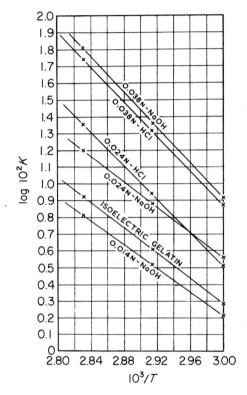

FIG. IV-8. The first order rate constant for decay of gel strength as a function of temperature [Croome (11)].

The C_n values of Table IV-3 are plotted in Fig. IV-10 as a function of the pH. The curve is reminiscent of Fig. IV-8, though not quite so symmetrical. It should be borne in mind that, as Courts and Stainsby have demonstrated (13), the C_n values do not necessarily correspond to molecular weights, particularly in the less degraded samples. For the same reason, the reduced viscosities may not follow the same molecular weight–viscosity function at all stages of the hydrolysis or at each pH. This behavior is evident in the crossover of the two curves in Fig. IV-11. Courts (12) pointed out a discrepancy between his results and those of Pouradier

TABLE IV-3 [a]

CHANGE IN N-TERMINAL RESIDUES OF LIMED OSSEIN GELATIN pH 5.1

pH of degradation [b]	1	2	3	4	5	7	9	10	11	12	Undegraded
N-Terminal residues											
Glycine	18.54	11.68	10.28	2.90	1.30	1.25	1.45	2.48	7.76	14.07	0.95
Serine	2.41	0.67	0.31	0.33	0.22	0.21	0.20	0.31	1.11	2.03	0.29
Threonine	2.53	0.58	0.36	0.21	0.16	0.14	0.13	0.21	0.42	1.26	0.12
Alanine	2.11	2.63	0.16	0.98	0.17	0.07	0.21	0.25	0.43	1.82	0.14
Aspartic acid	4.14	4.41	0.88	0.46	0.22	0.19	0.13	0.13	0.23	0.52	0.08
Glutamic acid	1.23	0.54	0.50	0.27	0.13	0.09	0.12	0.17	0.46	0.52	0.14
Others	0.82	0.45	1.10	0.23	0.05	0.05	0.00	0.05	0.22	0.41	0.00
Total	31.78	20.98	13.59	5.38	2.25	2.00	2.24	3.61	10.63	20.63	1.73
C_n [c]	3000	5000	7000	19,000	45,000	50,000	45,000	28,000	9000	5000	58,000
η_{red} 1/2% (close to $[\eta]$)	0.031	0.077	0.090	0.143	0.33	0.35	0.30	0.20	0.114	0.042	0.57
Rigidity (dynes/cm × 10^{-3})	---- did not set ----		----	1.7	—	31.4	16.7	----	did not set ----		75.4
$C_n/C_{n, original}$	0.055	0.082	0.13	0.32	0.77	0.87	0.77	0.48	0.16	0.084	1.00

[a] Data of Courts (12)

[b] Degradation at 75° for 24 hours.

[c] Number-average chain weight.

and Venet (*6*), who had found that M_n leveled off at about 20,000 following prolonged hydrolytic degradation. Courts reported C_n values that continued to drop as low as 3000 at extreme pH.

With the data for the appearance of specific amino-terminal amino acids as a function of temperature at constant pH, Courts (*12*) was able

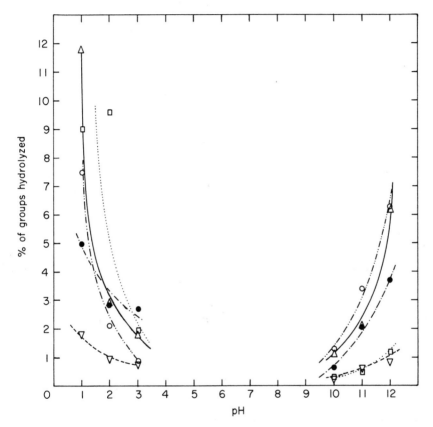

Fig. IV-9. Relative susceptibility of the amino group donor residues of peptide bonds to hydrolysis as a function of pH. Hydrolysis at 75° for 24 hours. Amino-terminal residues: ●, glycine; ○, serine; △, threonine; □, aspartic acid; ▽, glutamic acid [data from Courts (*12*)].

to determine the average activation energies for the hydrolysis of the peptide bonds involving the amino groups of the specified residues. These values are listed in Table IV-4 and are in very good agreement with the ranges determined by both Croome (*11*) and Pouradier and Venet (*6*), as well as the earlier values of Sheppard and Houck (*14*) and Greenberg and Burk (*15*), though each group used a different basis for assessing the degree of hydrolysis.

Paulson and Deatherage (*16–18*) found that Dowex-50, a sulfonated cross-linked polystyrene-type cation-exchange resin, was an effective acid catalyst for the hydrolysis of gelatins at elevated temperature. There were

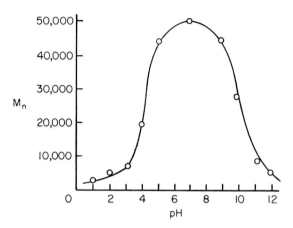

FIG. IV-10. Number-average chain weight of gelatin after degradation in solution for 24 hours at 75° at the indicated pH. Initial chain weight was 58,000 [Courts (*12*)].

no essential differences between the action of the strongly acidic resin and 1 N hydrochloric acid, with the one exception that the initial rate of degradation appeared to be more rapid in the hydrochloric acid than on the resin, whereas the rate of degradation was more rapid in the later

TABLE IV-4 [a]

ACTIVATION ENERGIES FOR THE HYDROLYSIS OF PEPTIDE BONDS
INVOLVING AMINO GROUPS OF THE LISTED AMINO ACIDS

Amino acid	Activation energy (cal/mole)
Serine	13,400
Threonine	13,400
Glycine	15,360
Aspartic Acid	22,670
Alanine	26,320
Average of all bonds	18,960

[a] Data of Courts (*12*).

stages on the resin column rather than in the hydrochloric acid. This discrepancy was probably an artifact of the method of assessing the rate of degradation. In spite of this difference the activation energies for both resin and free acid hydrolyses were the same.

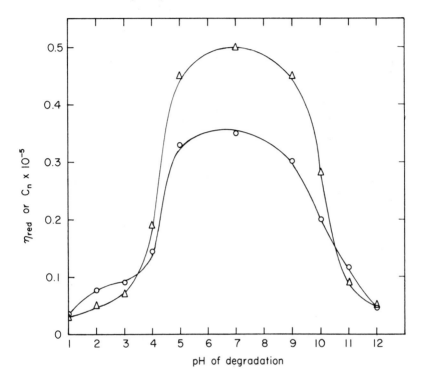

FIG. IV-11. Comparison of the changes in reduced viscosity, $\bigcirc$, and number-average chain weight, $\triangle$, following degradation at the indicated pH for 24 hours at 75° [Courts (12)].

Paulson and Deatherage (16) used Mihalyi's (19) equation relating the viscosity to the degree of hydrolysis in the form

$$\log \eta_t = (a - x)K_s + K_p \tag{32}$$

where

$$= x \frac{\log \eta_0 - \log \eta_t}{K_s - K_p} \tag{33}$$

In Eqs. 32 and 33, a represents the initial gelatin concentration, x the concentration of unhydrolyzed gelatin at time, t, and η_0 and η_t are the relative viscosities at times 0 and t, respectively. The constant K_s is the slope of a plot of log η_{rel} vs. the concentration of unhydrolyzed gelatin, and K_p is the slope obtained from a similar plot of log η_{rel} vs. the concentration of completely hydrolyzed gelatin. On the Dowex-50 column, the values of K_s and K_p were 0.0166 and 0.0015, respectively. In 1 N hydrochloric acid K_s was 0.0143 and K_p was 0.0024. The use of Eq. 32 to relate η_{rel} to the concentration suffers from the same error inherent in Croome's (11) use of the change in gel strength as a measure of degradation. The hydrolyzed fragments do not automatically have neither gel strength nor minimal viscosity.

E. Specific Hydrolytic Reactions with Nucleophilic Reagents: Hydroxylamine and Hydrazine

One of the more interesting developments in recent years has been the application of the limited reaction of hydrazine and hydroxylamine with specific groups in collagen and gelatin to determine the presence of ester-like linkages in the primary structure of the collagen. These reactions have been discussed in Chapter III in connection with the depolymerization of collagen fibers and the conversion of collagen to gelatin. There are additional insights that may be gained by reconsideration of this subject at this point.

Gallop et al. (20) noted that the reaction of both acid- and alkali-precursor gelatins with hydrazine or hydroxylamine at pH 10 and 40° appeared to proceed in two stages. The first fast reaction was nearly complete in about 90 minutes and resulted in a decrease of the molecular weight of the gelatin to about 20,000. If the hydroxylamine treatment was carried out at room temperature, the fast reaction was complete within 3 hours in the presence of 6 M urea. At this stage the acid-precursor gelatin contained 6 equivalents of bound hydroxamic acid or hydrazide groups per 10^5 gm. Similar treatment of the alkali-precursor gelatin resulted in a reduction of its molecular weight to 20,000, but only ~ 3 equivalents of bound hydroxamic acid were formed per 10^5 gm. Blumenfeld and Gallop (21) treated hydrazine-reacted ichthyocol gelatin with collagenase and isolated three hydrazide-containing peptide fragments from the digests by column chromatography. Each peptide fragment contained two hydrazide groups and the hydrazides were bound to aspartic acid in each case. From these analyses it was concluded that collagen was built from subunits of about 20,000 molecular weight and that the subunits were joined, by pairs of esterlike linkages involving aspartic acid residues. Lithium borohydride reduction studies indicated that about half the nucleophile-sensitive residues were linked to the α-carboxyl groups of aspartic acid, whereas the remaining half were linked to the β-carboxl groups. Blumenfeld and Gallop (21) therefore proposed that the three α-carboxyl-linked ester-like linkages marked the termini of three of the subunits of an α-peptide chain. The remaining three β-carboxyl-linked esterlike linkages thus could join the four α-peptide subunits into a single strand.

If one accepts these proposals it would appear that the prolonged exposure of collagen to alkali apparently leads to the hydrolysis of the non-cross-linking ester groups only, reducing the hydrazine- or hydroxylamine-sensitive linkages by one-half. If the intrapeptide chain cross-linking groups were hydrolyzed, then the maximum molecular weight obtainable for an extensively alkali-pretreated gelatin should be of the order of only 20,000. This is not the case and it does not agree with Ames' (8) observation that alkali-pretreated gelatins are fairly stable to alkaline hydrolysis, and substantially more stable than the acid-precursor gelatins.

Since Grassmann et al. (22) and Kono and Altman (23), as well as Blumenfeld and Gallop (21), all isolated amino alcohols from the lithium aluminum hydride or lithium borohydride reduction of collagen, it is clear that some ester linkages do occur in collagens and gelatins and it seems probable that the esters involve direct linkages to simple sugars. It is not clear, however, whether the sugars do in fact serve as cross-linking reagents within or between the peptide chains. The number of ester linkages occurring in various collagens and gelatins still remains to be quantitated. The value of 6 ester linkages per 10^5 gm collagen seems too high for the reasons cited in Chapter III.

III. ENZYMATIC DEGRADATIONS

A. Effects of General Proteolytic Enzymes

At elevated temperature in aqueous solutions all gelatins can be considered as essentially devoid of secondary structure. Each peptide chain is therefore able to take up a number of configurations of approximately equal energy and has no preferred orientation. It is not surprising, therefore, that the gelatin peptide segments can adapt themselves to the configurations of the active centers of enzymes and are quite susceptible to almost all proteolytic enzymes.

A typical study was that carried out by Courts (24), who followed the enzymatic degradation of an alkali-precursor ox bone gelatin, pI 5.1, at 37°. The number of amino-terminal residues, and their chemical nature were determined by the FDNB method; suitable controls were run without enzyme to assess the extent of thermal hydrolytic degradation. Crystalline papain, pepsin, chymotrypsin, and trypsin were used in this study. Pertinent data at the pH optimum of each enzyme are given in Table IV-5.

The specificities, or at least the primary specificities, of these enzymes have been determined. A useful tabulation is given by Dixon and Webb (25). Trypsin is the most specific of the four examined by Courts, splitting

TABLE IV-5 [a]

EFFECT OF PROTEOLYTIC ENZYMES ON GELATIN

	Enzyme				Undegraded
	Pepsin	Papain	Chymotrypsin	Trypsin	
pH	1.87	5.05	8.0	8.5	—
Temperature (°C) (time)	37° (19 hr)	37° (5 days)	37° (6 hr)	44° (2.5 hr)	—
N-terminal groups [b]					
Glycine	2.81	14.00	8.34	40.44	0.95
Serine	0.68	2.40	1.25	1.17	0.29
Threonine	0.72	4.00	0.71	1.36	0.12
Alanine	2.14	12.24	1.40	0.85	0.14
Aspartic acid	0.69	3.42	0.75	1.25	0.08
Glutamic acid	0.45	1.78	0.85	0.80	0.14
Others	2.00	1.50	2.20	1.30	0.00
Total	9.49	39.34	15.50	47.17	1.73
C_n [c]	10,500	2500	6000	2100	58,000
C_n (control)	43,300	44,000	—	—	—
Maximum number of residues available according to enzyme specificity	14.7	—	24.5	78.9	—
Minimum C_n for cleavage at sites of primary specificity	7440	—	4090	1270	—

[a] Data of Courts (24).
[b] Release, in terms of residues/10^5 gm gelatin.
[c] Number-average chain weight.

peptide bonds, esters, and amides involving the carboxyl groups of arginine and lysine. Chymotrypsin preferentially hydrolyzes bonds involving the carboxyl groups of tyrosine, phenylalanine, tryptophan, and methionine. Pepsin is much less specific but also preferentially hydrolyzes bonds containing aromatic residues. Papain is even less specific. The two rows below the dashed line in Table IV-5 give the calculated maximum number of amino-terminal residues that could be created by the enzymes according to their primary specificity as indicated above. The amino acid composition data on ox skin gelatin obtained by Eastoe (26) were used for these calculations. It is evident, particularly by comparison of the C_n values with the minimum values, that in no case did the proteolysis proceed to completion.

Because of the large number of basic groups in gelatin, trypsin is the most effective enzyme of the four studied. It is of particular interest that the tryptic digestion produces amino-terminal glycine in overwhelming amount, signifying that sequences Arg·Gly or Lys·Gly are especially prevalent. On a strictly statistical basis only one-third of the amino-terminal residues created by tryptic digestion should have been glycine residues. Grassmann, Hannig and Schleyer (27) came to a similar conclusion in a study in the breakdown of tropocollagen with highly purified trypsin. They separated the digest chromatographically, obtaining 114 peptides of which 55 were apparently homogeneous by a variety of criteria. End-group analyses showed that only lysine and arginine appeared as carboxy-terminal residues, and in nearly all the peptides the amino end was occupied by glycine. *In toto*, in all of the isolated peptides, glycine represented one-third of the total amino acids, indicating the uniform distribution of glycine throughout the collagen molecule.

Two other aspects of the work of Grassmann *et al.* (27) are pertinent to this discussion of enzymatic degradation. First, of the pure peptides isolated from the tryptic digest, 51 were subjected to quantitative amino acid analysis. It was found that there were apolar sequences with high concentrations of proline and hydroxyproline, and that these sequences alternated with polar regions containing few imino acids. The polar regions themselves contained subregions, some primarily acidic, the others basic. Second, end-group analyses of the chromatographically pure peptides revealed that many of these peptides contained 3 amino-terminal groups (all glycine) and 3 carboxy-terminal groups. A few typical peptides are illustrated in Table IV-6. It is evident that the majority of the collagen peptides have a three-chain structure and that the cross-linkages between the chains resist tryptic digestion. Furthermore, since there were many three-chain peptide fragments and since the process of isolation of

TABLE IV-6 [a]

COMPOSITION OF TYPICAL PEPTIDE FRAGMENTS FROM TRYPTIC DIGESTS OF TROPOCOLLAGEN

Peptide designation	Composition
S_{86} (proline-free sequence)	H-Gly-Asp-Glu-Hylys - [3 Gly, 7 Thr, 2 Glu, Asp] -ArgOH
S_5 (proline-containing)	H-Gly-(Asp, Glu, Ala) - $\begin{bmatrix} 7 \text{ Pro, } 2 \text{ Hypro, } 11 \text{ Gly,} \\ 5 \text{ Ala, } 2 \text{ Asp, } 5 \text{ Glu, Arg} \end{bmatrix}$ -ArgOH
N_{IV_1} (proline-containing)	H-Gly- H-Gly- $\left(\begin{matrix} \text{Gly, Ser,} \\ \text{Glu, Ala} \end{matrix}\right)$ - $\begin{bmatrix} 10 \text{ Pro, } 2 \text{ Hypro, } 13 \text{ Gly,} \\ 2 \text{ Ala, Val, Ser, Asp,} \\ 4 \text{ Glu, } 2 \text{ Lys, Arg} \end{bmatrix}$ -LysOH H-Gly- -LysOH -ArgOH
N_{IV_3} (proline-containing)	H-Gly- H-Gly- $\left(\begin{matrix} \text{Gly, Ala, Ser,} \\ \text{Thr, } 3 \text{ Glu, Asp} \end{matrix}\right)$ - $\begin{bmatrix} 5 \text{ Pro, Hypro, } 8 \text{ Gly,} \\ \text{Ala, Ser, } 2 \text{ Val,} \\ \text{Asp, } 2 \text{ Glu} \end{bmatrix}$ -LysOH H-Gly- -ArgOH -ArgOH

[a] Data of Grassmann et al. (27).

these peptides precluded any retention of secondary structure which might otherwise have prevented chain separation, there must also have been a correspondingly large number of covalent cross-linkages between the chains. These data, in part, lend credence to the discussions in Chapter III, pointing out the insolubility of limed and hydrazine-treated collagen fibers even though up to 18 equivalents of peptide bonds per gm collagen were hydrolyzed (28).

It has been generally considered that native collagen is resistant to the usual proteolytic enzymes. Hodge, Highberger, Deffner, and Schmitt (29), however, found that trypsin at pH 7.2 and pepsin at pH 3.5 would react with tropocollagen in its native state to a limited extent. Hodge et al. (29) pictured the tropocollagen as a rigid rod of three peptide strands with small single peptide strands extending from one, or both ends of the rod. In free solution these single-chain portions assumed a randomly contorted configuration and were, therefore, expected to be susceptible to the action of proteases. The rigid three-chain helical portion of the molecule, on the other hand, was expected to be resistant to the proteases. In line with these proposals, trypsin liberated a low molecular weight acidic peptide fraction. This fraction was rich in tyrosine as well as in the acidic amino acids and contained a small amount of hydroxyproline. The main body of the tropocollagen rod was not disrupted. The addition of adenosine triphosphate (ATP) to acid solutions of the trypsin-treated tropocollagen solutions resulted in the precipitation of segment-long-spacing (SLS) collagen. In the original untreated tropocollagen the addition of ATP resulted in the formation of many dimeric SLS spools; these dimers did not appear in the trypsin- or pesin-treated collagens. The ATP in this case produced only single SLS segments, and it was argued that the interaction of the "end chains" was necessary for the formation of end-to-end linear aggregates of tropocollagen. This argument leads to the suggestion that the gelatins obtained by thermal denaturation of neutral-salt-soluble collagen (α chains) may themselves be polarized, that is, the ends of the chains may bear opposite electrical charges. Kühn et al. (30) dispute these conclusions. They were able to purify collagen so that the tyrosine content was effectively reduced to zero. The purified tropocollagen was then intensively reacted with trypsin, but no changes in fibril formation or SLS formation patterns were observed. Kühn et al. (30) did note, however, that the end-to-end polymerization of tropocollagen should be attributed to electrostatic forces. At the moment there is no explanation for the discrepancy between these two reports.

B. Effects of Treatment with Collagenase

A "collagenase" is one of several enzymes of bacterial or insect origin that is a highly specific agent for the proteolysis of the peptide chains in native collagen. The term "collagenase" was first used by Ssadikow (31) for a pancreatic enzyme capable of digesting heat-denatured collagen. In her excellent review, Ines Mandl (32) stresses the point that the term collagenase should be restricted to the enzymes that, uniquely, attack native collagen. Only two enzymes, isolated from the bacteria Clostridium perfringens and Cl. histolyticum, have been established as true collagenases. However, there is evidence that Cl. capitovale (33) and the larvae of certain insects (34) elaborate collagenases. The collagenase from Cl. histolyticum has been examined in greatest detail and the methods for its preparation (35–38) and assay (39) have been standardized. Collagenase from Cl. histolyticum prepared by the method of Mandl et al. (37) is available commercially.

1. Specificity of Collagenase

Collagenase digests both collagen and gelatin but no other proteins have been found to act as substrates. Grassmann et al. (40) proposed that the sequence

$$X — Pro \cdot R \cdot Gly \cdot Pro — Y$$

in which X and Y are blocking groups and R any amino acid, is required for the enzyme action, the split taking place between R and Gly. Other investigations (*38, 41–49*) modified this sequence requirement to

$$X - Pro \cdot R_1 \cdot R_2 \cdot Pro - Y$$

In this sequence, the proline residues may be replaced by hydroxyproline (*50*) but the rate of cleavage is greatly reduced. Similarly, residues with bulky side chains or proline cannot replace glycine in the R_2 position (*47*). The most common residue replacing glycine at R_2 is alanine, and this residue has been noted as the amino-terminal group in collagenase digests by Manahan and Mandl (*41, 42*). Residue R_1 may apparently be any amino acid (*50*). So far, sequences involving hydroxyproline and alanine (*51, 41*) at R_1 have been isolated. Schrohenloher *et al.* (*51*) identified Gly·Pro·Hypro and Gly·Pro·Ala in collagenase digests of steer hide collagen. These two tripeptides accounted for 23% of the alanine, 14% of the glycine, 23% of the hydroxyproline, and 40% of the proline of the original steer corium.

The products of the digestion of collagen with *Cl. histolyticum* collagenase are peptides. Free amino acids were not produced (*32*). The peptides varied in size from tripeptides, as noted above (*41, 51*), to very large fragments containing as many as 30 residues. In accord with the work of Grassmann *et al.* (*27*) on the trypsin digestion of collagen, some of the larger peptides contained no, or very few, imino acid residues (*41*). Some peptides contained proline with no hydroxyproline and the reverse situation held for others (*52*). Mandl and co-workers (*32*) isolated two peptides of 21 and of 24 residues, each containing only two proline residues and no hydroxyproline. They also obtained a peptide fragment of 50 residues without either proline or hydroxyproline. A tropocollagen molecule contains about 3000 residues, an α chain about 1000. Thus the above 50-residue peptide indicates that at least 5% of one chain is completely free of imino acids (or that a group of three cross-linked chains each with approximately 17 residues exists). These observations are of particular importance in pointing out the intrinsic heterogeneity of gelatin. The peptide backbones of two peptide chains of equivalent molecular weight or degree of polymerization may very well be considerably different in their charge, charge distribution, chain extension in space, and solvent interaction properties. This heterogeneity must increase as the average degree of polymerization decreases.

2. *Kinetics of Collagenase Action*

Seifter *et al.* (*53*) examined the degradation of ichthyocol by a purified *Cl. histolyticum* collagenase. They followed the specific viscosity and optical rotation as a function of time at pH 7.5 in 0.05 *M* Tris buffer at 20°. It was found that the log of the specific viscosity was a linear function of the time of degradation, and that the slope of the line was directly proportional to the specific activity of the collagenase. The optical rotation, however, was found to decrease much more slowly with time than the specific viscosity. The relative changes in both $(\eta_{sp})_t$ and α_t are shown in Fig. IV-12. Seifter *et al.* proposed that these data could be explained by a two-step process:

$$\text{ichthyocol} \xrightarrow[\text{enzymatic}]{\text{(I)}} \text{folded polypeptides} \xrightarrow[\text{thermal}]{\text{(II)}} \text{randomized peptides}$$

The enzymatic reaction (I) cuts the organized chains into small segments, with a consequent large decrease in viscosity but without a corresponding loss of internal order or optical rotatory power. The slower disorganization or unfolding of the peptides was supposed to take place because of

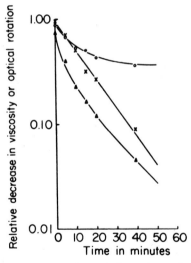

FIG. IV-12. Effects of collagenase on the optical rotation and viscosity of ichthyocol in solution. $\triangle$, $(\eta_{sp})_t/(\eta_{sp})_0$; $\times$, (c_t/c_0); and $\bigcirc$, $(a_t - a_\infty)/(a_0 - a_\infty)$. Here $(\eta_{sp})_t$ is the specific viscosity at any time t; c_t is the concentration of unreacted collagen at any time t; a_t is the specific rotation at time t; a_0 is the specific rotation of zero time control, $- 324°$; a_∞ is the specific rotation of the solution after the enzyme produces no further change in rotation (the actual time is approximately 4 hours), and is $- 90°$ at temperatures from 0° to 40° [Seifter *et al.* (*53*)].

the inherently lower stability of short peptides. An alternate explanation is possible, now that information is available on the nature of the peptides produced by collagenase. At least four, and probably six, amino acid residues in sequence are required to form a stable helix segment. Collagenase produces a mixture of tripeptides, tetrapeptides, and higher molecular weight polypeptides, thus leading to a mixture of ordered and disordered units, all of which, however, are of low viscosity. Some of the larger peptides cannot be degraded by collagenase because of their lack of the required sequence; hence, collagenase alone will not reduce the specific rotation of undenatured collagen to the value found for thoroughly denatured or disorganized gelatins of higher molecular weight.

Harrington, von Hippel, and Mihalyi (54) examined the kinetics of the collagenase degradation of ichthyocol at various temperatures, above and below the collagen → gelatin transition temperature (T_c). They depended primarily on pH-stat measurements to follow directly the number of peptide bonds created. At temperatures $T > T_c$ the reaction followed simple first order kinetics over its entire course. At $T < T_c$ a single first order rate constant could not be obtained. However, the rate data could be treated satisfactorily in terms of two first order reactions, one fast, the other substantially slower. At 20°, 26% of the hydrolyzable bonds of a gelatin were split in the fast reaction. At 10° only 10% of the enzyme-susceptible bonds were split in the fast reaction. In ichthyocol the fraction of bonds split in the fast reaction in the 10–20° range was constant at 35%. Harrington et al. (54) correlated the transfer of enzyme susceptibility from the fast to the slow reaction as the temperature was lowered with the formation of the so-called collagen-fold in the cooled gelatins. Enhancement of the fraction of bonds cleaved in the slow reaction coincided with the onset of large changes in the gelatin optical rotation.

Von Hippel et al. (55) extended these observations in a more detailed study. The action of collagenase was followed by pH-stat or colorimetric ninhydrin analyses with essentially identical results. Using the pH-stat, the number of equivalents of acid produced, P, was measured at various times. The maximal value of P, $P_{t=\infty}$, was determined from extrapolation of a plot of dP/dt vs. P. The first order plot of log $(P_\infty - P_t/P_\infty)$ vs. t is shown in Fig. 1V-13. Two straight lines can apparently represent these data. The dotted line with the filled circles represents the true course of the fast reaction, the values of the first straight line corrected for the simultaneous production of a small amount of acid by the slower reaction. The first order rate constants and related data from such runs at various temperatures are listed in Table IV-7. Von Hippel and Harrington (56) considered the question of the behavior of ichthyocol gelatin above and below the critical gelation temperature. As described in the preliminary note (*54*), at $T > T_c$ the rate data could be represented by a single first order rate

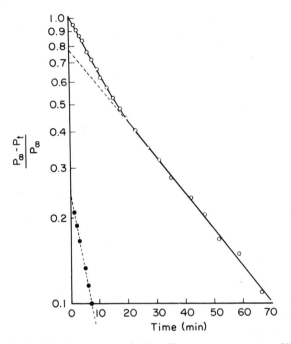

FIG. IV-13. Action of collagenase on soluble collagen at a temperature (19.55°, pH 8.0) below the collagen denaturation temperature. Fraction of total bonds cleaved is plotted as a function of time [von Hippel *et al.* (*55*)].

constant (Fig. IV-14), whereas two first order reactions were required when $T < T_c$ (Fig. IV-15). The activation parameters of Table IV-7 B indicate that the optimal configuration for the gelatin-collagenase complex is most readily achieved at $T > T_c$, since $\Delta S^{\ddagger}$ in this case is ~ 0 e.u. As ordered segments appear in the gelatin upon cooling, it becomes more difficult to force the ordered regions into the appropriate configuration to accept the collagenase; $\Delta S^{\ddagger}$ increases and a progressively greater expenditure of energy is required ($\Delta H^{\ddagger}$ increases to $+46$ kcal/mole in the collagen, and $\Delta S^{\ddagger}$ to 110 e.u.). Since $\Delta S^{\ddagger}$ and $\Delta H^{\ddagger}$ were always higher for the collagen reactions than for the corresponding cooled gelatin reaction, whereas the fractions of bonds split in the fast and slow reactions were the same for both materials, it was concluded that these differences were a measure of the relative "tightness" of the folding of the peptide

TABLE IV-7 [a]

SOME KINETIC PARAMETERS OF THE PROTEOLYSIS OF ICHTHYOCOL COLLAGEN BY COLLAGENASE

	(A) Rate constants		Bonds split (%)	
Reaction temperature	k' fast reaction ($\times 10^2$ min^{-1})	k' slow reaction ($\times 10^2$ min^{-1})	Fast reaction	Slow reaction
22.7	9.2	3.4	11	90
19.6	4.3	1.0	23	77
17.5	2.4	0.64	17	83
14.9	1.3	0.39	19	82
13.0	0.80	0.22	16	85
9.7	0.84	0.038	14	86

	(B) Activation parameters			
Reaction	ΔE_a^* (kcal/mole) [b]	$\Delta H^{\ddagger}$ (kcal/mole)	$\Delta F^{\ddagger}$ (kcal/mole)	$\Delta S^{\ddagger}$ (e.u.)
Ichthyocol gelatin above T_c ($> 27°$)	+15	+14	+14	$+1 \pm 7$
Ichthyocol collagen, $T < T_c$, fast reaction	+42	+41	+15	$+90 \pm 5$
Ichthyocol collagen, $T < T_c$, slow reaction	+47	+46	+15	$+110 \pm 6$
Ichthyocol gelatin, $T < T_c$, fast reaction	+23	+22	+14	$+30 \pm 4$
Ichthyocol gelatin, $T < T_c$, slow reaction	+30	+29	+15	$+51 \pm 4$

[a] Data of von Hippel et al. (55).
[b] Arrhenius plot.

chains. This argument implies that the ordered segments of the collagen and gelatin are similar in nature but vary in their accessibility to the enzyme.

Seifter et al. (53) had shown that the specific optical rotation of ichthyocol collagen did not decrease as rapidly as the intrinsic viscosity during the proteolysis of the collagen by collagenase. Von Hippel and Harrington (56) pointed out a similar difference between the rate of cleavage of peptide bonds and the rate of change of the optical rotation. On cooling gelatin the specific optical rotation became substantially more negative, but the change in levorotation was not very rapid and several hours were required for the development of maximum levorotation. Some typical ichthyocol rotation-time curves are shown in Fig. IV-16 for a gelatin heated at 40°, then cooled rapidly to 11.5°. A pH-stat collagenase proteolysis experiment could be completed within 90 minutes. Von Hippel and Harrington (56) found that the hydrolysis kinetics for a gelatin, quenched from 40° to 11.5° within a few minutes before the addition of

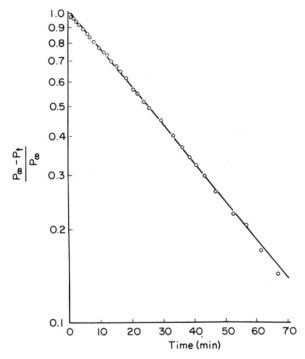

Fig. IV-14. Action of collagenase on ichthyocol gelatin at a temperature above the denaturation temperature. Fraction of total bonds cleaved as a function of time; pH 8.0 and 37.35°; gelatin, 0.28 mg/ml, collagenase, 0.017 units/ml [von Hippel and Harrington (56)].

the enzyme, showed the typical sequence of two first order reactions. In this case the treatment at 40° should have completely destroyed any secondary structure in the gelatin, and the proteolysis was essentially complete before any appreciable collagen-fold could have been restored. The rate constants for both the fast and slow proteolysis reactions in quenched (rapidly cooled) and unquenched (slowly cooled) gelatins were almost identical, and the activation parameters were unchanged. These data very strongly indicated that the configurational patterns responsible for the high levorotation of the gelatins have little effect on the susceptibility of peptide bonds to collagenase. On this basis, von Hippel and Harrington (56) suggested that there was an immediate, temperature-dependent's ordering of local regions of the imino acid-rich segments of the molecule (about

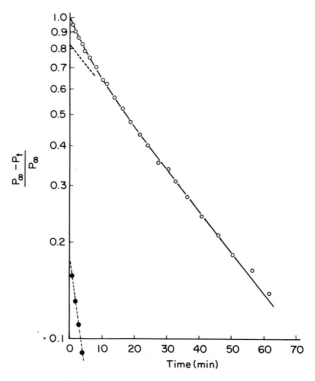

FIG. IV-15. Action of collagenase on ichthyocol gelatin at a temperature (14.25°) below the denaturation temperature. Conditions the same as in Fig. IV-14 except for the temperature [von Hippel and Harrington (56)].

20% of the total structure), and a slower formation of the collagen helix in the remainder of the structure. Since the enzyme acts essentially only on the sequence

$$X — Pro \cdot R_1 \cdot Gly \cdot Pro — Y$$

the spatial configuration of this chain segment must be involved in this fast, temperature-dependent structural organization. The nature of the chain folding in this region will be considered in detail in Chapter V, as it is intimately related to the mechanism of the gelation of gelatin sols.

IV. OXIDATIVE CHAIN CLEAVAGE

The oxidative breakdown of collagen and gelatin is a process that appears to be even more complex than the hydrolytic degradations. Nevertheless, several serious efforts have been made to elucidate the changes taking place in collagen and gelatin following reaction with a variety of oxidizing agents. Hydrogen peroxide, sodium periodate, sodium hypobromite, phenyliodosoacetate, and potassium ferricyanide have all been studied. It is probable that their reactions with gelatin may be quite different.

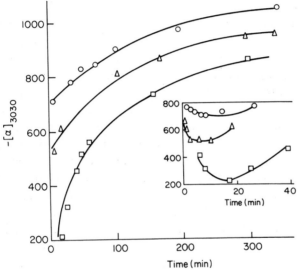

FIG. IV-16. Change in specific rotation of ichthyocol gelatin as a function of time after cooling rapidly from 40° to 11.5°; ⊙, gelatin, 1.42 mg/ml; △, gelatin, 0.47 mg/ml; ▣, gelatin, 0.28 mg/ml [von Hippel and Harrington (56)].

Sodium periodate is a relatively mild oxidizing agent and Gustavson (57) found it to have relatively little effect on collagen. He reacted insoluble limed collagen with 0.5 M periodate at pH 4.0, or 0.25–0.30 M periodate at pH 5–6, for 7–14 days at 20°, and found that only 5–10% of the collagen was solubilized. The remaining collagen was chemically modified, there being a decrease in the acid binding capacity from 92 × × 10^{-5} eq/gm to 82 × 10^{-5} eq/gm. The shrinkage temperature was reduced from 65° to 40°. However, the total nitrogen content, 18.0%, was unchanged. Gustavson attributed these results to the preferential destruc-

tion of hydroxylysine. Desnuelle and Antonin (*58*) also found that periodate destroyed the hydroxylysine of gelatin.

Grassmann and Kühn (*59*) compared the action of sodium periodate
and phenyliodosoacetate,

$$[\varPhi-\text{OIO}\overset{\overset{\displaystyle O}{\|}}{\text{C}}\text{CH}_3]^+\text{CH}_3\text{COO}^-$$

on steer corium collagen and calf skin tropocollagen. The reactions were
all carried out at 40° with a 2:1 weight ratio of protein to oxidizing
agent. The sodium periodate reactions were carried out at pH 8, the
phenyliodosoacetate reactions at pH 3.4. The two oxidizing agents appeared to be very similar in effect. The pertinent results are shown in
Table IV-8. The most striking observation was that in spite of the fact
that the fibrous corium collagen and the calf skin tropocollagen were
dissolved rapidly and after 6 days to the same extent, the oxidized
solubilized fibrous collagen was nondialyzable whereas the acid-soluble
tropocollagen was degraded to low molecular weight fragments. The
higher molecular weight fragments from the corium collagen behaved
electrophoretically as a single substance with an isoelectric pH of 9.2,
could not be dialyzed from solution, and formed gels even at very low
concentration. The acid-soluble collagen degradation products were not
electrophoretically homogeneous; they could be dialyzed, and did not form
gels even at high protein concentration. In spite of these differences, the
number of chain terminal groups per unit weight was similar in the two
degraded collagen preparations. Grassmann and Kühn (*59*) deduced,
through reaction of the degradation products with lithium borohydride,
that the carboxy-terminal groups of the acid-soluble collagen fragments
were free, while the corresponding groups in the solubilized corium collagen were esterified. In this case, 3.93 moles of amino alcohol were isolated per 10^5 gm oxidized protein compared to 3.94 moles/10^5 gm from
the unoxidized collagen. The amino alcohols were exclusively

$$\text{NH}_2\text{CH}_2\text{CH}_2\text{OH} \qquad \text{and} \qquad \underset{\underset{\displaystyle \text{NH}_2}{|}}{\text{CH}_3-\text{CH}-\text{CH}_2\text{OH}}$$

originating from glycine and alanine. Amino acid analyses of the degraded
collagen revealed only very slight differences in the composition of the protein, and it was therefore concluded that the oxidative degradation was
based on an attack on carbohydrates associated with the collagens. This
argument implies that the carbohydrates in fibrous collagen are much

TABLE IV-8 [a]

REACTION OF NaIO₄ AND PIA [b] WITH COLLAGEN AND ACID-SOLUBLE COLLAGEN

Substrate	Oxidizing agent	pH	% Protein dissolved after various reaction times (days)						% Dialyzable (% of soluble N)	N-Terminal groups (soluble N/amino N)
			1/2	1	2	3	4	6		
Corium collagen	NaOI₄	7–8	—	56.9	73.3	80.2	86.5	88.7	6.3	16.5
	PIA	3.4	—	62.7	79.2	88.0	90.5	91.2	9.8	16.3
Acid-soluble collagen	PIA	3.4	38	88.1	91.5	93.0	92.1	93.0	(2 days) 48.5	
									(72 hour) 71.4	15.0

[a] Data of Grassmann and Kühn (59)

[b] Phenyliodosoacetate[(Φ—OIOCCH₃)$^+$CH₃COO$^-$].

$$O$$

less accessible to, or less reactive with, the oxidizing agents than are similar carbohydrates in the acid-soluble collagen.

Hörmann and Fries (*60*) examined the reaction of periodic acid with acid-soluble collagen in more detail. In contrast to the phenyliodosoacetate oxidation, the periodate did not reduce the acid-soluble collagen to low molecular weight dialyzable fragments. There was little difference in the reactivity at 20°, where the acid-soluble collagen was in the native state, and at 40°, where the collagen was denatured. The collagen reacted almost immediately, with the consumption of 2.8 moles sodium periodate per 100 moles amino acid residues at 20°. More sodium periodate was consumed slowly over the remainder of the period examined (Fig. IV-17). This utilization of periodic acid was accompanied by a moderate

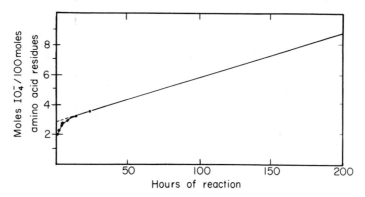

FIG. IV-17. Consumption of periodate as a function of time during the oxidation of acid-soluble collagen. Conditions: 0.7% collagen, 0.02 *M* periodic acid in 8% acetic acid; 20° [Hörmann and Fries (*60*)].

decrease in the number of free amino groups (van Slyke analysis), and a much more dramatic decrease in the hexose content (Fig. IV-18). The loss of amino groups was found to almost correspond to the decrease in hydroxylysine content of the acid-soluble collagen. There was an equivalent production of one mole ammonia and one mole formaldehyde per mole hydroxylysine destroyed (Fig. IV-19). Since the decrease in number of free amino groups was somewhat less than the ammonia production, it was evident that a limited hydrolysis of peptide bonds also took place.

In agreement with the report of Grassmann and Kühn (*59*), the acid-soluble collagen had a hexose content of 3.8×10^{-5} mole/gm. As shown in Fig. IV-18, this was reduced to a constant value of 0.8×10^{-5} mole/gm following prolonged reaction with the periodic acid. Since periodate oxidation did not decrease the molecular weight of the peptide chains following reaction at 40°, Hörmann and Fries (60) concluded that the periodic acid-susceptible hexoses were not incorporated within the peptide chains of gelatins, but were important in stabilizing the collagen structure. These conclusions were essentially confirmed by Gustavson (57), who also reported that there was an increase of about 50% in the ability of periodate-

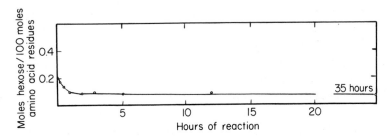

FIG. IV-18. Decrease in hexose content of acid-soluble collagen during periodate oxidation. Conditions as in Fig. IV-17 [Hörmann and Fries (60)].

oxidized limed collagen to fix or bind sulfitochromates and basic chromium perchlorates. These reagents are thought to bind to hydroxyl groups, and Gustavson therefore proposed that the hexoses (or aldehydes or other reductones) might be present as cross-linking groups involving the hydroxyl group of hydroxyproline.

Hydrogen peroxide is a much more powerful oxidizing agent than per-

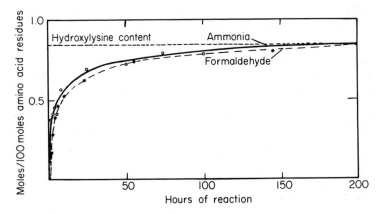

FIG. IV-19. Release of formaldehyde and ammonia during the periodate oxidation of acid-soluble collagen. Upper dashed line shows the final decrease in hydroxylysine content after 150 hours of oxidation [Hörmann and Fries (60)].

iodic acid. Gallop, Seifter and Meilman (61) found that citrate-extracted ichthyocol was not affected by 1.7 M hydrogen peroxide at pH 7 and 0°, but was completely dissolved in several hours at 37°, the dissolved gelatin having a molecular weight of 10,000 or lower. In a more complete study, ichthyocol gelatin was incubated with 0.8 M hydrogen peroxide at pH 7.5 for 21 hours at 50°. Aliquots of the solution were periodically freed of peroxide by addition of catalase and the samples analyzed. It was found that the oxidized solutions contained free ammonia, formaldehyde, and higher molecular weight aldehydes. Sedimentation velocity measurements indicated clearly that peptide chain cleavage was occurring.

Gallop et al. (61) found that potassium ferricyanide, in the range 0.1–1.0 M, caused changes in the gelatin very similar to those occasioned by hydrogen peroxide. Some control experiments in which potassium ferri-cyanide was reacted with pure amino acids showed that, in 24 hours at pH 7.5 and 37°, 1 M potassium ferricyanide was capable of oxidizing hy-droxyproline, arginine, proline, lysine, serine, threonine, and glycine. The amino acids are listed in the order of their susceptibility to oxidation, hy-droxyproline being the most readily oxidized. Even in this case, however, only a very small fraction ($\sim 2\%$) of the hydroxyproline was oxidized. Gallop et al. (61) suggested that the observed peptide chain splitting was probably the result of destruction of hydroxyproline, proline, serine, and threonine, whereas the formaldehyde and ammonia originated from oxi-dation of hydroxylysine and carbohydrate.

In a study similar to that of Gallop et al. (61), Courts (62) obtained significantly different results. In one phase of the study a purified ox bone collagen was treated with 1.7 M hydrogen peroxide at 21° in water and in the presence of lyotropic reagents. In water, the peroxide system came to equilibrium at pH 5.5 and only about 1% of the collagen was dissolved. Substantially higher amounts, indicated in Table IV-9, were dissolved in the presence of the lyotropic reagents, 4.0 M sodium salicylate being the most effective. It is interesting to note that 4.0 M lithium bromide, which alone had a very substantial solubilizing power at 21°, was not as effective as salicylate or 8.0 M urea, neither of which had significant solubilizing effect in the absence of hydrogen peroxide. In these latter cases, the col-lagen-peroxide-reagent systems equilibrated at pH 8.0, suggesting that the solubilizing reaction might have been base-catalyzed. At 60°, 1.7 M hy-drogen peroxide alone was able to dissolve a portion of the collagen as a relatively high molecular weight gelatin with the ability to form gels. The amino-terminal group content was determined for the insoluble residues of the 60° extractions. The native collagen had no such amino-terminal

TABLE IV-9 [a]

SOLUBILITY OF COLLAGEN IN SOLUTIONS CONTAINING 1.7 M H_2O_2
AND VARIOUS LYOTROPIC REAGENTS AT 21°

Reagent	Equilibrium pH	Collagen dissolved (%)	Collagen dissolved (reagent blank, no H_2O_2)
H_2O_2 (1.7 M)	5.5	1	—
Na salicylate (4.0 M)	8.0	80	3
Urea (8.0 M)	8.0	58	1
CaCl$_2$ (8.0 M)	?	53	3
LiBr (4.0 M)	5.5	48	17

[a] Data of Courts (62).

residues, the 60° water-extracted (3 hours) collagen had 0.28×10^{-5} residue/gm, and the 1.7 M peroxide-treated collagen extracted at 60° for 2.5 hours had 0.72×10^{-5} residue/gm. Thus, there was only a very limited oxidative degradation of the collagen. In marked contrast to the report of Gallop et al. (61), Courts did not report that evolution of ammonia or formaldehyde accompanied the collagen solubilization. Amino acid analyses of the peroxide-extracted gelatins showed no decrease in hydroxylysine, proline, serine, threonine, or hydroxyproline contents. In fact the serine, threonine, and tyrosine contents were all higher than those of the control bone gelatin. The analyses did show losses of 4.5×10^{-5} residue of methionine and 3.5×10^{-5} residue of histidine per gm gelatin. Glycine, serine, threonine, proline, hydroxyproline, methionine, histidine, and glycylglycine were all reacted with 1.7 M hydrogen peroxide at 60°. No alterations were detected by paper chromatographic analyses in any of these compounds except methionine and histidine. The reacted methionine chromatogram showed that the methionine had completely disappeared and was replaced by a spot corresponding to threonine. The histidine spot was reduced in intensity compared with an untreated control, and a second spot corresponding to serine appeared on the chromatogram. These observations with the pure amino acids appear to account for the enhanced serine and threonine contents of the gelatin obtained by extraction from the collagen in the presence of hydrogen peroxide. Courts (62) favors the view that the tyrosine found in native collagen is present in a noncollagen impurity. He argues that the higher content of tyrosine ($\sim 0.5\%$) in the peroxide-extracted gelatin indicates that peroxide treatment is an effective method for purification of the residual undissolved collagen.

In comparing the two reports *(61, 62)* on the effect of hydrogen peroxide on gelatin, it is difficult to find an experimental reason for the discrepancy. Gallop *et al. (61)* apparently used milder conditions, 0.8 *M* peroxide, 50°, than did Courts *(62)*, 1.5 *M* peroxide, 60°. Gallop *et al.* buffered their systems at pH 7.5 whereas Courts did not control the reaction pH. In spite of this, Gallop *et al.* noted considerably greater oxidative degradation.

The oxidation of gelatin with hypobromite has been studied chiefly in regard to the deguanidination reaction and its effect on the gelation of gelatin sols. Grabar and Morel *(63)* showed that potassium hypobromite reacted with gelatin to produce nitrogen gas and a degraded gelatin that would no longer set to a gel. The principal reaction was presumed to be the deguanidination of the arginine residues. The arginine residues were therefore linked with the gelling properties of gelatin. This aspect of the subject will be dealt with in Chapter V. The present discussion is concerned with the direct chemical effects of the oxidation. Davis *(64, 65)* confirmed the deguanidination reaction. Figure IV-20 shows the decrease

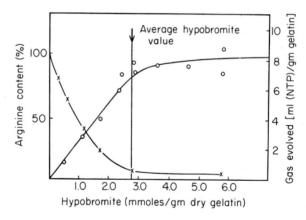

Fig. IV-20. Deguanidination of gelatin with hypobromite. The nitrogen gas evolution and arginine loss level off at the same point of hypobromite consumption (straight vertical line); gas evolution expressed as ml at standard temperature and pressure [Davis *(64)*].

in arginine content as a function of the amount of hypobromite consumed for an alkali-precursor gelatin reacted with 0.5 *M* potassium hypobromite, in the presence of 0.5 *M* potassium bromide and 0.8 *M* potassium hydroxide for 2 minutes at 40°. The evolution of nitrogen gas (the upper curve in Fig. IV-20) paralleled the destruction of the guanidino group. On a residue basis, 3.3 moles hypobromite were required per mole of guanidine destroyed, in good agreement with the stoichiometry of the oxidation. However, a larger amount of hypobromite was consumed in the overall reaction (65). In examining this problem, Bello (66) repeated the hypobromite oxidation by the Davis (65) procedure. After 130 seconds at 39° Bello neutralized the reaction mixture with 1 N acetic acid to pH 5.0–5.2. He found that 80% [in agreement with Davis (65)] of the arginine was destroyed and that 2.5–2.6 mmoles hypobromite were used per gm gelatin. Since gelatin contains only about 0.5 mmole arginine per gram, the stoichiometry requires that only 1.2 mmoles hypobromite could have been consumed in the guanidine oxidation. Thus, the remaining 1.3–1.4 mmoles hypobromite must have been consumed in other reactions. Bello found that the intrinsic viscosity of his gelatin was reduced from 0.47 to 0.095 dl/gm during the oxidation, and concluded that these other oxidation reactions led to peptide chain degradation. Bello did not attempt to identify the possible sites of oxidative attack on the peptide backbone.

REFERENCES

1. W. Kuhn, *Z. physik, Chem.* **A159**, 368 (1932).

2. W. Kuhn, *Kolloid-Z.* **58**, 2 (1934).

3. J. W. Williams, W. M. Saunders, and J. S. Cicerelli, *J. Phys. Chem.* **58**, 774 (1954).

4. H. Boedtker and P. Doty, *J. Phys. Chem.* **58**, 968 (1954).

5. G. Scatchard, J. L. Oncley, J. W. Williams, and A. Brown, *J. Am. Chem. Soc.* **66**, 1980 (1944).

6. J. Pouradier and A. M. Venet, *J. Chim. Phys.* **49**, 238 (1952).

7. J. Cohen and A. Veis, unpublished results (1959).

8. W. M. Ames, *J. Soc. Chem. Ind., (London)* **66**, 279 (1947).

9. J. H. Northrop, *J. Gen. Physiol.* **3**, 715 (1921).

10. J. H. Northrop, *J. Gen. Physiol.* **4**, 57 (1921).

11. R. J. Croome, *J. Appl. Chem. (London)*, **3**, 280 (1953).

12. A. Courts, *Biochem. J.* **58**, 74 (1954).

13. A. Courts and G. Stainsby, *in* "Recent Advances in Gelatin and Glue Research" (G. Stainsby, ed.), p. 100. Pergamon Press, New York, 1958.

14. S. E. Sheppard and R. C. Houck, *J. Phys. Chem.* **36**, 2319 (1932).

15. D. M. Greenberg and N. F. Burk, *J. Am. Chem. Soc.* **49**, 275 (1927).

16. J. C. Paulson and F. E. Deatherage, *Arch. Biochem. Biophys.* **56**, 363 (1955).

17. J. C. Paulson and F. E. Deatherage, *J. Biol. Chem.* **205**, 909 (1953).

18. J. C. Paulson, F. E. Deatherage, and E. F. Almy, *J. Am. Chem. Soc.* **75**, 2039 (1953).

19. E. Mihalyi, *J. Biol. Chem.* **201**, 197 (1953).

20. P. M. Gallop, S. Seifter, and E. Meilman, *Nature* **183**, 1659 (1959).

21. O. O. Blumenfeld and P. M. Gallop, *Biochemistry* **1**, 947 (1962).

22. W. Grassmann, H. Endres, and A. Steber, *Z. Naturforsch.* **9b**, 513 (1954).

23. K. Konno and K. I. Altman, *Nature* **181**, 995 (1958).

24. A. Courts, *Biochem. J.* **59**, 382 (1955).

25. M. Dixon and E. C. Webb, "Enzymes," pp. 266-272. Longmans, Green, New York, 1958.

26. J. E. Eastoe, *Biochem. J.* **61**, 589 (1955).

27. W. Grassmann, K. Hannig, and M. Schleyer, *Z. Physiol. Chem.* **322**, 71 (1960).

28. R. de la Burde, L. Peckham, and A. Veis, *J. Biol. Chem.* **238**, 189 (1963).

29. A. J. Hodge, J. H. Highberger, G. G. S. Deffner, and F. O. Schmitt, *Proc. Natl. Acad. Sci. U. S.* **46**, 197 (1960).

30. K. Kühn, J. Kühn, and K. Hannig, *Z. Physiol. Chem.* **326**, 50 (1961).

31. W. S. Ssadikow, *Biochem. Z.* **181**, 267 (1927).

32. I. Mandl, *Advan. Enzymol.* **23**, 163 (1961).

33. J. Tancous, *J. Am. Leather Chemists' Assoc.* **56**, 106 (1961).

34. I. H. Maseritz, *A. M. A. Arch. Surg.* **28**, 589 (1934).

35. R. DeBellis, I. Mandl, J. D. MacLennan, and E. L. Howes, *Nature* **174**, 1191 (1954).

36. N. H. Grant and H. E. Alburn, *Arch. Biochem. Biophys.* **82**, 245 (1959).

37. I. Mandl, H. Zipper, and L. T. Ferguson, *Arch. Biochem. Biophys.* **74**, 465 (1958).

38. S. Seifter, P. M. Gallop, L. Klein, and E. Meilman, *J. Biol. Chem.* **234**, 285 (1959).

39. P. M. Gallop, S. Seifter, and E. Meilman, *J Biol. Chem.* **227**, 891 (1957).

40. W. Grassmann, H. Hörmann, A. Nordwig, and E. Wünsch, *Z. Physiol. Chem.* **316** 287 (1959).

41. J. Manahan and I. Mandl, *Biochem. Biophys. Res. Commun.* **4**, 268 (1961).

42. J. Manahan and I. Mandl, in preparation (1963).

43. W. Grassmann, A. Nordwig, and H. Hörmann, *Z. Physiol. Chem.* **323**, 48 (1961).

44. Y. Nagai and H. Noda, *Biochim. Biophys. Acta* **34**, 298 (1959).

45. K. Heyns and G. Legler, *Z. Physiol. Chem.* **315**, 288 (1959).

46. K. Heyns and G. Legler, *Z. Physiol. Chem.* **321**, 184 (1960).

47. K. T. Poroshin, T. D. Kozarenko, V. A. Shibnev, and V. G. Debakov, *Bull. Acad. Sci. U.S.S.R., Div. Chem. Sci. (English Transl.)* No. 3, **550** (1960).

48. O. V. Kozakova, V. N. Orekhovich, and V. O. Shpikiter, *Doklady Acad. Nauk S.S.S.R.* **122**, 657 (1958).

49. S. Michaels, P. M. Gallop, S. Seifter, and E. Meilman, *Biochim. Biophys. Acta* **29** 450 (1958).

50. P. M. Gallop and S. Seifter, *in* "Collagen" (G. Ramanathan, ed.), p. 249. Wiley (Interscience) New York, 1962.

51. R. E. Schrohenloher, J. D. Ogle, and M. A. Logan, *J. Biol. Chem.* **234**, 58 (1959).

52. E. Meilman, P. M. Gallop, and S. Seifter, *in* "Recent Advances in Gelatin and Glue Research" (G. Stainsby, ed.), p. 260. Pergamon Press, New York, 1958.

53. S. Seifter, P. M. Gallop, and E. Meilman, *in* "Recent Advances in Gelatine and Glue Research" (G. Stainsby, ed.), p. 164. Pergamon Press, New York, 1958.

54. W. F. Harrington, P. H. von Hippel, and E. Mihalyi, *Biochim. Biophys. Acta* **32**, 303 (1959).

55. P. H. von Hippel, P. M. Gallop, S. Seifter, and R. S. Cunningham, *J. Am. Chem. Soc.* **82**, 2774 (1960).

56. P. H. von Hippel and W. F. Harrington, *Biochim. Biophys. Acta* **36**, 427 (1959).

57. K. H. Gustavson, *in* "Recent Advances in Gelatine and Glue Research" (G. Stainsby, ed.), p. 259. Pergamon Press, New York, 1958.

58. P. Desnuelle and S. Antonin, *Compt. Rend.* **221**, 206 (1946).

59. W. Grassmann and K. Kühn, *Z. Physiol. Chem.* **301**, 1 (1955).

60. H. Hörmann and G. Fries, *Z. Physiol. Chem.* **311**, 19 (1958).

61. P. M. Gallop, S. Seifter, and E. Meilman, *in* "Recent Advances in Gelatine and Glue Research" (G. Stainsby, ed.), p. 82. Pergamon Press, New York, 1958.

62. A. Courts, *Biochem. J.* **81**, 356 (1961).

63. P. Grabar and J. Morel, *Bull. Soc. Chim. Biol.* **32**, 643 (1950).

64. P. Davis, *in* "Recent Advances in Gelatine and Glue Research" (G. Stainsby, ed.), p. 225, Pergamon Press, New York, 1958.

65. P. Davis, *Trans. Faraday Soc.* **53**, 1390 (1957).

66. J. Bello, *Trans. Faraday Soc.* **55**, 2130 (1959).

The Gelatin ⟶ Collagen Transition

I. Introduction:
A Molecular Interpretation of Gel Formation

When an aqueous solution of a reasonably high molecular weight gelatin is cooled below 40°, certain characteristic changes can be detected. In all cases the specific optical rotation becomes more negative and the reduced viscosity increases. Depending upon the concentration of the gelatin, pH, and ionic strength, the solution may become more turbid and/or may set to a gel. X-ray diffraction analysis of a typical gel would yield a pattern similar to a powder diffraction pattern, indicating the formation of locally ordered regions (crystallites) but no crystallization or secondary long-range ordering of the crystallites. The characteristic spacings would be those of the collagen wide-angle x-ray diffraction pattern. Stretched films of the gelatin gel after drying would also show the infrared dichroism characteristic of oriented bundles of collagen fibers.

Consideration of these characteristic changes accompanying gel formation has led most investigators to propose that gel formation is the result of a partial, random return of the disordered gelatin to the collagen structure. This partial reordering has been treated in terms of both the "renaturation" of gelatin and the reintroduction of a characteristic "collagen-fold" in the ordered regions, but these terms have not been adequately defined. With the detailed information now available on collagen, gelatin, their macromolecular constituents, and their chemical composition, as developed in the previous chapters we are in position to be more specific in considering the gelation phenomena. The framework for the ensuing discussions of gelation is embodied in the following model.

As outlined in Fig. III-11, the ideal case of the collagen → gelatin transition would be the disordering of the macromolecular monomer, tropocollagen, and the separation of its component chains to form a mixture of α-, β-, and γ-gelatin units without hydrolysis of covalent bonds. Let us consider first a system containing predominantly α chains in such dilute solution that intermolecular interactions may be neglected. The chemical nature of the individual peptide strands is non-uniform in the sense that the amino acid sequence divides the α chain into contiguous segments of alternating polar and nonpolar character, on the one hand, and into segments rich and poor in imino acid residues on the other hand. It is probable that the consequent alterations in backbone chain properties are not regular, so that a stretched out α chain would be asymmetric in a fashion similar to the SLS form of collagen. Upon cooling, the specific optical rotatory power of a solution increases rapidly to a limiting value substantially lower than that of the tropocollagen. The reduced viscosity also increases, but much more slowly than does the optical rotation. The optical rotatory power changes may be interpreted as being the result of an *intra*molecular rearrangement of *limited* regions of the single peptide strand α unit. For a variety of reasons, it appears that this rapid change is related to the folding or helical winding of the imino acid-rich chain segments, and that the resulting chain configurations are similar to the configurations of these same segments when in the collagen structure. Therefore, we may term the intramolecular reorganization of the imino acid-rich portions of a single peptide strand as the building of the "collagen-fold" in gelatin, a more restricted definition than is generally used.

The single-strand α-gelatins exist as random coils in solution, each with a root-mean-square average chain extension that defines the domain of the molecule. A solution may be considered dilute when the volume of the solution is larger than the volume encompassed by the sum of all the unperturbed volumes of the molecular domains. A solution may be thought of as concentrated when the molecular domains overlap, and contacts between chain elements of different chains become as probable as contacts between elements of the same chain. For the α-gelatins, at neutral pH and moderate ionic strength, the concentration at which this overlap of molecular domains occurs is $\sim 0.5\%$. Solutions more dilute than this will not form gels. The mechanism of gelation probably involves the nonspecific interaction (hydrophobic bonding, hydrogen bonding, and electrostatic forces all being important) of the ordered segments on different, intimately entangled α strands. These aggregated chain elements, two ordered segments on two adjacent strands being all that is required to form a stable junction point, create the crystallites which are responsible for the wide-angle diffraction pattern of the gelatins. In the present view, this random gelation process does not correspond to a real regeneration of the collagen structure and should not be confused with the "renaturation" process. The terms "gelation" and "renaturation" are not synonyms.

The collagen molecule very clearly can be considered as having two levels of structural order. At the first level is the helical winding of the individual peptide strands into their characteristic collagen-fold configuration. At the second level is the apparently very precise alignment of the three peptide strands to provide complementary interaction of both side-chain functional groups and nonpolar-chain backbone segments. The term "renaturation" applies only to the processes whereby gelatins may be induced to attain both levels of structural organization. The complete renaturation of a gelatin-containing solution would lead to the formation of tropocollagen rods or highly asymmetric polymers of the tropocollagen, and not to the formation of isotropic three-dimensional gel networks; thus renaturation and gelation are competing processes. It is highly improbable that a solution containing only α chains could be renatured, because of the difficulty in simultaneously getting three strands into the correct juxtaposition; indeed, such a renaturation has never been observed. The probability of achieving renaturation grows as the α chain polymers are formed. Solutions rich in γ-gelatin are readily renaturable. Since the usual types of high molecular weight gelatin contain covalently cross-linked multichain units, some partial renaturation may occur under conditions which also favor gelation. Both reactions must be kept in mind in assessing much of the experimental data on systems undergoing gelation.

II. DEVELOPMENT OF THE COLLAGEN-FOLD: INTRAMOLECULAR ORGANIZATION

A. The Collagen-Fold

The essential features of the x-ray diffraction patterns of both collagen and gelatin were determined in the early 1930's by Herrmann, Gerngross, and Abitz (1) and Katz and co-workers (2, 3). Both collagen and gelatin showed the same three spacings, at 2.85, 4.5, and 11 Å. Katz and Derksen (3) reported that the apparent crystallinity of gelatin films depended on the method of film preparation. A dry gelatin film obtained from a gel prepared by cooling a concentrated gelatin solution before drying was more crystalline than a film obtained by drying the same solution at elevated temperature, avoiding the gelation step. It was almost twenty years before the significance of these data was fully appreciated. A typical study was that of Bradbury and Martin (4), who extended these observations. They found that "hot" films gave evidence of crystallinity, but that the 2.85 Å spacing was much weaker and the side spacing of 11 Å was both weaker and much more diffuse than in corresponding "cold" films. Films of cold gelatin examined with the x-ray beam parallel to the film surface gave much sharper diffraction patterns than when the beam was oriented perpendicular to the surface or than hot films in either orientation. It was argued from this that the crystallites in the films were asymmetric and similar in character in both hot and cold films, but that those in cold films were larger and oriented with their long axes parallel to the film surface. In hot films the crystallites appeared to be randomly oriented. In confirmation of these conclusions, Bradbury and Martin (4) found that oriented cold films would exhibit sharp thermal contraction to about two-thirds of their length and width when exposed briefly to boiling methanol, whereas hot films did not change dimension. Upon prolonged heating in methanol both hot and cold films would gradually elongate under their own weight, but the cold film would always contract first. The x-ray diffraction diagrams of the thermally contracted cold film were identical with those of the hot film. The crystallinity and orientation of the best cold films were considerably less than those of native collagen fibers. Under similar treatment a collagen fiber would shrink to about one-fourth of its original length before undergoing stress relaxation.

Tensile strength and extension studies (4) showed that cold films were uniformly stronger than comparably conditioned hot films, as anticipated from the higher crystallinity and orientation in cold films. The tensile strengths and extensions at break were strongly dependent on the relative humidity for both hot and cold films. The extensions at break were small in each case until a relative humidity (R.H.) of 65% was attained. Then the two films deviated markedly (Fig. V-1). The hot film extension increased sharply at this point. At this relative humidity and higher, the hot film exhibited a remarkable elasticity. It would, for example at 85% R.H., return to its original length upon removal of the load after being extended to 130% of its length. The low extensibility of the cold film was attributed to the alignment of rigid asymmetric units parallel to the film surface, in contrast to the random orientation of the peptide chains in the hot film, and to a larger number of interchain junction points in the cold film. The marked change in properties of the films at R.H. > 65% was ascribed to the fact that at this point the peptide chains had absorbed very nearly their maximum amount of firmly bound water (a 20–30% weight regain), and further hydration caused the rupture of interchain junctions.

The work of Bradbury and Martin (4) has been discussed in detail because it delineates three of the essential events of systems undergoing gelation:

1. The formation of asymmetric chain elements.

2. The establishment of interchain junction points.

3. An increase in the crystallinity or ordering of the gelatin system.

The first of these three events is an intramolecular process, whereas the latter two depend on intermolecular interactions.

In concurrent investigations Ambrose and Elliott (5–7) and Robinson and Bott (8) used polarized infrared spectrometry and optical rotation to examine these same events accompanying gelation. As a part of their extensive investigation of infrared spectra and the structure of the fibrous proteins, Ambrose and Elliott (5) showed that the two chief items of information obtainable from the collagen infrared spectrum are the C=O and N—H stretching frequencies. In native collagen, $\nu_{C=O} = 1660$ cm^{-1}

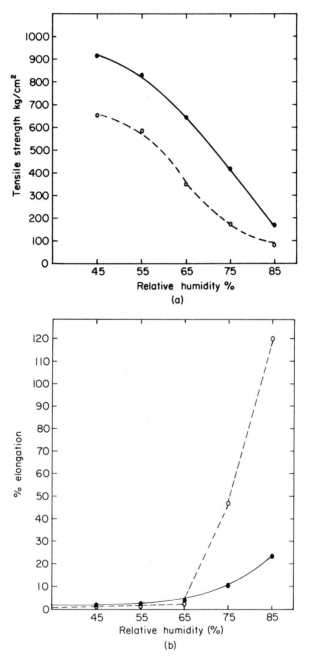

FIG. V-1. Properties of gelatin films as a function of relative humidity: (a) tensile strength, (b) % elongation; ●, "cold" film; ○, "hot" film [Bradbury and Martin (4)].

and $v_{NH} = 3330$ cm^{-1} and both absorption maxima show perpendicular dichroism with respect to the direction of collagen fiber long axis orientation. In the keratin series, the chracteristic frequency maxima occur at 1660 and 3300 cm^{-1} but the dichroism of the α and β forms are opposite. Ambrose and Elliott (5–7) discussed these differences in terms of an α-fold and β-fold of the peptide chains, and suggested that the peptide chains in collagen had their own particular collagen-fold which was stabilized by interchain hydrogen bonds. Comparing cold and hot gelatin films, Robinson and Bott (8) found that v_{NH} for cold films was 3330 cm^{-1}, whereas v_{NH} for hot films was only 3310 cm^{-1}. Oriented cold films exhibited perpendicular dichroism similar to collagen, but stressed hot films did not. The obvious conclusion was that the gelation step involved the formation of chain segments with the collagen-fold and intersegment hydrogen-bond stabilization. Optical rotatory power changes appeared to accompany the formation of the collagen-fold (8, 9). The data of Table V-1 clearly show that the hot film has the same optical rotatory power as a hot gelatin solution and no collagen-fold as measured by the N—H stretching frequency maximum. Cold films, on the other hand, have both a greatly enhanced negative optical rotation and the collagen-fold N—H frequency. Ferry and Eldridge (10) had shown that the change in $[\alpha]_D$ on cooling gelatin solutions was independent of the gelatin concentration in the range 2–6%. Robinson (9) worked down from 2% to 0.11% gelatin and found thet even in this range the concentration had only a small sec-

TABLE V-1 [a]

COMPARISON OF SPECIFIC ROTATION AND N-H
ABSORPTION OF HOT AND COLD GELATIN FILMS

State of gelatin during measurement	Specific rotation, $[\alpha]_D$	N-H stretching frequency (cm^{-1})
5% solution (40°)	—128°	—
5% solution (18°, 3 days)	—262°	—
Hot film [b]	—125°	3310
Cold film [c]	about —1000°	3330

[a] Data of Robinson (9).
[b] Solids 90%, evaporated at 55°.
[c] Solids 90%, evaporated at 18° after 3 days at 18° in gel form.

ondary effect at the very lowest temperatures. It is important to note however, that both Ferry and Eldridge and Robinson made their measurements on solutions first cooled and aged at 0° for 24 hours and then warmed to the measurement temperature for 1.5 hours. They were thus looking at the stability of aggregates or structures resulting from the common exposure to low temperature, rather than at the temperature sensitivity of aggregate or structure formation. There is a substantially higher activation energy for structure breakdown than for structure formation; hence, the procedure of cold quenching and rewarming does not give true equilibrium states over short time periods even when apparently constant properties are observed. Nevertheless, Robinson (9) argued from these data that the optical rotatory power changes observed were not primarily connected with the crystallinity of cold films, as might be inferred from the data of Bradbury and Martin (4). He concluded that the optical rotatory power and the v_{NH} maximum at 3330 cm^{-1} were related to the intramolecular organization of the peptide chains into their characteristic asymmetric chain elements. The magnitude of each of these observed changes was such that every molecule had to participate in the structural reorganization, or folding on gelation, even though the gel crystallinity (or long-range order) remained at a low level. The perpendicular infrared dichroism of oriented cold films indicated that interchain hydrogen bonds were forming between the internally organized asymmetric chain elements to provide strong interchain junction points, which lead to the creation of the three-dimensional gel network. This interpretation is strongly supported by the earlier observation of Gerngross, Herrmann and Lindemann (11), that although concentrated gelatin solutions set to a rigid gel immediately after cooling, the sharp x-ray diffraction rings did not appear for many hours. More than 3 days of aging were required before the diffraction patterns could be seen in 17–40% gelatin gels. In contrast, the optical rotation changes were virtually complete within 2 hours (12).

The primary event on cooling a gelatin solution thus appears to be an intramolecular reorganization of parts of the gelatin peptide chains to a configuration called the collagen-fold. Operationally, the collagen-fold is characterized by a negative optical rotation and an N — H stretching frequency absorption maximum of 3330 cm^{-1}. The fact that collagen-fold formation in gelatins is accompanied by the rapid development of the N—H stretching frequency characteristic of hydrogen bonding in collagen suggests that, although the process is concentration independent and apparently intramolecular, segments within a single molecule must be required to form hydrogen bonds during fold formation. A slower process is the formation of aggregates which lead to increased solution viscosity and ultimately the formation of rigid gels. Oriented gels exhibit the N—H and C=O stretching frequency dichroism. Finally and still more slowly, the gel aggregates age and crystallites develop, giving rise to the x-ray diffraction patterns of the matured gels.

Cold films containing gelatin in the collagen-fold configuration are less soluble than hot films. Pinoir and Pouradier (13) first observed that films dried at 60° would dissolve completely at 25°, or even at 18° if finely divided. However, at 10° there was evidence of a configurational transition. A hot film dissolved at the edges and began to swell; after only a small amount had dissolved swelling continued but dissolution stopped. Robinson (9) obtained similar results, except that he found a limit to solution of the gels at 18°. This behavior was interpreted as being the result of the formation of the collagen-fold and the concurrent development of a gel network. There is thus a substantial amount of free rotation or thermal motion of chain segments in highly hydrated, gelatin systems, even at low temperature. This is in agreement with the progressive increase in crystallinity of gels upon maturation, but further suggests that water plays an important role in stabilizing the collagen-fold.

B. Synthetic Polypeptides as Models of the Gelatin System

Gustavson (14) was among the first to suggest that proline and hydroxyproline residues might play a decisive role in controlling the structure and stability of both collagen and gelatin. This was amply borne out by the subsequent finding (15, 16) that the x-ray diffraction pattern of poly·L-proline was very similar to that of collagen. Indeed, the analysis of the poly-L-proline structure provided the basic framework for the interpretation of the more complex collagen diffraction patterns. It was natural, therefore, that extended investigations of the solution behavior of poly-L-proline and poly-L-hydroxyproline were carried out with the express object of explaining the behavior of gelatin systems. Polyglycine was also examined with a similar intent. These investigations have proven to be very fruitful.

1. *Synthesis of Polyglycine, Poly-L-proline, and Poly-L-hydroxyproline and Their Structures in the Solid State*

a. *Synthetic Methods.* Poly-L-proline was first synthesized by Berger, Kurtz, and Katchalski (17) by polymerization of N-carboxy-L-proline anhydride in nonaqueous systems with bases as initiators, or directly in pyridine. The anhydride synthesis preferred by these workers (*18*) involve the treatment of L-proline (I) with phosgene in dioxane to form an *N*-carbonyl chloride (II) which can be cyclized to the anhydride (III) in acetone solutions in the presence of silver oxide.

$$
\begin{array}{c}
\text{CH}_2\text{—CH—COOH} \\
| \\
\text{CH}_2 \qquad \\
\backslash \\
\text{CH}_2\text{—NH} \\
\text{(I)}
\end{array}
\quad \xrightarrow{\text{COCl}_2} \quad
\begin{array}{c}
\text{CH}_2\text{—CH—COOH} \\
| \\
\text{CH}_2 \qquad \\
\backslash \\
\text{CH}_2\text{—N—COCl} \\
\text{(II)}
\end{array}
\quad + \text{ HCl}
$$

$$\downarrow \text{Ag}_2\text{O}$$

$$
\begin{array}{c}
\text{CH}_2\text{—CH—C}=\text{O} \\
| \qquad \backslash \\
\text{CH}_2 \qquad \quad \text{O} \\
\backslash \qquad \quad / \\
\text{CH}_2\text{—N — C} \\
\qquad \qquad \backslash \\
\text{(III)} \qquad \quad \text{O}
\end{array}
\quad + \text{ HCl}
$$

$$\left. \begin{array}{c} \text{diethyl amine + dioxane} \\ \overline{\qquad\qquad\qquad} \\ \text{pyridine} \end{array} \right| \downarrow$$

$$
\left[
\begin{array}{c}
\qquad\qquad\quad \text{O} \\
\qquad\qquad\quad \parallel \\
\text{CH}_2\text{—CH—C—} \\
| \\
\text{CH}_2 \qquad \\
\backslash \\
\text{CH}_2\text{—N—}
\end{array}
\right]_n
\quad + \text{ CO}_2
$$

poly-L-proline

This method of synthesis yielded poly-L-proline with a molecular weight of the order of 10,000–20,000. Blout and Fasman (*19*) increased the degree of polymerization by resorting to strong base initiation. In the best cases the sodium methoxide-initiated polymerization of *N*-carboxy-L-proline anhydride in acetonitrile yielded polymers with weight-average molecular weights as high as 90,000.

The synthesis of poly-L-hydroxyproline is similar to that of poly-L-proline with the added complication that the hydroxyl group of the monomer must be blocked during polymerization. This has been accomplished by O-acetylation (*20*) and O-tosylation (*18*). After polymerization the problem is to remove the blocking groups. Kurtz *et al.* (*18*) treated the O-acetylated polymer with aqueous ammonia and obtained poly-L-hydroxyproline in fair yields, but even more drastic conditions, e.g. sodium in liquid ammonia, failed to yield a pure poly-L-hydroxyproline from the O-tosyl derivative. The poly-L-hydroxyprolines were of low average molecular weight.

Polyglycine is readily synthesized from N-carboxy-glycine anhydride. Copolymers of proline or hydroxyproline with glycine were prepared by Kurtz *et al.* (*18*) by mixing the desired ratios of the monomer N-carboxy anhydrides under the conditions required for the synthesis of poly-L-proline.

The three polymers, polyglycine, poly-L-proline, and poly-L-hydroxyproline, have a common property. When films of these materials are cast from solution and examined by x-ray diffraction methods, two distinct crystallographic patterns are observed for each polymer, the pattern developed being dependent upon the solvent system.

b. *Polyglycine structures.* Polyglycine films cast from acid solution (trifluoroacetic or dichloroacetic acid) exhibit x-ray diffraction maxima at 4.4 and 3.45 Å. If the polyglycine is precipitated from concentrated aqueous lithium bromide or calcium chloride the diffraction pattern exhibits a strong 4.15 Å reflection (*21, 22*). The acid-cast polyglycine is said to be in the polyglycine I configuration, the salt-precipitated form is termed polyglycine II. The polyglycine I spacings are typical of the β-structure of the KMEF group of proteins (keratin–myosin–epidermin–fibrinogen). The peptide chains are almost fully extended and hydrogen bonds are established between neighboring chains to form either parallel or antiparallel sheets (*22*). Form II, however, does not fit either the α- or β-structure. Crick and Rich (*23*) proposed a structure in which all the chains are parallel and packed in hexagonal array with each chain being hydrogen-bonded to each of its six nearest neighbors. This configuration is illustrated in Fig. V-2, in which the hydrogen bonding is indicated by the dashed lines. In this configuration each chain has a threefold screw axis. Two features sharply distinguished from the form I configuration are that the coiled chains are less extended along the chain axis, and that the hydrogen bonds run in several directions. The projection of the structure with the screw axis vertical (Fig. V-3) shows the hydrogen bond situation more clearly. The peptide groups at the bottom of the figure are inclined at an angle of 35° to the helix axes, and the hydrogen bonds formed run in an infinite sequence directly perpendicular to the plane of the paper. At the next set of carbonyl groups, another connecting plane of hydrogen bonds runs out at a different angle to the plane of the paper, and so on. The hydrogen bonding planes are separated by 3.1 Å along the chain axes, and the threefold axis thus has a repeat of 9.3 Å. The hydrogen bond length, nitrogen to oxygen, is 2.76 Å, and the chain packing is such that there is no room in the lattice for side chains unless some of the hydrogen bonds are broken. There is essentially no intrachain stabilization; the structure is created and stabilized solely by the interchain interactions. When polyglycine II precipitates are oriented, the chains readily elongate to the more extended form I-β configuration. Since there are no asymmetric car-

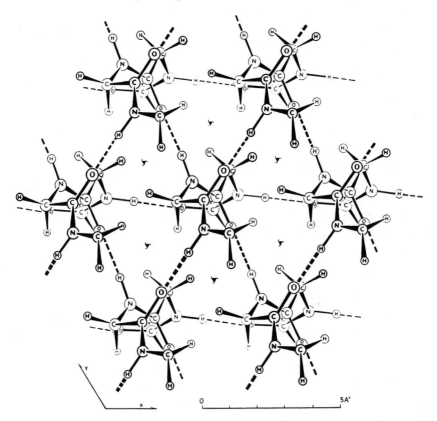

FIG. V-2. Axial projection of polyglycine II structure showing three residues of each chain: the dashed lines represent hydrogen bonds and show that each chain is hydrogen-bonded to its six nearest neighbors [Crick and Rich (23)].

bon atoms in polyglycine, the chains in form II may have either a right- or left-handed screw sense, and can be combined in both parallel and antiparallel arrays. Models have shown that it is possible to remove a chain from the structure and replace it with a chain running in the opposite direction, without disturbing either the number of hydrogen bonds or the x-ray diffraction pattern spacings.

Films of polyglycine cast from organic acid solutions are always in the form I-β configuration. However, Meggy and Sikorski (*24*) found that the form of the precipitates from aqueous salt solution was dependent on the precipitation temperature. If the polyglycine was precipitated from saturated calcium chloride solution at 20° by dilution with water, polyglycine II was the exclusive product. If the precipitation was carried out at 100°

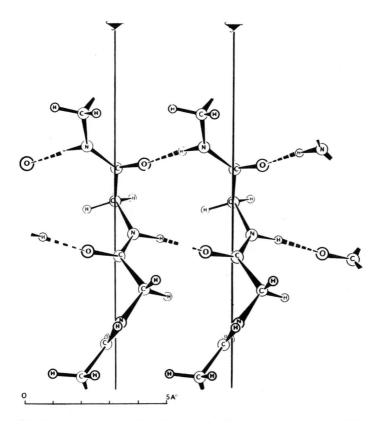

FIG. V-3. Projection of polyglycine II structure with the screw axis vertical. The x-axis indicated in Fig. V-2 points towards the reader; hence, the chain on the right is somewhat in front of the chain on the left. The hydrogen bonds indicated by dashed lines are almost perpendicular to the paper [Crick and Rich (*23*)].

by the same procedure, the more extended form I resulted. Precipitation at temperatures between 100° and 60° yielded mixtures of forms I and II. Polyglycine does not appear to assume any particular stable configuration in either acid solutions or concentrated aqueous salt solutions.

c. *Poly-L-proline structures.* Poly-L-proline precipitated from its basic polymerization mixture by addition of ether gives the characteristic infrared spectrum shown in Fig. V-4 a (*19*). A similar spectrum can be obtained if the precipitate is dissolved in glacial acetic acid and immediately cast into a film from that solvent. However, a second form of the spectrum is observed if the polymer is allowed to stand in glacial acetic acid at room temperature for several days, or if such a solution is heated to 100° for a few hours, or if the polymer is dissolved in a stronger acid than glacial acetic, e.g. trifluoroacetic acid. Every absorption band of the second spectrum (Fig. V-4 b), has a counterpart in the first spectrum, the most prom

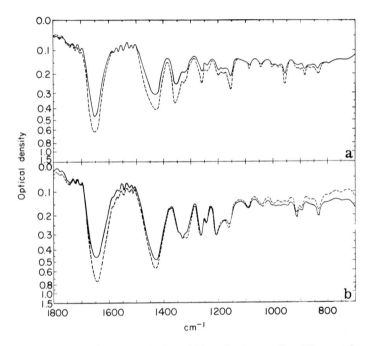

FIG. V-4. The infrared spectrum of oriented films of poly-L-proline. Films cast from acetic acid on silver chloride. (a) Form I. (b) Form II. Solid line: electric vector parallel to direction of orientation. Dashed line: electric vector perpendicular to direction of film orientation.

inent being C—H stretching modes at 2950 and 2860 cm^{-1}, C=O stretch at 1650 cm^{-1}, and a strong C—H vibration at 1435 cm^{-1} associated with the pyrrolidine ring. The first spectrum, however, has two additional strong absorption bands at 1355 cm^{-1} and at 960 cm^{-1}. Blout and Fasman (*19*) interpreted these data as indicating that there were two different interconvertible forms of poly-L-proline. The form resulting from direct precipitation of the polymer from the polymerization mixture was called poly-L-proline I, the form resulting from the action of acids on I was designated poly-L-proline II. The infrared spectra of forms I and II both showed weak perpendicular dichroism of the C=O bond at 1650 cm^{-1} and the pyrrolidine C—H band at 1435 cm^{-1}. The carbonyl dichroic ratios for I and II were 1.4 and 1.7, respectively.

The two forms of poly-L-proline show striking differences in solubility. Form I is insoluble in salt-free water, form II is readily soluble in cold water but precipitates from solution at temperatures above 65° (19). This phenomenon is completely reversible; the precipitates of II redissolve readily when the temperature is lowered, and the temperature recycling precipitation can be repeated indefinitely (18, 19). Form II poly-L-proline is soluble in many simple organic acids, such as formic, acetic, and propionic acids, however, trichloroacetic acid at 7.5–10% concentration will precipitate II from aqueous solutions. Anhydrous perchloric acid, periodic acid, hydrobromic acid, and sulfuric acid in glacial acetic acid will all precipitate I or II from acetic acid solutions. During perchloric acid precipitation the poly-L-proline binds about one-third of an equivalent of perchloric acid per proline residue (18).

Poly-L-proline I is soluble in chloroethanol but, as in glacial acetic acid, converts to form II. Similarly, poly-L-proline I converts to form II in 2.0–4.0 M potassium thiocyanate, 2.0–8.0 M urea, and 8.0 M guanidine hydrochloride. In the presence of these reagents the poly-L-proline does not precipitate upon heating to temperatures as high as 85°. In water solution the solubility of form II is not affected by variation of pH in the range 2–13 (19).

In spite of the differences in solubility of poly-L-proline I and II in water or aqueous salts, there is strong absorption in the infrared region at 3480 cm^{-1} in both forms. Blout and Fasman (19) found that on very thorough drying of the polyproline films this absorption band completely disappeared, and concluded that the band was due to very firmly adsorbed water. Bradbury et al. (25) found a similar strong band at 3450 Å in collagen preparations. The band intensity was a direct function of the humidity or water content of the collagen.

While Crick and Rich (23) were working out the structure of polyglycine II, Cowan and McGavin (15) were similarly engaged in an x-ray diffraction analysis of poly-L-proline II. It is of interest that the backbone chain structure proposed for poly-L-proline II is very similar to the polyglycine II backbone. The poly-L-proline II structure consists of polypeptide chains situated at trigonal positions, each chain having three equivalent residues related by an exact threefold screw axis. The residue repeat in the direction of the peptide chain axis is 3.12 Å. The density of such a structure was calculated to be 1.36 gm/ml for a unit cell of three proline residues. The experimentally determined density was 1.32 gm/ml.

The amide group in a peptide bond may have either a *cis* or *trans* configuration, the normal situation being that of a planar *trans* amide. *Cis* and *trans* models of poly-L-proline were constructed; the *cis* model gave a residue repeat of 2.83 Å and since a considerable distortion of bond angles was necessary to stretch the structure to give a 3.12-Å repeat, the *cis* structure was considered improbable. There was no difficulty in constructing the planar pyrrolidine ring, planar amide group *trans* structure with the appropriate coordinates, if a small distortion was allowed at the α-carbon atom. This strain can be relieved by puckering the pyrrolidine portion of the structure to take the α-carbon atom out of the plane of the ring by 0.4 Å. The structure is illustrated in Fig. V-5. The left-handed form of the helix is required for L-proline (*26*).

The poly-L-proline II structure is not stabilized by hydrogen bonding; rather it appears that steric factors and mutual repulsion of the partially charged carbonyl oxygens on successive residues favor the extended *trans* configuration. In contrast to polyglycine II, the polyproline non-hydrogen-bonded helix appears to be stable enough to maintain itself in solution, although in films or powders interchain van der Waals interactions determine the packing of the unit cells. The proposed model does account for the observed dichroism of the C=O stretching frequency, since the carbonyl groups extend perpendicularly from the helix axis. Sasisekharan (*27*) has confirmed all the essential features of the Cowan and McGavin model (*15*).

Poly-L-proline I can be obtained as powders and films sufficiently good for study by infrared techniques, but good oriented films suitable for detailed x-ray diffraction analysis have not yet been prepared. Consequently the crystal structure of poly-L-proline I has not been established in all details. Two preliminary reports, one by Cowan and Burge (*28*) and the other a personal communication by Rich and Crick, have been quoted by Harrington and von Hippel (*29*). Both reports suggest that the diffraction patterns of poly-L-proline I are compatible with a right-handed helix consisting of *cis*-prolyl residues. In the Cowan and Burge model there are three residues per turn with an axial repeat of 6.3 Å. The Rich and Crick model has three and one-eighth residues per turn with a lesser pitch to give an axial repeat of 5.85 Å. The *cis* model is illustrated in Fig. V-6 and suggests the weaker infrared perpendicular dichroism of the carbonyl stretching noted previously (*19*).

d. *Poly-L-hydroxyproline structure.* Poly-L-hydroxyproline is readily soluble in water at room temperature but, unlike poly-L-proline, is not soluble in pyridine, glacial acetic acid, or formic acid, nor is it soluble in the

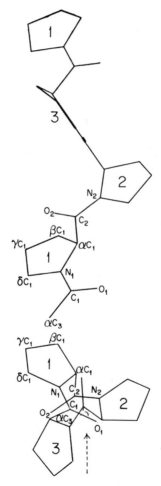

FIG. V-5. Projections of poly-L-proline II structure [Cowan and McGavin (*15*)].

usual nonpolar organic solvents. At elevated temperature poly-L-hydroxyproline is soluble in formic and glacial acetic acids. The derivatives, poly-O-acetyl-L-hydroxyproline and poly-O-*p*-tolylsulfonylhydroxy-L-proline, both show greater similarity to poly-L-proline than to the parent poly-L-hydroxyproline. Both derivatives are insoluble in water but soluble in pyridine, formic acid, and glacial acetic acid at room temperature (*18*).

The infrared spectrum of poly-O-acetyl-L-hydroxyproline is similar to that of poly-L-proline, except of course for the addition of the ester carbonyl absorption (*30*). The strong C=O stretching frequency is found at

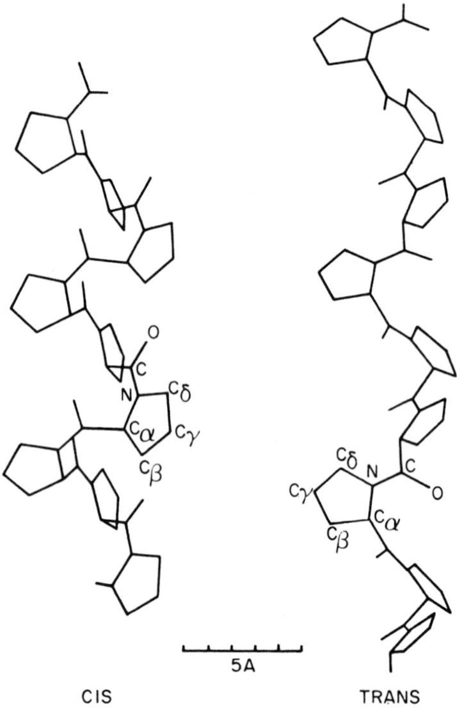

FIG. V-6. A comparison of poly-L-proline I and II structures. Poly-L-proline I (left) has each peptide bond in the *cis* configuration. Poly-L-proline II (right) has each peptide bond in the *trans* configuration. In both structures the neighboring ring planes are nearly perpendicular to each other [Harrington and von Hippel (*29*)].

1650 cm^{-1}. In poly-L-hydroxyproline, however, the C=O stretching maximum is lowered to 1620 cm^{-1}. Kurtz *et al.* (*30*) suggested that this shift was the result of intermolecular hydrogen bonding. The sharpness of the 1620-cm^{-1} absorption band indicated that the majority of the carbonyl groups participated in the hydrogen bonding. This conclusion was supported by studies of the molecular weight of poly-L-hydroxyproline in aqueous solution. From end-group titrations the degree of polymerization of a sample was determined to be 51, equivalent to a number-average molecular weight of 5750. Osmotic pressure and sedimentation-diffusion measurements lead to a molecular weight of 10,600, strongly indicating the formation of hydrogen bond-stabilized dimers (*30*). The end-group and osmotic pressure molecular weights of poly-L-proline were much closer and did not indicate significant association of the polymers in solution.

The x-ray diffraction pattern of poly-L-hydroxyproline was studied by Sasisekharan (*31*). He examined films and powders obtained by evaporation of aqueous poly-L-hydroxyproline solutions. The diffraction patterns were found to be very similar to that of poly-L-proline II. The peptide chains were packed in a hexagonal array of left-handed helices and the unit cell required three peptide chains, as in collagen. Sasisekharan (*31*) could find no evidence for the existence of another crystal form of poly-L-proline I. There is evidence for such forms of the acetylated and tosylated polymer. It is probable that any form I poly-L-hydroxyproline that might be synthesized during polymerization is isomerized to the more stable and extended form II during removal of the O-blocking group.

e. *Comparison of chain configurations.* The three amino acids, glycine, proline, and hydroxyproline, consitute more than 54% of the total residue content of collagen. The similarities between the structures which polymers of these three amino acids can assume in the solid state are remarkable. Both the polyglycine II and poly-L-proline II structures have a threefold screw axis with an exact 120° residue rotation. Polyglycine II has a residue repeat, from one α-carbon atom to the next, of 3.1 Å. More precise measurements on poly-L-proline II (*27*) place its residue repeat at 3.12 Å. The coordinates of the carbonyl carbon, oxygen, and nitrogen atoms are also extremely close in the two polymer systems.

Poly-L-hydroxyproline, in its stable form II configuration, and polyglycine II are both capable of forming interchain hydrogen bonds. In polyglycine II these hydrogen bonds provide the main structure-stabilizing forces. In form II poly-L-hydroxyproline, the structure-stabilizing effects of the interchain hydrogen bonds are superimposed on the intrinsic backbone-chain stability resulting from restricted rotation in the *trans* form of the Pro · Hypro peptide bond.

One can easily imagine that glycine-proline-hydroxyproline copolymers would readily assume the common structure regardless of the monomer weight ratios, and that the copolymers would tend to stabilize in the form II configuration since the polyglycine I and poly-L-proline I structures are quite dissimilar. The compatibility of the polyglycine II and poly-L-

proline II structures is undoubtedly of major importance in regulating the
organized configurations of collagen and gelatin peptide chains.

2. *Mutarotation of Poly-L-Proline and Poly-L-Hydroxyproline*

The early studies on poly-L-proline very quickly and clearly established
that the two forms of poly-L-proline could be differentiated by their optical
rotatory properties in solution just as readily as they could be differentiated by infrared and x-ray diffraction measurements in the solid state.
It was quite evident from the infrared studies cited earlier that the
polymer form was determined by the nature and properties of the solvent
system, and that the configurational transitions did not occur with equal
rapidity in all solvents upon transfer of poly-L-proline from one solvent
environment to another. Analyses of the optical rotatory changes accompanying the configurational transitions provide a very sensitive and con-
venient measure for these systems. It is well to bear in mind, however, that
the optical rotation data are interpreted in terms of the structures deduced
from the x-ray diffraction and infrared data on poly-L-proline and polyglycine in the solid state.

Poly-L-proline, precipitated with ether in form I from the basic polymerization mixture, gives an $[\alpha]_{546}^{25}$ of $+40$ when dissolved in glacial
acetic acid (*19*). The transition to form II proceeds slowly and, as shown
in Fig. V-7, the mutarotation is not complete even after 100 hours. After
heating a poly-L-proline solution in glacial acetic acid to 100° for 5 hours,
the final stable value of $[\alpha]_{546}^{25}$ was -730, and infrared examination of a
dried film from this solution showed that the poly-L-proline was entirely
in form II. The rotatory dispersions of the two forms (Fig. V-8), are distinctly different. Drude plots of the dispersion data of form II in various
solvents are all simple (i.e. linear) with a dispersion constant $\lambda_c = 206$ mμ.
The b_0 terms do vary (Fig. V-9).

The I → II poly-L-proline transition also alters the hydrodynamic
behavior in line with the predictions that might be made from the models
deduced from the diffraction data. The *cis* configuration of form I is more
highly folded and compact than the extended *trans* configuration of form
II. Accordingly, the reduced viscosity increases from about 1.0 to 1.43
during the I → II transition in glacial acetic acid (*19*) (Fig. V-7). Blout
and Fasman (*19*) determined the intrinsic viscosity and optical rotation of
form II poly-L-proline in a number of solvents; these data are plotted in
Fig. V-10. The organic and aqueous systems have different effects. All
the organic acids give higher viscosities than the aqueous solutions of

equivalent optical rotation. In the aqueous systems there appears to be a direct linear relationship between $[\eta]$ and $[\alpha]$, with urea and guanidine causing the higher viscosities and more negative specific rotations. The effect of concentrated potassium thiocyanate in lowering both rotation and viscosity of aqueous poly-L-proline is especially noteworthy. In gelatin-containing systems thiocyanate and urea are used interchangeably as denaturants. Obviously, their interaction with the gelatin must be different.

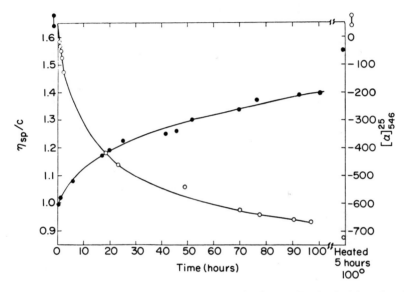

FIG. V-7. Reduced viscosity and specific rotation of poly-L-proline in glacial acetic acid as a function of time at 25° during form I → II mutarotation [Blout and Fasman (19)].

As is evident in Fig. V-10, water alone is sufficient to isomerize poly-L-proline from form I to form II. This was shown more strikingly by Kurtz et al. (18, 32), who followed the mutarotation of poly-L-proline upon dilution of the pyridine polymerization solution with water. Water concentrations above 10% led to mutarotation to form II. The mutarotation was faster in water than in glacial acetic acid (18, 19, 32), but dichloroacetic acid and formic acid converted form I to form II almost instantaneously. On the other hand, the mutarotation was considerably slower in propionic acid than in glacial acetic acid (33).

All the isomerizations noted above have been termed "forward" mutarotation–from form I to form II. For some time all attempts at reversing the mutarotation failed, but Steinberg, Berger and Katchalski (34) finally accomplished this by the addition of *n*-propanol or *n*-butanol to formic acid solutions of poly-L-proline II. The reverse mutarotation to form I was confirmed by the infrared spectra of ether precipitates of 90% propanol solutions. Ethanol and methanol were also effective in bringing about the reverse mutarotation, but when $[\alpha]_D^{25}$ reached a value of about

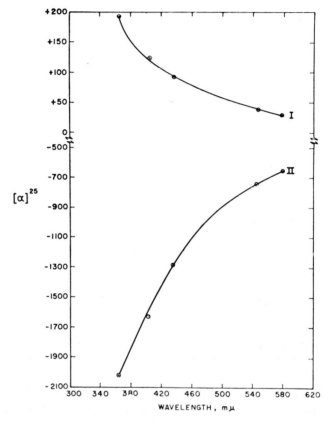

FIG. V-8. Optical rotatory dispersion of poly-L-proline in glacial acetic acid, concentration 0.2%. Upper curve: form I, 19°; lower curve: form II, 25° [Blout and Fasman (19)].

—250° the polymer precipitated from solution and the isomerization stopped. As might have been expected from the more rapid forward mutarotation in formic acid, the reverse mutarotation was more rapid in glacial acetic than in formic acid. The reversibility of the specific rotation of poly-L-proline was very strong evidence that form I ⇌ form II transitions involved only configurational changes rather than more deep-seated chemical modification of the polymer.

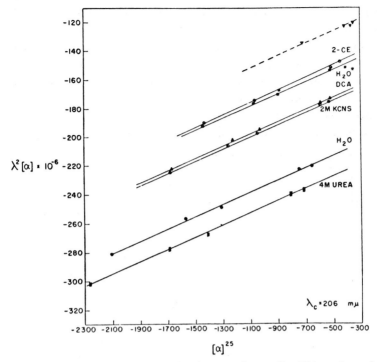

FIG. V-9. Drude plot of rotatory dispersion data on poly-L-proline II in various solvents. Polymer concentration 0.2%. 2-CE, 2-chloroethanol; DCA, dichloroacetic acid. H_2O^* is a low molecular weight sample as compared with a high molecular weight sample, H_2O. Dashed line represents rotatory dispersion data on ichthyocol at pH 3.7 [Blout and Fasman (*19*)].

The x-ray diffraction and infrared data indicate that the form I → form II transition is the conversion of a right-handed poly-L-proline helix with peptide bonds in the *cis* configuration to a left-handed helix with peptide bonds in the *trans* configuration. The *cis* configuration (I) may be defined as that configuration of the peptide bond in which adjacent α-carbon atoms are *cis*, whereas these α-carbons are *trans* in the *trans* configuration (II):

Alternatively, one may say that in the *cis* configuration the δ-carbon of proline is *cis* with respect to the carbonyl oxygen. Using the theory of Fitts and Kirkwood (*35, 36*) and the diffraction model parameters (*15, 28*) of the two poly-L-proline structures, Harrington and Sela (*37*) computed the rotations to be expected. For poly-L-proline II the left-handed *trans* helix contribution to $[\alpha]_D$ was calculated to be —230°. The right-handed *cis*-poly-L-proline I contribution was estimated at +204°. These values, combined with an estimated residue rotation of —250° to —300°,

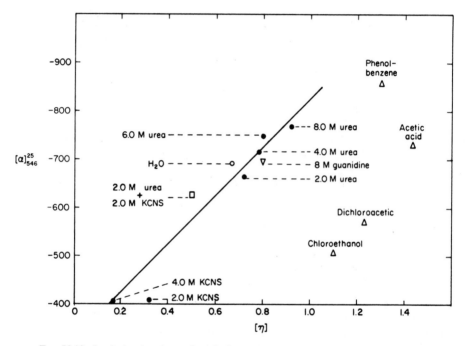

Fig. V-10. Intrinsic viscosity and optical rotation of poly-L-proline in various solvents [Blout and Fasman (*19*)].

gave satisfactory agreement with the observed $[\alpha]_D$ values for the two forms, and served as one verification that the transitions in solution were related to the configurations of poly-L-proline in the solid state.

Rotatory dispersion data gave linear $\lambda^2[\alpha]$ vs. $[\alpha]$ plots at every stage of the mutarotation in water (*37*). The values of λ_c obtained from the slopes of these plots are shown in Fig. V-11 as a function of $[\alpha]_D$; λ_c increased steadily from ~ 100 mμ for form I to ~ 200 mμ for form II, but two different reactions were evident. Harrington and Sela (*37*) interpreted the point of change in slope in the λ_c vs. $[\alpha]_D$ plot as marking the region at which all structure was lost, that is, the $[\alpha]_D$ of $\sim -250°$ corresponded to the intrinsic residue rotation of amorphous polyproline. The variation in λ_c on either side of this point is then a measure of the right-handed *cis* or left-handed *trans* helix content. The first reaction of forward mutarotation, accordingly, is the collapse of the form I structure. The linearity of the two branches of the plot of Fig. V-11 was taken to signify that extended helical segments of form II were not built until the majority of the *cis* configurations had been isomerized.

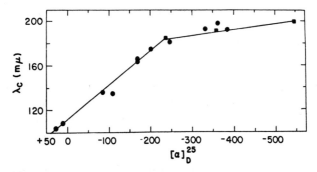

FIG. V-11. The rotatory dispersion constant of poly-L-proline as a function of the specific rotation: ●, data taken during mutarotation of poly-L-proline I; ■, data obtained from poly-L-proline II in varying concentrations of lithium bromide [Harrington and Sela (*37*)].

Downie and Randall (*38*) agreed with the conclusion that the mutarotation was a *cis-trans* isomerization, but disputed the contention that the mechanism involved the formation of an essentially amorphous intermediate. Their kinetic studies suggested that the intermediate stage consisted of molecules with many short sequences of *cis* and *trans* residues in which neither helical structure was developed. During forward mutarotation the *cis* helical contribution to $[\alpha]$ diminishes but the *trans* helix contribution steadily increases. These structure effects are superimposed on the intrinsic changes in optical properties that would be seen in an isolated pair of residues. Downie and Randall, therefore, concluded that the change in specific rotation could not be directly proportional to the fraction of polymer isomerized, and that the reaction order could not be determined from a plot of log $(d[\alpha]/dt)$ vs. log $([\alpha] - [\alpha]_\infty)$ for the mutarotation observed at a single poly-L-proline concentration. The reaction order would, however, be determined by observing the mutarotation rate at several poly-L-proline concentrations.

Defining $[\alpha]_\infty$ as the specific rotation of the polymer at completion of mutarotation, $[\alpha]$ as the observed specific rotation at time t, c_0 as the initial polymer residue concentration (in the I form), c as the concentration of unisomerized residues at t, and x as the fraction c/c_0, Downie and Randall (38) then set $([\alpha] - [\alpha]_\infty)$ to be a function of x only, $f(x)$, from which it followed that

$$\frac{d[\ln([\alpha] - [\alpha]_\infty)]}{dt} = \frac{f'(x)x}{f(x)c} \frac{dc}{dt} \tag{1}$$

Assuming that the reaction is first order with respect to the polymer concentration, then $1/c\ (dc/dt)$ is the rate constant k and

$$\frac{d[\ln([\alpha] - [\alpha]_\infty)]}{dt} = k \frac{f'(x)x}{f(x)} = kF(x) \tag{2}$$

If $f(x)$ is a function only of x, the fraction of bonds unisomerized, $f(x)$, should be independent of temperature and c_0 so that $F(x)$ should also be a constant for any given value of $[\alpha] - [\alpha]_\infty$. Studies on the forward mutarotation of poly-L-proline in glacial acetic acid at various temperatures and varying polymer concentrations verified the validity of these assumptions. The mutarotation appears to be a first order reaction with respect to the polymer concentration. A plot of log $kF(x)$ vs. the reciprocal of the temperature yielded a straight line from which the activation energy was determined to be 22.9 kcal/mole of isomerizing residues, assuming that each residue reacts independently. The frequency factor for the isomerization reaction was of the order of $10^{11} - 10^{12}$ sec^{-1}, in the normal range for a single process. If the isomerization were a cooperative phenomenon involving simultaneous isomerization of several residues, the frequency factor should have had an abnormally high value. The amide group had a decided double-bond character and is stabilized by a resonance energy of about 21 kcal/mole (39). In the absence of steric effects the cis-trans isomerization of a normal peptide bond should be of the order of the resonance energy. The activation energy found for the mutarotation of poly-L-proline is thus just that expected for the cis-trans isomerization uncomplicated by steric factors.

In support of their mechanism (complete collapse of structure), Harrington and Sela (37) reported that the reduced viscosity of poly-L-proline in water went through a distinct minumim during the forward mutarotation, the minimum occurring at a point corresponding to a mixture $[\alpha]_D$ of $-100°$ to $-150°$. Downie and Randall (38) found that in their glacial acetic acid system the reduced viscosity increased throughout the mutarotation. This discrepancy suggests that the mechanism of mutarotation was substantially different in the two solvent systems, although the end result in both cases was the conversion of the right-handed *cis* form I helix to the left-handed *trans* form II helix.

Steinberg *et al.* (*33*) confirmed the experiments of Downie and Randall (*38*) in most particulars. However, Steinberg *et al.* did find that a plot of log $([\alpha]_t - [\alpha])$ vs. log $(d[\alpha]/dt)$ was linear for the mutarotation in glacial acetic acid. The slope of the line indicated the reaction order to be 4/3 at constant polymer concentration. The reaction was first order with respect to polymer. The activation energies were determined for both forward and reverse mutarotation. The two values were essentially identical, $\Delta H_F^{\ddagger} = 20.6$ kcal/mole peptide bond and $\Delta H_R^{\ddagger} = 20.2$ kcal/mole peptide bond, which led to the conclusion that the enthalpy change in the mutarotation was practically zero.

The profound effect of the solvent on the mutarotation, and particularly the effect of water, was demonstrated by the marked change in kinetics observed in acetic acid-water mixtures or in water alone as compared with the glacial acetic acid system. The rate of forward mutarotation was constant in acetic acid-water up to the completion of two-thirds of the isomerization reaction. A value of $\Delta H^{\ddagger} = 24$ kcal/mole was obtained for the mutarotation in a 7 : 3 (v/v) acetic acid-water system. As in the glacial acetic acid system, the rate of mutarotation at a given temperature and solvent composition was independent of the polymer molecular weight. The viscosity behavior was also different in the two solvent systems. As in the work of Downie and Randall (*38*), the reduced viscosity increased at all points in the forward mutarotation in glacial acetic acid, while the viscosity decreased first in the acetic acid-water system (Fig. V-12). As is evident in Fig. V-12, the value of $[\alpha]_D$ does not uniquely predict the hydrodynamic properties of poly-L-proline. These data suggest that Downie and Randall (*38*) were correct in asserting that $[\alpha]_D$ is not a parameter that unambiguously measures the *cis/trans* ratio. Nevertheless Steinberg *et al.* (*33*) used exactly this assumption for the analysis of the kinetics of the mutarotation.

The assumption was made that each individual L-proline residue associated with a *cis* or *trans* peptide bond contributed to the observed specific rotation of the system according to the specific rotations of each form $[\alpha]_I$ and $[\alpha]_{II}$, such that

$$[\alpha] = \frac{c_{cis}}{c_0} [\alpha]_I + \frac{c_{trans}}{c_0} [\alpha]_{II} \tag{3}$$

In this equation c_{cis} and c_{trans} are the concentrations of the *cis* and *trans* peptide bonds, respectively, and $c_0 = c_{cis} + c_{trans}$. Equation 3 can be rearranged to

$$\frac{c_{cis}}{c_0} = \frac{[\alpha] - [\alpha]_{II}}{[\alpha]_I - [\alpha]_{II}} \tag{4}$$

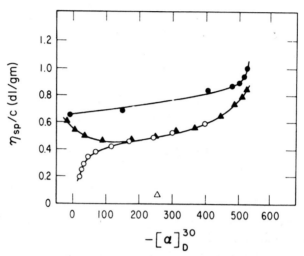

FIG. V-12. Reduced viscosity of poly-L-proline during mutarotation: ⊖, I → II mutarotation in glacial acetic acid; ▲, I → II mutarotation in acetic acid-water (7:3 v/v); ○, II → I mutarotation in acetic acid-propanol (2:8 v/v); △, value in aqueous 12 M lithium bromide [Steinberg et al. (33)].

Since c_0, $[\alpha]_I$, and $[\alpha]_{II}$ are fixed, then $d[\alpha]/dt$ is a direct measure of dc_{cis}/dt. Assuming further that the mutarotation is a spontaneous cis-trans transformation dependent only in c_{cis}, then

$$-\frac{dc_{cis}}{dt} = Kc_{cis} \tag{5}$$

As in the kinetic analysis of Downie and Randall (38), the "reaction constant" K is not necessarily a constant during the entire course of the mutarotation but varies with the degree of conversion. That is, one should obtain constant K's at constant $[\alpha]$'s in any particular solvent system. K is thus a function of the degree of conversion, $f(c_{cis}/c_0)$, or, equivalently, of the reaction time, $\Phi(t)$. Expressed in terms of a reaction of a given order, β, Eq. 5 becomes

$$-\frac{dc_{cis}}{dt} = k\left(\frac{c_{cis}}{c_0}\right)^{\beta-1} c_{cis} \tag{6}$$

which can be integrated and reduced to

$$k(t) = \frac{k}{1 + k(\beta - 1)t} \tag{7}$$

Equation 7 indicates the manner in which the apparent first order reaction constant varies during the course of the mutarotation. When $\beta > 1$, as in the case for the forward mutarotation in glacial acetic acid ($\beta = 1.35$), $k(t)$ decreases with time. When $\beta = 1$, exemplified by the reverse mutarotation in acetic acid-propanol, $k(t)$ is constant. Finally, when $\beta < 1$, $k(t)$ increases with time. In the special case of zero order kinetics, as observed in the initial stages of the mutarotation in acetic acid-water, $k(t) = k/(1 - kt)$. In spite of the limitations inherent in the basic assumptions, it appears that this kinetic analysis is capable of serving as a means for classifying various mechanisms of mutarotation.

Steinberg et al. (33) found that the addition of strong mineral acids, such as perchloric, sulfuric, hydrobromic, and periodic acids, catalyzed both forward and reverse mutarotation in the aliphatic acids. Very small amounts, as shown in Fig. V-13, markedly increased the rate of mutarotation of both

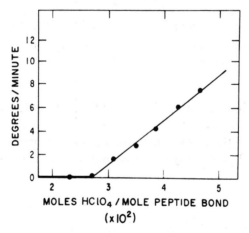

FIG. V-13. Effect of the binding of perchloric acid on rate of I → II mutarotation of poly-L-proline. Reaction at 30°. Rotation as $[\alpha]_D$ [Steinberg et al. (33)].

poly-L-proline and poly-O-acetyl-hydroxy-L-proline. A variety of measurements showed that the mineral acids were firmly bound to the polymer. Precipitates of both poly-L-proline I and poly-L-proline II obtained upon addition of anhydrous perchloric acid were found to have 0.26–0.31 mole of bound perchloric acid per mole peptide bond. Titration of poly-O-acetylhydroxyproline with perchloric acid in acetic anhydride gave a sharp end point when 37% of the imide nitrogens were titrated.

When poly-O-acetylhydroxyproline is dissolved in acetic anhydride, form I is favored and $[\alpha]_D = +40°$. In the presence of perchloric acid in the equivalence range of 0.3 mole per mole peptide bond, form II is favored with $[\alpha]_D = -130°$. With lesser amounts of perchloric acid intermediate values of $[\alpha]_D$ are obtained, as shown in Fig. V-14, which

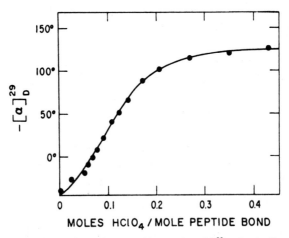

FIG. V-14. Equilibrium values of the specific rotation $[a]_D^{29}$, of poly-O-acetylhydroxy-L-proline in acetic anhydride as a function of the binding of perchloric acid [Steinberg *et al.* (*33*)].

are stable equilibrium values. These equilibrium studies and the catalytic effect of strong mineral acids on the mutarotation led to the postulate that the mutarotation proceeded through a protonated form of the imide bond. The imide bond can be considered as resonating between the four structures

$$
\begin{array}{cccc}
\underset{(A)}{
\begin{array}{c}
\text{C} \qquad \text{C} \\
\diagdown \; \diagup \\
\text{C—N} \\
\parallel \quad \diagdown \\
\text{O} \qquad \text{C}
\end{array}
}
&
\underset{(B)}{
\begin{array}{c}
\text{C} \qquad \text{C} \\
\diagdown \; \diagup \\
\text{C=N} \\
\mid \quad \overset{+}{} \diagdown \\
\text{O}_- \qquad \text{C}
\end{array}
}
&
\underset{(C)}{
\begin{array}{c}
\text{C} \qquad \text{C} \\
\diagdown \; \diagup \\
\text{C=N} \\
\mid \quad \overset{+}{} \diagdown \\
\text{OH} \qquad \text{C}
\end{array}
}
&
\underset{(D)}{
\begin{array}{c}
\text{C} \quad \text{H} \;\; \text{C} \\
\diagdown \; \mid \diagup \\
\text{C—N} \\
\parallel \quad \overset{+}{} \diagdown \\
\text{O} \qquad \text{C}
\end{array}
}
\end{array}
$$

with $\xrightarrow{\;+H^+\;}$ and $\xleftarrow{\;-H^+\;}$ between B and C

pictured, the latter two being protonated. Free rotation about the C—N bond is possible only in forms A and D, and the protonation requirement suggests that the *cis-trans* isomerization proceeds through form D. Poly-L-proline II is the more extended configuration and hence would be

favored by the electrostatic repulsion between successive protonated peptide bonds, as is the case. Further support for the protonation mechanism can be found in work on the nuclear magnetic resonance (n.m.r.)
of N-methylacetamide (40) and N, N-dimethylacetamide in neutral a-
queous solution. The latter compound shows the presence of two N—C
methyl lines in the n.m.r. spectra because of the nonequivalence of the
cis- and trans-N-methyl groups. Acidification of the solution collapses the
doublet to a single line characteristic of that in N-methylacetamide, indicating the onset of free rotation.

All of the data and experiments cited above demonstrate that the mutarotation of poly-L-proline in aliphatic organic acids, water-acid or al-
cohol-acid mixtures, involves the cis-trans isomerization of the imide peptide
group at the —C=O—N$\diagdown$ bond and requires the protonation of the bond.
The activation energy is of the order of 21 kcal/mole of peptide bond
stabilization. The frequency factor is also in the normal range, $\sim 10^{11}$,
and the reaction proceeds slowly, in accord with the high activation energy,
unless strong mineral acid catalysts are present. As a result of the protonation of the peptide bond the extended trans configuration is favored in
acidic and aqueous media. Basic proton acceptors favor the reverse mutarotation to the cis form and attenuate the effect of acid catalysts. Blout
and Fasman (19) pointed out that concentrated aqueous salt solutions had
a significantly different effect on the mutarotation than the aqueous acid
solvent systems. Harrington and Sela (37) and Steinberg et al. (33) explored the concentrated aqueous neutral salt effects in detail and concluded (33) that the cis-trans peptide bond isomerization could not explain
their data. In particular, the effect of the salts on the specific rotation
and intrinsic viscosity of form II poly-L-proline was immediate. The equilibrium values were reached within the brief time interval required for
measurement. Further, the intrinsic viscosity of the polymer in concentrated salt solutions was always significantly lower than in the alcohol-
acid systems favoring the reverse mutarotation.

Steinberg et al. (34) proposed that the neutral salts effected the isomerization at the C_a—C=O bond, the only other bond in polyproline aside
from the peptide C—N bond capable of rotation. They examined the system by following the mutarotation of a 5% poly-L-proline II solution in
12 M lithium bromide when that solution was diluted 50-fold with water
to form 0.2 M solution. In the original concentrated salt solution $[\alpha]_D =$
—250° and the final value in the dilute salt approached —540°. A typical set of kinetic data is shown in Fig. V-15. Upon dilution $[\alpha]_D$ immediately changed to —400°; the kinetic data refer only to the slower proc-

ess covering the range in $[\alpha]_D$ from $-400°$ to $-540°$. The Arrhenius plot (lower straight line in Fig. V-15) showed the activation energy to be 20.6 kcal/mole, similar to that of the previously noted peptide bond isomerization, but the reaction induced by neutral salt dilution was about 10^3 times faster. Application of the transition state theory to these data led to estimates of the entropy of activation, $\Delta S^{\ddagger}$, for the acid-catalyzed and salt dilution-induced reactions, of -12.5 and -0.84 e.u., respectively. That the peptide bond was not involved in the dilution-induced re-

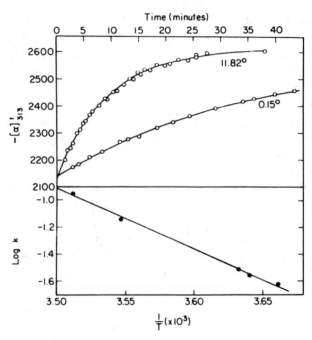

FIG. V-15. Kinetics of I → II mutarotation in aqueous lithium bromide solutions, upon dilution from 12.0 M to 0.2 M lithium bromide. Upper figure, kinetic data; lower figure, Arrhenius plot [Steinberg et al. (33)].

actions was demonstrated by the persistence of the characteristic peptide bond doublet in the n.m.r. spectra of poly-L-proline in concentrated lithium bromide and sodium thiocyanate.

A study of space-filling atomic models of poly-L-proline (33) showed that there is a definite restriction to rotation about the C_a—C=O bond. Steinberg et al. (33) pointed out that if the peptide bond is in the *trans* configuration, the C_a—C=O bond can assume two positions. These are illustrated in Fig. V-16. In the first position the hydrogen on the α-carbon is *cis* to the oxygen and this is designated *cis'*. In the second, the *trans'* configuration, the hydrogen on the α-carbon is *trans* to the carbonyl oxygen. Similarly, as illustrated, there are two *cis* peptide bond configurations, *cis-cis'* and *cis-trans'*. The poly-L-proline II left-handed helix described by Cowan and McGavin (*15*) and Sasisekharan (*27*) corresponds to the *trans-trans'* arrangement. A *trans-cis'* configuration would require a

Trans peptide bond

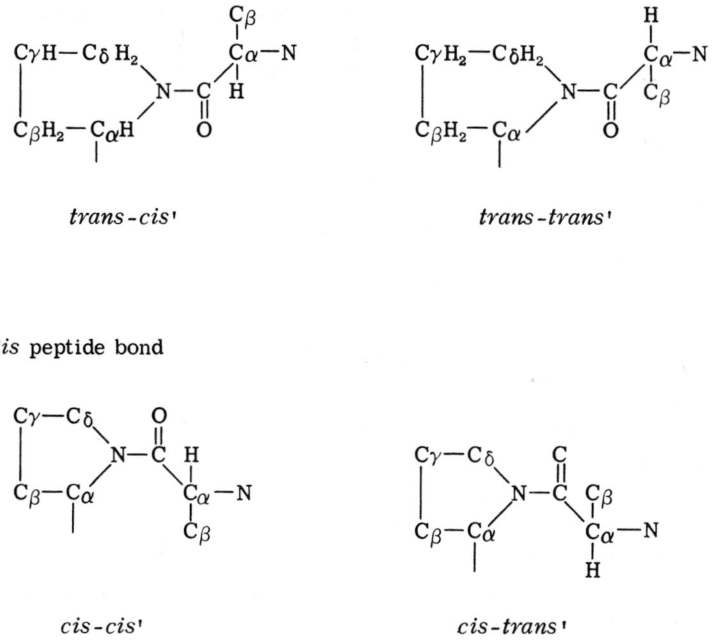

trans - cis'   trans - trans'

Cis peptide bond

cis - cis'   cis - trans'

FIG. V-16. Stereochemical arrangements of proline–proline peptide bonds.

right-handed helix and this is clearly incompatible with all of the data on the structure of poly-L-proline II. A right-handed helix can be built from the combinations *cis-trans'* and *trans-cis'*. Since the poly-L-proline I structure has its peptide bonds in the *cis* configuration, the organized form I helix must have the *cis-trans'* combination. The neutral salts, at high concentration, then, appear to bring about a very rapid *trans'-cis'* isomerization, leaving the peptide bonds in the *trans* configuration. The polymer in this form has no helical character and has a very compact structure and, consequently, a low intrinsic viscosity compared with that of either the right- or left-handed I and II helices.

We can turn now to reexamine the data collected by Harrington and Sela (*37*) on the optical rotatory dispersion and specific rotation of poly-L-proline in aqueous salt systems. The pertinent data are in Fig. V-11 and Table V-2. Additional data of Blout and Fasman (*19*) are shown in Fig. V-10. In water and in dilute salt solution the poly-L-proline stable

TABLE V-2 [a]

OPTICAL ROTATION AND ROTATORY DISPERSION OF SOME AQUEOUS POLY-L-PROLINE SYSTEMS

Solvent	$[a]_D^{25}$ (degrees)	λ/c ($m\mu$)	Structure type
KCl (0.1 *M*)	−540	202	*trans-trans'*
Urea (8.0 *M*)	−546	210	
Guanidine-HCl (6.0 *M*)	−516	206	
LiBr (6.45 *M*)	−364	192	*trans-cis'*
LiBr (10 *M*)	−250	—	
LiBr (12.9 *M*)	−243	185	
CaCl₂ (satd.)	−233	—	
LiClO₄ (satd.)	−215	—	
Pyridine (satd. with LiBr)	−237	185	
KSCN (5 *M*)	−250	—	
H₂O (form II polyproline)	−540	210	*trans-trans'*
H₂O (form I polyproline)	+ 33	100	*cis-trans'*

[a] Data of Harrington and Sela (*37*).

configuration is that of form II with the *trans-trans'* arrangement. This arrangement is also assumed by the polymer in the protein denaturants, 8.0 *M* urea and 6.0 *M* guanidine hydrochloride. These denaturing reagents apparently have no effect on the stability of the *trans-trans'* Pro · Pro peptide sequence. On the other hand, the concentrated neutral salts "unlock" the C_a—C=O *trans'* configuration to produce a highly folded *trans-cis'* structure.

All of the remarks relating to the configuration of poly-L-proline probably apply with equal validity to poly-L-hydroxyproline. Experiments on the forward mutarotation of the poly-L-hydroxyproline have not been possible because of the highly acidic nature of the aqueous medium required for deacetylation of the polymerization mixture. During deacetylation the conversion to form II is essentially complete. The poly-L-hydrox-yproline is also insoluble in the organic acid-alcohol mixture used to bring about the reverse mutarotation. However, the addition of 6.0 M lithium bromide to poly-L-hydroxyproline in aqueous solution lowers $[\alpha]_D$ from $-384°$ to $-168°$ and λ_c from 206 mμ to 191 mμ in exact analogy to the behavior of poly-L-proline II. Chemically modified poly-L-hydrox-yprolines which are soluble in the acid-alcohol mixtures exhibit the mutarotary phenomena of poly-L-proline (33).

C. Intramolecular Effects in the Formation of the Collagen-Fold in Dilute Gelatin Solutions

1. Mechanism of Collagen-Fold Formation

We now turn our attention to gelatin systems to examine the development of the collagen-fold from the disorganized random gelatin structure found in warm aqueous evironment. In this discussion we shall be concerned primarily with the intramolecular events associated with the formation of the collagen-fold as outlined earlier in Section II A. The secondary slower intermolecular aggregation will be treated later. Most of the early work, typified by that of Smith (12) and Ferry and Eldridge (10), was carried out at gelatin concentrations sufficiently high so that the gelatin solutions set to gels shortly after cooling, indicating the formation of interacting chain networks. The principal contributions to the question of the intramolecular mechanism of the development of the collagen-fold have come from the collaborative investigations by Harrington and von Hippel (41–43), in which the gelatin concentrations were kept well below the minumum concentrations required for gelation.

Von Hippel and Harrington (41) found that the kinetics of the degradation of ichthyocol collagen by collagenase were strongly temperature dependent. Above the ichthyocol denaturation temperature the collagenase action could be described by a single first order rate constant for all bonds split. Below the denaturation temperature the reaction kinetics were more complex, but could be adequately explained by two simultaneous first order reactions. (See Fig. IV-14 and 15 and Section III B 2 of Chapter IV for discussion of the experimental details.) The onset of the complex kinetics was immediate upon cooling the ichthyocol below 27° and was independent of the method of cooling. That is, quick quenching was no less effective than slow cooling in inducing the complex kinetics.

Optical rotation measurements were carried out to determine if there was a correlation between the kinetic mechanism and the peptide chain configuration (41). Ichthyocol gelatin was formed by heating an ichthyocol solution in 0.5 M calcium chloride, pH 6.0–6.5, for 5 minutes at 40°. The solution was quenched, i.e. cooled rapidly, to the desired low temperature. The specific rotation increased slowly to more negative values over a time span of several hours (Fig. V-17). In a parallel experiment collagenase was added to the gelatin solution immediately after quenching and the

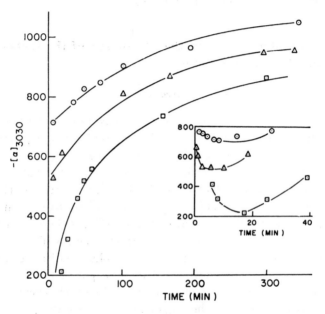

FIG. V-17. Formation of the collagen-fold as indicated by change in specific rotation upon quenching an ichthyocol gelatin solution from 40° to 11.5°: ○, gelatin concentration 0.147%; △, 0.047%; □, 0.028% [von Hippel and Harrington (41)].

specific rotation measured as a function of time. In this case (Fig. V-18) the specific rotation decreased as expected, but the lowest value of $[\alpha]$ due to proteolysis was reached within about 90 minutes. As with the pH-stat data (Chapter IV), the rate of change of the specific rotation could be represented as the sum of two first order reactions. Setting $[\alpha]$ as the specific rotation at time t, $[\alpha]_i$ as the initial rotation, $[\alpha]_\infty$ as the final rotation, $[\alpha]_0 = [\alpha]_i - [\alpha]_\infty$, and k as the apparent first order rate constant, then the integrated first order rate equation becomes

$$\ln \left[\frac{([\alpha] - [\alpha]_\infty)}{([\alpha]_i - [\alpha]_\infty)} \right] = - kt \qquad (8)$$

Combining Eq. 8 with its differential form

$$\frac{d[\alpha]}{dt} = - k([\alpha] - [\alpha]_{\infty}) \qquad (9)$$

Harrington and von Hippel arrived at Eq. 10

$$\ln \left(\frac{d[\alpha]}{dt} \right) = \ln \left[(- k[\alpha]_0) - kt \right] \qquad (10)$$

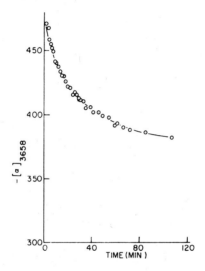

FIG. V-18. Action of collagenase on ichthyocol gelatin at 12°. Solution quenched from 40° just prior to addition of collagenase [von Hippel and Harrington (*41*)].

which predicts that a plot of log $(d[\alpha]/dt)$ vs. t will be linear. Typical data are illustrated in Fig. V-19. The upper curve is the rate data plotted as obtained according to Eq. 10. The linear portion of the plot in the region when the reaction was nearing completion was used to calculate the rate constant of the slow reaction. The change in $[\alpha]$ resulting from the slow reaction was then computed and used to calculate the change in $[\alpha]$ and the corresponding rate terms of Eq. 10 occasioned by the first rapid reaction. The two linear plots in the lower part of the figure represent the result of these computations. The transfer of collagenase-susceptible bonds from the fast reaction, characteristic of collagenase action on gelatin above the melting temperature of gelatin gels, to the slow reaction was substantially complete within 20 minutes, and the entire reaction was concluded within 120 minutes. These studies, and similar analyses of viscosity and light scattering data, clearly indicated that the configurational arrangements leading to the high levorotation and high viscosity of cooled gelatins were preceded by some other very rapid intramolecular transition.

Inasmuch as the specificity of collagenase involves the sequence

$$X—Pro \cdot R_1 \cdot Gly \cdot Pro—Y$$

and since the rapid intramolecular transition was clearly related to the collagenase-susceptible chain regions, von Hippel and Harrington proposed that the transition involved was the "local" establishment of the *trans-*

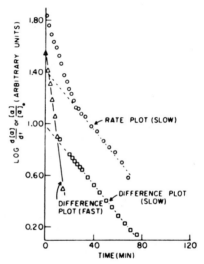

FIG. V-19. Rate of change of specific rotation during collagenase digestion of ichthyocol gelatin at 12° [von Hippel and Harrington (41)].

trans' configuration at each Pro · Hypro peptide bond. Following the "locking in" of the *trans-trans'* configuration, the remainder of the peptide chains were considered to slowly assume the poly-L-proline II-type helix because the stable *trans-trans'* regions make this the most stable overall configuration. Since the specific optical rotation of dilute gelatin solutions does not reach the value of the rotation observed for undenatured ichthyocol even after long cooling, the poly-L-proline II helix must be developed only in the regions vicinal to the Pro · Hypro bonds. The cooled gelatin molecules do not, therefore, take on the character of extended rigid rods. The viscosity and particle weight increased slowly, however, as long as the gelatin solutions were kept cool, indicating that interaction of the ordered helical regions was probably occurring.

It is relatively easy to accept the idea that poly-L-proline and poly-L- gly-cine, neither of which can establish intrachain hydrogen bonds, can, never-theless, establish stable helical chain configurations. In the first case, there is a common restriction to rotation at every peptide bond and C_a—C=O bond. In the second, systematic $interchain$ hydrogen bonds at every car-bonyl and amide position support the structure. The situation is striking-ly different in gelatin. The pyrrolidine residues constitute about 25 res-idue % of the peptide backbone but only a much smaller percentage of the peptide bonds are specifically in the Pro · Hypro sequence, which provides both structural stability and nucleation sites. The scattered re-maining pyrrolidine residues $prevent$ the formation of intramolecularly hydrogen-bonded helices and, in any event, the poly-L-proline II helix does not have the proper dimensions for such bonds. The question therefore becomes, how can a stable structure form at all in dilute systems where both systematic interchain and intrachain hydrogen bonds are not pos-sible? Harrington and von Hippel (43) found their answer to this question in the fact that high concentrations of urea or guanidine hydrochloride (which do not disrupt the $trans$-$trans'$ configuration, Table V-2) prevented the formation of organized gelatin structures, clearly implicating hy-drogen bonding in the structure stabilization. Experiments with ichthyocol gelatin in D_2O and H_2O confirmed this implication. In connection with a study of the secondary and tertiary structure of ribonuclease, Herman and Scheraga (44) found that the denaturation temperature for the protein was about 4° higher in D_2O than in H_2O. They explained this on the basis that a peptide —C=O- -D—O— bond is stronger in D_2O than is the corresponding —C=O- -H—O— bond in H_2O. If hydrogen bonds are important in stabilizing the collagen-fold, then, Harrington and von Hip-pel (43) argued, the melting temperature of gelatin should be higher in D_2O than in H_2O. The appropriate experiments are illustrated in Fig. V-20. In these experiments ichthyocol gelatin was dissolved in 0.5 M calcium chloride in D_2O or H_2O at 45°. The solutions were quenched and held at 3° for 1 day (solid lines in the figure) or 6 days (dashed lines); then the solutions were heated and the optical rotation measured as a function of temperature. The solutions were held at each temperature until a constant rotation was obtained. The temperature of the midpoint of the melting transition, T_c, is a measure of the structural stability. As in the case of Herman and Scheraga (44), T_c was higher in D_2O than in H_2O by about 3.7°. This presumably demonstrated that solvent hydrogen bond-ing does play some role in the stabilization of the collagen fold.

Burge, Cowan and McGavin (45) analyzed the x-ray diffraction models for collagen in terms of the incorporation of solvent into the structure. In the three-chain model of Rich and Crick (46) only one-third of the carbonyl oxygens and amide nitrogens are involved in hydrogen bonding between the three chains, leaving a large number of unbonded polar groups. Burge et al. (45) calculated, assuming one water molecule for each polar group, that 19.7 gm water could be bound per 100 gm collagen. Rougvie and Bear (47), however, found that kangaroo tail tendon had a primary binding water content of only 13.3 gm per 100 gm collagen.

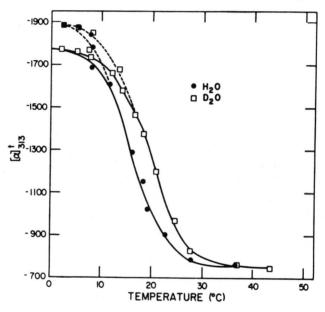

FIG. V-20. The melting curves of ichthyocol gelatins in H_2O and D_2O. Gelatin concentration 0.167% in 0.5 M calcium chloride. Solid lines, melting after 24-hr quenching at 3°. Dashed lines, after holding the gelatins at 3° for several days [Harrington and von Hippel (43)].

Burge et al. (45) suggested that this value was close to one water molecule per polar side chain plus one for every two carbonyl groups. According to the model, a single water molecule could form two hydrogen bonds simultaneously in only two ways—with successive oxygens of adjacent chains in a clockwise (right-handed) direction or with adjacent carbonyl groups on the same chain. However, neither arrangement was entirely satisfactory stereochemically. Water molecules could be placed comfortably in the structure only if they were bonded singly to each polar group. Bradbury et al. (48) followed this line by calculating the diffraction pattern for the collagen II structure on the assumption that the collagen held one water molecule per polar group. The optical transforms for this structure were compared with the experimental diffraction pattern and with the *trans* forms for the anhydrous collagen II structure. The agreement of the hydrated model with the experimental collagen pattern was better than the agreement of the anhydrous model with the collagen pattern. The agreement of the hydrated model was not so good as to rule out other possibilities, but clearly indicated that a regular arrangement of water within the collagen structure was very likely.

Esipova *et al.* (*49*), in a study similar to that of Burge *et al.* (*45*), correlated moisture sorption with the changes in intensities of collagen fiber diffraction patterns. They found that hydrated collagen was actually more crystalline than completely dehydrated collagen. They proposed that water molecules were disposed in a semiregular fashion along the peptide chains, one possibility being that in which the carbonyl oxygens are connected with water bridges:

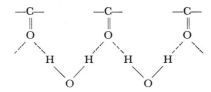

These water bridges were thought to increase the crystallinity of the collagen and stabilize the chains in the crystalline regions. The crystalline regions are those of essentially nonpolar or short side-chain character. The polar regions probably do not bind water along the peptide backbone. The carbonyls of the imide bonds could participate in this form of backbone hydrogen-bond stabilization. Harrington and von Hippel (*43*) adopted this model, pictured in Fig. V-21, in which the water bridges wind around the collagen peptide chains.

If, as proposed (*41–43*), the Pro · Hypro sequences nucleate the formation of the collagen-fold, then collagens with different imino acid contents should form the collagen-fold at different rates. Comparison of dogfish shark gelatin, ichthyocol gelatin, and calf skin gelatin showed this to be the case. Table V-3 lists the imino acid content of each of these gelatins and data related to their formation of the collagen-fold upon quenching. Figure V-22 shows the specific rotation-time data after quenching. It is most interesting to note that the final value of $[\alpha]$ attained after prolonged aging of the quenched solution is independent of the imino acid content,

TABLE V-3 [a]

FORMATION OF THE COLLAGEN-FOLD IN GELATINS WITH DIFFERING CONTENTS OF IMINO ACIDS

Gelatin	Imino acid content (residues per 1000)	T_c [b] (°C)	Initial rate of collagen-fold formation [c] ($[\alpha]_{313}$, deg/min)	Final value of specific rotation [d] (degrees)
Dogfish shark	158	11	0.39	—1940
Ichthyocol	197	16	4.8	—1900
Calf skin	232	23	13.1	—1972

[a] Data of Harrington and von Hippel (43).
[b] Midpoint of collagen-fold breakdown.
[c] Upon quenching to 3.7° in H_2O.
[d] After quenching and aging.

whereas the initial rate of collagen-fold formation varies more than 30-fold for these gelatins. For each gelatin Harrington and von Hippel (43) found that the rate of change of $[\alpha]$ during collagen-fold formation was independent of the gelatin concentration. The invariance of the final value of $[\alpha]$ for the three gelatins led to the conclusion that after nucleation in the imino acid-rich regions, the remainder of the peptide chains were forced

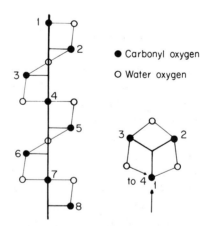

● Carbonyl oxygen

O Water oxygen

FIG. V-21. Two schematic views of the poly-L-proline II helix completely surrounded by the proposed water bridges. The central vertical line represents the backbone of the polypeptide chain and the numbers designate the carbonyl oxygen atoms of the successive amino acid residues: ●, carbonyl oxygen; O, water oxygen. The hydrogens of the water molecules are located on the lines joining the carbonyl and the water oxygens, but are not shown [Harrington and von Hippel (43)].

to assume the poly-L-proline II structure. It was further concluded from the nondependence of the rate on gelatin concentration that the specific configuration responsible for the mutarotation developed intramolecularly, that is, along each individual peptide chain, the poly-L-proline II structure in the nonpolar side-chain regions of the gelatin being stabilized by water hydrogen-bond bridges linking neighboring backbone carbonyl groups.

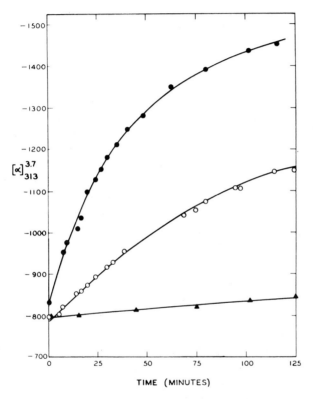

TIME (MINUTES)

FIG. V-22. Specific rotation of three different species of gelatin at 3.7° as a function of time after quenching from 45°. Solvent: 0.5 M CaCl$_2$ in H$_2$O; ●, calf skin gelatin; ○, ichthyocol gelatin; ▲, dogfish shark gelatin [Harrington and von Hippel (43)].

The mechanism described above for the nucleation of the collagen-fold by the temperature-dependent formation of *trans-trans'* configurations at Pro · Hypro sequences, followed by organization of vicinal chain segments into the poly-L-proline II structure stabilized by water bridges between adjacent carbonyl groups, is very attractive. However, there is evidence which does not entirely substantiate this mechanism. First, as mentioned earlier, the doubly hydrogen-bonded water structure does not lead to a stereochemically satisfactory overall structure and was rejected on these grounds by Bradbury *et al.* (*48*). Harrington and von Hippel (*43*) emphasized the apparent stoichiometry of water binding and one of the models of Esipova *et al.* (*49*) in choosing the doubly hydrogen-bonded structure. However, the data of Esipova *et al.* (*49*) are consistent with *any* semiregular disposition of water molecules close to the collagen macromolecule (*50*). Furthermore, correlation of the doubly hydrogen-bonded structure with the observed primary water binding of 13.3 gm per 100 gm protein would require that every possible backbone site on the collagen was hydrogen-bonded in this fashion. As we have seen, the collagen-fold does not extend along the entire chain and only the nonpolar regions are probably those involved in the collagen-fold formation. The polar regions with long side chains probably do not have the doubly hydrogen-bonded water structure. Furthermore, in the collagen structure proposed by Ramachandran *et al.* (*51*) in which two-thirds of the carbonyl groups are intramolecularly hydrogen-bonded, the only stabilizing water molecule bridge that could be formed is one joining one unbonded N—H with the lone unbonded C=O group at the same level in each chain triad. Ramachandran pointed out that it is not necessary to postulate that water molecules are involved in stabilizing the collagen structure, though water may well be bound to the structure.

Recently Berendsen (*50*) examined the nuclear magnetic resonance spectrum of the hydration water of bovine Achilles tendon as a function of degree of hydration, and the orientation of the collagen fibers with respect to the direction of the magnetic field. The resonance signal was shown to be dependent on the fiber-field orientation and exhibited the characteristic doublet shape for proton-pair interaction. This interaction was attributed to the two protons of a single water molecule. Interactions of protons on different water molecules were ruled out because three or five resonance peaks would then have been observed. The data were best explained if the water molecules were assumed to form chains in the fiber direction and with the potential to rotate about the chain axis. Water molecules bound by single hydrogen bonds to —C=O or —N—H groups and rotating about that bond axis were not compatible with the observed resonance angular dependence. Similarly, motionless water molecules bound to the protein by two hydrogen bonds (the model favored by Harrington and von Hippel) would have required that the observed line splitting increase with increasing water sorption at higher relative humidity. This was not the case. Berendsen proposed that water chains in the ice I structure surrounded the collagen molecule. The suggested chain arrangement is indicated in Fig. V-23. A number of possible water arrangements within a chain are shown in Fig. V-24. In the temperature range 17–38° the a-axis repeat of the ice I structure is 4.74 Å, with a hydrogen bond length of 2.9 Å. The collagen repeat of 28.6 Å equals six a-axis repeats, with an accuracy of 2% in this temperature range. The formation of occasional hydrogen bonds at sites along the collagen fiber may stabilize the existence of water chains parallel to the collagen fiber axis. A single chain of water molecules could be bound to two collagen

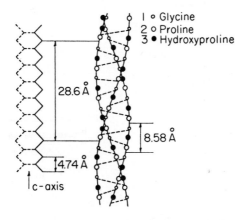

FIG. V-23. Relation between collagen macromolecule, schematically represented (right), and water chains (left); the dashed lines make an ice-I structure as seen along the c-axis. Distances in the water lattice are values for ice extrapolated to 25° [Berendsen (50)].

molecules (see Fig. V-24), making water of major importance in intermolecular interactions. However, though the collagen–ice I structural relationship may stabilize the ice structure, the nuclear magnetic resonance data require extensive free water chain rotation, so that the lifetime of an individual water chain is expected to be short. At very high relative humidities, and perhaps in aqueous solution, enough water is present to form related three-dimensional structures with dimensions compatible with the collagen helix. In this case as well, however, Berendsen points out that the structure must have many lattice defects and be in an intermediate solid-liquid state. The existence of short water chains in the nonpolar, short side-chain gelatin regions could account for the primary water-binding data of Rougvie and Bear (47) and the x-ray diffraction data of Esipova et al. (49).

Flory and his colleagues (52, 54) take issue with the interpretations of

Harrington and von Hippel on still different grounds. As described in detail in Chapter I, Flory and Garrett (53) describe the thermal shrinkage of collagen as a first order phase transition. They found that if the melting temperature, T_m, was plotted as a function of collagen concentration over a range from 80% collagen to high dilutions in ethylene glycol, no

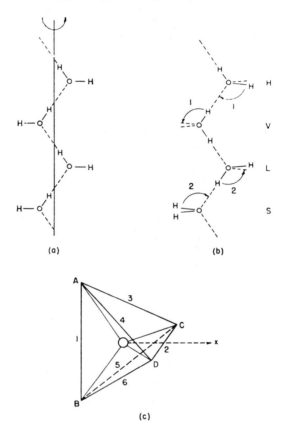

(a)   (b)

(c)

Fig. V-24. Chains of water molecules: (a) structure of a chain; (b) four possible orientations of the water molecules in a chain: H(igh), V(ertical), S(ide), and L(ow), and coupled proton jumps of types 1 and 2 that produce reorientations; (c) possible proton positions A–D for a water molecule with oxygen nucleus at O. Lines 1–6 indicate directions of possible proton interactions [Berendsen (50)].

discontinuities were observed at any concentration, indicating that the fiber shrinkage and the dilute solution transformation represent the same melting process. Since observations in ethylene glycol and in water showed that the transitions in the two media were very similar, Flory (52) suggested that ethylene glycol could stabilize the collagen-fold about as well as water, but that it was difficult to imagine an ethylene glycol "ice." Von Hippel, however, claimed (42) that the similarity in results with ethylene glycol and water stemmed from the fact that it is very difficult to achieve totally anhydrous conditions in ethylene glycol.

Flory and Garrett (52, 53) also proposed an alternate explanation for the correlation between the total proline and hydroxyproline content and the increased melting temperature. Assuming that the melting process is an equilibrium phase transition, then $T_m = \Delta H_f / \Delta S_f$, where ΔH_f and ΔS_f are the enthalpy and entropy of fusion. T_m may be affected by a change in either quantity. Flory and Garrett (53) suggested that an increase in the proline and hydroxyproline content should lower the entropy change on melting, because the random coil form would have reduced configurational freedom owing to restricted rotation about the pyrrolidine rings. ΔS_f, therefore, should decrease and T_m must increase. This appears to be a much more satisfactory argument for the increase in T_m than that given by Harrington and von Hippel (43), particularly since Harrington and von Hippel had shown that for the three gelatins of different total proline and hydroxyproline content the final values of the specific optical rotation were identical. These data indicate that the total collagen-fold content was the same in the three gelatins at low temperature after equilibration. In this state each of the gelatins should be stabilized by an equivalent amount of structurally related solvent and, since the melting out of the collagen-fold is a cooperative phenomenon characterized by a high activation energy, the melting points of the three equivalent structures should have been the same. The Flory and Garrett analysis does not, however, vitiate the implication that the rate of collagen-fold formation is profoundly influenced by the content of Pro · Hypro sequences which can "lock" in the *trans-trans'* configuration and nucleate the folding process.

Flory and Weaver (54) examined the kinetics of the denaturation and collagen-fold formation of soluble rat tail tendon collagen in aqueous systems. The collagen used in this study was prepared by an unusual procedure developed by Dumitru and Garrett (55). Fresh rat tail tendons were soaked in ethanol, then immersed in 0.5 M sodium dihydrogen phosphate for 12 hours at 5°. Following this treatment the tendons dissolved almost completely in distilled water at 5° after the salt was washed away. The isothermal rate of transformation of the collagen to gelatin was examined in a fashion similar to the method of Weir (56) (see Chapter I). Solutions of collagen in distilled water were heated very rapidly to fixed temperatures within a few degrees of the melting temperature, and then the optical rotation and viscosity were measured as a function of time. Typical transformation curves are shown in Fig. V-25. There was very rapid decrease in both η_{red} and $[\alpha]_D$ in the first half-hour of heating, followed by very slow decrease in both quantities. Three conclusions were drawn from these data: first, the rate of transformation was found to be finite, although the temperature range over which the transformation could be measured was small; second, the temperature coefficient for the transformation was very large; and third, in the range 35–38° the transformation did not go to completion, a small fraction of the collagen remaining untransformed. The temperature coefficient was too large, however, to permit the final mixture

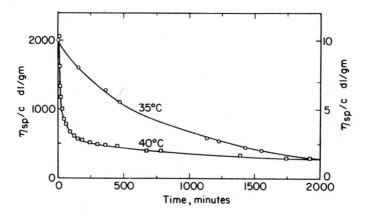

Fig. V-25. Isothermal melting of the collagen-fold in native collagen in water at 35° (left-hand ordinate scale) and at 40° (right-hand ordinate scale). Collagen concentration 0.0586 gm/100 ml [Flory and Weaver (54)].

to have contained distinct forms such as tropocollagen rods and completely random coils. It was, therefore, inferred that certain parts of each gelatin molecule were not completely disorganized at 38°.

Collagen-fold formation was studied by a quenching process. The collagen was converted to gelatin by heating at 80° for 30 minutes in pure water. The solutions were filtered into polarimeter tubes or viscometers and quenched to the desired low temperature. The appropriate data were taken as a function of time. As in other similar work (41), the rotation was found to level off much more rapidly than the solution viscosity which even at a concentration of ∼ 0.2 gm/100 ml, continued to rise indefinitely (Fig. V-26). The specific optical rotation regained 40–70% of its initial, native-collagen value, depending on the temperature, whereas the reduced viscosity increased to only a small fraction of its original value. Reexamination of the melting temperature of the gelatin in the collagen-fold configuration (a second collagen-fold → gelatin transformation) showed that the equilibrium transformation temperature was the same ($\sim 40°$) as in the native collagen, although the transition was less abrupt. This was further confirmation of Flory and Garrett's (53) contention that the (collagen-fold)$_{\text{gelatin}}$ → amorphous gelatin transformation was identical in nature to the (collagen-fold)$_{\text{collagen}}$ → amorphous collagen transformation.

Having shown that the collagen-fold to gelatin transition was a reversible process, Flory and Weaver (54) explored possible formulations for the equilibrium equation. On the basis that tropocollagen has a three-

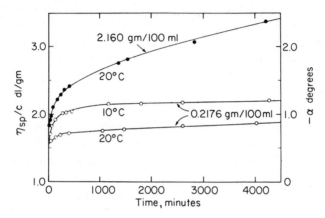

FIG. V-26. Collagen-fold formation in quenched gelatin solutions as a function of time of quenching at the indicated temperatures: ○, specific optical rotation; ●, reduced viscosity [Flory and Weaver (54)].

chain structure in which interchain (but intramolecular) hydrogen bonds are involved at one-third of the possible hydrogen-bonding sites, the reversible reaction was assumed to be

$$\text{3-strand helix} \rightleftarrows \text{3 random coil chains} \tag{11}$$

with an equilibrium constant, K, defined by

$$K = \frac{c_0^2 \alpha^3}{1 - \alpha} \tag{12}$$

In this equation c_0 is the total concentration, and α the degree of conversion of collagen to gelatin. As indicated earlier, K has a very large temperature coefficient. The temperature coefficient is determined by the enthalpy change during transformation, and this enthalpy change is of the order of 1.5 kcal/mole peptide unit (*53*) or about 3000 kcal per collagen molecule. Therefore, K must change by a factor greater than 10^6 per degree. A change in K of this magnitude would not permit the observed breadth of the temperature interval (35–38°) in which it was noted that the transition did not go to completion. Intrinsic differences in stabilities of the individual molecules are required to account for this observed breadth of the temperature range of collagen denaturation, a situation which appears extremely likely in view of the demonstrated molecular heterogeneity of every collagen preparation so far examined (see Chapter III).

In considering the kinetics of the reversion process (right to left in Eq. 11), the principal problem was that of reconciling the apparent first order concentration dependence of the rate on the gelatin concentration with the conclusion that even at high dilution the "reverted collagen" or collagen-fold form gelatin had to have the organized fraction of its structure in the triple-strand compound helix form. The essential postulate leading to the resolution of this difficulty was the assumption that an intermediate was formed by unimolecular rearrangement of a single random coil molecule, this step being rate-controlling, with the concentration of intermediate always being very small compared to that of the random coil molecules (*54*). With the symbols C, I, and H representing, respectively, random coil, intermediate, and native helix, and the k's the appropriate rate constants, the reversion process may be represented as

$$C \underset{k_1}{\overset{k_1'}{\rightleftharpoons}} I \underset{k_2}{\overset{k_2'}{\rightleftharpoons}} 1/3\ H \qquad (13)$$

Assuming that the formation of I is the rate-controlling step, then

$$rate\ of\ reversion\ =\ R'\ =\ k_1'\ C \qquad (14)$$

In Eq. 13, the assumption that I is present only in very low concentration compared to C requires that $n\Delta F_1' \gg 0$, where $\Delta F_1'$ is the standard state free energy change for the process per peptide unit, and n is the number of units involved in each segment transition. On the other hand, the free energy change for the overall process $\Delta F'$ must be negative but small in the neighborhood of T_m, so that I must also be unstable with respect to H as well as C. The overall transition is also characterized by a negative ΔH of ~ -1.5 kcal per peptide unit and it is reasonable to suppose that the C → I transition also has $\Delta H_1' < 0$. On balance then, $\Delta S_1'$ must be a large negative quantity, as expected, since the intermediate

I is the more ordered form. These values for $\Delta H_1'$ and $\Delta S_1'$ lead to the observed unusual situation of a negative activation energy but a large positive free energy of activation for the random coil $\rightarrow$ helix transition.

Another point gleaned from the reversion studies was that the rate of change of the rate of reversion with respect to temperature was not constant. That is, an Arrhenius plot of $\log t_{1/2}$ vs. $1/T$ was not linear and the negative activation energy of the process, therefore, increased as the reversion temperature approached T_m. Flory and Weaver (54) pointed out that this behavior was typical of nucleated crystallizations in other polymer systems (57) and, in these terms, determined the form of the rate constants for both steps of Eq. 13. They assumed that the intermediate I consisted of a helical segment comprising n consecutive peptide units, and that three such helical segments of the same length combined to form a triple-compound helix with imperfections in secondary structure at the juncture between helical and random coil regions. The free energy change, $\Delta F_2'$, for this process (step 2 of Eq. 13) may be written

$$(\Delta F_2')_{3n} = 3(n\Delta F_2' + 2\sigma) \tag{15}$$

where $\Delta F_2' = \Delta S_2' \Delta T = -\Delta S \Delta T$ in which ΔS is the overall entropy change per peptide unit; $\Delta T = T_m - T$, the degree of undercooling; and σ is an excess free energy for each traversal of a peptide chain through the imperfection region at the protofibril segment ends. The compound helical segment will become stable relative to C when $(\Delta F_2')_{3n} < 0$; consequently there is a minimum segment length n^*, such that when $n = n^*$, $(\Delta F_2')_{3n} = 0$, below which the compound helix could not exist. Values of $n \gg n^*$ are not likely in view of the difficulties of organizing very long sequences, so as a first approximation one can set $n = n^*$ and from Eq. 15

$$n^* = \frac{2\sigma}{\Delta S \, \Delta T} \tag{16}$$

If $(\Delta F_1') T_m$ is the standard free energy change per peptide unit for step 1 at T_m, then the free energy change for step 1 at temperature T is

$$n^*[(\Delta F_1') T_m - \Delta S_1 \Delta T] = \frac{2\sigma}{\Delta S} \left[\frac{(\Delta F_1') T_m}{\Delta T} - \Delta S_1 \right] \tag{17}$$

The free energy change for the rate-determining step, i.e. the activation energy of the overall process, may thus be put in the simple form

$$\Delta F^* = \frac{A}{\Delta T} - B \tag{18}$$

where A and B are constants. Hence k', the overall rate constant for the reversion process, becomes

$$k' = (\text{constant}) \left(e^{- \frac{A}{kT \Delta T}} \right) \qquad (19)$$

so that a plot of the log of the rate constant vs. $1/T \Delta T$ should be linear. The reversion data represented in this fashion are shown in Fig. V-27 and are in accord with the several assumptions and the general model. Examination of Eq. 16 shows that as the temperature approaches T_m the minimum segment size, n^*, required for the formation of a stable segment becomes larger, and hence the formation of such stable segments becomes less likely.

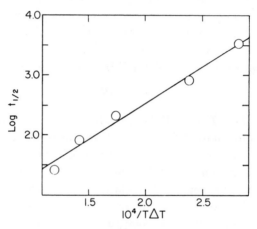

FIG. V-27. Logarithm of the half-time for collagen-fold formation of a gelatin vs. $1/T \Delta T$, where $\Delta T = T_m - T = 308 - T$ in °K [Flory and Weaver (54)].

The most crucial point in the collagen-fold formation or "reversion" mechanism proposed by Flory and Weaver (54) is the necessity for the formation of triple-chain compound helical segments. On the other hand, the reversion experiments on which the model was based were carried out at concentrations below 0.1 gm/100 ml, where intermolecular interactions were unlikely to have played a very significant role in the compound helix formation. This apparent conflict suggests that the compound helix segments might be formed intramolecularly from different transient intermediate segments of n^*. Intramolecular compound helix formation would have two direct consequences. First, it would account for the observation that the solution viscosity increases to only a small fraction of its native tropocollagen value, while the optical rotation regains almost

70% of its native value. In dilute solution, gelatins containing collagen-fold segments aggregated intramolecularly would be compact structures, with a lower viscosity than would be expected for stiffened random coils or rods. Second, the formation of intramolecular aggregates would require that the compound helix formation be limited in extent (n^* small) and lacking in the interchain specificity characteristic of the native interchain alignments. The difficulty in aligning or winding random chains suggests that the compound helices would not be wound fully but would extend only for the minimum distance compatible with stability. Thus, the rate of collagen-fold formation should be most rapid at low temperature, as noted, where n^* is smallest. A structure such as the one proposed would have many lattice imperfections and a low degree of crystallinity, even though predominantly in a folded form.

Presumably, the *inter*helix bonds are hydrogen bonds, and the chief stabilization of the single-chain segment intermediates comes from the immediate formation of the compound helixes. Thus the Flory and Weaver model (54) adequately explains the effect of reagents which interfere with hydrogen bond formation and does not call upon as crucial a role for the solvent as does the model of Harrington and von Hippel (42, 43). It appears that the Flory and Weaver reversion mechanism (54) can account for all of the data of Harrington and von Hippel (41–43), except perhaps that relating to the rates of collagen-fold formation in D_2O and H_2O. However, if ice-like chains of water molecules can contribute to the stabilization of the collagen-fold segments as suggested by the data of Berendsen (50), then D_2O ice would enhance the stability of the intermediate I relative to the random coil form C, giving rise to more crystallization nuclei of $n^*_{D_2O}$ segments where $n^*_{D_2O} < n^*_{H_2O}$. Under these conditions the rate of formation of H in D_2O should be greater than in H_2O and, since the minimum number of peptide units in a segment required for stability is smaller in D_2O, the melting temperature or denaturation temperature should also be greater for H in D_2O.

Bensusan (58) has followed the deuterium-hydrogen exchange of the amide (peptide bond) hydrogens by following shifts in the N—H and N—D stretching frequencies in the infrared. There was a direct correlation, during collagen-fold formation, of the optical rotatory changes and the conversion of fast exchanging hydrogens to slow ones. It thus appears that the formation of a polyglycine-like fold, stabilized by amide-to-carbonyl hydrogen bonds, is involved in collagen fold formation. Such bonding clearly requires intersegment interaction as a primary event in the gelatin → collagen-fold transition.

2. Effect of Macromolecular Composition on Collagen-Fold Formation

Both Harrington and von Hippel (*41–43*) and Flory and his colleagues (*52–54*) neglected the factor of intrinsic molecular weight heterogeneity in their studies of the collagen-fold formation mechanism, although, as shown in Chapter III, even the most carefully prepared gelatins are not homogeneous. In the ideal cases where gelatins are prepared by denaturation of tropocollagens with a minimum of hydrolytic degradation, the resulting systems may best be described as pauci-disperse. These systems contain the specific molecular species α, β, and γ in varying amount. One may certainly anticipate that the existence of the two- and three-chain gelatins might very well be important in collagen-fold formation. Before exploring the studies that have been carried out in this area, however, it seems profitable to examine the two mechanisms of collagen-fold formation to see what each might predict.

In the model proposed by Harrington and von Hippel (*42, 43*), the essential feature is that the collagen-fold is developed along single peptide strands which then attain, through the cooperative hydrogen bonding of water bridges at every available site on the backbone, a decided stability and finite life. The formation of hydrogen bonds between peptide strands to form crystallites or compound helices therefore requires a release of some of the backbone-bound water, suggesting that the interchain association would be a slower process than single-strand collagen-fold formation and "that the additional increment of stability arising from interactions between the individual strands of the triple helix might be quite small, and therefore that the melting temperatures of the postulated single-chain and three-chain structures might be very similar" (*42*). On this basis, we should predict that the presence of multichain gelatins would have little effect on the rate of collagen-fold formation or on the ultimate values of [α] and [η] which could be attained after collagen-fold development.

The essence of the Flory and Weaver (*54*) mechanism is that the single-strand helix intermediate, formed as proposed by Harrington and von Hippel by the locking in of the poly-L-proline II structure over short peptide unit segments, could have only a transitory existence. The collagen-fold is noted and becomes stabilized only when favorably situated intermediates, created by statistical mechanical configurational fluctuations, interact to form intersegment hydrogen bonds. On this basis, we should predict that the presence of multichain gelatins would have a profound effect in enhancing the rate of collagen-fold formation and on the ultimate values of [α] and [η] which could be attained after collagen-fold development.

Engel (*59*) investigated the transformation (or denaturation) and collagen-fold formation reactions with the specific intent of determining the
effect of peptide strand separation on the kinetics of both. An acid-soluble
calf skin tropocollagen preparation was used in all phases of his study. Such
preparations generally contain 6–10% γ, 20–40% β, and the remainder
α after denaturation. The weight-average molecular weight (M_w) of the
native tropocollagen was found to be 360,000 by light scattering measurement at concentrations below 0.025%. When this tropocollagen was denatured isothermally at 35° at pH 3.7 in 3.075 M sodium citrate, M_w
decreased at a finite rate to a limiting lower value of 190,000. The molecular
weight decay was determined by light scattering measurements at various
time intervals after the collagen solutions were warmed to 35°. The angular dependence of scattering was also measured. Engel obtained the
unusual result that the second virial coefficient was zero (compare with
Boedtker and Doty (*60*) who found $B = 3 \times 10^{-4}$ ml-mole/gm^2 at pH
3.7), and hence made all calculations from runs at single protein concentrations without extrapolation to infinite dilution. As anticipated, the an-

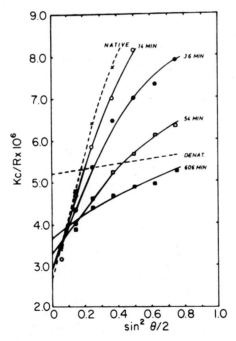

Fig. V-28. Molecular weight decay as indicated by the angular scattering envelope
during isothermal denaturation of acid-soluble collagen at 35°. Collagen concentration
0.018% [Engel (*59*)].

gular scattering envelope changed along with the molecular weight decay, indicating a lessening of the molecular asymmetry. Plots of $Kc/R(\theta)$ vs. $\sin^2 \theta/2$ during the denaturation are shown in Fig. V-28 and 29. Figure V-28 refers to the isothermal denaturation at 35°, Fig. V-29 to the same process at 39°. The initial slope of each of the plots, divided by the intercept, is directly related to the Z-average molecular dimension in each

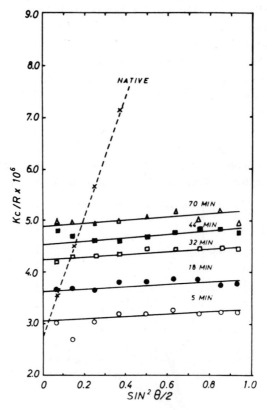

FIG. V-29. Isothermal denaturation of acid-soluble collagen at 39.0°. Collagen concentration 0.0125% [Engel (59)].

case. Initially, the slope/intercept ratio yielded a length of 3700 Å for the tropocollagen rods, whereas the final random coil mean diameter was 400 Å. At 35° the average dimension and M_w decreased at approximately the same rate. At higher temperatures, however, the rate of dimensional and configurational change was markedly more rapid than the rate of change of M_w. Thus the collapse of the collagen-fold at temperatures close to T_c, the melting temperature, clearly precedes peptide strand separation. The intrinsic viscosity, $[\eta]$ (in this case determined by extrapolation to infinite dilution!), decreased at the same rate as the (initial slope/intercept) factor and the specific optical rotation decreased at a similar rate. Assuming that the denaturation is a two-step process, collagen-fold collapse *followed* by peptide chain separation, one can readily determine the kinetics of the second step since changes in M_w are a measure of the second step only. Setting N_0 as the number of undissociated molecules at the beginning of the denaturation, and N_t as the number remaining undissociated at time t, then

$$\frac{N_0}{N_t} = \frac{M_{w,\,t=0} - M_{w,\,t=\infty}}{M_{w,\,t=t} - M_{w,\,t=\infty}} \tag{20}$$

where $M_{w,\,t=0}$ is the molecular weight of the undissociated molecules, and $M_{w,\,t=\infty}$ is the weight-average molecular weight at the end of the reaction. A plot of the logarithm of either side of Eq. 20 vs. t was found to be linear, indicating that the strand separation followed first order kinetics. The first order rate constants were: 6.9×10^{-4} sec^{-1} at 39°, 2.7×10^{-4} sec^{-1} at 37°, and 0.7×10^{-4} sec^{-1} at 35°. The energy of activation was ~ 108 kcal.

Collagen-fold formation was followed by an identical set of molecular weight, viscosity, and optical rotation measurements (59). The collagen was first denatured at 40° for 20 minutes, that is, under conditions which lead to complete strand separation and loss of collagen-fold configuration. The collagen solutions were then quenched to 4° and the appropriate measurements made. These data are summarized in Fig. V-30 a, b, c, d and several points can be made readily. First, as in the many other studies already cited, the specific rotation attained its maximum value within a few hours and this maximum was independent of gelatin concentration (Fig. V-30 d). The maximum $[\alpha]$ corresponded to about 65% regain of rotation compared with the native value. Second, the regain in rotation is followed by an increase in the initial slope of the angular scattering envelope. Unlike the rotatory power changes, this change was concentration dependent. Furthermore, at a gelatin concentration of 0.01%, the initial slope increased to less than 10% of its value for native collagen (Fig. V-30 a). Since the initial slope provides a Z-average dimension it is extremely sensitive to the presence of even a few large or asymmetric particles. Hence very few, if any, if the collagen fold regions evidenced by the specific rotation values could have led to extensive formation of rodlike native structures. Third, the molecular weight change was also concentration dependent, and increased with time even for the lowest concentration studied (0.01%). At higher concentration ($\sim 0.06\%$) the values of M_w exceeded the molecular weight of the original collagen. Finally the reduced viscosity changes generally followed the changes in the light scattering angular envelope in the early stages of the collagen-fold formation reaction. At later stages, and at the higher gelatin concentrations, the changes in η_{red} were related to the increase in M_w. However, even in those cases

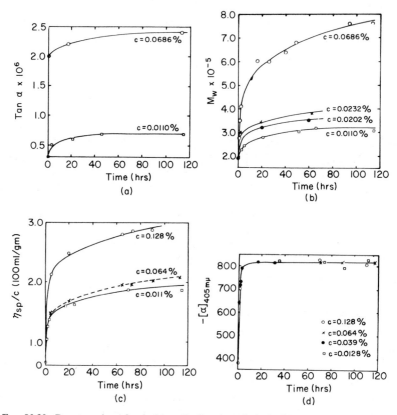

FIG. V-30. Renaturation of gelatin at 4° after the gelatin had been denatured at 40° for 20 minutes. (a) Increase of initial slope of the angular dependence of light scattering as a function of time. (b) Increase of weight-average molecular weight, M_w, measured by light scattering. (c) Increase of reduced viscosity. (d) Increase of optical rotation [Engel (59)].

at high concentration ($\sim 0.06\%$), where M_w was greater by a factor of 2 or 3 than the original tropocollagen weight, the reduced viscosity was a small fraction of its original native value.

In an additional and enlightening experiment Engel (59) compared the rate of collagen-fold formation as a function of peptide strand separation. Tropocollagen was denatured for 11 minutes and 90 minutes at 38°.

After 11 minutes the intrinsic viscosity and optical rotation had been reduced to their lowest values, but M_w had decreased only to about 270,000. After 90 minutes M_w was reduced to its final low value of 190,000. Upon quenching to 4° the 11-minute denatured preparation increased in viscosity much more rapidly than did the 90-minute denatured preparation, and the final viscosity was higher (Fig. V-31). Crosby and Stainsby (*61*) reported similar observations on a eucollagen preparation.

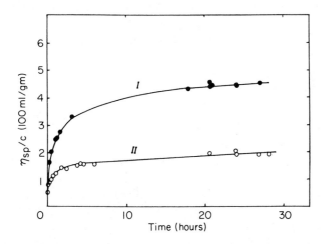

F<small>IG</small>. V-31. Renaturation rate as a function of chain dissociation. Increase of reduced viscosity at 4° following cooling of denatured collagen solutions: curve I: denatured 11 minutes at 38.0°; curve II: denatured 90 minutes at 38.0°; $c = 0.058\%$ [Engel (*59*)].

Engel (*59*) interpreted his data in terms of the collagen-fold formation mechanism of Harrington and von Hippel (*42, 43*). He took this as a three-step mechanism involving: (1) local establishment of nucleation sites in the poly-L-proline II configuration, (2) folding of the remainder of the *individual* chains in the poly-L-proline II helix, and (3) the association of the individual helices to form larger particles. Engel, taking his data as pertinent to the elucidation of step 3, concluded that the aggregates of helices could not have the rodlike structure of the native macromolecules, although other features are similar to native collagen. Further, he concluded that interchain interactions did affect the rate of collagen-fold formation to a marked degree. Having reached these conclusions, it would have been more profitable for Engel to have considered his data in the context of the Flory and Weaver (*54*) mechanism for, as indicated above, these unambiguous conclusions are not compatible with the Harrington and von Hippel collagen-fold formation mechanism. On the other hand, Engel's data and conclusions appear to fit the Flory-Weaver proposal in every detail. In particular, the highly folded compact nature of the collagen-fold-rich molecule and the extreme tendency to form aggregates even at very low concentration clearly indicate that the initial collagen-folded intermediates are highly unstable with respect to the compound helix form.

Having established that some high molecular weight gelatins were multichain in character (62, 63) and that the interchain covalent linkages were those in the native collagen fibers (64, 65), Veis and Cohen (66) and Veis et al. (67–69) studied the collagen-fold formation of gelatins rich in the intramolecularly cross-linked γ component. The premise of these investigations was that if interchain interactions were the crucial factors in stable collagen-fold formation, as subsequently proposed by Flory and Weaver (54), then those gelatins containing cross-linkages that held the random chains in the proper register with each other at reasonable intervals should generate a completely ordered molecule indistinguishable from the native structure. In other words, if random interchain contacts were prevented following the nucleation of collagen-fold formation, then complete renaturation should occur. This situation would prevail, however, only if interchain interactions provided an additional stability to the individual peptide chains in the poly-L-proline II folded configuration.

Veis and Cohen (66) extracted an isoionic suspension of bovine corium collagen for 1 hour at 60°. The resultant gelatin (about 7% of the corium dissolved) was fractionated by the ethanol-sodium chloride coacervation procedure into six fractions. The criterion used for ascertaining the success of a renaturation trial was the direct preparation of fibrous precipitates that exhibited the cross-striated pattern typical of native collagen fibers when viewed in an electron microscope. The one possibility for error in such an examination could arise only if some collagen fibrils were carried in suspension through the extraction, fractionation, and recovery procedures. Extreme precautions were taken to avoid this possibility and only the third of the six fractions, completely and readily water-soluble, was used. The gelatin was dissolved at 40° in 0.1 M potassium chloride, centrifuged at 40° for 1.5 hours at 144,000 g, and the supernatant collected. This clear supernatant was quenched to 4° and held at that temperature for 20 hours. The clear gel which formed was then reheated, without shaking, to 40°. Within 12 minutes, and as the gel melted, a fibrous precipitate formed. The fibers were collected, and when shadowed and viewed in an electron microscope were clearly identical in structure with native collagen fibrils. Subsequent fractionation and ultracentrifuge studies (67) indicated that the isoionic extract gelatin was a pauci-disperse system containing three principal components, identified as α, γ, and δ with weight-average molecular weights of 1.35×10^5, 4.4×10^5, and 12.3×10^5, respectively. The fraction renatured by Veis and Cohen (66) was particularly rich in the γ component. Veis, Anesey and Cohen (68) established, again by ultracentrifuge studies, that of the mixture, only γ and δ components were renaturable. Once renatured, the γ component behaved as did native tropocollagen preparations. The renatured fibers were soluble in dilute acetic acid, had an intrinsic viscosity of 13, a specific rotation, $[\alpha]_D^{15}$, of $-346°$, and yielded typical SLS precipitates upon the addition of ATP to the acetic acid solutions.

Light scattering analyses were used to elucidate the nature of the factors which governed the renaturation process by the quenching-heat precipitation technique (68). The gelatin used in this study was an unfractionated, 60°, pH 6.6, bovine corium extract. A deionized stock solution was prepared and various solutions were made up to provide systems at different gelatin concentration, ionic strength, and pH. One solution was made to contain 6.0 M urea. All solutions were centrifuged at high speed for optical clarification and pipetted into individual light scattering cells which were then sealed. Two duplicate sets of light scattering cells were prepared in this fashion and the turbidity of each cell determined. All solutions were then cold quenched and rewarmed to 40°. One set of cells was held at 40° for 8 days and their turbidities were determined daily. The other set of cells was cooled to 4° and rewarmed to 40° for 2 hours each day prior to turbidity measurement. Fiber precipitation occurred only in the isoelectric pH range 6.5–9.2. Precipitation was completely inhibited at pH < 5 and pH > 10. Fiber precipitation was also completely inhibited at high ionic strength (> 1.0) and in 6.0 M urea. In 1.0 M potassium chloride and 6.0 M urea, there was gradual decrease in turbidity due to hydrolytic degradation (Fig. V-32). In the zero ionic strength solutions, the turbidity decreased and fiber precipitation was very rapid. The rate of precipitation decreased as the salt content increased and the turbidity function became more complicated. In the presence of 0.1 M potassium chloride the relative turbidity increased and fiber flocculation was limited. However, centrifugation of the solution at the conclusion of the experiment showed that about 20% of the gelatin had been renatured.

The gelatin concentration also affected the amount of precipitate harvested after the final centrifugation on the eighth day. About 90% of the gelatin was collected as fibers at initial gelatin concentrations $< 2 \times 10^{-3}$ gm/ml. The amount of precipitate dropped off sharply as the concentration was increased, so that at $c = 4 \times 10^{-3}$ gm/ml only about 50% of the gelatin formed fibers.

The temperature effect is indicated in Fig. V-33 where the turbidity measured (at 40°) after centrifugation on the eighth day is plotted as a function of the holding temperature for a series of cells at zero ionic strength and $c = 4 \times 10^{-3}$ gm/ml. The best range for renaturation was 30–40°. At temperatures above 40° hydrolytic degradation decreased the fiber yield. At temperatures lower than 30° general gelation of the solutions seemed to inhibit fiber formation.

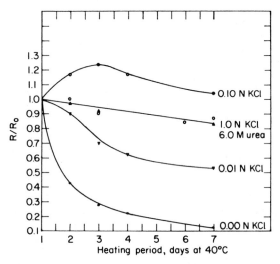

FIG. V-32. Effect of salt concentration and time on collagen-fold formation and fiber precipitation at 40° as measured by the relative turbidity of an unfractionated gelatin containing the γ component [Veis *et al.* (*68*)].

The time scale on which the above observations were made appears to preclude application of these data to the interpretation of the intramolecular events during collagen-fold formation and renaturation. A few conclusions are in order at this point, however. In the reversion mechanism proposed by Flory and Weaver (*54*), the rate-limiting step is the nucleation of the poly-L-proline II structure along short segments of individual peptide chains, and the aggregation of these nuclei to give the collagen-fold compound helix is more rapid. Accordingly, the complete renaturation should have occurred as rapidly as the nucleation process, and all of the γ units should have precipitated at once warming. Gross and Kirk (*70*) have shown that in the heat precipitation of native neutral-salt-soluble collagen all of the collagen is precipitated in fibril form within an hour after heating. This does not appear to be the case in the renaturation experiments cited. A further indication that the complete renaturation step is slower than the collagen-fold nucleation step was found in the observation that several successive cooling and heating cycles would lead to the formation of successive crops of fibrils (68). As many as four crops of fibers could be obtained by temperature cycling in a γ-rich gelatin fraction. An explanation of these data can be drawn from the extreme dependence of the renaturation on gelatin concentration, high gelatin concentration apparently inhibiting the complete renaturation. The optical rotation data of Smith (12), Ferry and Eldridge (10), and others (9, 43, 54) all show

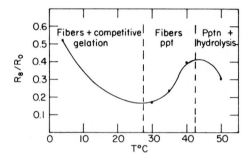

Fig. V-33. Effect of temperature on precipitation of collagen from an unfractionated gelatin containing the γ component [Veis et al. (68)].

that in the usual nonrenaturable gelatins, collagen-fold formation, up to about 70% recovery of structure, is independent of concentration in the range studied ($< 1\%$ gelatin). It is likely, therefore, that in quenching the renaturable gelatins for nucleation of the collagen-fold a number of random, nonspecific inter- or intrachain compound helices are formed and that these prevent the complete renaturation of the γ units. The more low molecular weight gelatin present to competitively aggregate with the γ-gelatin strands, the more difficult renaturation becomes. Support for this proposal comes from electron microscope investigations of the fibers produced during renaturation (68). At low gelatin concentration in 0.01–0.1 ionic strength potassium chloride and at a renaturation temperature of 40°, the fibers were very clean and the cross-striations sharply indicated. At lower salt concentration at 40° or at lower renaturation temperatures, the fibers appeared to be coated or masked by amorphous material. Furthermore, under these conditions the yields of precipitate were larger than the γ component content of the unfractionated gelatin mixture. The lack of coprecipitated gelatin in 40° renaturations at moderate ionic strength must mean that during the heating the random compound helical aggregates melt out, while the native collagen-fold segments achieve the more stable completely renatured form via recreation of new individual chain poly-L-proline II unstable intermediates, this final structure having enhanced stability because of specific localized interchain interactions. A confirmation of the difference in rate between collagen-fold formation and complete renaturation, and of the efficacy of temperature cycling in permitting the reorganization of random chain contacts to the native alignments, has been presented recently by Engel in a preliminary note (71). Engel found that better reformation of the collagen structure could be obtained by alternating temperatures between 4° and 22° than by a constant 4° isothermal renaturation.

Altgelt, Hodge and Schmitt (72) isolated a γ-gelatin from a calf skin tropocollagen preparation by renaturation, and then examined the kinetics of its renaturation compared directly with mixtures containing only α- and β-gelatin components. It was shown conclusively by both optical rotation and viscosity studies that both the rate of collagen-fold formation and the maximum recovery of structure were greater for the γ-gelatin unit. Figure V-34 shows the recovery of specific optical rotation as a function of time for the various gelatins. The rate and extent of recovery of the unfractionated tropocollagen (TC in the figure) parallel the curve

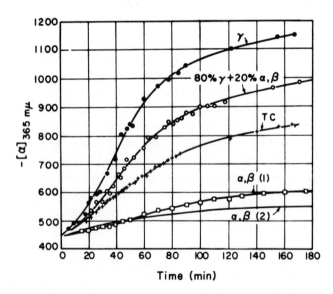

Fɪɢ. V-34. Optical rotation recovery of gelatins containing differing proportions of γ component. Concentrations were in the range 0.05–0.3% [Altgelt *et al.* (72)].

shown in Fig. V-22 for unfractionated denatured calf skin tropocollagen, whereas the data for the mixtures containing only α and β are similar to the Harrington and von Hippel (43) data on dogfish shark gelatin. On the other hand, the pure γ fraction renatured more rapidly and completely. In the case treated by Altgelt et al. (72), the total pyrrolidine ring content of each fraction was probably very close (73) and therefore the explanation of the differing collagen-fold formation rates advanced by Harrington and von Hippel could not apply. These data thus provide direct evidence that interchain interactions do play a major role in the organization of the collagen-fold. The very slow formation of the collagen-fold in γ-poor gelatins at low concentration indicates also the importance of specific interaction patterns in stabilizing the collagen-fold compound helix aggregates.

Drake and Veis (74–77) approached this problem differently. A buffalo fish swin bladder ichthyocol was prepared and analyzed for its subunit structure following denaturation. This particular preparation was 80% α and 20% β with no trace of a γ component (74, 76). All attempts to completely renature this gelatin were fruitless. Very dilute solutions of the native ichthyocol were prepared, at pH 2.8 in acetic acid or at pH 7 in 0.5 M calcium chloride, and reacted with formaldehyde to form covalent intramolecular cross-linkages. The ichthyocol was freed from excess formaldehyde, denatured by heating to 40°, and its subunit composition determined by sedimentation analysis. The intramolecular cross-linking caused the formation of a typical γ-gelatin, and the reaction could be carried out so as to give nearly quantitative yields of pure γ (Fig. V-35). Approximately ten cross-linkages, presumably methylene bridges, were introduced per γ unit (or per tropocollagen unit) (76). The γ-gelatin prepared in this way was readily renaturable to either the native fibrous or SLS forms. In addition to showing that the reactive groups capable of aldehyde cross-linking are sufficiently close for intramolecular bonding in the native structure, these studies provide, by synthesis, a proof that the "natural" γ-gelatins are intramolecularly bonded by covalent cross-linkages. Kinetic studies (77) of the collagen-fold formation in α, β mixtures as compared with γ very closely duplicated the results of Altgelt et al. (72), again showing that collagen-fold formation in dilute solutions of α-gelatins is very slow while the complete renaturation of pure γ-gelatin is very rapid, emphasizing the importance of interchain interactions in collagen-fold formation. One puzzling aspect of the kinetic studies, seen in a comparison of the rotation and viscosity data in Figs. V-36 and 37, is that, even in the case of complete renaturation with α- and β-free γ-gelatin, the optical rotation changes were more rapid than the viscosity changes. Altgelt *et al.* (*72*) made similar note of the difference in the two measures of collagen-fold formation.

Interesting and informative as kinetic data are, they do not present an entirely satisfactory base for the description of a system. Complementary data on the equilibrium states of a system are also highly desirable. In the case of the gelation of gelatin, however, very little direct information

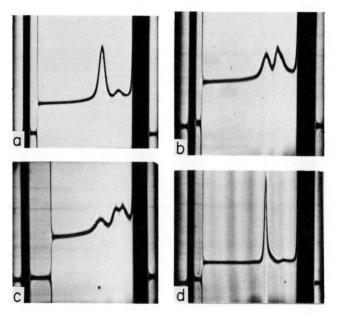

FIG. V-35. Synthesis of a γ component by the reaction of formaldehyde with buffalo fish swim bladder ichthyocol. (a) Zero reaction time: 80% α, 20% β; (b) 20-hour reaction: α, accentuated β, and first appearance of γ; (c) 30-hour reaction: α diminished, β, and γ; (d) 72-hour reaction: γ predominates, no α or β. Small fast peak is γ-dimer [Veis and Drake (*76*)].

relating to the equilibrium content of the collagen-fold has been obtained. A common feature of the kinetic studies has been that the collagen-fold formation rates were measured following the quenching of hot gelatin solutions to a temperature well below the melting temperature, so that the observations related to the process of the transition of supercooled gelatin to the collagen-fold along an irreversible reaction path. Although some of the reaction parameters changed rapidly following quenching, many hours or even days were required for these parameters to attain stable values, if such values were reached. Slow cooling methods were

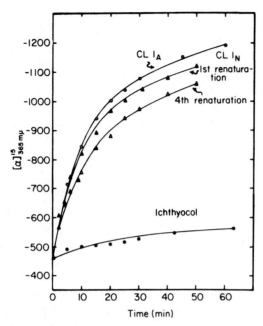

FIG. V-36. Recovery of specific optical rotation of synthetic γ-gelatin compared with the original α, β mixture. The degradation of γ-gelatin during successive denaturations and renaturations lowers rate of recovery of rotation. CLI_A cross-linked in acid. CLI_N, cross-linked in 0.5 M calcium chloride. Renaturation at 15° [Drake and Veis (77)].

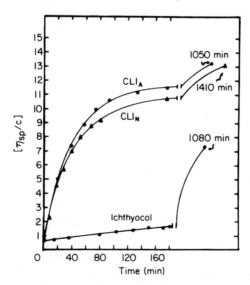

FIG. V-37. Recovery of reduced viscosity with time at 15°. Synthetic γ-gelatin compared with α, β mixture. CLI_A and CLI_N as in Fig. V-36 [Drake and Veis (77)].

not used because of the difficulty of achieving reproducible results. Some studies (9, 10) made use of gradual warming from a cold quenched and annealed gelatin solution, but these data are difficult to interpret in terms of collagen-fold formation because the aged solutions contained aggregates in addition to the collagen-fold units. The work of Harrington and Sela (37) and Steinberg et al. (33) on poly-L-proline showed that the poly-L-proline II helix content was governed by a rapid temperature-dependent equilibrium. These data suggested to Veis and Legowik (78) the possibility that optical rotation measurements at low wavelength (where the specific rotation is several-fold greater than at the sodium D line) might be able to pick up small changes in rotation during the primary stages of collagen-fold formation at temperatures near T_c. Accordingly, gelatin solutions of known molecular species distribution were cooled from T_c in small temperature decrements and the specific rotations determined at wavelength 365 mμ.

The nature of the results with all gelatin preparations is illustrated in Fig. V-38 for a γ-rich gelatin at pH 7. There was an almost instant change in $[\alpha]_{365}^t$ to a stable value characteristic of the lower temperature, but within about 5 minutes the specific rotation began a slower time-dependent

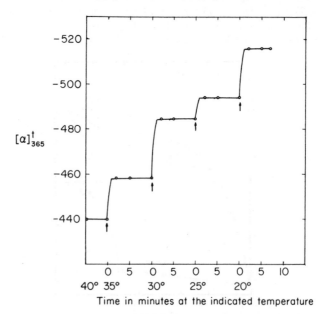

FIG. V-38. Equilibrium specific rotations during fold formation for a γ-containing gelatin cooled at pH 7.0 in 0.1 ionic strength phosphate buffer (Na$_2$HPO$_4$, NaH$_2$PO$_4$, NaCl) Arrows indicate points of temperature change [Veis and Legowik (78)].

change. This latter change became more rapid as the system temperature was lowered. By working with a system permitting rapid temperature change, the temperature could be dropped by 5 degrees in steps every 5 minutes in the range 40–20°. At temperatures below 20° the secondary changes were so rapid that a stable plateau value of the specific rotation could not be observed. However, in the 40–20° range the 5-minute plateau values of $[\alpha]_{365}^t$ were highly reproducible. On the assumption that these plateau values corresponded to the collagen-fold-nucleating poly-L-proline II helix content, and the additional assumption that the specific optical rotation of native tropocollagen represented a 100% poly-L-proline II configuration, the equilibrium content of nuclei was computed in terms of an equilibrium constant K_n, at each temperature. Such measurements and computations were made for an acid-precursor commercial gelatin (essentially α chains, pI 9), an alkali-precursor commercial gelatin (essentially α chains, pI 5), and a γ-rich bovine corium collagen extract (pI $\sim$ 9). Each gelatin was studied at pH's from 5 to 9. Collagen-fold nuclei formation in the two commercial gelatins was essentially identical, and there was no significant pH dependence in this limited pH range. The γ-rich gelatin, however, showed a much enhanced nuclei formation which was maximal at the isoionic pH. As anticipated for an equilibrium process, a plot of ln K_n vs. $1/T$ was linear in each case (Fig. V-39), and the enthalpy change for poly-L-proline II nuclei formation, ΔH_n, was determined from the slopes of the appropriate lines. Since K_n was known, ΔF_n and ΔS_n could also be calculated and these parameters are listed in Table V-4. As anticipated, since the nucleation step involved only a fraction of the total structure in each case, the values of ΔF_n are all positive and small. However, the formation of nuclei was clearly more favorable in the γ-gelatin. The enthalpy changes were negative as also expected for the formation of the more stable structure, but the energy involved in the random gelatin-nuclei transition was reduced by a factor of almost 2 in the γ-gelatin, indicating perhaps that at the isoionic pH particularly there are interchain interactions even in the random or disordered γ-gelatin molecule. The sharply reduced values of ΔS_n for the γ-gelatin are in clear agreement with the presence of interchain interactions and interchain organization in the disordered γ-gelatin solutions at $T \geqslant 40°$.

The fact that the equilibrium content of collagen-fold nuclei at any given temperature was greater in the γ-gelatin at its isoionic pH than at other pH's, whereas there did not appear to be significant pH dependency for either of the α-type gelatins, strongly suggests that specific electrostatic interactions were involved in establishing the *native* type of collagen-fold nuclei.

The Harrington and von Hippel collagen-fold formation mechanism (*43*) emphasizes that the fold is developed along single peptide chains and that the individual fold-containing chain segments have almost the same stability as would be expected for a collagen triple helix (*42*). If this were the case and the collagen-fold nucleation step was indeed taking place in independent chain regions, then ΔS_n should have been identical in all three gelatin systems. Veis and Legowik (*78*) therefore concluded that their

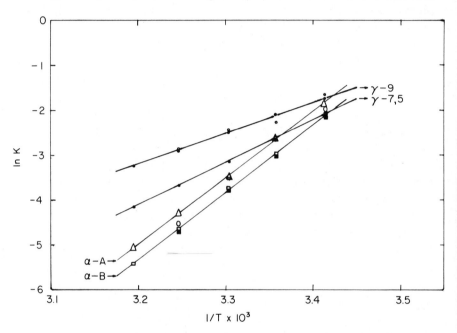

FIG. V-39. Van't Hoff plots of equilibrium rotation data. α-A and α-B represent pH-independent data for acid-precursor and alkali-precursor α-component gelatins; γ-9: γ-rich gelatin at its isoionic pH of 9.0; γ-7,5: γ-rich gelatin at pH 7 and pH 5 [Veis and Legowik (*78*)].

data were not compatible with the Harrington and von Hipple reversion mechanism, and that the nucleation step in collagen-fold formation involved the immediate formation of interchain compound helix segments, as proposed in the kinetic studies of Flory and Weaver (*54*).

While it is easy to accept different values of ΔS_n for the α- and γ-gelatins, it is much more difficult to understand why ΔH_n should be so dependent upon the molecular character of the gelatins. Spurr (*79*) and Flory and Garrett (*53*) have determined that the enthalpy change in the melting of native collagen to random gelatin is of the order of —1 to

TABLE V-4 [a]

THERMODYNAMIC PARAMETERS FOR POLY-L-PROLINE II HELIX
NUCLEI FORMATION IN VARIOUS GELATINS

Gelatin	ΔH_n (cal)	T (°C)	ΔF_n (cal)	ΔS_n (e.u.)
Acid-precursor	—7550	40	+3150	—34.1
(pH 5–9)		35	2622	—33.0
		30	2073	—31.7
		25	1559	—30.6
		20	1044	—29.3
Alkali-precursor	—7635	40	+3377	—35.2
(pH 5–9)		35	2846	—34.0
		30	2288	—32.7
		25	1766	—31.5
		20	1235	—30.2
γ-Gelatin	—4743	40	+2592	—23.4
(pH 5–7)		35	2251	—22.7
		30	1896	—21.9
		25	1564	—21.1
		20	1218	—20.3
γ-Gelatin	—3459	40	+1995	—17.4
(pH 9.0)		35	1744	—16.9
		30	1484	—16.3
		25	1240	—15.7
		20	995	—15.2

[a] Data of Veis and Legowik (78).

—1.5 kcal per peptide unit. Comparing this value with the ΔH_n values for the reverse process, one might say that the minimum number of peptide units required for stable collagen-fold formation is reduced in the γ-gelatin, or in terms of the analysis of Flory and Weaver (54), n^*, the number of peptide units necessary to form a stable, propagating intermediate, I, is greater for the α-gelatin than for the γ-gelatin. As suggested in the previous paragraph, this situation might arise from the possibility that specific interchain interactions partially organize randomized γ-gelatin. Another interpretation is possible, however. The kinetic studies with D_2O and H_2O (43) and the nuclear magnetic resonance data (50) as well as the crystallographic studies (45, 48, 49) all point to participation of water in the stabilized collagen-folded chain regions. According to Berendsen (50), the collagen-fold might assist in the organization of water molecules into chains with the ice-I structure. A part of the enthalpy change of the collagen-fold formation in α-gelatins might, therefore, come from the building of these ice-I chains. The more rapid rate of collagen- fold formation in γ-gelatins (72, 77) suggests that the interchain cross-linkages are located in or near the chain regions where the collagen-fold nucleates. Since the nucleating regions are essentially nonpolar, tending to organize water into pentagonal ice-like arrays (the ice-I form) (80–83), interchain junctions in these regions may increase the water organization of the "denatured" gelatin, leading to a smaller enthalpy change upon reorganization into the collagen-fold and a less negative ΔS_n. This interpretation of the data is admittedly speculative but it indicates at least one direction for further research. More work on the thermodynamics of the collagen-fold formation process is certainly warranted.

3. A Model for Collagen-Fold Formation in Single-Strand α-Gelatins at High Dilutions

The kinetic and thermodynamic analyses of collagen-fold formation described in the preceding section can be boiled down to a simple sequence of reactions, which can serve as a model for the prediction and correlation of the behavior of systems undergoing gelation. Recalling the sequence studies of Grassmann et al. (84), it was shown that peptides could be isolated from collagens with regions rich in pyrrolidine and other nonpolar residues, or rich in the polar amino acids. The polar regions contained subregions, some primarily acidic, the others basic. We may therefore imagine that upon collagen-fold nucleus formation, each poly-L-proline II single-chain intermediate segment is characterized by a particular charge distribution at each end and behaves more or less as a dipole. Other dipoles of appropriate length and charge distribution will be attracted, become oriented, and lead to the formation of collagen-fold compound helices stabilized by interchain hydrogen bonds, electrostatic interactions, and organized water structure surrounding the compound helix segment. This scheme is pictured in Fig. V-40 as it might apply to collagen-fold formation in a single-strand α-component gelatin. It does not seem to be necessary, a priori, to require that stable or metastable compound helix segments be limited to aggregates of three peptide chains interacting simultaneously. Indeed, the slow reorganization leading to increased crystallinity of gelatin gels or higher viscosities of dilute gelatin solutions might very well take place by dissociation of the metastable compound helix segments into short-lived intermediates, and reaggregation of these into more stable form. Such a rearrangement reaction could take place without change in net optical rotatory power of the system, and if the better organization led to larger helical segments $[\alpha]_\lambda$ might increase slightly.

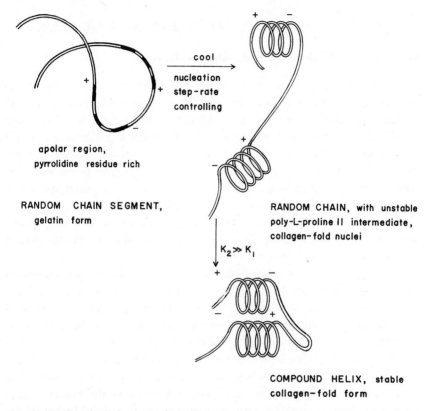

apolar region,
pyrrolidine residue rich

RANDOM   CHAIN   SEGMENT,
gelatin form

RANDOM CHAIN, with unstable
poly-L-proline II intermediate,
collagen-fold nuclei

$K_2 \gg K_1$

COMPOUND   HELIX, stable
collagen–fold form

FIG. V-40. Hypothetical scheme for collagen-fold formation in a single-strand α-gelatin.

The most questionable aspect of this proposal is the suggestion that electrostatic forces are involved in the structural orientation. As discussed in Chapter I, Weir (56) concluded that salt-links were of little importance in stabilizing the collagen structure. Furthermore, dilute salts have relatively little effect on fold formation and specific ions, rather than the solution ionic strength, determine the effectiveness of the salts. Veis et al. (68), on the other hand, showed that varying the concentration of potassium chloride from 0.01 to 0.10 M did change the course of the fold formation reaction. What is proposed is that while the electrostatic interactions do not cause the formation of the compound helix segments, the charge pattern at the end of each folded unit prohibits the interaction of certain segments or, alternatively, selects the proper segmental alignments and chain directions in the interacting unit.

III. INTERMOLECULAR ORGANIZATION IN GELATION

A. Fiber Formation from Soluble Collagen

As Engel's light scattering experiments indicate (71), it is almost impossible to find an experimentally feasible concentration so low that interchain aggregation does not occur upon cooling a gelatin solution below its equilibrium melting temperature. In the preceding discussion it has been suggested that for complete renaturation a certain degree of specificity of charge pairing is required for stable aggregate formation. The maximal effect of the long-range aggregating forces and their specificity can be seen by a consideration of the conditions which lead to the reconstitution* of native fibrils from tropocollagen solutions. This subject has been examined in detail by Bensusan and his colleagues (85–88), Wood and Keech (89), and Wood (90, 91).

The reconstitution of collagen fibers from tropocollagen was examined in terms of the process of heat gelation of tropocollagen at neutral pH, as first described by Gross and Kirk (92). In this procedure a tropocollagen solution is brought to the desired pH and ionic strength at low temperature ($\sim 1°$) and then rapidly warmed. Upon warming, native-type (~ 700-Å spacing) fibrils are formed in a random gel network. As the gel forms the turbidity of the suspension increases and this parameter has been taken as an appropriate quantitative measure of the extent of precipitation. Typical optical density-time curves are illustrated in Fig. V-41, where it can be seen that they have the characteristic shape of growth curves with a pronounced lag period, a rapid, nearly linear growth phase, and a subsequent period where the gel formation is complete. In all investigations a good correlation was observed between duration of the lag phase and rate of growth in the linear phase, so that it suffices to consider only the quantitatively more reliably determinable linear-phase growth rate. In general, the growth rate sharply decreased upon increasing the

---

* The term "reconstitution" is used to describe the process of the recombination of fully organized soluble tropocollagen into native-type fibrils, in contrast to the term "renaturation" which describes the organization of disorganized gelatin into the tropocollagen structure.

ionic strength at all pH's examined. Bensusan and Hoyt (*85*) routinely used 0.085 ionic strength tris [tris-(hydroxymethyl)-aminomethane] buffer at pH 8.1 as providing a 100% rate of fiber precipitation at 28°; all of their values are expressed relative to this ionic strength and rate. The inorganic cations behaved exactly as predictable from the Hofmeister series for the lyotropic swelling of collagen, the relative rates of fiber formation being in the order $K^+ > Na^+ > Li^+ > Mg^{++} > Ca^{++} > Ba^{++}$ for the chlorides of these cations. Even K^+, however, markedly decreased the rate (to $\sim 30\%$) when added to give an increment of only 0.02 to the ionic

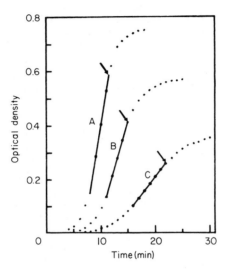

Fig. V-41. Increase in optical density during heat precipitation of collagen as a function of time. Protein concentrations were: curve A, 0.022%; curve B, 0.016%; curve C, 0.010% [Bensusan and Hoyt (*85*)].

strength of the solution. Ca^{++} decreased the rate of fiber precipitation to 10% at the same relative concentration. The anions had a more unusual effect, reversing their order in the Hofmeister series (Fig. V-42). Bensusan and Hoyt (*85*) measured the electrophoretic mobilities of collagen in each salt, and concluded that the effect of the anions on decreasing the rate of coagulation followed the order of their increasing extent of binding to the protein, for example, sulfate shifted the mobility at pH 8.3 from 0.0 in 0.5 N sodium chloride to -0.21 in 0.05 N sodium sulfate. In an analogous way the addition of 0.05 N barium chloride to collagen shifted the collagen mobility to $+0.27$, a clear indication that the effect of the cations on coagulation also follows the order of the extent of binding.

Divalent phosphate (HPO$_4^=$) appears to have a particularly strong inhibitory effect on fiber precipitation (87). Figure V-43 shows plots of the logarithm of the rate of precipitation during the growth phase as a function of the ionic strength of added sodium salts of various anions. Gross and Kirk had noted (92), in contrast to Bensusan and Hoyt (85), that

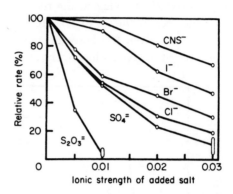

FIG. V-42. Effect of various anions at increasing ionic strength on rate of fiber formation. The basic environment contained tris buffer at a final ionic strength of 0.085. Sodium was the cation in all cases [Bensusan and Hoyt (85)].

thiocyanate ion at low concentration accelerated fiber formation in systems buffered by phosphate rather than tris. Bensusan (87) confirmed this and explained these data on the basis that HPO$_4^=$ was strongly bound to two sites on the protein, inhibiting fiber formation. The addition of low concentrations of the slightly inhibitory thiocyanate ion (see Fig. V-42) to the phosphate system appeared to competitively remove some of

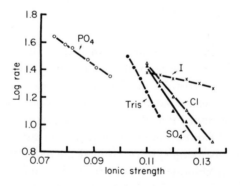

FIG. V-43. Ionic strength and specific ion effects in heat precipitation as measured by rate of fiber formation. The pH of the phosphate buffer was 7.2. The basic environment was 0.1 M NaCl. The pH of the tris buffer was 8.2. No other salt was present [Bensusan (87)].

the bound phosphate, leading to a net increase in the rate of precipitation in the growth phase. This effect would not be noted in other buffer systems where binding of the buffer ions was less specific and addition of thiocyanate ion merely increased the ionic strength.

At low concentration ($< 0.1\ M$) the aliphatic alcohols inhibit fiber formation, whereas at higher concentration the same alcohols accelerate fiber precipitation (86). In order of increasing inhibitory power the alcohols studied were methyl < ethyl < isopropyl < t-butyl < n-propyl. This inhibitory series does not correlate with either the electronegativity or the dielectric increment of the alcohols, but appears to be a function of the interaction of the alcohols with hydrophobic sites on the protein. These data may indicate that nucleation of fiber growth requires protofibrillar aggregates that are organized by long-range electrostatic forces, but stabilized by hydrophobic or hydrogen bonding between the nonpolar regions of the molecule. The inhibition of fiber growth by urea (92) at concentrations below the denaturing concentration of urea may result from the fact that urea interferes with the hydrophobic bonding between tropocollagens rather than with hydrogen bonding (83). In view of the current fluid situation with regard to the effect of urea (83, 93–95) on hydrogen bonds in aqueous solutions, great caution must be used in interpreting the experimental data on urea denaturation of proteins in general.

Two amino acid side chains have been shown to have a specific effect on fiber formation (86, 88). Bensusan and Scanu (86) iodinated tyrosine to increase the acidity of the phenolic hydroxyl group, and found marked increase in the rate of fiber formation and sharp decrease in the activation energy. A companion study (88) was undertaken to determine which of the basic groups might have some specific effect. Two tropocollagen derivatives were prepared, guanidinated TC and acetylated TC. Both deivatives were prepared without denaturation of the parent molecule. Acetylation, of both the lysine and hydroxylysine ε-amino groups, markedly-decreased the rate of fiber formation, as measured by the time required for formation of a fibrous clot. Electron microscope examination of the precipitated fibers showed a progressive loss of fine structure with increasing acetylation until, at 40% acetylation, only amorphous fibers were obtained. On the other hand guanidination, which converted lysyl residues to homoarginyl residues, increased the rate of fiber formation. In this case also, however, increasing the extent of guanidination decreased the electron microscopically visualized substructure of the fibers when they were stained with phosphotungstic acid. No substructure was evident in the heat-precipitated fibers when the extent of guanidination was increased above 20%. In contrast, SLS preparations from 22% guanidinated TC demonstrated a markedly sharpened substructure which agreed within 2% with the position of each sub-band in unmodified TC. The clotting time for 20% guanidinated collagen in the heat-precipitation process was less than one-eighth that for unmodified TC. Bensusan et al. (88) concluded from these observations that the arginyl residues in the native unmodified TC were responsible for the directing forces involved in formation of the native 700-Å spacing collagen fibrils. By comparing electron micrographs of phosphotungstic acid-stained unmodified TC and acetylated TC, five loci particularly rich in arginine were uncovered; these are approximately equidistantly spaced along the rod backbone of the TC. Competition between these loci and the new, randomly spaced homoarginyl residues in guanidinated TC for presumably uniformly spaced complementary acidic side chains leads to the more ready formation of structureless fibers. Further support for these postulates comes from the work of Gross and Kirk (92). These workers reported that the addition of small amounts of guanidine to tropocollagen solutions effectively inhibited fiber formation.

The above data serve as a useful framework within which we can examine the intermolecular interactions between gelatin molecules, leading to the formation of infinite gel networks.

B. Aggregate Formation in Dilute Gelatin Solutions

Light scattering studies, which permit the independent but simultaneous determination of molecular weight, radius of gyration, and second virial coefficient, are particularly well suited for the examination of the nature and extent of aggregate formation in dilute gelatin solutions under conditions which normally (at sufficiently high gelatin concentration) lead to gelation. Such studies have been carried out by Boedtker and Doty (96) and Beyer (97).

Boedtker and Doty (96) found, as Engel subsequently confirmed (71), that the aggregation of gelatin molecules was readily discernible even in extremely dilute solutions that were incapable of gelation. This aggregation was temperature dependent but was noted at all temperatures below the equilibrium melting temperature. The aggregate size, however, was dependent not only on the temperature but on the thermal path by which the gelatin solution was brought to the measurement temperature. In order to achieve reproducible results a standard quenching procedure, the forerunner of that used in the later collagen-fold formation experiments of Harrington and von Hippel, was used. In this procedure, each gelatin solution was prepared separately at the desired concentration, centrifuged for optical clarification, heated at 40° for 1 hour to erase the "thermal history" of the solution, quenched to 4° for 1 day, and finally brought to the desired final measurement temperature and held at that temperature for 18 hours. Two thoroughly characterized, essentially equivalent Knox P-111-20 gelatin preparations (see Chapter II) were used. The weight average molecular weight of the molecularly dispersed gelatin at 40° was 97,000 and the isoelectric pH was 5.1. The nature of the light scattering data is indicated in Fig. V-44, where the reduced intensity of 90° scattering is plotted vs. gelatin concentration. Each solid line connecting a set of points in the figure, except for the lowest line labeled 19° (dilution at constant temperature), refers to the size of the aggregates

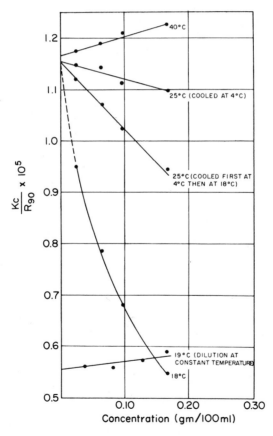

FIG. V-44. Aggregation in gelatin solutions at various temperatures. Reduced intensity of scattering in 0.15 M NaCl at the isoelectric point, pH 5 [Boedtker and Doty (96)].

formed at different concentrations but finally equilibrated at the indicated temperature. A vertical line at constant concentration drawn through the four upper curves thus represents the variation of aggregate size with temperature at constant concentration. The difference between the upper and lower 25° curves shows the effect of the thermal history on the aggregation. The solutions held at 18° for 18 hours before being equilibrated at 25° contained aggregates of larger size than solutions equilibrated directly at 25° after the 4° quenching. Casual perusal of the curves might suggest that the aggregates dissociate upon dilution, but the lowest curve (19°, dilution at constant temperature) indicates that this is not the case. These data were obtained by successive dilution at 19° of the solution represented

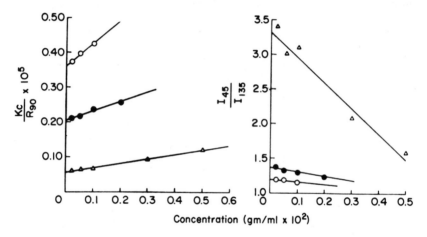

FIG. V-45. Light scattering by gelatin aggregates at 10°: ○, $c = 0.0010$ gm/ml; ●, $c = 0.0020$; △, $c = 0.0050$. Abcissa: gelatin concentration, gm/ml × 10^2. Dissymmetry of scattering shown by second graph [Beyer (97)].

by the highest concentration point. If very long times, of the order of hundreds of hours, were used a partial decrease in aggregate size was noted, but in practical terms the aggregates were irreversible at constant temperature. Beyer (97) obtained essentially identical results with dilute gelatin solutions finally equilibrated at 10° (Fig. V-45), and also concluded that, within a span of several hours, gelatin aggregates did not dissociate on dilution.

Boedtker and Doty (96) determined the aggregate size, from Zimm plots of the light scattering intensities at various angles and concentrations, in several different solvent environments at a constant temperature of 18°. To determine the effect of ionic strength, the scattering intensities were compared in 1.0 M sodium chloride and in 0.15 M sodium chloride at pH 5.1 and were found to be identical. However, in 1.0 M potassium thiocyanate at 18° the scattering intensity was unchanged from that observed for the unaggregated gelatin at 40° in dilute salt solution. From this comparison, Boedtker and Doty concluded that electrostatic forces did not play an important role in the aggregation process, and that the efficiency of the thiocyanate ion in inhibiting aggregate formation was the result of some specific effect, unrelated to ionic strength. Electrostatic effects could not be entirely excluded from consideration, however, since adjustment of the pH to 3.1 in 0.15 M sodium chloride caused marked decrease in aggregate size, whereas deionization at pH 5.1 led to greatly enhanced aggregate formation as compared with the aggregation in pH 5.1, 0.15 M sodium chloride. The weight-average molecular weights and Z-average radii of gyration, as well as other pertinent data, are listed in Table V-5

TABLE V-5 [a]

MOLECULAR WEIGHTS OF GELATIN AGGREGATES AT 18° IN VARIOUS SYSTEMS

System	pH	c (gm/ml) $\times 10^2$	M_w $\times 10^{-6}$	R_g (Å)	M/R_g^2	B (ml-mole/gm²) $\times 10^4$
NaCl (0.15 M)	5.1	0.54	5.9	1480	2.71	0.35
NaCl (0.15 M)	3.1	0.75	1.65	850	2 29	1.25
Isoionic	5.1	0.58	40.0	4260	2.21	—0.33

[a] Data of Boedtker and Doty (96).

for these three latter situations. The sharp concentration dependence of the aggregation, indicated in Figs. V-44 and 45, makes the comparison between the pH 5.1 and pH 3.1 data even more striking. Boedtker and Doty were unable to determine the aggregate size in 0.755% gelatin solution in 0.15 M sodium chloride at pH 5.1 because the data could not be extrapolated to a positive $Kc/R(0)$ intercept, indicating that an infinite network structure was formed rather than a set of large but independent aggregate units. Even in the relatively unfavorable case at pH 3.1 the aggregate size was quite large, with an average of more than 16 molecules per aggregate unit.

Measurements of the reduced viscosities of aggregated solutions at 18° indicated that $[\eta]$ was approximately proportional to $M^{1/2}$ (96). From Zimm plot data the radii of gyration of the various aggregates were calculated, and it was found that the ratio M_w/R_g^2 was also approximately constant. These two facts suggested to Boedtker and Doty (96) that the best model for the aggregate was a branched "brush heap" structure in which the individual gelatin molecules were held together at randomly occurring points. Within the "brush heap" the chain mobility was restricted, but the average chain segment distribution about the aggregate center of gravity was still close to that of a linear randomly coiled molecule of appropriate molecular weight. The second virial coefficient was increased, in 0.15 M sodium chloride, on going from pH 5.1 to 3.1, although M_w decreased. This increase was probably the result of both repulsions between chain segments within the aggregate and repulsions between segments on different aggregates. Beyer (97) examined the viscosity–aggregate molecular weight relationship in more detail, and found that $[\eta] = 3.6 \times 10^{-3} M_w^{0.41}$ for gelatin aggregates formed at 10°.

Aggregates formed in water at the isoelectric point presented a substantially different picture (96). Particle weights were higher (Table V-5) particle densities were higher (compare M/R_g^2), and the second virial coefficient was negative. In addition, the reduced specific viscosity for an aggregate with a particle weight of 40 million was less than that of an aggregate in 0.15 M sodium chloride with a particle weight of 1 million. Aggregate formation was detected even in solutions prepared at concentrations as low as 3×10^{-5} gm/ml (0.003%). Obviously, electrostatic interactions between oppositely charged chain segments greatly enhanced intermolecular associations and the formation of very compact spherical aggregates.

Boedtker and Doty (96) pointed out the close comparison between the melting of polycrystalline polymers and the gelatin aggregates. Since the melting of a crystalline polymer is endothermic, the equilibrium melting temperature must decrease with increasing dilution. In a polycrystalline polymer the distribution of crystallite sizes leads to progressive melting of the crystallites upon dilution at constant temperature. The melting temperature of gelatin gels decreases in this fashion with dilution, and the decreased aggregate size in diluted gelatin sols is consistent with this view. The stability to dissociation on dilution of the aggregates formed at high concentration is attributed to formation of relatively large crystallites involving many amino acid residues, and a consequent large activation energy for the dissociation reaction. In the light of our previous discussion we may clearly identify the crystallites in the gel aggregates as multiple-chain segments in the collagen-fold configuration.

C. Gel Formation: The Infinite Three-Dimensional Network

Ferry (98) pointed out the similarity of the gelation of gelatin to the gelation of celluloses and many synthetic linear polymers. Under appropriate conditions these polymers form random interchain contacts stabilized by either primary or secondary bonds. As long as the number of interchain contacts is below some critical number per polymer chain, the polymer system retains its solubility. When the critical points is reached there is a sharp transition which corresponds to formation of an infinitely large network of polymer chains. This network is insoluble, though it may contain many times more solvent than polymer on a weight basis. Immediately upon its formation the polymer network exhibits a well-defined rigidity and the entire polymer-solvent system is immobilized or "sets" to form a gel. Network systems stabilized by secondary forces such as hydrogen bonds, rather than by primary covalent bonds, exhibit a strong dependence upon the solvent environment and the system temperature. They represent a delicate balance between solute-solvent and solute-solute interactions.

In general the structure of a network gel is determined by the mode of gel formation. For example, if network formation is brought about rapidly or at high polymer concentration, random chain contacts and polymer chain entanglements lead to the formation of fine chain network structures. On the other hand, slow formation of interchain contacts in dilute polymer solutions permits a greater ordering of the interacting segments, leading to the development of large crystallites in which chains are aligned for relatively long distances, and the formation of coarse networks. Tempering a gel formed as a fine network at some point close to its critical melting temperature would permit a gradual rearrangement to a more ordered structure, and a consequent gradual structure transition to a coarser network.

In network gels stabilized by secondary forces, one of the most characteristic properties is that of exhibiting a relatively sharp melting temperature, T_g. T_g depends on the relative number of bonds involved in each set of interacting chain segments, increasing as the number of bonds per segment increases and becoming more sharply defined. The sharpness of T_g is related directly to the fact that the disruption of an interacting pair of chain segments is a cooperative phenomenon involving simultaneous rupture of several bonds. Fine network gels might therefore be expected to have both a lower T_g and a broader melting range than an equivalently bonded coarse network gel.

Eldridge and Ferry (*99*) examined the relationship between T_g and the concentration and molecular weight in some well-characterized fractionated gelatin systems. The gelatin fractions were derived from the alkali-pretreated ossein gelatin described by Scatchard, Oncley, Williams, and Brown (*100*) (see Chapters II and IV) and had molecular weights of 72,000–33,400. A very simple but clever scheme was used to obtain the gel melting temperatures. Gels were formed at pH 7 in 0.15 M sodium chloride by quenching a standard volume of solution at 40° to 0° for 24 hours in uniform test tubes. These tubes were stoppered, inverted, and placed in a water bath warmed at a constant rate of 12° per hour. The temperature at which the gel loosened at the edges and fell to the bottom of the tube, reproducible to $\pm$ 0.2°, was taken as T_g. For reasons which will be evident shortly,

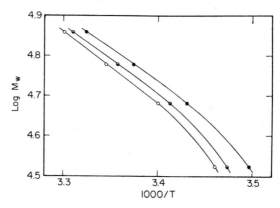

FIG. V-46. Relation between weight-average molecular weight and absolute temperature of melting; ◖, ◗, ●, denote gelatin concentration values of 55, 40, and 25 gm/liter, respectively. All gels chilled at 0° [Eldridge and Ferry (*99*)].

Eldridge and Ferry (*99*) represented the basic data as illustrated in Fig. V-46, in which the logarithm of the weight-average moledular weight, M_w, is plotted vs. the reciprocal of the absolute melting temperature, T_g. It is immediately evident that T_g is a pronounced function of both M_w and concentration, c. These dependencies are emphasized in Fig. V-47, a set of plots of log c vs. $1/T_g$ at constant M_w.

Eldridge and Ferry (*99*) noted a tempering effect similar to that observed by Boedtker and Doty (*96*). When the gels were chilled at 15° rather than 0°, the 15° set gels melted at higher temperatures than the 0° set gels and the concentration dependence of T_g was reduced. The stability of a gel against thermal disruption was increased when the gel was formed slowly (cooled gradually rather than quenched), or when a quench-

ed gel was annealed before melting, or when the temperature of a quenched gel was raised at a slower rate than 12° per hour.

The gel point is that point at which a sufficient number of interchain
bonds are formed so that an infinite three-dimensional chain network
first appears. This point, p_c, is given by Eq. 21 (*101*)

$$p_c = \frac{1}{\varrho \, (\lambda_w - 1)} \tag{21}$$

in which λ_w is the weight-average number of monomer units in a macromolecule, and ϱ is the fraction of these capable of forming cross-links
by, in this case, secondary bonds. The gel point thus represents the frac-

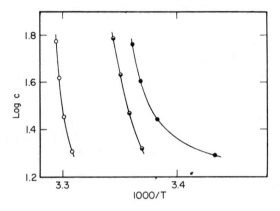

Fig. V-47. Relation between gelatin concentration and absolute temperature of melting;
○, ◓, ●, denote M_w values of 72,100, 52,700, and 48,000, respectively. All gels chilled
at 15° [Eldridge and Ferry (*99*)].

tion of cross-linkable units that have actually formed cross-linkages. The
only fruitful cross-linkages, so far as network formation is concerned, are
those which are intermolecular rather than intramolecular or "cyclic."
When cyclic structures are present $p_c > 1/\varrho \, (\lambda_w - 1)$. When $\lambda_w \gg 1$ then

$$m_{cl} \geqslant c/2M_w \tag{22}$$

where m_{cl} is the concentration of cross-links (two cross-linking groups per
cross-link) in moles liter at the gel point, M_w is the weight-average molecular weight, and c the concentration of macromolecules in gm/liter.
Whether or not the equality or inequality holds depends upon the presence or absence of cyclic structures. According to the light scattering data
on dilute solutions (*96, 97*), aggregates are formed prior to the formation

of the gel network, indicating the presence of many cyclic cross-links. Eldridge and Ferry (99) assumed, however, that a coefficient f could be defined representing the fraction of fruitful noncyclic cross-linkages and that the equation

$$f\, m_{cl} = \frac{c}{2\, M_w} \tag{23}$$

would then be valid at the gel point. Assuming next that the reaction involved was

$$2 \text{ moles cross-linking loci} \rightarrow 1 \text{ mole cross-links} \tag{24}$$

and using the term m_1 to indicate the concentration of free cross-linking loci, then an equilibrium constant K was defined as

$$K = m_{cl}/m_1^2 \tag{25}$$

K is a function of the temperature and M_w and possibly other variables, but the other variables appeared to have a one-to-one correspondence with M_w. Hence, Eldridge and Ferry (99) combined Eqs. 23 and 25 with van't Hoff's law and obtained

$$\left(\frac{d \ln c}{dT}\right)_{M_w} \left[1 - 2\, \frac{\partial \ln m_1}{\partial c}\right] = \frac{\Delta H^\circ}{RT^2} + \left(\frac{\partial \ln f}{\partial T}\right)_{M_w} 2 \left(\frac{\partial \ln m_1}{\partial T}\right) \tag{26}$$

with ΔH° representing the enthalpy change in Reaction 24. Assuming that the proportion of cross-linking loci actually linked is always small, even at $T_g < T_m$, as suggested by the fact that the dilute solution aggregates have a random-coil-like structure (87), then $\partial \ln m_1 / \partial \ln c \approx 1$ and $\partial \ln m_c/\partial T \approx 0$. Furthermore, $(\partial \ln f/\partial T)_{M_w} = 0$, or the ratio of noncyclic cross-links to the total number of cross-links is assumed to be unchanged when the gelatin solution at T_g is warmed but c is increased to keep the system at the gel point. This assumption is warranted if one assumes that the heat of reaction is the same for cyclic and noncyclic cross-linking, and that the concentration of noncyclic cross-links is proportional to the same power of the concentration as the total number of cross-linkages. This latter assumption is the most doubtful of the set, particularly if the gelatin chains are highly cross-linked. At the gel point, and with the above assumptions, it is reasonable to expect that the total number of cross-linkages is proportional to c^2. Using this relationship and the various simplifying assumptions, Eq. 26 may be integrated to the form

$$\log c = \frac{\Delta H^\circ}{2.303\, RT_g} + \text{constant} \tag{27}$$

so that a plot of log c vs. $1/T_g$ should yield a straight line. This behavior is approximated for gelatins of high molecular weight equilibrated at 15° (Fig. V-47), and for even lower molecular weight gelatins equilibrated at 0°. Eldridge and Ferry (99) suggested that the deviations from linearity noted at low concentration might indicate that cross-links having lower heats of reaction must be formed, in addition to the more stable cross-linkages, to effect infinite network formation. Heats of cross-linking obtained through the application of Eq. 27 are listed in Table V-6 for gels formed at

TABLE V-6 [a]

HEATS OF REACTION FOR CRYSTALLITE FORMATION AS A FUNCTION OF MOLECULAR WEIGHT

$M_w \times 10^{-3}$	$-\Delta H°$ (kcal/mole of cross-links)	
	Gels chilled at 0°	Gels chilled at 15°
72.1	73	220
60.0	60	—
52.7	62	130
48.0	56	120
33.4	49	—

[a] Data of Eldridge and Ferry (99).

both 0° and 15°. These data were interpreted as showing that all of the cross-linkages do not have equivalent stabilities and that tempering, or slow gel formation, allows the more stable cross-links to be established at the expense of the weaker bonds. Rapid chilling causes a more haphazard formation of weaker, or less well-organized, cross-linked regions. These data, then, represent a quantitative statement of the importance of the thermal history of a gelatin aggregate or gel on its stability. Returning to the concept that the crystallite or cross-linked regions represent chain segment pairs or triads in the collagen-fold configuration, the data of Table V-6 indicate either that the tempered gels or gelatin aggregates contain collagen-folded segments 2–3 times the size of the random aggregates of untempered gels, or that the interchain contacts are more perfectly arranged so that hydrogen bonds or hydrophobic bonds are maximized.

Equation 26 and the resulting approximation of Eq. 27 are based on the relation between T_g and c at constant M_w. The T_g vs. M_w data at constant c provide an alternate and independent view of the problem of network formation. Qualitatively one would expect T_g to increase as M_w

increases, at constant c, since p_c is inversely proportional to the degree of polymerization or M_w. An infinite three-dimensional network is formed when there is one cross-link per polymer unit (Eq. 24) and the larger the polymer the fewer cross-linkages are required. As indicated in Fig. V-46, the logarithm of M_w is nearly a linear function of $1/T_g$. A very approximate analysis of the van't Hoff relationship, linking K and T_g at constant c but varying M_w, leads to Eq. 28

$$\log M_w = \frac{\Delta H^\circ}{16\,RT_g} + \text{constant} \tag{28}$$

in which ΔH° has the same meaning as in Eq. 27. This equation predicts the linearity of a plot of log M_w vs. $1/T_g$. Application of Eq. 28 to the data gives values of $\Delta H^\circ \approx -50$ kcal/mole for gels chilled at 0°, in reasonable agreement with the values indicated in Table V-6.

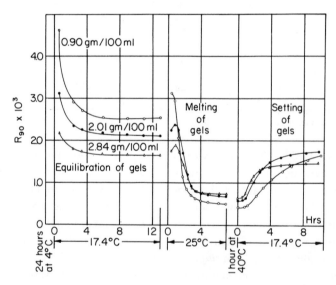

FIG. V-48. Aggregate formation and melting in an alkali-precursor gelatin in 0.15 M NaCl, pH 6.5 solution as a function of temperature and time [Boedtker and Doty (96)].

Boedtker and Doty (96) explored the aggregation during gel formation and gel melting by a further refinement of their light scattering tecnique. Figure V-48 illustrates the variations in scattering intensity during manipulation of three different concentrations of an unfractionated Knox-P-111-20 alkali-precursor ossein gelatin ($M_w = 97,000$) in 0.15 M sodium chloride at pH 6.5. First the solutions, at the indicated concentrations, were quenched at 4°, then equilibrated at 17.4° until constant 90° scattering intensities, R (90), were observed. This required a minimum of about 8 hours in each case. The ordered nature of the gels was evident in the fact that the more concentrated gels scattered substantially less light than the more dilute gels. Upon raising the temperature to 25°, above T_g for these gels, there was an immediate decrease in order, marked by an increase in R (90) followed by a decline in R (90), as the aggregates dissociated until, as expected, R $(90)_{c=0.9\%} < R$ $(90)_{c=2.8\%}$. The melting of the gels was accomplished relatively rapidly, but the stable sols at 25° still contained aggregates that were not dissociated until the sols were heated to 40° for an hour. Reformation of the gels by cooling the 40° solutions to 17.4° was accompanied by slow increase in R (90), in which the relative magnitude of the scattering intensities was again reversed, $(R$ $(90)_{c=0.9\%} > R$ $(90)_{c=2.8\%})$. Although the gelation was a much slower process in general than the melting process, concentrated gels attained their 17.4° equilibrium scattering values more rapidly than the more dilute gels. The R (90) values in each case were indistinguishable from the previous equilibrium gel scattering intensities after about 70 hours at 17.4°.

Zimm plots, (Fig. V-49) were constructed from measurements of the angular dependence of scattering of a series of preparations at pH 5.1 in 0.15 M sodium chloride at 18°, but traversing in gelatin concentration the range in which only aggregates were formed through the range in which stable gels appeared. As indicated in Fig. V-49, the aggregate plots were "normal," i.e. Kc/R (θ) was a linear function of $\sin^2$ $(\theta/2) + k'c$ and the average aggregate size increased as c increased. At the gel point, however, Kc/R (θ) was no longer linear in $\sin^2$ $(\theta/2)$, curving upward at low angles, and the Kc/R (θ) values increased rapidly as c increased. The behavior of the gel systems is typical of that which arises when ordering of the scattering centers occurs. The high angle scattering values are changed relatively little from those for the independent aggregate scattering of similar-size scattering centers, but the low angle values are changed markedly. If the scattering centers were fixed in space as would be the case if the entire gel structure were composed of rigid particles, then the expectation would have been that the low angle scattering would be unaffected while the greatest deviations would have been noted at high angle (102). Boedtker and Doty (96) considered that the absence of this effect implied that the scattering centers in gelatin gels were not rigidly fixed, and they assigned the cause of the alteration of shape of the angular scattering envelopes to the ordering of the scattering centers, due to the spatial volume-filling capacity of the centers.

Boedtker and Doty (*96*) encountered their greatest difficulty in interpreting the concentration dependence of the gel scattering intensity. One could attribute the decrease in R (0) as c increased to decrease in the average size of the scattering units. They argued, however, that there was no reason to expect that the regular increase in aggregate size noted in dilute quenched gelatin solutions with increasing concentration should reverse

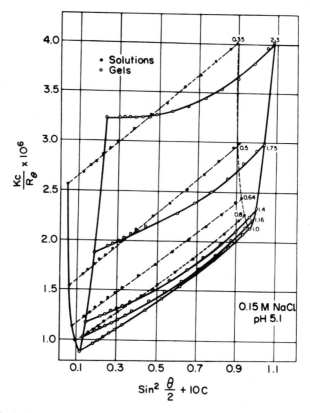

Fig. V-49. Reciprocal angular scattering envelopes of a gelatin system in the solution and gel states. Sols and gels measured at 18° [Boedtker and Doty (*96*)].

itself during gelation and, hence, that the observed behavior was the result of external interference as a consequence of the ordering of the system indicated by the angular scattering dependence. In support of this view, Boedtker and Doty analyzed the concentration dependence to be expected from a dense gas of very large hard spheres, on the assumption that the distribution of aggregates (the scattering centers) in the gel was approximately like that which would have occurred if the gelatin strands connecting the aggregates were severed so that the aggregates were kinetically independent. Computations based on this model were shown to predict a maximum in a plot of R (0) vs. c (Fig. V-50), for a hard sphere gas with particles 795 Å in diameter and $M = 5.9 \times 10^6$. The conclusion was reached that a collection of scattering centers not greatly different from the crystallite-like aggregates observed in dilute solution could, if distributed in space in a regular fashion as in a dense gas of volume-filling hard spheres, give rise to scattering intensities at zero angle similar to those observed for the gelatin gels.

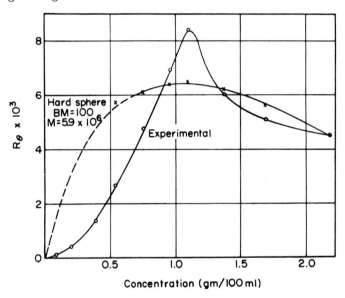

FIG. V-50. Comparison of the concentration dependence of the reduced scattering intensity of gelatin gels with that predicted for a hard sphere fluid [Boedtker and Doty (96)].

As indicated above, the key argument was that the aggregate size in the cooled gelatin systems, in the concentration range covering the sol-gel transition point, was a monotonously increasing function of the concentration. As Ferry (98) pointed out, however, the character of a network gel is determined by the conditions of network formation. Rapid gel formation at high polymer concentration favors the formation of fine networks, with relatively many interchain junction points as compared with the network formation in more dilute systems. One should therefore anticipate that the average crystallite size is less in a quenched gel formed at high concentration than in an equally rapidly quenched gel formed at lower concentration. In the latter case gel formation occurs more slowly.

This appears to be the situation, illustrated in Fig. V-48, where the 4° quenched gels formed at 2.84% gelatin concentration have a lower scattering than the 0.9% gels. Upon melting and regelation the concentrated solutions again form gels more rapidly (right-hand set of curves in Fig. V-48), and quickly attain the average crystallite size characteristic of the fine network structure. Regelation of the dilute gelatin system, however, is slower and a coarse network of larger aggregates is built. Assuming, with Boedtker and Doty, that the aggregates in the dilute gel are not fixed rigidly in space, then the slow gelation at 18° provides the opportunity for self-tempering of the loose gel so that larger crystallites are formed at the expense of the less perfectly ordered aggregates. Thus, the experimentally determined $R(0)$ curve in Fig. V-50 may indeed be a reflection of a decrease in average aggregate size as the gel concentration is increased, rather than a qualitative correspondence with the hard sphere model as proposed by Boedtker and Doty (96). This matter will be examined again in Section V of this chapter from the point of view of the rheological properties of gels.

IV. Gel Stability

Before entering into a discussion of the factors which influence and control gel stability, we might well pause to ponder over the various ideas that have been developed in the preceding sections regarding the nature of gelatin aggregates and gels. The one indispensable event in gelation is the initial development of the collagen-fold involving portions of each gelatin molecule. Collagen-fold formation in that process in which peptide chain segments, of uncertain and probably varying length, assume a stable helical configuration similar to the helical conformation of the peptide chains in native collagen. The evidence cited so far seems to favor the proposition that an individual peptide chain segment cannot form a stable helix, although there are powerful arguments which suggest that this may indeed be the case. Assuming, however, that at least two chain segments are required to form the stable collagen-fold unit, it is nevertheless clear that collagen-fold formation can be an intramolecular reaction. The apparent concentration independence of collagen-fold formation may be explained on the basis that, even at the high dilutions at which investigations have been carried out, the chain segment density within the domain of a single random coil is relatively high. For example, the α-gelatin ($M_w \sim$ 90,000) examined by Boedtker and Doty (96) was found to have a Z-average radius of gyration of 165 Å at infinite dilution at 40°, pH 5.1, in 0.15 M

sodium chloride. Taking into account the polydispersity of the system, the weight-average end-to-end chain extension was 258 Å and, therefore, the weight concentration within the polymer domain was 2.1×10^{-3} gm/ml. Thus a gelatin chain segment is never in an environment less concentrated than about 0.2%. Furthermore, at total gelatin concentration greater than 0.2%, the molecular domains must necessarily overlap so that intermolecular contacts are equally probable as intramolecular contacts. Because of the great effective volume of each molecule, it is a practical impossibility to examine gelatin systems at concentrations so low that intermolecular interactions can be ruled out, though intra-molecular events will predominate at concentrations less than 0.2%. In this context the argument, that since collagen-fold formation proceeds at the same rate at 0.08% total gelatin concentration as at 0.5%, the transition must involve only the configurational change in a single peptide strand, is untenable.

The chain segments primarily involved in the collagen-fold are the nonpolar regions rich in proline and hydroxyproline. During collagen-fold formation in single-strand α-gelatins, there does not appear to be any specificity to the intersegment interaction so that any random contact between nonpolar chain segments might lead to the formation of a collagen-folded unit. However, all folded units randomly formed will not have the same intrinsic stability. Studies on the renaturation of the multichain gelatins (γ-gelatins) suggest that there are specific groupings of ionic side chains which are complementary on different chains and which direct the selective formation of the most stable collagen-fold-containing regions in favorable cases. As a result of the lack of specificity in the intersegment interaction in collagen-fold formation, this process should be relatively independent of pH and ionic strength, whereas complete renaturation should be much more dependent on these parameters. In contrast to collagen-fold formation, network gel formation via random segment interactions is concentration dependent and is favored at high concentration. Conversely, renaturation is competitively inhibited by random collagen-fold formation and network formation, so that renaturation proceeds most efficiently at gelatin concentrations less than 0.2%.

The collagen-folded segments have been identified as the "crystallites" which form the basis of the aggregates in dilute gelatin systems and the network junction points in gels. The rigid, structured collagen-folded aggregates are joined by flexible, unstructured individual peptide chains. At temperatures near the collagen-fold equilibrium melting temperature, both aggregates and gels are subject to aging or tempering, during which a reorganization process progressively alters the average aggregate size in sols and increases the stability of gels. This reorganization can apparently take place without a major change in net content of collagen-folded units under any particular set of conditions. Thus the imperfectly ordered, randomly formed collagen-folded segments are in a temperature-sensitive dynamic equilibrium with the disordered random chain segments.

Gel formation and gel melting are different types of processes operating through distinctly different kinetic mechanisms. Gel formation is the concentration-dependent sum of reactions involving rotations about specific peptide bonds, random collisions, ordering and stabilization of individual chain elements. Gel melting has all the aspects of a cooperative transition requiring simultaneous rupture of several weak bonds, followed by rapid randomization of the chain elements. Both processes, however, depend on a common set of parameters whose influence can be considered from two points of view. One can examine the environmental conditions in terms of their effect on the primary intersegment interaction, or in terms of their effect on enhancing or inhibiting the development of the specific peptide chain configuration characteristic of the collagen-fold. Restated in terms of the Flory-Weaver model of collagen-fold formation (54), we can ask whether or not a particular set of conditions affects the structure or size of the transient intermediate, or affects the establishment of bonds between such intermediates. Our discussion of gel stability must therefore encompass both of these questions and must draw on the data relating to gel network and collagen-fold formation, as well as on gel melting.

A. pH Effects

The early work on the effect of pH on both the formation and melting of gelatin gels was inconsistent and frequently contradictory, probably due to the lack of clear definition of the gelatins involved and general disregard for the importance of the thermal history of the gels. The most reliable investigations appear to be those of Lloyd (103) and Pleass (104), who determined the minimum gelatin concentrations necessary to form a gel at various specified pH's and temperatures. Pleass (104) found that at temperatures below 18°, the minimum concentration required for gelation was near 0.5% and was independent of the pH in the range 4–8. At higher temperatures higher gel concentrations were required and, at 25°, a sharp minimum concentration was found at pH 5, the isoelectric point of the gelatin being studied. Kraemer and Fanselow (105) also found a pI 5 gelatin to have maximum stability at pH 5 and observed that at this point the gelatin had a maximum negative specific rotation. Kraemer and Dexter (*106*) later found a very pronounced maximum in the turbidity at the isoelectric pH in salt-free 1% gelatin solutions at temperatures below 30°.

Bello, Bello and Vinograd (*107*) have recently reexamined the pH and concentration dependence of the melting points of various gelatins and chemically modified gelatins. In this study, the melting point was determined on solutions which were first heated to 50° for 3–10 minutes and then quenched to 0° for 20 hours. The value of T_g was determined as the gels were heated at a constant rate of 5° per hour. Figures V-51 and 52 illustrate the results for pI 9.2 and pI 5.0 gelatins, respectively. In both

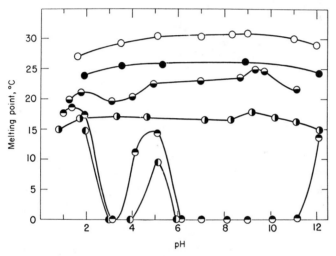

Fɪɢ. V-51. Melting points of an acid-precursor pig skin gelatin as a function of pH at various concentrations. Deionized: ○, 5%; ●, 1.2%; ◐, 0.7%; ◑, 0.6%; ◑, 0.6% with 0.1 *M* sodium chloride added. Nondeionized: ◔, 0.73% [Bello *et al.* (*107*)].

cases, high gelatin concentration in the absence of salt and low gelatin concentration in the presence of salt, the melting temperature was more dependent on gelatin concentration than on the pH at which the measurements were made over the entire range pH 1–12. However, at concentrations less than 1.0%, deionized gelatins in the absence of salt exhibited very striking changes in T_g with pH. In the acid-precursor gelatin with pI 9.2, 0.7% gelatin solution did not form a gel at pH 6–11. Swelling, turbidity, and electrophoretic data (*106–108*) usually indicate that the isoelectric range of acid-precursor gelatins lies between pH 6.5 and 9.0, so that the extended minimum in T_g of pH 9–11 must have been the result of some other factor. This is emphasized in Fig. V-52, where a pI 5 gelatin at 0.57% concentration is also seen to have a minimum in T_g in just this pH range, in addition to a distinct minimum at pH 4.5–5.0. A second minimum at pH 3.0 in the acid-precursor gelatin is not duplicated by the alkali-precursor gelatins. The specific rotation of the acid-precursor gelatin was measured as a function of pH (Fig. V-53) and the data are particularly revealing. In the range from pH 5, the position of a T_g maximum for the 0.7% gelatin solution examined, to pH 12, there was only slight variation in $[\alpha]_D^4$ from a maximum value of —290°. However, at pH 3, the acid T_g minimum, $[\alpha]_D^4$ was only —250°. Thus the alkaline T_g mini-

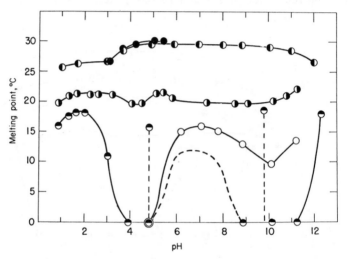

FIG. V-52. Melting points of alkali-precursor gelatins as a function of pH. Deionized: ◑, 5% calf skin; ●, 5% ossein; ◓, 0.57% calf skin (dotted curve indicates that weak gels formed at pH 6, 7, and 8 but that gel strengths were not measured; vertical dashed lines show the effect of 0.1 M sodium chloride); ○, 0.7% calf skin. Nondeionized: ◐, 0.7% ossein [Bello *et al.* (*107*)].

mum occurred without a reduction in collagen-fold formation, whereas the acid T_g minimum was caused by a lessened extent of collagen-fold formation. Consequently, at low gelatin concentration cyclic aggregates rather than network-forming aggregates must be favored in the alkaline range. An alternate way of making this same statement would be to specify that the term f in Eq. 23 is pH and ionic strength dependent. A concentration of only 0.15 M sodium chloride is sufficient to completely eliminate the pH dependence of f. On the other hand, the pH 3 minimum in T_g can be interpreted on the basis that the m_{cl} term in Eq. 23 was decreased in the absence of salt. Again, 0.15 M sodium chloride completely suppressed the pH dependency of m_{cl}. Bello *et al.* (*107*) noted that as the solutions which did not gel were allowed to age at $0°$, T_g rose in both acid and alkaline pH ranges until, in about 11 days, the pH dependence was effectively erased and the value of T_g approximated that of 1-day-old gels formed at the same gelatin concentration in 0.15 M sodium chloride. Thus the inhibition of gelation appeared to result from a decrease in the *rate* of collagen-fold formation in the acid range. The equilibrium collagen-fold content was unchanged. Conversely, the increase in T_g in the alkaline range must have been the result of a tempering effect, a rearrangement to a more stable crystallite distribution. Bello *et al.* (*107*) did not determine the specific optical rotation of the alkali-precursor gelatin as a function of pH or time.

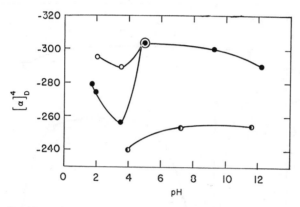

FIG. V-53, Specific rotation of acid-precursor gelatin gels as a function of pH: ●, 0.7% pI 9.2 gelatin after 20 hours at 4°; ○, same after 10 days at 4°; ◉, 0.7% esterified gelatin after 20 hours at 4° [Bello *et al.* (*107*)].

It is likely, that both minima in Fig. V-52 are caused by variations in f with pH, and that aging would have permitted tempering and network formation.

Acetylation of the amino groups of the acid-precursor gelatin, by methods which did not lead to a decrease in the average molecular weight of the gelatin, had little effect on the pH-T_g relationship indicated in Fig. V-51, although the alkaline T_g minimum was narrowed slightly at the lowest gelatin concentration (*107*). Esterification of the carboxyl groups, however, completely eliminated the alkaline T_g minimum at pH 6–11, shifting this to pH > 11 (Fig. V-54). Equally interesting was the fact, shown in Fig. V-53, that the specific rotation was lower for the esterified gelatin at pH 4–12 than for the corresponding unesterified gelatin, although T_g was higher for the esterified gelatin at pH 6–11.

Bello *et al.* (*107*) concluded that ionic effects were unimportant in gelation at high gelatin concentration and at moderate ionic strength, and that the amino groups were unimportant even in dilute salt-free gelatin systems, but that whatever ionic group effects were noted at low gelatin concentration were inhibitory with regard to the rate of gelation. It seems possible to make a somewhat more definite assignment of the role of the ionic interactions at high pH. As pointed out earlier, the optical rotation data showed that collagen-fold formation was *not* inhibited at high pH. Thus we may fix the effect of ionic interactions as decreasing the number of fruitful network-forming interchain contacts. That is, cyclic intramolec-

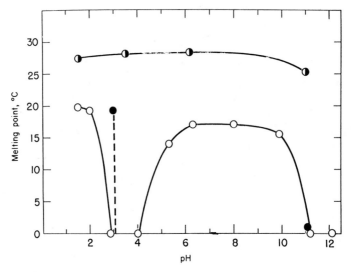

FIG. V-54. Melting points of a carboxyl-esterified gelatin as a function of pH. ◑, 5%; ○, 0.7%; ●, 0.7% with 0.1 *M* sodium chloride added [Bello *et al.* (*107*)].

ular interactions are favored. It is easy, from this point of view, to see why the T_g minimum is so much broader for acid-precursor gelatins than for alkali-precursor gelatins. Veis *et al.* (*108*) showed that the acid-precursor gelatins were multi-chain molecules, much more compact than alkali-precursor gelatins of equivalent molecular weight, and suggested that acidic and basic side chains were constrained, by interchain cross-linkages, to reside in nearby regions within the molecular domain of the random gelatin molecular network. Ion binding was enhanced by this situation and internal salt-linkages were also favored. This picture is in agreement with the data of Grassmann *et al.* (*84*), showing the polar groups in collagen to be localized in specified regions and the probability (76, 109) that the cross-linkages occur in the polar regions. Thus collagen-fold formation in dilute acid-precursor gelatin systems at high pH leads to partial renaturation (f low) rather than to network formation. Highly cross-linked gelatins, such as γ-gelatin, renature completely (maximal cyclic aggregation) and precipitate out from solution. The commercial acid-precursor gelatins and gelatins with low average molecular weight and low degree of cross-linking cannot form perfect collagen structures and, therefore, slowly form networks upon tempering. The importance of cyclic collagen-fold formation in competing with network collagen-fold formation is clearly indicatd by the increased network formation in esterified gelatins with lower net content of collagen-fold aggregate units.

Earlier investigations, similar in intent to the researches of Bello et al. (107), agree in eliminating the side-chain carboxyl and amino groups from having any important bearing on gelation at gelatin concentrations greater than 1%, but several reports have suggested a specific role for the guanidino groups in gelation. The very basic guanidino groups would not be affected by pH variations between 1 and 12. Grabar and his co-workers (110, 111) were the first to suggest that destruction of the guanidino groups of arginine inhibited the gelation of gelatin. Using the same technique of hypobromite oxidation, Davis (112, 113) also found that the amount of hypobromite consumed was directly proportional to the decrease in arginine content and to the decrease in ability of 2.5% gelatin solutions to set to gels. Berger et al. (114) deguanidinated gelatin by reacting anhydrous gelatin with metallic sodium in liquid ammonia. The modified gelatin reaction product was found to contain only 1.0–1.2% arginine. This gelatin failed to gel even at 20% concentration at room temperature and set only to a very weak gel at 0° at that concentration. The conclusion drawn in each of these investigations was that the arginine side chain was required for gelation, but each argument rested upon a relatively poorly supported claim that the degradative treatment did not significantly reduce the gelatin molecular weight. Bello (115) effectively refuted this claim with evidence that the gelatin molecular weight was significantly reduced during the hypobromite oxidation reaction. Bello et al. (116) reexamined the role of specific side-chain functional groups in gelation, paying special attention to the molecular weights of the chemically modified gelatins. A pI 9.2 pig skin gelatin was used in this study. The original weight-average molecular weight was determined by ultracentrifugal approach-to-equilibrium methods to be 220,000. The gelatin was degraded for various times by hydrolysis at pH 5 and 100° and M_w was redetermined. The intrinsic viscosity of each gelatin was also determined and the M_w-$[\eta]$ relationship was found to be $[\eta] = 4.8 \times 10^{-4} M_w^{0.56}$. One sample each of carboxyl-methylated, amino-acetylated, hydroxyl-acetylated, and guanidino-nitrated gelatins was also taken for both M_w and $[\eta]$ evaluation. In each case except that of the guanidino-nitrated gelatin the $[\eta]$-M_w values fit the Staudinger relationship given above. The intrinsic viscosity of the nitrated gelatin was too low for the observed M_w. This observation may be contrasted with that of Berger et al. (114), who reported that the reduced viscosity of a 1% gelatin rose from an original value of 0.33 to 0.45 after deguanidination. The nitration reaction was carried out with dry gelatin dissolved in a mixture of concentrated sulfuric and nitric acids. Under one set of conditions 50% of the guanidino groups were nitrated along with 75% of the hydroxyl groups. A second preparation yielded a 70% nitrated, 36% hydroxyl-sulfated gelatin.

Having shown that the intrinsic viscosity was a reliable measure of molecular weight for the modified gelatins (in the worst case, the calculated M_w would be too low), Bello et al. (116) plotted T_g vs. $[\eta]$. The resulting plot, (Fig. V-55) showed that at 5% gelatin concentration the carboxyl-esterified and amino-acetylated gelatins had melting points equal to those of unmodified gelatins of similar molecular weight, confirming the conclusion that these groups are of no importance in gelation. The situation was less clear-cut for the guanidino-nitrated gelatins. The 50% nitrated–75% sulfated gelatin had a T_g much lower than anticipated, but a sulfated, non-nitrated gelatin had a similar melting point. The 70% nitrated–36% sulfated gelatin had only a slightly lower T_g than anticipated. In both cases, therefore, the lowering of T_g was attributed to the hydroxyl-sulfation rather than to blocking of the guanidino groups, and Bello et al. concluded that the guanidino groups are of relatively little importance in the formation and stabilization of concentrated gels.

Small but experimentally significant deviations from the behavior of unmodified gelatins were noted for hydroxyl-acetylated gelatins. Gelatins acetylated with acetic acid and acetic anhydride in perchloric acid had T_g's higher than normal. Those acetylated with acetic anhydride in trifluoroacetic acid had lower than normal T_g values. In both systems, acetylation was 96–100% complete. It was thought that an acyl shift-type rearrangement occurred during acetylation in the presence of trifluoroacetic acid. Deacetylation reversed this effect and T_g returned to its normal value. The slight increase in T_g upon acetylation without chain rearrangement is consistent with the thought that polar and ionic group interactions tend to inhibit gel formation. The O-sulfation, which must have drastically al-

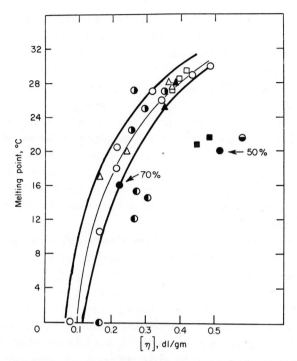

Fig. V-55. The melting point–viscosity relationships of gelatin and modified gelatin: O, standard gelatin; ●, guanidine-nitrated; ■, hydroxyl groups quantitatively sulfated; ◑, hydroxyl-acetylated in perchloric acid; ◐, hydroxyl-acetylated in trifluoroacetic acid; □, amino-acetylated; △, carboxyl-methylated (methanol + HCl); ▲, carboxyl-methylated (methanol + thionyl chloride) [Bello *et al.* (*116*)].

tered the net charge and polar character of the gelatin, clearly led to marked inhibition of gelation.

These studies, then, do not point to the specific participation of either ionic or polar groups in collagen-fold formation and confirm the view that only the nonpolar chain regions are involved in both collagen-fold and network formation. In a negative sense, having ruled out the utilization of chain segments containing polar groups, the data do suggest the essential identity of the collagen-fold regions and the chain segments in aggregate form, whether the aggregates are cyclic or network-forming.

B. Specific Salt Effects

In spite of the conclusion that pH and ionic strength are relatively unimportant in gelation, and that the polar groups may also be disregarded, the fact that neutral salts at high concentration do affect gelation is well documented (98). The neutral salts may either increase or decrease T_g just as they may increase or decrease the melting temperatures of collagen fibers (see Chapter I). Sodium sulfate, for example, raises T_g at 1 M concentration whereas 1 M sodium chloride lowers T_g. Evidently the explanation of these neutral salt, or lyotropic, effects must be sought in terms of direct stabilization or disruption of the collagen-folded nonpolar chain segments. The lyotropic effects can conceivably occur in either of two ways; the salts may act by changing the character of the stabilizing hydrogen bonds or water structure, or they may interact directly with the peptide backbone, imposing configurations at the peptide bonds which prevent the chains from even assuming transiently the poly-L-proline II helix configuration.

Using the well-characterized acid-precursor gelatin described above (pI 9.2, $M_w = 220,000$), Bello, Riese and Vinograd (117) examined the effect of a number of ions on the melting points of 5% gels. Table V-7 lists the melting points of the gelatin in a number of sodium salts in relation to the melting temperature of a salt-free 5% gel. The various anions have markedly different power in potentiating gelation. The melting point reduction, for most of the salts investigated, was a linear function of the salt concentration in the range 0.1–1.0 M. As previously shown by Ferry (98) and Gordon and Ferry (118), the large polarizable anions had the greatest effectiveness as melting point reducers. An interesting new observation was that in a series of mono- and dicarboxylic acids there was first an increase in T_g with increasing chain length, followed by lowering of T_g (Fig. V-56).

Bello et al. (117) compared various cation-anion combinations and noted that the effect of each ion could be represented individually by a characteristic molar melting point depression, α. The net effect of any given salt could then be determined by merely adding the α values of the individual ions. The agreement was generally very good even in mixtures of several salts. Urea and formamide fit in the same scheme, as did a number of salts of the guanidinium ion.

Stock deionized gelatin solutions were held at 37° and pH 7.3, and salt solutions, also adjusted to pH 7.3, were added. After brief equilibration the pH of the mixture was determined. In every case, as shown in Fig. V-57, the pH shifted and the magnitude of the shift correlated well with the change in gel melting point. Raised pH values indicate anion binding, lowered values cation binding. The site of the ion binding was examined by comparing the molar melting point reduction of the various salts in

TABLE V-7

Additive (No salt)	Concentration (moles/liter)	M.p. (°C)
Fluoride	1.0	34.5
Maleate	0.5	33.7
Succinate	0.25	32.3
Fumarate	0.50	31.5
Methanesulfonate	1.0	31.5
None	—	30.4
Chloride	1.0	28.0
Chloroacetate	1.0	26.6
Trimethylacetate	1.0	26.5
Trifluoroacetate	1.0	24.1
Bromide	1.0	22.8
Nitrate	1.0	22.3
Dichloroacetate	1.0	19.6
Dibromoacetate	1.0	16.3
Thiocyanate	1.0	16.0
Iodide	1.0	16.0
Benzenesulfonate	1.0	15.5
Trichloroacetate	1.0	12.7
Diiodoacetate	1.0	12.3
Salicylate	1.0	no gel
Tribromoacetate	1.0	no gel
Acetyltryptophan	0.75	13.7
Acetylenedicarboxylate	0.5	19.4

[a] Data of Bello et al. (117).

5% N-acetylated or O-nitrated gelatins. The data, (Table V-8), unambiguously show that the binding of anions at basic or hydroxyl groups cannot account for the melting point reductions. Similarly, the melting point reductions due to the presence of calcium ions were identical for normal gelatin and a gelatin with 70% of its carboxyl groups esterified. The only case where carboxylate ion binding was definetely indicated was with the ferric ion. Ferric ions were found to rise the gel melting temperature at low concentration and reduce T_g at higher concentration. In the example cited, a 5% gelatin solution, made 0.13 M in ferric ion, gelled at room temperature and, after aging at 0° for 20 hours, T_g was raised by 4°. A similar solution, 1.0 M in ferric ion, did not gel at room temperature and after

TABLE V-8 [a]

EFFECTS OF SODIUM SALTS ON MELTING POINTS OF GELATIN AND MODIFIED GELATINS

Type of gelatin	Salt [b]	Concentration of salt (molar)	M.p. change, (°C)
Original	Thiocyanate	0.5	−7.1
Nitrated	Thiocyanate	0 5	−7.2
Original	Lithium diiodosalicylate	0.06	−7.0
Nitrated	Lithium diiodosalicylate	0.06	−7.0
Original	Acetate	0.25	+1.0
Acetylated	Acetate	0.25	+0.9
Nitrated	Acetate	0.25	+0.9
Original	Succinate [c]	0.25	+1.9
Acetylated	Succinate [c]	0.25	+2.0
Nitrated	Succinate [c]	0.25	+1.6
Original	Dibasic phosphate [c]	0.25	+2.8
Acetylated	Dibasic phosphate [c]	0.25	+2.6
Nitrated	Dibasic phosphate [c]	0.25	+2.8
Original	Fluoride	0.25	+1.1
Acetylated	Fluoride	0.25	+1.3
Nitrated	Fluoride	0.25	+1.4

[a] Data of Bello et al. (117).
[b] At pH 7 unless otherwise noted.
[c] At pH 8.9.

aging T_g was found to have been lowered by 8°. The same treatment of a carboxyl-esterified gelatin led to a melting point reduction in 0.13 M ferric ion corresponding to the 8° molar melting point reduction in 1.0 M ferric ion for the original gelatin. Apparently at low concentration ferric ions coordinate with two or more carboxyl groups, acting as a reversible cross-linking or network-forming agent. It would be interesting to know if optical rotation changes accompany the iron-induced gelation but such data are not available. Bello et al. (117) concluded that, with the exception of iron (III), the neutral salts exert their effects by direct interaction with peptide bonds.

Another indication that the neutral salts might act directly on the peptide bond can be seen in the work of Harrington (119). He examined the specific optical rotation and the rotatory dispersion of gelatins in 2 M potassium thiocyanate and high concentrations of lithium bromide. As indicated in Chapter II, both collagen and gelatin in water or dilute acid have the same value for the Drude constant, $\lambda_c = 220$ mμ, whereas $[\alpha]_D^{25} = -350°$ for collagen and $[\alpha]_D^{40} = -110°$ for gelatin. The gelatin specific rotation at $40°$ supposedly represents the intrinsic residue rotations of the constituent amino acids, with a minimal configurational contribution. Harrington estimated that there was a small residual left-handed asymmetry, in conformity with the *trans* peptide bond configuration and screw sense of poly-L-proline II, in these gelatin systems. In the presence of either thiocyanate or concentrated lithium bromide, as shown in the third and

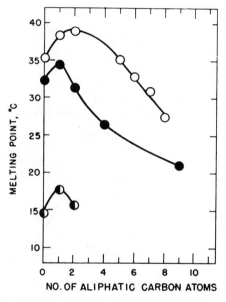

Fig. V-56. Melting point of 5% gelatin containing sodium salts of carboxylic acids; effect of aliphatic chain length: ●, monocarboxylic acids; ○, dicarboxylic acids; ◐, phenyl-substituted monocarboxylic acids. Abscissa is number of aliphatic carbon atoms exclusive of carboxyl groups [Bello *et al.* (*117*)].

fifth columns of Table V-9, there was a decided right-handed contribution to the specific rotation, and possibly a small decrease in λ_c. These data were taken as evidence that the neutral salts brought about *trans-cis* isomerization at the proline-hydroxyproline peptide bonds. However, in view of the later work of Harrington and Sela (*37*) and Steinberg *et al.* (*33*) on poly-L-proline (summarized in Table V-2), the neutral salts probably brought about isomerization at the O=C—C$_\alpha$ bond to form the *trans-cis'* configuration at each proline-hydroxyproline sequence. Bello and Bello (*120, 121*) have deduced from the behavior of *N*-methylacetamide, *N*,

N-dimethylacetamide, and some model peptides in lithium bromide that in concentrated solution the lithium ion probably interacts directly with the carbonyl oxygen in a bond such as

$$—C=O \text{ - - - } Li \text{ - - - } O=C—$$

or

$$—C=O \cdots H—O \text{ - - - } Li \text{ - - - } O—H \cdots O=C—$$

with H atoms above the two O—H oxygens.

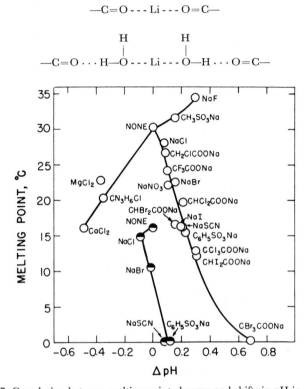

FIG. V-57. Correlation between melting point changes and shifts in pH in a 5% gelatin system. All salts added to make 1 *M* solution. CN₃H₆Cl is guanidinium chloride; ◐, data for amino-acetylated gelatin [Bello *et al.* (*117*)].

while the bromide ion may interact with an amide hydrogen in a complex interaction of the type

$$—C=O \text{ - - - } Li \text{ - - - } O—H \cdots Br \cdots H—N—$$

with an H below the O—H oxygen,

or

$$—N—H \cdots O—H \cdots Br \cdots$$

with an H below the O—H oxygen.

In these diagrams the short dashes represent ion-dipole interactions, the dots represent hydrogen bonds. Much work remains to verify these specific

TABLE V-9 [a]

EFFECT OF LITHIUM BROMIDE AND POTASSIUM THIOCYANATE ON
OPTICAL ROTATORY PROPERTIES OF COLLAGEN AND GELATIN

Material	Solvent system	$[\alpha]_D^{25}$ (degrees)	λc (mμ)	$[\alpha]_D$, configuration (degrees)
Rat tail tendon				
Collagen	Water	—289	217	—200
Gelatin	Water	—118	217	— 30
	LiBr (12 M)	— 35	207	+ 53
Ichthyocol				
Collagen	Citrate (pH 3.7)	—330	204	—240
Gelatin	Citrate (pH 3,7, 41°)	—110	204	— 20
	KSCN (2 M)	— 86	204	+ 4
	LiBr (12 M)	— 56	202	+ 34
Bovine				
Collagen	KCl (0.2 M)	—350	220	—258
Gelatin	KCl (0.2 M)	—146	217	— 54
	LiBr (8.5 M)	— 60	198	+ 32

[a] Data of Harrington (119).

interaction schemes, but it is apparent that specific ion interactions at the peptide bond could prevent the intersegment hydrogen bonding or the water-carbonyl bridge hydrogen bonding required for the stabilization of the collagen-fold.

In contrast to the studies of Bello *et al.* (117), and in line with the hypothesis that collagen-fold formation involves only single peptide chains stabilized by organized water structures, von Hippel and Wong (122) examined neutral salt effects on the rate of formation and stability of the collagen-fold in solutions so dilute that gelation did not take place. Von Hippel and Wong studied a purified acid-soluble carp swim bladder ichthyocol that was essentially all of an α component character. The gelatin concentrations were held to 1–2 mg/ml and, as might have been anticipated (107), even very dilute salts had marked influence on the rate of collagen-fold formation. Heated gelatin solutions were made up at appropriate salt concentration and pH. These were pipetted directly into a cooled polarimeter tube and the optical rotation was measured as a function of time during quenching to 4°. Measurements were begun within 1 minute after the gelatin was charged into the polarimeter tube. Figure V-58 shows the initial rate of mutarotation, $d[\alpha]_{313}/dt$, in degrees per minute during

quenching at various calcium chloride concentrations. As also shown by
Bello et al. (107), von Hippel and Wong (122) found that the final equilibrium value of the specific optical rotation was not dependent on salt concentration when the solutions were aged for many days. Another point
of agreement was that the rate of mutarotation was practically independent
of pH. The exception to this statement, shown in Fig. V-58, was that, at
pH 2.5 and very low calcium chloride concentration, the rate of collagen-
fold formation markedly decreased. This may be due to the fast that hydrogen ions themselves act as melting point reducers, with a higher molar
melting point reduction capability than sodium ions (117). Von Hippel

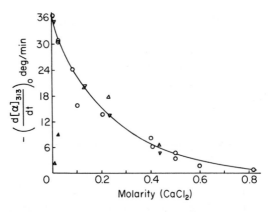

FIG. V-58. Initial rate of mutarotation of ichthyocol gelatin at 4° as a function of CaCl₂
concentration. Quenched from 40° to 4° at zero time. Protein concentration = 1.56 mg/ml;
⊙, CaCl₂ (pH 7); △, CaCl₂ + 0.02 M glycine (pH 2.5); ▽, CaCl₂ + 0.02 M glycine
(pH 10.5) [von Hippel and Wong (122)].

and Wong noted that a plot of $\log d[\alpha]/dt$ vs. the molarity, m, of calcium
chloride was linear over the entire salt concentration range, so that, setting $d[\alpha]/dt = \gamma$, they could represent these data by

$$\log \gamma = \log \gamma_0 + k_0 m \tag{29}$$

in which γ_0 is the rate of fold formation at $m = 0$. Equation 29 was shown
to represent the behavior of all salts examined (Fig. V-59), and the slope
of each line, k_0 (liters/mole), was therefore taken as the characteristic
parameter for comparison of the behavior of the various salts.

After the gelatin solutions had been quenched at 5° for 24 hours, the
solutions were heated by small increments and the transition temperature,
T_m, the temperature of the midpoint between initial and final rotation

values in each case, was determined. It proved to be the case that T_m could also be represented as a linear function of m, such that

$$T_m = T_m^\circ + Km \tag{30}$$

for any particular salt. The slope $K(^\circ\text{C/mole/liter})$, therefore was taken as a measure of the stability of the collagen-fold in a particular salt environment. Table V-10 lists the values of K and k_0 for the various salts in which collagen-fold formation was observed. As is evident from the table,

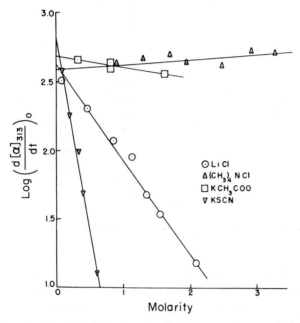

FIG. V-59. Logarithm of initial rate of mutarotation of ichthyocol gelatin at 3° as a function of molarity of added salt; pH 7, protein concentration $\simeq 1.2$ mg/ml [von Hippel and Wong (122)].

and the representation of the same data in Fig. V-60, there was an excellent correlation between K and k_0. This should not have been unexpected, however, since, as von Hippel and Wong pointed out, the melting temperature was measured after a 24-hour quenching period, a time interval which did not correspond to complete collagen-fold formation. In every case, except at the very highest salt concentrations, all of the gelatin-salt systems developed the same final change in $[\alpha]$, $\Delta[\alpha]$, after standing for very long periods, which was independent of the molarity of the particular salt (T_m° differed for different salts). Thus the observed T_m, measured

TABLE V-10 [a]

KINETIC AND EQUILIBRIUM PARAMETERS RELATED TO NEUTRAL SALT
EFFECTS ON COLLAGEN-FOLD FORMATION IN ICHTHYOCOL GELATIN

Salt	K (°C/mole/liter)	k_0 liters/mole
$(NH_4)_2SO_4$	+3.8	+0.12
$(CH_3)_4NCl$	+2.2	+0.04
$(CH_3)_4NBr$	—0.4	—0.08
$K(CH_3COO)$	—0.8	—0.08
NH_4Cl	—	—0.28
RbCl	—	—0.37
KCl	—1.4	—0.42
NaCl	—1.6	—0.41
CsCl	—1.8	—0.52
LiCl	—4.1	—0.66
KBr	—	—0.71
KNO_3	—	—1.03
$MgCl_2$	—	—1.07
$CaCl_2$	—8.8	—1.82
KSCN	—10.0	—2.85
$BaCl_2$	—	—3.23

[a] Data of von Hippel and Wong (122).

at constant gelatin concentration and constant quenching time, would appear to be a rate term, indicative of the fraction of gelatin chain segments potentially capable of being converted to the collagen-fold that were actually converted, rather than a true equilibrium parameter characteristic of the final number of collagen-fold chain segments formed at the quenching temperature. Nevertheless, one may take K as a measure of the molar effectiveness of various salts in reducing the rate of collagen-fold formation. The melting point data of Bello et al. (117) on 5% gels refer to exactly the same type of pseudoequilibrium measurements, and their values can be compared directly with those of von Hippel and Wong (122). Such a comparison is shown in Table V-11. The correspondence between the results obtained for the transition temperatures in dilute solutions and in concentrated gels is quite clear. In making this comparison von Hippel and Wong attributed the small difference between ichthyocol and calf skin gelatins to their different proline and hydroxyproline contens, and pointed to the similarity in amino acid composition of the two mammalian gelatins.

TABLE V-11

COMPARISON OF THE MOLAR EFFECTIVENESS OF VARIOUS SALTS
IN REDUCING THE COLLAGEN-FOLD ⇌ GELATIN TRANSITION TEMPERATURE

Salt	K (degrees/mole added salt)		
	Pig skin [a] (5% gels)	Ichthyocol [b] (0.1% solution)	Calf skin [b] (0.1% solution)
NaSCN	—14.4	—10.2	—14.8
CaCl$_2$	—14.2	— 8.8	—12.8
LiCl	— 5.0	— 4.1	— 6.0
NaCl	— 2.4	— 1.8	— 2.6

[a] Bello *et al.* (*117*).
[b] von Hippel and Wong (*122*).

Von Hippel and Wong (*122*) emphasized that the observation that the change in melting point per mole salt was independent of gelatin concentration was of major importance, demonstrating that the neutral salts must exert their effect on the melting temperature via an intramolecular mechanism. They further concluded that the salts acted "directly on the struc-

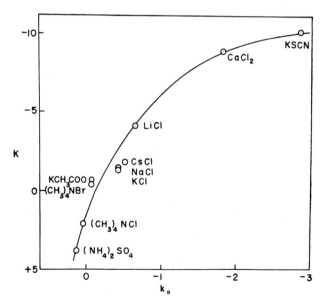

FIG. V-60. Relation between the kinetic parameter, k_0, and the equilibrium parameter, K, for various salts; k_0 measured at ~ 3° [von Hippel and Wong (*122*)].

ture of the collagen-type helix lying *between* cross-links, rather than attack-
ing the interchain cross-links themselves." For the reasons we have considered in previous discussions this statement is difficult to accept, particularly since we have repeatedly seen the correspondence between collagen-
folded chain segments and junction points in gel networks, that is, the
collagen-fold exists at the interchain junctions (cyclic or network-forming)
and is stabilized by the interchain interaction. Keeping this reservation
in mind, we shall, nevertheless, follow in the next few paragraphs the interesting treatment given by von Hippel and Wong to the development of
a detailed mechanism of neutral salt action.

The three possibilities for neutral salt action considered were: (1) a
general electrostatic or ionic strength effect, (2) a specific and direct ion-
protein interaction or binding, and (3) a specific salt effect on the water
associated directly with the gelatin chains. The ionic strength effect was
immediately eliminated because salts of the same valence type altered
both K and k_0 in such widely different ways. Interactions of the salts with
specific side-chain functional grops were also ruled out on the basis of
the data of Bello *et al.* (*107, 117*). The choice thus narrowed quickly to a
consideration of the possibility of direct ion binding to the peptide backbone as suggested by Bello *et al.* (*117*), as compared with the ion-solvent interaction.

Von Hippel and Wong (*122*) described the ion-peptide backbone interaction by an equilibrium constant K_{eq}, such that

$$K_{eq} = \frac{[SG]}{[S][G]} \tag{31}$$

where [S] = concentration of free salt, [G] = molar concentration of
free gelatin binding sites, and [SG] = molar concentration of filled binding sites. Assuming that the binding sites are the peptide bonds, and taking the average residue weight in gelatin as 100, then a 5% gel is 0.5 M
in G and a 0.1% solution is 0.01 M in G. Von Hippel and Wong (*122*)
examined Eq. 31 under four different extreme situations. First, they supposed that both K_{eq} and G were large, that is, that a relatively large fraction of the peptide bonds could bind ions, and that most of these sites were
filled. Such a situation could not lead to the observed non-dependence of
T_m on the gelatin concentration since one should be able to saturate the
effective binding sites with only a small excess of salt. Consequently, this
combination of K_{eq} and [G] would require that the salt concentration at
which helix formation was completely suppressed should vary directly with
gelatin concentration. A second variation, with K_{eq} large and [G] small,

would lead to the same result, since at low gelatin concentrations small amounts of salt should have completely inhibited collagen-fold formation. At the other extreme, one may suppose that K_{eq} is small and [G] is large. In this case, since [SG]/[G] would be small and little affected by the gelatin concentration, the nondependence of T_m on G would be expected. Von Hippel and Wong ruled out this case, however, on the ground that suppression of helix formation was found to go to completion when the salt concentration was of the same order of magnitude as the potential salt binding sites, and that this should not have been possible for the stipulated conditions. This argument would seem to require some knowledge of both K_{eq} and the number of filled binding sites necessary to prevent collagen-fold formation. The final case treated was that of K_{eq} being small with G also small. The interpretation again hinged on the observation that complete suppression of collagen-fold formation can be brought about at any given temperature by addition of neutral salts to gelatin. In other words, it is apparently possible to fill all of the potential binding sites. Von Hippel and Wong interpreted Eq. 31 as stating that the addition of successive aliquots of salt should alter T_m in some manner following a simple adsorption isotherm, the effect per aliquot decreasing progressively with increasing salt concentration. The melting temperature, T_m, should not have been a linear function of m in this instance.

Von Hippel and Wong (122) concluded that ion-binding effects at peptide bonds could not have given rise to the entire set of T_m and initial rate of collagen-fold formation data, and were left with the final proposal that the ions affected the collagen-fold indirectly by interacting with structurally bound water molecules. The particular structural model involved is that proposed by von Hippel and Harrington (41, 43), in which single water molecules form two hydrogen bonds, bridging adjacent carbonyl oxygens along single gelatin peptide chains in the poly-L-proline II configuration. The bridging water molecules, and the barrier to free rotation and, consequently, to isomerization, about the peptide bind combine to "lock" the gelatin chain into the poly-L-proline II structure. Both the hydrogen bond bridges and the peptide bond isomerization have low activation energies and, hence, the configurational stabilization is enhanced as the system temperature is decreased. It was further proposed that "nucleation" of the collagen-fold and the growth of the configuration along the peptide backbone were distinct processes, nucleation occurring only at the proline-hydroxyproline sequences. Qualitatively, the effect of salts is twofold. By preventing organization of the water in general, the neutral salts also inhibit the incorporation of the water into the stabilizing double hydrogen-bond bridge preventing nucleation. In addition, the growth phase is slowed by the same factors.

The data on the initial rate of collagen-fold formation suggested an exponential relationship between the rate of the nucleation step, ν, and salt concentration of the form

$$\nu/\nu_0 = \mathcal{N}^*/\mathcal{N}_0 = e^{k_0 m} \tag{32}$$

where $\mathcal{N}^*$ is the number of active growth nuclei at temperature T and salt concentration m, and $\mathcal{N}_0$ the corresponding number of growth nuclei at T but with $m = 0$. From the fact that no initial lag phase in collagen-fold formation was noted in any case, von Hippel and Wong suggested that all nuclei which were going to grow (exceed their critical size for stability) began to do so at zero time, and that the effect of the salt was to alter the number of active growth nuclei according to Eq. 32. This interpretation assumed that all of the active nuclei, $\mathcal{N}^*$, grow at an initially constant rate. Alternatively, they suggest that the number of nuclei may be unchanged but that the average initial rate is changed in accordance with Eq. 32. The latter interpretation seems more satisfactory, since after very long times the same final fraction of the gelatin is in the collagen-fold configuration at any particular temperature with a given salt, irrespective of its concentration.

There is abundant evidence in the recent literature (80–83, 123) to substantiate the fact that ions do have a profound effect on the properties of liquid water. Liquid water exists in hydrogen-bonded clusters, whose average size depends upon the temperature. Inside the clusters the water is tetrahedrally coordinated in a pentagonal ice-like structure of relatively low density. Nonpolar molecules, and bulky organic ions such as the tetramethylammonium ion, have the effect of increasing the organization of the water, causing a transfer of water molecules at the hydrophobe-water interface into the ice-like phase. Small ions, conversely, attract the water molecules into more dense arrangements at their surface and tend to decrease the amount of water in the ice-like phase. These observations would seem to be in agreement with the ideas of von Hippel and Wong (122), particularly in view of their data (Table V-12) showing that the tetramethylammonium ion raises the melting point, giving positive values of K_{eq} and k_0. In contrast the ammonium ion has little effect, while the lithium ion is very potent in reducing T_m and gives highly negative values for K_{eq} and k_0. The situation is not clear-cut, however, since measurements with tetraethyl-, tetrapropyl-, and tetrabutylammonium ions indicate that

TABLE V-12

Salt	Concentration (molar)	$d[\alpha]_{313}/dt$ (deg/min)
$(CH_3)_4NBr$	1.0	—8.2
$(C_2H_5)_4NBr$	1.0	—2.8
$(C_3H_7)_4NBr$	1.0	0
$(C_4H_9)_4NBr$	1.0	0

[a] Data of von Hippel and Wong (122).

the higher aliphatic homologs have less effect than the tetramethylammonium ion. In fact the latter two ions, as the bromide, completely inhibit
collagen-fold formation at 7°. These data are very similar to the case of
aliphatic organic acids (117) depicted in Fig. V-55.

Bello (124) takes rather sharp issue with the argument that the inhibition of collagen-fold formation by neutral salts cannot be attributed to
ion-binding effects at the peptide backbone. Bello agrees that the two cases
cited by von Hippel and Wong, with K_{eq} large, are correctly analyzed in
terms of Eq. 31, but objects to the conclusions cited for the cases in which
K_{eq} is assumed to be small. The argument is couched in terms of two
questions. What fraction of peptide groups needs to be involved in binding
to inhibit collagen-fold formation? What values of K_{eq} will provide this
fraction of bound peptide groups at the gelatin concentrations concerned?
Bello et al. (116) and Bello and Vinograd (125) had shown that divalent
copper and nickel ions had a very marked effect in drepressing the melting point of 5% gels. As indicated in Fig. V-61, gelation was completely
suppressed in 0.03 M copper (II) solutions. At the point of complete gel
suppression, only about one copper ion is present for every 18 peptide bonds
and each copper is assumed to be either tetra- or penta-coordinated to the
protein, but not bound at the pyrrolidine peptide bonds. Thus, when
only one of every four to five peptide bonds is bound to copper, suppression of collagen-fold formation is complete. Bello (124) pointed out that
this number was in agreement with the studies of Yaron and Berger (126),
demonstrating, with polyprolyl residues grafted to a poly-DL-lysine, that
incipient poly-L-proline II helix formation required at least a pentaprolyl
side chain and that complete helix formation did not occur until six proline
residues were in each side chain. Bello suggested that in gelatin, with only

about one-fourth the residues being proline or hydroxyproline, at least six and possibly a greater number of residues were required to form a stable collagen-fold unit. Further, binding at any particular bond would therefore prevent helix formation in the three to four residues on either side of the residue binding the ion. Thus in considering the binding of independent monovalent ions, Bello concluded that binding of the order of 0.1–0.2 of the peptide bonds might be sufficient to completely suppress collagen-fold formation at 0°. None of the simple salts treated by von Hip-

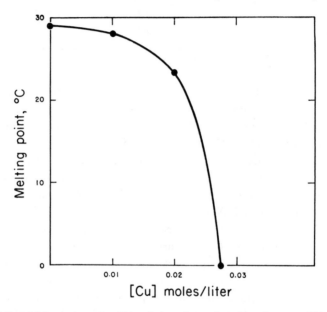

FIG. V-61. Melting points of a 5% gelatin gel as a function of copper (II) at pH 11 [Bello *et al.* (*116*)].

pel and Wong (*122*) had this effectiveness, and therefore the binding, if it existed, need have been much less than this. Using Eq. 31, Bello (*124*) computed [G]/[GS], the ratio of free peptide bonds to salt-bound peptide bonds, for given values of K_{eq}, $[G]_{total}$, and $[S]_{total}$. Some examples are listed in Table V-13. These examples particularly illustrate two points. First, at 1.0 M salt concentration, a value of $K_{eq} = 0.2$–0.3 is sufficient to provide binding in excess of 20–25% at the peptide bonds independent of the gelatin concentration. Binding of this magnitude would supposedly yield complete suppression of collagen-fold formation at 0°. Since the majority of salts listed by von Hippel and Wong were not this effective, Bello suggested that values of K_{eq} of the order of 0.1 could account for

TABLE V-13 [a]

SALT-BINDING RATIOS AT VARIOUS GELATIN CONCENTRATIONS ACCORDING TO EQUATION 31

K_{eq} [b]	Total gelatin peptide bonds (moles/liter)		Total salt (moles/liter)	[G]/[GS]
0.03	1.0	(10% gelatin)	1.0	35
	0.1	(1% gelatin)	1.0	32
	0.01	(0.1% gelatin)	1.0	32
0.10	1.0		1.0	10.7
	0.1		1.0	10.7
	0.01		1.0	10.0
	1.0		0.2	55
	0.1		0.2	49
	0.01		0.2	49
0.20	1.0		1	5.9 [c]
	0.01		1	5.0 [c]
0.30	1.0		1	4.1 [c]
	0.01		1	3.4 [c]

[a] Data of Bello (124).
[b] Assumed value.
[c] Range of site occupancy > 20%.

their data. Second, assuming a K_{eq} of 0.1, the ratio [G]/[GS] is practically constant over the gelatin concentration range examined, possibly explaining the observed nondependence of T_m on $[G]_{total}$.

The argument, that the linearity of T_m as a function of m would not agree with the case of K_{eq} small and $[G]_{total}$ small (122), also does not appear to follow from Eq. 31. Bello (124) plotted the ratio of free peptide bonds to total peptide bonds as a function of $[S]_{total}$ for various values of K_{eq} and $[G]_{total}$ (Fig. V-62). For the lower values of K_{eq} this ratio is essentially a linear function of $[S]_{total}$, as observed. Accordingly, ion-peptide bond interactions cannot be ruled out as an explanation of the effects of neutral salts on the rate of collagen-fold formation.

In spite of its apparent utility, Eq. 31 is obviously a gross simplification. For example, at least two independent equilibria must be involved, since each cation and anion has a characteristic effect as a melting point reducer

and these are additive in any particular case. Hence the binding sites may
be different in each case, and this may be particularly true in comparing
large organic ions with small, high charge-density inorganic ions. Another
oversimplification may lie in the fact that a number of groups on the same
molecule, e.g. peptide bonds, compete for or are in equilibrium with a
given number of free ions. As in other types of multiple equilibria, the bonding affinity at any particular site may be a function of the average number
of ions already bound. Since the system is in a state of dynamic equilibrium, a particular set of binding sites (barring very stable or specific
interactions) is not occupied at all times, the net or average number of

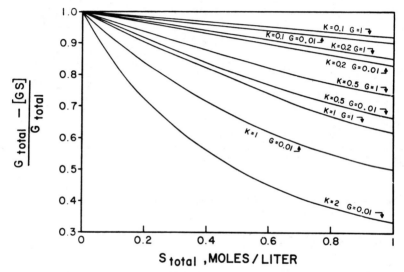

Fig. V-62. The fraction of helical segments intact as a function of total salt (S) concentration for various values of the salt-binding equilibrium constant, K [Bello (124)].

bound ions being shared statistically among all groups with essentially
equal intrinsic binding affinity. Such a picture of the interacting system
may explain the fact, obvious in the work of both Bello *et al.* (107) and von
Hippel and Wong (122), that neutral salts with low binding affinity inhibit the rate of collagen-fold formation during quenching, but do *not* alter
the final equilibrium content of collagen-folded segments, which depends
only on the equilibration temperature. This point alone eliminates the
24-hour T_m data as representing an equilibrium parameter for gelation.
    Suppose that all peptide bonds in gelatin have an equal affinity for a
given pair of salt ions, but that only certain of these peptide bonds in the
vicinity of proline-hydroxyproline sequences can participate in the growth

of collagen-fold nuclei. The presence of a bound ion at such a bond will prevent collagen-fold formation in that particular chain segment, but statistically this bond will be occupied by the salt ion only a fraction of the time, depending on the value of K_{eq} and [S]. During a salt-binding fluctuation the peptide bond may be freed, and the group of chain elements may lock into the more stable collagen-fold by interaction with water molecules or a neighboring chain element similarly free. This would in effect reduce $[G]_{total}$, but, as we have seen in Table V-13, at low K_{eq} the fraction of peptide bonds bound is effectively independent of $[G]_{total}$. More and more collagen-fold-forming bonds would be removed from the competitive ion-binding equilibria at a slower and slower rate, but since the total number of collagen-folded bonds in the typical quenched α-gelatins does not approach 100%, the ion-binding equilibria are maintained throughout the reaction, with progressive involvement of the peptide bonds which cannot be reordered into the collagen-fold for steric reasons. This point of view reinforces the thought expressed earlier, that T_m or T_g, as obtained after only 24-hour quenching, should be viewed as another measure of the rate of collagen-fold formation rather than as a measure of intrinsic collagen-fold stability in a particular salt environment.

As discussed in Chapter I, Flory and Garrett (53) determined equilibrium melting temperatures for both collagen and gelatin in ethylene glycol-water mixtures. They found that the melting point for each material was almost exactly the same at the same solvent medium composition. From this it was concluded that the thermodynamic stability of the crystalline aggregates in gelatin was quantitatively almost identical with that in native collagen. The latent volume changes in the melting of the gelatin gels, however, were much smaller than in the melting of collagen, and obviously the degree of crystallinity of the gelatin was low. These data suggest that once a stable collagen-fold segment is formed, its intrinsic stability is comparable to that of a similar-size segment in the native tri-helical structure. In this light, we should consider one additional parameter, that has not yet been examined quantitatively, the sharpness of the melting transition zone. Almost every investigator who has determined the melting point of gelatins has noted that the temperature range over which melting occurred was substantially broader than that observed for collagen denaturation. It is tempting to relate sharpness of the melting transition to stability of the collagen-fold in the particular environment under which melting occurred. However, it seems more likely that the breadth of melting range refers primarily to the average size of collagen-fold segments. This can be seen most clearly by comparing Figs. V-63 and 64. Figure V-63 shows the data of von Hippel and Wong (*122*) on specific rotations of ichthyocol gelatins as a function of temperature and calcium chloride concentration. As salt concentration is increased, T_m decreases and the range over which melting can be observed increases. Figure V-64 shows similar data of Doty and Nishihara (*127*), comparing the melting transitions of three soluble collagens of obviously different stability due to their differing chemical composition. These three collagens cover a wider range of melt-

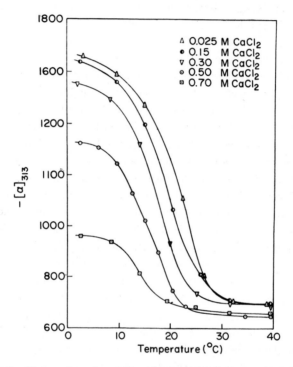

Fig. V-63. Specific rotation of samples of ichthyocol gelatin at various $CaCl_2$ concentrations as a function of temperature, after 24 hours at 5°; pH 7; protein concentration = 1.6 mg/ml [von Hippel and Wong (*122*)].

ing temperatures than that occasioned by addition of calcium chloride to the ichthyocol gelatin, yet even the cod skin collagen exhibited a very sharp denaturation temperature transition range. The sharpness of the melting range, therefore, is probably a measure of the activation energy for the melting transition and this, in turn, is probably related to the average size of the collagen-folded segment. Since melting of the collagen-fold structure is a cooperative phenomenon, the larger the organized structure, the higher the activation energy and the more abruptly melting sets in.

As defined by von Hippel and Wong (122), T_m is the temperature read from a plot of some structurally related parameter at the value of that parameter half-way between its initial and final values. As indicated in Fig. V-63, the final value for the specific rotation of gelatin in the disordered state is practically independent of salt concentration, whereas the initial value, corresponding to the degree of folding, is dependent on salt concentration. The less sharp transition range resulting from the low activation energy of the smaller collagen-folded regions therefore lowers the position of the temperature at the transition midpoint. Again we see that T_m is a kinetic rather than a true thermodynamic parameter. This is borne out

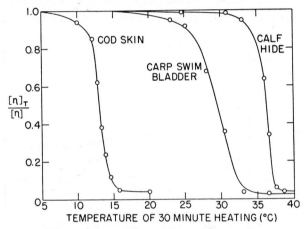

FIG. V-64. The collagen-gelatin transition as represented by the intrinsic viscosity of solutions heated for 30 minutes at temperature shown on abscissa. The intrinsic viscosity values are divided by the constant value observed at temperatures below the transition. Soluble collagens from three sources are shown [Doty and Nishihara (127)].

further by von Hippel and Wong's observation that in the transition region very long time periods were required to achieve a stable value for the optical rotation, a stable value being a reading that did not change more than 0.002° (direct instrument reading) in 30 minutes. A definitive experiment to show whether T_m was a valid measure of the intrinsic stability of a collagen-fold unit would be to determine T_m and the sharpness of the melting transition as a function of salt concentration after the gelatin solutions had attained their maximal collagen-fold content upon prolonged aging. Then $\Delta[\alpha]_{transition}$ would be the same in each case, and any difference in T_m would have to be ascribed to changes in the effect of the environment on the intrinsic stabilizing energy of the collagen-folded segments.

C. Nonaqueous Solvent Systems

Very little attention has been given to the properties of gelatin in non-aqueous systems although the use of nonaqueous solvents presents many interesting possibilities for varying the behavior of gelatin solutions. The limited work reported indicates that there are two distinct classes of non-aqueous solvents with respect to their effect on collagen-fold formation. The work of Flory and Garrett (53) on collagen and gelatin in ethylene glycol, discussed in detail in Chapter I and elsewhere in the present chapter, indicates that melting and collagen-fold formation take place in much the same fashion as in water. Folded, organized gelatin segments can be reversibly broken and reformed in ethylene glycol, and the identity of the

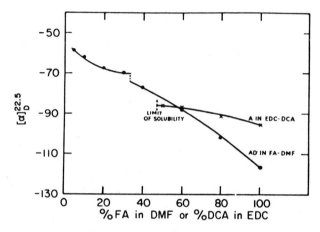

Fig. V-65. Specific rotation of gelatin as a function of the nonaqueous solvent composition: ●, in formic acid (FA)–dimethyl formamide (DMF) mixture; ×, in dichloroacetic acid (DCA)–ethylene dichloride (EDC) mixture. The notations A and AD refer to an acid-precursor gelatin, nondeionized, and a deionized preparation of the same gelatin, respectively [Veis and Anesey (128)].

equilibrium melting temperature of a refolded gelatin-ethylene glycol gel is identical with that of native collagen in ethylene glycol. Thus the collagen-fold units formed in ethylene glycol must have the same *trans-trans'* conformation at imide linkages as in aqueous systems. More interesting are mixed solvent systems such as formic acid–dimethyl formamide (128) and formic acid–*n*–propanol (33).

Veis and Anesey (128) examined the specific rotation of gelatin at constant concentration at varying mixing ratios of formic acid (FA) and dimethyl formamide (DMF) and found, as illustrated in Fig. V-65, that

$[\alpha]_D$ assumed more positive values as the DMF content was increased. In 100% FA, $[\alpha]_D^{25.5}$ was $-116°$, characteristic of gelatin in the random form. At the lower limit of gelatin solubility in 5% FA–95% DMF, $[\alpha]_D^{25.5}$ had decreased to $-58°$, similar to the value observed by Harrington (119) for gelatin in 8.5 M lithium bromide. Steinberg et al. (33) similarly found an $[\alpha]_D$ of $-59.8°$ for bovine gelatin in 12% FA–88% n-propanol solution. In both cases it was suggested that the decrease in rotation was the result of a conformational change about the bonds joining the pyrrolidine rings, leading to a poly-L-proline I type structure due to trans → cis isomerization (128) or due to rotation about the C_α—C=O bond (33).

Veis and Anesey (128) noted that there was a rather abrupt configurational transition at a solvent composition corresponding to a 1 : 1 mole ratio of FA to DMF. When DMF is in excess, the viscosity rises sharply, Fig. V-66, indicating that asymmetric structures are formed. Light scattering molecular weight determinations showed that the viscosity increase could not be ascribed to aggregation even at FA concentrations as low as 5%. The viscosity increase noted when FA was increased so that FA/DMF > 1 was interpreted as a typical polyelectrolyte effect arising from FA salt formation with the basic groups on the protein and, possibly, direct binding of FA at peptide bonds. Measurements of conductivity and viscosity of FA-DMF mixtures definitely suggest that the reaction

$$\begin{array}{c} CH_3 \\ \diagdown \\ N—C \\ \diagup \quad \diagdown \\ CH_3 \quad\quad H \end{array} \overset{O}{\diagup} + HO—\overset{O}{\overset{\|}{C}}—H \rightleftharpoons \left[\begin{array}{c} CH_3 \\ \diagdown \\ N=C \\ \diagup \quad \diagdown \\ CH_3 \quad\quad H \end{array} \overset{OH}{\diagup} \right]^+ + [O—\overset{O}{\overset{\|}{C}}—H]^-$$

takes place. When FA is in excess, the dielectric constant is increased from 26 to 57 and the salt dissociation constant is increased by a factor of 100. Peptide bonds can probably react to form salts in the same fashion. The formation of such ions at the peptide bond would facilitate the isomerization required to go from the normal collagen-fold form to the poly-L-proline I type of structure.

When the gelatin was precipitated from an FA-DMF mixture by adding a large excess of DMF and then washed with more DMF to remove all traces of FA, the final precipitate was found to be water-insoluble. About one-third of the precipitate dissolved in aqueous potassium thiocyanate at 40°, but the soluble gelatin had a higher molecular weight than the orginal gelatin. Unfortunately, the optical rotation of this aggregated and possibly form-I gelatin was not measured. The DMF-precipitated gelatin was readily soluble in FA, and after solution and dialysis to form an aqueous acid-free system the gelatin behaved normally. It would obviously be very interesting to pursue the behavior of aqueous form-I gelatin solutions in more detail.

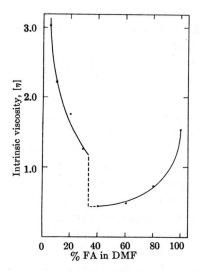

FIG. V-66. Intrinsic viscosity of gelatin in formic acid–dimethyl formamide mixtures [Veis and Anesey (128)].

V. RHEOLOGY OF GELATIN GELS

At the gel point, p_c, as defined by Eq. 20, a continuous network is formed throughout a polymer system. Even if the chain segments between or at junction points have no intrinsic rigidity, the network structure immediately takes on a new mechanical property, it resists deformation. The resistance to deformation for gelatin gels generally follows Hook's Law and is characterized by a shear modulus or modulus of rigidity, G, for small deformations. G is the ratio of shear stress to shear strain, where shear stress is the force per unit area producing lateral motion, and shear strain is the lateral displacement per unit height or its equivalent, the angular deformation (true only for small angles). Since the strain is dimensionless, G has the units of force per unit area. G is related to Young's modulus, Υ (linear elasticity), by the equation

$$\Upsilon = 2G(1 + \sigma) \tag{33}$$

in which σ is Poisson's ratio, the ratio of transverse contraction of a body per unit dimension to elongation per unit length when subject to a tensile stress. Poisson's ratio has a value near 0.5 so that, to a good approximation, $\Upsilon = 3G$. For an aqueous system with density near that of water the minimum rigidity must be of the order of 10^3 dynes/cm² to resist deformation by gravitational forces.

The rigidity and elasticity which develop upon network formation in linear polymer systems have been examined by many investigators, most particularly in terms of the behavior of gum rubber and vulcanized or cross-linked rubber. Flory (129) has reviewed these developments in detail. Qualitatively, the resistance to deformation exhibited by a gel may be considered to arise from two sources, the entropy decrease accompanying the decreased randomness of chain segments in the deformed or perturbed network, and the increase in internal energy of the system occasioned by reordering of the environment of the random chain segments. The behavior of gelatin gels has been analyzed in terms of these two potential effects.

Finally, it has been observed that stressed or deformed gels gradually require less stress to be maintained at a given strain or deformation. This phenomenon, known as stress relaxation, is a measure of internal reorientation of junction points within the network. Useful insights may be gained by considering the stress relaxation in gelatin gels.

The static rigidity of a gel may be measured in a number of ways. Gels cast in the form of bars, strips, or cylinders may be stretched (130, 131) or bent. Alternatively, such cylinders may be compressed (132). These simple measurements yield Young's modulus but present some difficulties experimentally in terms of the method used to support or confine the gels. Another early technique yielding G directly was utilized by Sheppard et al. (133). These investigators rotated a cylinder of gel at constant speed from one end. The other end to the gel was supported by a plate to which a restoring torque could be applied. The torque required to deform the gel could be measured from zero strain up to the point where the gel ruptured. These measurements require that the gel dimensions be known precisely. Similar data have been obtained more conveniently by using a concentric cylinder apparatus (134–138). In the apparatus described by Schremp et al. (136), the gel was formed between coaxial stainless steel cylinders separated by a gap of 0.125 inch. The outer cylinder could be rotated through a small angle, θ_A. The inner cylinder was suspended by a very stiff torsion wire from which a very small distortion angle, θ_B, could be determined. The static rigidity was computed from the equation

$$G = \frac{k\,\theta_B}{b\,(\theta_A - \theta_B)} \tag{34}$$

The torsion constant, k, was known from the instrument calibration with known torques, and the constant b was related to the dimensions of the concentric cylinders. In the experiments of Miller et al. (137) with this apparatus, θ_A was of the order of 0.015 radian, θ_B was usually less than 0.0005 radian. In addition to providing values for G this apparatus also permitted ready determination of the stress relaxation. Miller et al. held θ_A constant and followed the change in θ_B with time. Since $\theta_B \ll \theta_A$ and the strain was proportional to $(\theta_A - \theta_B)$ (Eq. 34), the observed change in θ_B represented the stress relaxation at constant strain. Kinkel and Sauer (135), on the other hand, held the torque constant in a similar apparatus and measured the resulting creep or flow and permanent deformation of the gel as a function of time at constant stress.

Saunders and Ward (139) determined G by setting a gelatin gel in a glass tube. The gel column was sufficiently long to adhere firmly to the wall of the glass tube and prevent slip. Air pressure was applied at one end and the volume displacement of mercury along a capillary tube at the other end was a good measure of the distortion at the gel meniscus. The shear stress was a maximum at the wall and zero at the gel cylinder axis. This method was adapted from an apparatus devised by Kinkel and Sauer (135).

The dynamic rigidity was measured by Ferry and his colleagues (10, 140–143) from the velocity of propagation of transverse waves through the gel. In this case the wavelength of the transverse vibration is determined by observing the strain double refraction at various frequencies. If v is the velocity, λ the wave length, ν the frequency, and ϱ the density of the gel, then

$$G = v^2\varrho = \nu^2\lambda^2\varrho \tag{35}$$

Ferry and Eldridge (10) found no evidence for any frequency dispersion of the rigidity.

A. Rigidity and Gelatin Concentration

The early investigations of the rigidity–gelatin concentration relationship all showed remarkable agreement in concluding that G was very nearly proportional to c^2 over a very wide range of gelatin concentration and for a variety of gelatins (130, 131, 144), of reasonably high (but unspecified) molecular weight. Both Sheppard and Sweet (144) and Kinkel and Sauer (135) found highly degraded gelatins to deviate from this rule, with the concentration exponent becoming greater than 2.

Ferry (*142*) and Ferry and Eldridge (*10*) examined the concentration dependence of the rigidity of some well-characterized gelatins at constant ionic strength (0.15 M sodium chloride), pH (7.0), and fixed temperature. Ferry (*142*) reported that at a given temperature $G^{1/2}/c$ was a constant in the gelatin concentration range 2.3–5.75 gm/100 ml. The subsequent studies (*10*) indicated some deviation from the c^2 rule at lower gelatin concentration. This was confirmed by Saunders and Ward (*139*), who examined the rigidity of a high molecular weight alikali-precursor calf skin gelatin over the range from the minimum concentration required for gelation after aging the gelatin solution at 10° for 17 hours to a maximum concentration of 25% gelatin. Their data (Fig. V-67), also showed that relatively minor

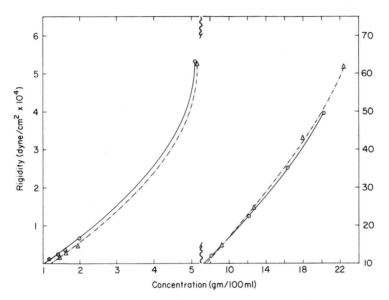

FIG. V-67. Gel rigidity as a function of gelatin concentration; ⊙, deionized gelatin; △, gelatin containing normal ash content [Saunders and Ward (*139*)].

concentration of salts decreased the rigidity at high gelatin concentration. The two lowest concentration points in Fig. V-67 cover the range examined by Ferry and Eldridge (*10*). The same type of deviation from linearity in the G-c^2 plot was noted for an acid-precursor pig skin gelatin (*139*). At very high gelatin concentration (> 20–30%) the deviations become positive rather than negative (*138*).

B. Rigidity and Molecular Weight

Ferry (*142*) and Ferry and Eldridge (*10*) determined the rigidites of a series of low molecular weight gelatins prepared by hydrolytc degradation of a high molecular weight alkali-precursor ossein gelatin. The weight-average molecular weights, computed from osmotic pressure data as described in Chapter IV, were 33,400–72,100. At any particular temperature and constant concentration there was a direct linear relationship, depicted in Fig. V-68, between $G^{1/2}$ and M_w. G increased by a factor of almost 20 as M_w doubled at constant temperature. From these data, Ferry and Eldridge (*10*) deduced the empirical relationship

$$\frac{G^{1/2}}{c} = 1.22 \times 10^{-4} [M_w - 3.1 \times 10^{10} \exp(-7900/RT)] \qquad (36)$$

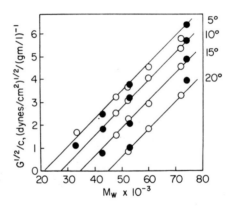

FIG. V-68. Relationship of rigidity to molecular weight at various temperatures for low molecular weight gelatins. Open and filled circles represent independent experiments [Ferry and Eldridge (*10*)].

Ferry (*142*) examined mixtures containing equal weight concentrations of gelatins with known rigidities. The mixture rigidity, at all temperatures, was found to be the average of values of G to the one-half power rather than the arithmetic average of G. $(G)^{1/2}$ is thus a function of the weight-average molecular weight of the gelatins in this low molecular weight range, as implied by Eq. 36.

Saunders and Ward (*139*) examined a series of gelatins of higher molecular weights in which fractions of varying weight were obtained from undegraded high molecular weight gelatins by coacervation fractionation. These data showed that, at temperatures substantially lower than the gel melting point, the rigidity was practically independent of the molecular weight for any particular gelatin preparation. The molecular weights in this case were taken as being proportional to the intrinsic viscosity of the gelatin fraction at 40°. Degradation of the gelatin by enzymes, or by hydrolysis at pH 1.7 and 60°, indicated, as illustrated in Fig. V-69, that there was a definite "rigidity plateau" over a wide molecular weight range (145), beginning with gelatins having an intrinsic viscosity greater than 0.4. The low molecular weight gelatins examined by Ferry (10, 142) would fit the rapidly increasing, low viscosity portion of the curve in Fig. V-69. Courts

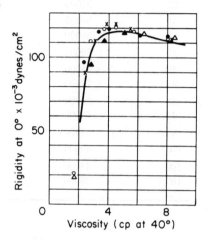

FIG. V-69. Rigidity of various gelatins as a function of molecular weight over an extended weight range. The gelatins were prepared from a common high molecular weight gelatin by enzymatic or acid degradation as indicated: $\triangle$, $\blacktriangle$, papain (0–20 hr); $\bigcirc$, trypsin (0–23 hr); $\bullet$, chymotrypsin (0–23 hr); $\times$, pepsin (0–9 hr); solid line, acid degraded (pH 1.7, 60°) [Saunders and Ward (145)].

(146) determined the average chain weights of similar fractionated and variously degraded gelatins by his end-group analysis technique, and attempted to correlate these average chain weights, C_n, with rigidity measurements of 5.65% gels at 10°. In a series of fractions prepared from the same gelatin, Courts verified that the rigidity at low temperature was practically independent of C_n and of the intrinsic viscosity (range 0.4–0.92). It must be pointed out, however, that there was also no correlation between C_n and viscosity in this range; all gelatins gave C_n values of 55,000–70,000. When gelatins of varying origin were compared it was evident that each gelatin had a different rigidity plateau, and that there was no correlation between plateau rigidity and either C_n or viscosity. The rigidity plateau values are listed in Table V-14 in relation to the two parameters C_n and

TABLE V-14 [a]

CORRELATION BETWEEN PLATEAU RIGIDITY AND MOLECULAR PARAMETERS FOR GELATINS
OF DIFFERENT ORIGIN

Pretreatment of ossein [b]	Extraction temperature (°C)	Plateau rigidity (dynes/cm²)	C_n	LVN
NaOH, Na₂SO₄	55	99000	74000	52
	65	95000	85000	53
Ca(OH₂)₂	55	94000	72000	48
	65	89000	77000	43
NaOH, Na₂SO₄	75	78000	73000	76
Ca(OH)₂	75	76000	80000	51
	85	71000	73000	54
NaOH, Na₂SO₄	85	66000	69000	81
	95	65000	62000	68
Ca(OH)₂	95	51000	73000	62
NaOH, Na₂SO₄	100	49000	66000	82
Ca(OH)₂	100	43000	81000	80
	100	26000	59000	45

[a] Data of Courts (146).
[b] For 16 days at 20°.

LVN, the logarithmic viscosity number (equivalent to 100 $[\eta]$), and the pretreatment and extraction conditions. The same situation is evident in Fig. V-70, in which the rigidity–intrinsic viscosity relationship is compared for two gelatins at two temperatures. Once again it can be seen that the complete history of a gelatin preparation is an absolute necessity in order to relate its behavior to that of other gelatins. A particular gelatin and its fractions and degradation products will generally exhibit a consistent pattern of characteristic properties; however, the behavior of a second gelatin preparation of similar viscosity or average molecular weight but of different extraction history will not duplicate the pattern of the first gelatin upon similar treatment. More detailed molecular weight *distribution* data are probably required for adequate comparison.

C. Rigidity and Temperature

The conclusions drawn in the previous section were restricted to those situations in which rigidities were measured at temperatures well below the gel melting point and at relatively high gelatin concentration. At gelatin concentrations of the order of 2% a rigidity–molecular weight plateau could not be observed even at 0° (*141*). Similarly, as the temperature of measurement approached the gel melting point a rigidity plateau could not be detected even at 11%. In spite of these complexities in the molecular weight–concentration–rigidity relationships, Ferry and Eldridge (*10*) found that the temperature dependence of the rigidity was independent of the gelatin molecular weight. Thus, in Fig. V-68, plots of $G^{1/2}/c$ vs. M_w

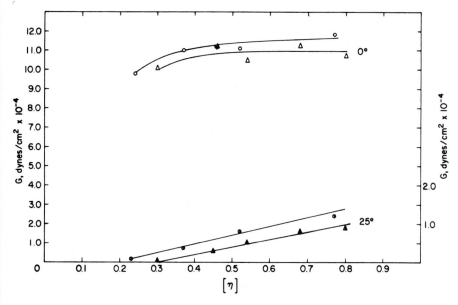

Fig. V-70. Effect of the history of extraction and pretreatment on the rigidity-intrinsic viscosity relationship for two "similar" gelatins: ○, ◐ acid-precursor gelatin; △, ▲ alkaliprecursor gelatin; left-hand ordinate refers to 0°; right-hand ordinate to 25° [Taken from data of Courts (*146*)].

at several temperatures form a family of straight lines of constant slope. The exact form of the temperature dependence is given by the exponential term in Eq. 36. Implicit in the use of $G^{1/2}/c$ in Eq. 36 is the fact that the temperature dependence of the rigidity should be independent of gelatin concentration. The data of Ferry (*142*) (Fig. V-71), confirm this point, showing a superposition of rigidity-temperature data obtained at six different gelatin concentrations.

Having found the rigidity–molecular weight maxima on plateaus for high molecular weight gelatins, Saunders and Ward (*145*) questioned the validity of Ferry's findings (*10, 142*) for the higher weight gelatins. As indicated earlier, Ferry's gelatins were prepared by hydrolytic degradation rather than fractionation and, therefore, were thought by Saunders and Ward to contain low molecular weight components incapable of participating in gel formation. Saunders and Ward therefore examined the rigidity-temperature behavior of a series of well-characterized fractions obtained by alcohol coacervation from a first-extract limed ox hide gelatin.

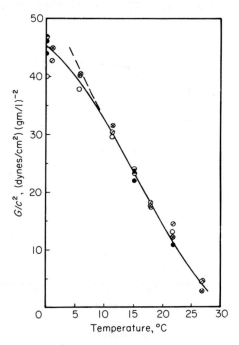

FIG. V-71. Temperature dependence of the rigidity as a function of gelatin concentration. Gelatin concentrations in gm/liter: ○, 57.5; ●, 46; ◐, 40; ◓, 34.5; ⊗, 25; ◖, 23 [Ferry (*142*)].

Their data, assembled in Table V-15, are not strictly comparable with that of Ferry and Eldridge (*10*), as the gels were aged at different temperatures for different periods in the two studies. However, plots of these data as $G^{1/2}$ vs. M_w (Fig. V-72) indicate an entirely different behavior than that indicated in Fig. V-67, with the $G^{1/2}$ vs. M_w relationship a definite function of temperature in the molecular weight range 50,000–150,000. Another point worthy of note is that in each G vs. M_w or $G^{1/2}$ vs. M_w plot there is a maximum in G, and the molecular weight at which the maximum is observed is shifted to higher and higher molecular weights as the temperature is increased. One interpretation of these data which readily comes to mind is that the character of the gel network varies with molecular weight in such a way that the networks formed at higher molecular weight and low temperature are finer and less well organized, although containing more (small) network junction points, than the less entangled lower molecular weight gelatins. However, the melting temperatures, listed in Table V-15, are higher for the higher molecular weight gelatins, indicating more collagen-fold units, and the optical rotation data also quoted are in agreement. Thus the fraction of the gelatin chains in collagen-fold form does not appear to uniquely determine the gel rigidity.

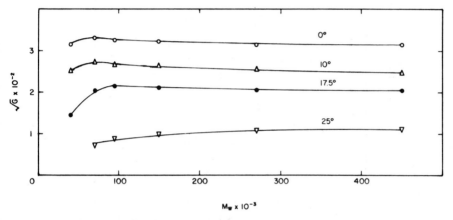

FIG. V-72. Relationship of rigidity to molecular weight at various temperatures for a series of gelatin fractions from a common gelatin extract. In the low molecular weight range $G^{1/2}$ is a decided function of M_w and temperature (taken from data of Saunders and Ward (*145*)].

In the discussion of gel melting points, the dependence of T_g on annealing, tempering, or aging of the gel was emphasized. Similarly, Ferry (*98*) found that rigidity was a function of age of the gel and annealing temperature, but that this was less pronounced an effect than with either T_g or optical rotatory power of the gel. For example, annealing a 4.17% gel at 15° for 24 hours rather than at 0° for 24 hours caused a decrease in T_g from 30.2° to 29.0°. The rigidity of the 0° tempered gel at 15° was 3.85 $\times$ 10⁴ dynes/cm². The corresponding value for the 15° tempered gel at 15° was 2.78 $\times$ 10⁴ dynes/cm². However, when the temperature was raised to only 19° both gels (with different melting points) had identical rigidities and this held true to within a few degrees of the lower melting temperature.

TABLE V-15 [a]

RIGIDITY OF LIMED OX HIDE GELATIN FRACTIONS AND RELATED PARAMETERS

Gelatin fraction molecular weight (weight-average)	$[\ln \eta_{rel}/c]_{40°}$	Gel m.p. [b]	Rigidity [b] (G at indicated T) (dynes/cm² × 10⁻³)			
			0°	10°	17.5°	25°
450,000	1.01	32.2	99	62	42	12
270,000	0.81	31.0	100 (−323) [c]	64 (−300)	43	11.5 (−213)
150,000	0.64	30.2	105 (−314)	69 (−290)	44	10 (−196)
95,000	0.53	30.0	106	71	46	8
70,000	0.44	28.8	109 (−309)	74 (−290)	42	5 (−190)
40,000	0.31	26.0	100	63	41	0
Unfractionated						
190,000	0.62	30.7	112 (−314)	72 (−295)	46	11.5 (−208)

[a] Data of Saunders and Ward (145).

[b] At 0°, 5.8% gel, 18-hour aging.

[c] Figures in brackets represent values of $[\alpha]_D^t$, pH 5.9.

D. Stress Relaxation

Using a coaxial cylinder apparatus, Miller *et al.* (*137*) determined the static rigidities of the low molecular weight gelatins whose rigidities had been previously determined by the dynamic method of velocity of propagation of transverse waves (*10*). The static rigidities, measured over a period of several minutes, were identical within experimental error with the dynamic rigidities measured at several hundred cycles second. Thus, there were no elastic mechanisms with relaxation times between 10^{-3} and 10^{2} seconds that were contributing to the rigidity.

The stress relaxation was determined in the same apparatus. A gelatin solution warmed at 37° for at least 1 hour to erase its thermal history was introduced into the annular space. Some appropriate cooling schedule was applied to reduce the gel rapidly or slowly to the desired temperature; the gel was then aged and stressed and the stress relaxation observed. Two cooling schedules were used. In the first series the initial rate of cooling to the measurement temperature was varied, but the aging period was held constant. In the second series all initial cooling rates were constant, but the aging time at which stress was applied was varied. The nature of the data in each case is illustrated in Fig. V-73 and 74, respectively. In the first case, variable cooling rate and constant aging time, the static rigidity was the same in each case within the experimental precision, but the relaxation times varied. The more rapidly the gel was cooled to the measurement temperature, the more *slowly* the gel appeared to relax un-

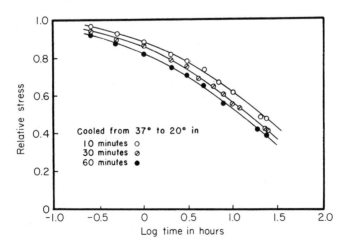

FIG. V-73. Stress relaxation of gels as a function of cooling rate. Gels cooled from 37° to 20° over the periods indicated and then aged for 24 hours [Miller *et al.* (*137*)].

der stress. On the other hand, variation of aging time after uniform cooling caused major changes in both initial static rigidity and rate of stress relaxation. Although the three plots of Fig. V-74 appear to be different, Miller *et al.* (*137*) showed that all of the data, plotted as relative stress vs. log $t/t_{1/2}$, fell on the same curve, the shape of which was determined by the aging temperature. The half-time for stress relaxation, $t_{1/2}$, the time required for the relative stress to fall to one-half its initial value, was therefore taken as the characteristic parameter for the relaxation process, and considered to be the inverse of the average rate of network bond rupture.

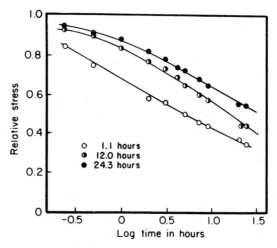

FIG. V-74. Stress relaxation of gels cooled at a uniform rate but aged at 16.2° for the periods indicated [Miller *et al.* (*137*)].

Plots of $t_{1/2}$ vs. aging time are shown in Fig. V-75. In spite of these evident differences in $t_{1/2}$, the rigidities were not nearly so markedy a function of aging. For example, at 20.2° G increased by 15–20% upon increasing the aging period from 12 to 24 hours. In contrast, $t_{1/2}$ increased by 65% in the same time interval. The relative constancy of the rigidity signifies that the total number of gel network junction points is increasing slowly and only to a small extent during the annealing process. Thus stress relaxation is accompanied by rapid reformation of unstressed network junction points of noncyclic character. Strengthening of the gels via annealing is seen to proceed more rapidly at high temperature than at low temperature [$(t_{1/2})T_1 > (t_{1/2})T_2$ when $T_2 > T_1$].

The concentric cylinder apparatus permitted one more type of measurement. After stress relaxation had been allowed to proceed for a speci-

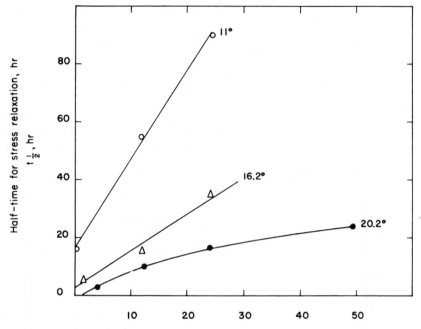

Fig. V-75. The half-time for stress relaxation as a function of the aging temperature [taken from data of Miller *et al.* (*137*)].

fied period, the gel could be stressed in the opposite direction and the re-laxation time of bonds formed during the annealing process could be de-termined. Figure V-76 shows such reverse relaxation data plotted as relative stress vs. log $t/t_{1/2}$, along with the initial relaxation data. At each tempera-ture the forward and reverse relaxation plots had the same shape and were superimposable. Miller *et al.* (*137*) concluded from this that the bonds formed during annealing were similar in distribution of strength and dis-tribution of relaxation times to the bonds formed in comparably aged un-stressed gels. The viscoelastic mechanisms associated with the annealing and stress-relaxing process appear to have relaxation times of 10^3–10^6 seconds at low temperature. These times shift to shorter values as the temperature approaches T_g.

E. Rigidity and Solvent Environment

While several investigations of the relationship between solvent compo-sition and gel rigidity have described, particularly in the early literature, the data are of relatively little use in terms of interpreting gelation on a molecular level. The most often quoted work is that of Gerngross (*147*), who found that the rigidity of an alkali-precursor gelatin following a standard low temperature aging process was independent of pH of the gel over a considerable range. At 10% gelatin concentration, G was constant from pH 4.4 to 9.0. As the gelatin concentration was decreased, the pH range of constant G was reduced on the high pH side of the isoelectric point (pH ∼ 5). More recently Cumper and Alexander (*138*) examined the rigidity of a 2.7% gel of an alkali-precursor gelatin at a rather marginal temperature for gelation, 25°. The gels were cooled to 25° and aged at that

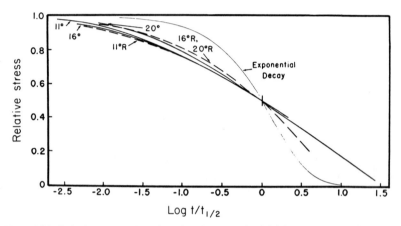

FIG. V-76. Relative stress plotted against log $t/t_{1/2}$ for initial and reverse relaxations at various temperatures, compared with the corresponding plot for simple exponential decay of stress [Miller *et al.* (*137*)].

temperature. Under these conditions gelation was a slow process and it is not surprising that a pH-rigidity dependence was observed. The rigidities are plotted vs. pH in Fig. V-77. These data are reminiscent of the pH-T_g data of Figs. V-51 and 52, which indicate marked pH dependence of the melting point for low concentration gels. As in that case, it is likely that the pH dependence of rigidity could be ironed out by tempering or prolonged aging of the gels. The data of Cumper and Alexander, however, indicate that the rate of gel network formation is greatest in the range pH 5–8, whereas the melting point data of Bello *et al.* (*107*) imply the opposite behavior. The data are too sparse to indulge in argument on this point.

At pH 5.0 the rigidity of dilute gels at 25° was found to vary with the ionic strength, (I) (*138*). In sodium chloride the direct relationship

$$G = G_0 \left[1 - 0.77 \, (I)^{1/2} \right] \tag{37}$$

was found to hold from zero ionic strength up to concentrations as high as 3.0 M. The maximum rigidity, G_0, was found to be that of the deionized gelatin at its isoionic pH.

Various alcohols (*144*), sugars (*132, 144*), and glycerine (*132, 144*) all have been found to increase the modulus of rigidity. Formaldehyde cross-linking also increased rigidity (*132*). In each of the above cases the data are not sufficiently detailed for further evaluation.

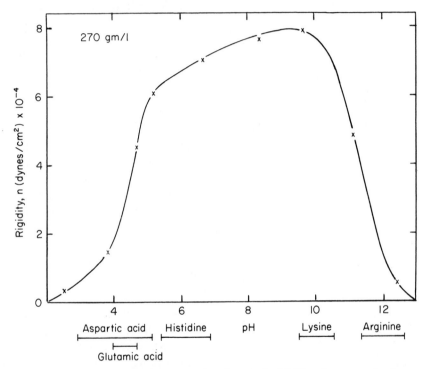

Fig. V-77. Rigidity of gelatin gels as a function of gels pH. Titration ranges for the various functional groups are indicated along the pH abscissa [Cumper and Alexander (*138*)].

F. Rigidity and Collagen-Fold Formation

All the conditions which apply to the development of the collagen-fold seem also to apply to the development of rigidity in a gelatin gel. Up to this point, however, a clear-cut relationship between the two properties has not been drawn. Indeed, the data of Saunders and Ward (*145*), presented in Table V-15, raise some serious questions. The specific rotations did not correlate with gel rigidities. While the deviations are small, the differences between various G's in a given series and between corresponding $[\alpha]_D$

values were greater than the deviations that could be ascribed to experimental error.

Todd (*148*) specifically examined the relationship between rigidity and specific optical rotatory power in three very similar high molecular weight alkali-precursor gelatins. A 5.5% solution of each gelatin at pH 7.0 was prepared at 40°; one portion was used to fill a polarimeter tube, another portion to fill a rigidity tube of the type described by Saunders and Ward (*139*). Each device was then subjected to an identical quenching and heating schedule. The quenching rapidly reduced the temperature to 0°, and after 24-hour aging the 0° reading was taken. Subsequent heating was carried out in 10° steps and measurements were made after 3 hours at 10, 20, and 30° and after 65 minutes at 40°. At the three intermediate temperatures Todd found both G and $[\alpha]_D$ to be changing slowly and approximately linearly with time. Readings were taken at various time intervals and extrapolated to the 3-hour value. The three gelatins all had intrinsic viscosities between 0.61 and 0.64 at pH 7 and 40° in 1.0 M sodium chloride. In spite of this similarity, there was a striking difference in rotatory power of each gelatin at each temperature below 40°, and a variation of 5° in T_g (Fig. V-78). There was a correpondingly large deviation in the values for G at any particular temperature. The best correlation between these data was obtained in a plot of $[\alpha]_D$ vs. $G_{1/2}$ (Fig. V-79). Todd's conclusion was that the modulus of rigidity of a gelatin gel is determined by the amount of chain folding and that "the 'rigidity factor' defines the capacity of a gelatin molecule to fold in a regular fashion." If one were to plot the data of Table V-15 on the same graph, those data referring to the unfractionated gelatin would fit the correlation line very nicely, that is, as well as Todd's own data. However, the data cited for the fractions form a set of parallel lines and only data for the fraction with intrinsic viscosity of 0.64 (fraction 3) fall directly on the Todd plot. Interestingly, the unfractionated gelatin examined by Saunders and Ward (*145*) also had an intrinsic viscosity of 0.62.

If we take the specific optical rotation of a gelatin as being the parameter which directly measures the fraction of gelatin in the collagen-fold configuration, then, from the "fraction" data of Saunders and Ward (*145*), we can conclude that high molecular weight gelatins form the collagen-fold more readily and to a greater extent than lower molecular weight gelatins. On the other hand, according to the theory outlined by Ferry (*98*), the rigidity can be considered as a measure of the number of network junction points in the gel. Consequently the decrease in G above a critical value of M_w, noted by Saunders and Ward and verified by Pouradier et al. (*149*),

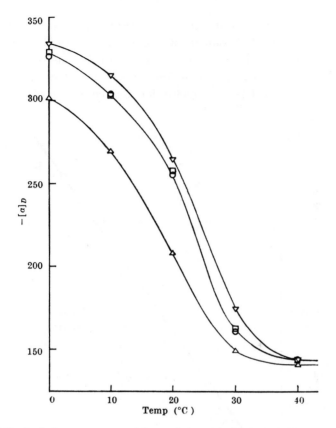

Fig. V-78. Optical rotatory power of three gelatins of similar intrinsic viscosity as a function of temperature [Todd (*148*)].

signifies a decrease in network-forming properties for the higher molecular weight gelatins. Taken together, these arguments imply that the very high molecular weight gelatins ($M_w > 10^5$) tend to form cyclic or non-network-forming chain segments with the collagen-fold configuration. Gelatins with molecular weights greater than the weight of an α chain must, of necessity, be of multichain character with covalent cross-linkages joining the peptide strands. As shown earlier, chain juxtaposition in the region of a cross-link enhances collagen-fold formation and regeneration of the collagen structure. This type of folding can be considered as cyclic, removing chain segments from potential use in network junction points and competitively inhibiting the development of rigidity. Writing the relationship found by Todd as

$$[\alpha] = CG^{1/2} + I \tag{38}$$

we can interpret the constant C as a measure of the cross-link content (and cyclic collagen-fold content) of a particular gelatin. The second constant, I, is a measure of the intrinsic residue rotation and will depend on the source and amino acid composition of the gelatin. The larger the value of C, the smaller will be the rigidity for a given degree of collagen-fold formation.

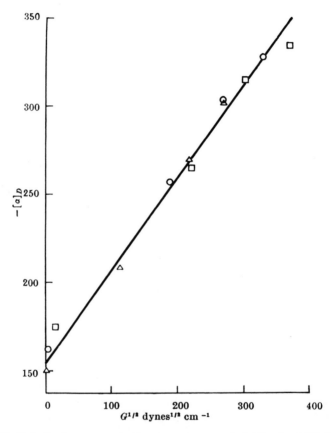

FIG. V-79. Relation between optical rotatory power and rigidity for 5.5% gels. The different symbols indicate the specific gelatins depicted in Fig. V-78 [Todd (*148*)].

Courts (*150*) has used the viscosity rather than optical rotation as a measure of the reversion of gelatin to the collagen-fold form. One interesting result was that the citrate ion was found to have a special effect in promoting the viscosity increase in dilute gelatin solutions upon cooling from 40° to 20° as compared with acetate and lactate ions at comparable ionic strength and pH. There was a pH dependence of the viscosity increase which was accentuated by aging (Fig. V-80). In plots of viscosity as a function of time at 20°, Courts noted that after an initial rapid increase in relative viscosity over a period of about 1 day, there was a second, lower velocity stage of viscosity development during which η_{rel} was linear with time. This linear phase covered 7 or 8 days of gel maturation. The slope of the line, r, was taken as the characteristic parameter for collagen-fold formation, and was expressed in arbitrary viscosity units per day. Courts

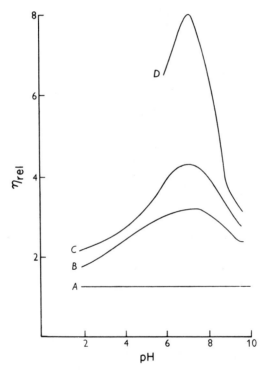

Fig. V-80. Effect of pH on the increase in gelatin viscosity brought about by the presence of citrate ion. The effect of aging is also shown: (A) initial, zero time pH–viscosity relation; (B) after 1 day; (C) 2 days; (D) 4 days [Courts (*150*)].

determined r for a number of gelatins of varying character and then determined the modulus of rigidity for each of the gelatins at 5.65% concentration and 10° after the gels were matured at 10° for 18 hours. As illustrated in Fig. V-81, Courts found that the gelatins with the greater rate of viscosity increase in citrate also had the higher rigidities. A plot of log G vs. log r was linear, indicating a relationship of the type

$$G = K r^\alpha \tag{39}$$

Under the particular gel aging conditions and with the viscosity units utilized, K was found to have a value of $93,500 \pm 2,000$, and α was 0.15. Every gelatin studied, regardless of its origin, fitted Eq. 39 with the indicated values of the constants.

Courts found that there was no relationship between r and intrinsic viscosity of the gelatins examined, but pointed out that r was smallest for gelatins with the highest intrinsic viscosity. Since these high viscosity, low r gelatins also had very low rigidities, Courts concluded that the relation-

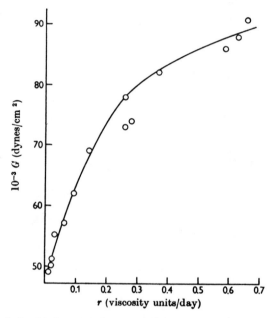

Fig. V-81. Relationship between the rate of viscosity increase, r, in citrate systems and the rigidity modulus, G, for various gelatins [Courts (*150*)].

ship between G and r expressed in Eq. 39 indicates that both the viscosity increase and rigidity are governed by the same factor, the extent to which the molecules can become organized in helical form. On the basis of his earlier work (*146*) (Table V-14), demonstrating that G was maximal for gelatins when $M_w/C_n = 1$ and decreased as M_w/C_n became greater than 1, Courts (*150*) proposed that single-chain molecules not only gave the greatest rigidity, but that single-chain gelatins, showing in this study the greatest rate of viscosity increase, also formed the collagen-fold most readily. This conclusion ignores the data relating to cyclic collagen-fold formation in multichain gelatins (*59, 66, 72, 76, 78*).

The electrostatic factor in collagen-fold formation, which was proposed earlier but largely ignored in this discussion, is evident in the work of Janus (*151*). In experiments paralleling those of Bensusan et al. (*88*) with collagen aggregation, Janus guanidinated a moderate molecular weight gelatin and then determined the setting rate and 24-hour, 0° rigidity of the gels produced from gelatins with different degrees of guanidination. There was rapid increase in setting rate with increasing guanidination when the modified gelatins were compared with gels formed from unmodified gelatin of equivalent molecular weight. However, there was no increase in rigidity of the tempered gels with increasing guanidination. Electrostatic interactions of a very localized nature would appear to be playing an important role in directing the orientation of the apolar regions into configurations which permit the organization of interchain collagen-fold units.

REFERENCES

1. K. Herrmann, O. Gerngross, and W. Abitz, Z. *Physik. Chem.* **B10**, 371 (1930).

2. J. R. Katz, J. C. Derksen, and W. F. Bon, *Rec. Trav. Chim.* **50**, 725 (1931).

3. J. R. Katz and J. C. Derksen, *Rec. Trav. Chim.* **51**, 513 (1932).

4. E. M. Bradbury and C. Martin, *Proc. Roy. Soc.* **A214**, 183 (1952).

5. E. J. Ambrose and A. Elliott, *Proc. Roy. Soc.* **A205**, 47 (1951).

6. E. J. Ambrose and A. Elliott, *Proc. Roy. Soc.* **A206**, 206 (1951).

7. E. J. Ambrose and A. Elliott, *Proc. Roy. Soc.* **A208**, 75 (1951).

8. C. Robinson and M. J. Bott, *Nature* **168**, 325 (1951).

9. C. Robinson, *in* "Nature and Structure of Collagen" (J. T. Randall, ed.), p. 96. Butterworths, London, 1953.

10. J. D. Ferry and J. E. Eldridge, *J. Phys. Chem.* **53**, 184 (1949).

11. O. Gerngross, K. Herrmann, and R. Lindemann, *Kolloid-Z.* **60**, 276 (1932).

12. C. R. Smith, *J. Am. Chem. Soc.* **41**, 135 (1919).

13. R. Pinoir and J. Pouradier, *Compt. Rend.* **227**, 190 (1948).

14. K. H. Gustavson, "The Chemistry and Reactivity of Collagen". Academic Press, New York, 1956.

15. P. M. Cowan and S. McGavin, *Nature* **176**, 501 (1955).

16. P. M. Cowan, S. McGavin, and A. C. T. North, *Nature* **176**, 1062 (1955).

17. A. Berger, J. Kurtz, and E. Katchalski, *J. Am. Chem. Soc.* **76**, 5552 (1954).

18. J. Kurtz, A. Berger, and E. Katchalski, *in* "Recent Advances in Gelatin and Glue Research" (G. Stainsby, ed.), p. 131. Pergamon Press, New York, 1958.

19. E. R. Blout and G. D. Fasman, *in* "Recent Advances in Gelatin and Glue Research" (G. Stainsby, ed.), p. 123. Pergamon Press, New York, 1958.

20. W. Sakami and G. Toennies, *J. Biol. Chem.* **144**, 203 (1942).

21. K. H. Meyer and Y. Go, *Helv. Chim. Acta* **17**, 1488 (1934).

22. C. H. Bamford, L. Brown, E. M. Cant, A. Elliott, W. E. Hanley, and E. R. Malcolm, *Nature* **176**, 396 (1955).

23. F. H. C. Crick and A. Rich, *Nature* **176**, 780 (1955).

24. A. B. Meggy and J. Sikorski, *Nature* **177**, 326 (1956).

25. E. M. Bradbury, R. E. Burge, J. T. Randall, and G. R. Wilkinson. *Discussions Faraday Soc.* **25**, 173 (1958).

26. J. M. Bijvoet, A. F. Peerdeman, and A. J. van Bommel, *Nature* **168**, 271 (1951).

27. V. Sasisekharan, *Acta Cryst.* **12**, 897 (1959).

28. P. M. Cowan and R. E. Burge, discussion *in* "Recent Advances in Gelatin and Glue Research", The British Gelatin and Glue Research Association, G. Stainsby, ed. London, 1958, p. 16.

29. W. F. Harrington and P. H. von Hippel, *Advan. Protein Chem.* **16**, 16 (1962).

30. J. Kurtz, G. D. Fasman, A. Berger, and E. Katchalski, *in* "Recent Advances in Gelatin and Glue Research" (G. Stainsby, ed.), p. 270. Pergamon Press, New York, 1958.

31. V. Sasisekharan, *Acta Cryst.* **12**, 903 (1959).

32. J. Kurtz, A. Berger, and E. Katchalski, *Nature* **178**, 1066 (1956).

33. I. Z. Steinberg, W. F. Harrington, A. Berger, M. Sela, and E. Katchalski, *J. Am. Chem. Soc.* **82**, 5263 (1960).

34. I. Z. Steinberg, A. Berger, and E. Katchalski, *Biochim. Biophys. Acta* **28**, 647 (1958).

35. D. D. Fitts and J. G. Kirkwood, *Proc. Natl. Acad. Sci. U. S.* **42**, 33 (1956).

36. D. D. Fitts and J. G. Kirkwood, *J. Am. Chem. Soc.* **78**, 2650 (1956).

37. W. F. Harrington and M. Sela, *Biochim. Biophys. Acta* **27**, 24, (1958).

38. A. R. Downie and A. A. Randall, *Trans. Faraday Soc.* **55**, 2132 (1959).

39. L. Pauling and J. Sherman, *J. Chem. Phys.* **1**, 606 (1933).

40. A. Berger, A. Loewenstein, and S. Meiboom, *J. Am. Chem. Soc.* **81**, 62 (1959).

41. P. H. von Hippel and W. F. Harrington, *Biochim. Biophys. Acta* **36**, 427 (1959).

42. P. H. von Hippel and W. F. Harrington, *in* "Protein Structure and Function," *Brookhaven Symp. Biol.* **13**, 213 (1960).

43. W. F. Harrington and P. H. von Hippel, *Arch. Biochem. Biophys.* **92**, 100 (1961).

44. J. Herman, Jr. and H. A. Scheraga, *Biochim. Biophys. Acta* **36**, 534 (1959).

45. R. E. Burge, P. M. Cowan and S. McGavin, in "Recent Advances in Gelatin and Glue Research" (G. Stainsby, ed.), p. 25. Pergamon Press, New York, 1958.

46. A. Rich and F. H. C. Crick, *J. Mol. Biol.* **3**, 483 (1961).

47. M. A. Rougvie and R. S. Bear, *J. Am. Leather Chemists' Assoc.* **48**, 735 (1953).

48. E. M. Bradbury, R. E. Burge, J. T. Randall, and G. R. Wilkinson, *Discussions Faraday Soc.* **25**, 173 (1958).

49. N. G. Esipova, N. E. Andreeva, and T. V. Gatovskaia, *Biofizika* **3**, 529 (1958).

50. H. J. C. Berendsen, *J. Chem. Phys.* **36**, 3297 (1962).

51. G. N. Ramachandran, V. Sasisekharan, and Y. T. Thathachari, *in* "Collagen" (N. Ramanathan, ed.), p. 81, Wiley (Interscience), New York, 1962.

52. P. J. Flory, *in* "Protein Structure and Function," *Brookhaven Symp. Biol.* **13**, 229 (1960) (discussion of paper by von Hippel and Harrington, *42*).

53. P. J. Flory and R. R. Garrett, *J. Am. Chem. Soc.* **80**, 4836 (1958).

54. P. J. Flory and E. S. Weaver, *J. Am. Chem. Soc.* **82**, 4518 (1960).

55. E. T. Dumitru and R. R. Garrett, *Arch. Biochem. Biophys.* **66**, 245 (1957).

56. C. E. Weir, *J. Am. Leather Chemists' Assoc.* **44**, 108 (1949).

57. L. Mandelkern, *Chem. Rev.* **56**, 903 (1956).

58. H. B. Bensusan, private communication (1963).

59. J. Engel, *Arch. Biochem. Biophys.* **97**, 150 (1962).

60. H. Boedtker and P. Doty, *J. Am. Chem. Soc.* **78**, 4267 (1956).

61. N. T. Crosby and G. Stainsby, *Nature* **190**, 80 (1961).

62. A. Veis, D. N. Eggenberger, and J. Cohen, *J. Am. Chem. Soc.* **77**, 2368 (1955).

63. A. Veis and J. Cohen, *J. Am. Chem. Soc.* **78**, 6238 (1956).

64. A. Veis, J. Anesey and J. Cohen, *in* "Recent Advances in Gelatin and Glue Research" (G. Stainsby, ed.), p. 155. Pergamon Press, New York, 1958.

65. A. Veis and J. Cohen, *J. Phys. Chem.* **62**, 459 (1958).

66. A. Veis and J. Cohen, *Nature* **186**, 720 (1960).

67. A. Veis, J. Anesey, and J. Cohen, *J. Am. Leather Chemists' Assoc.* **55**, 548 (1960).

68. A. Veis, J. Anesey, and J. Cohen *Arch. Biochem. Biophys.* **94**, 20 (1961).

69. A. Veis, J. Anesey, and J. Cohen, *Arch. Biochem. Biophys.* **98**, 104 (1962).

70. J. Gross and D. Kirk, *J. Biol. Chem.* **233**, 355 (1958).

71. J. Engel, *Z. Physiol. Chem.* **328**, 94 (1962).

72. K. Altgelt, A. J. Hodge, and F. O. Schmitt, *Proc. Natl. Acad. Sci. U.S.* **47**, 1914 (1961).

73. K. A. Piez, M. S. Lewis, G. R. Martin, and J. Gross, *Biochim. Biophys. Acta* **53**, 596 (1961).

74. M. P. Drake and A. Veis, *Federation Proc.* **21**, 405 (1962).

75. M. P. Drake, Ph.D. Dissertation, Northwestern University, 1962.

76. A. Veis and M. P. Drake, *J. Biol. Chem.* **238**, 2003 (1963).

77. M. P. Drake and A. Veis, *Biochemistry* (1964) in press.

78. A. Veis and J. T. Legowik, *Abstr. 7th Ann. Meeting Biophys. Soc., New York, ·1963* TA13.

79. O. K. Spurr, Ph.D. Dissertation, Cornell University, 1958.

80. I. M. Klotz, *Science* **128**, 815 (1958).

81. G. Némethy and H. A. Scheraga, *J. Chem. Phys.* **36**, 3382 (1962).

82. G. Némethy and H. A. Scheraga, *J. Chem. Phys.* **36**, 3401 (1962).

83. G. Némethy and H. A. Scheraga, *J. Phys. Chem.* **66**, 1773 (1962).

84. W. Grassmann, K. Hannig, and M. Schleyer, *Z. Physiol. Chem.* **322**, 71 (1960).

85. H. B. Bensusan and B. L. Hoyt, *J. Am. Chem. Soc.* **80**, 719 (1958).

86. H. B. Bensusan and A. W. Scanu, *J. Am. Chem. Soc.* **82**, 4990 (1960).

87. H. B. Bensusan, *J. Am. Chem. Soc.* **82**, 4995 (1960).

88. H. B. Bensusan, V. W. Mumaw, and A. W. Scanu, *Biochemistry* **1**, 215 (1962).

89. G. C. Wood and M. K. Keech, *Biochem. J.* **75**, 588 (1960).

90. G. C. Wood, *Biochem. J.* **75**, 598 (1960).

91. G. C. Wood, *Biochem. J.* **75**, 605 (1960).

92. J. Gross and D. Kirk, *J. Biol. Chem.* **233**, 355 (1958).

93. I. M. Klotz and J. Franzen, *J. Am. Chem. Soc.* **84**, 3461 (1962).

94. J. A. Gordon and W. P. Jenks, *Biochemistry* **2**, 47 (1963).

95. M. Levy and J. P. Magoulas, *J. Am. Chem. Soc.* **84**, 1345 (1962).

96. H. Boedtker and P. Doty, *J. Phys. Chem.* **58**, 968 (1954).

97. G. L. Beyer, *J. Phys. Chem.* **58**, 1050 (1954).

98. J. D. Ferry, *Advan. Protein Chem.* **4**, 1 (1948).

99. J. E. Eldridge and J. D. Ferry, *J. Phys. Chem.* **58**, 992 (1954).

100. G. Scatchard, J. L. Oncley, J. W. Williams, and A. Brown, *J. Am. Chem. Soc.* **66**, 1980 (1944).

101. W. H. Stockmayer, *J. Chem. Phys.* **11**, 45 (1943); **12**, 125 (1944).

102. G. Oster, *Rec. Trav. Chim.* **68**, 1123 (1949).

103. D. J. Lloyd, *Biochem. J.* **16**, 530 (1922).

104. W. B. Pleass, *Proc. Roy. Soc.* **A126**, 406 (1930).

105. E. O. Kraemer and J. R. Fanselow, *J. Phys. Chem.* **29**, 1169 (1925).

106. E. O. Kraemer and S. T. Dexter, *J. Phys. Chem.* **31**, 764 (1927).

107. J. Bello, H. R. Bello, and J. R. Vinograd, *Biochem. Biophys. Acta* **57**, 214 (1962).

108. A. Veis, J. Anesey, and J. Cohen, *in* "Recent Advances in Gelatin and Glue Research" (G. Stainsby, ed.), p. 155. Pergamon Press, New York, 1958.

109. O. O. Blumenfeld and P. Gallop, *Biochemistry* **1**, 947 (1962).

110. P. Grabar and J. Morel, *Bull. Soc. Chim. Biol.* **32**, 643 (1950).

111. J. Moul and P. Grabar, *J. Chim. Phys.* **48**, 632 (1951).

112. P. Davis, *in* "Recent Advances in Gelatin and Glue Research" (G. Stainsby, ed.), p. 225. Pergamon Press, New York, 1958.

113. P. Davis, *Trans. Faraday Soc.* **53**, 1390 (1957).

114. A. Berger, J. Kurtz, and J. Noguchi, *in* "Recent Advances in Gelatin and Glue Research" (G. Stainsby, ed.), p. 271. Pergamon Press, New York, 1958.

115. J. Bello, *Trans. Faraday Soc.* **55**, 2130 (1959).

116. J. Bello, H. R. Bello, and J. R. Vinograd, *Biochim. Biophys. Acta* **57**, 222 (1962).

117. J. Bello, H. C. A. Riese, and J. R. Vinograd, *J. Phys. Chem.* **60**, 1299 (1956).

118. R. S. Gordon, Jr. and J. D. Ferry, *Federation Proc.* **5**, 136 (1946).

119. W. F. Harrington, *Nature* **181**, 997 (1958).

120. J. Bello and H. R. Bello, *Nature* **190**, 440 (1961).

121. J. Bello and H. R. Bello, *Nature* **194**, 681 (1962).

122. P. H. von Hippel and K. Wong, *Biochemistry* **1**, 664 (1962).

123. H. S. Frank and M. W. Evans, *J. Chem. Phys.* **13**, 507 (1945).

124. J. Bello, *Biochemistry* **2**, 276 (1963).

125. J. Bello and J. R. Vinograd, *Nature* **181**, 273 (1958).

126. A. Yaron and A. Berger, *Bull. Res. Council Israel* **A10**, 46 (1961).

127. P. Doty and T. Nishihara, *in* "Recent Advances in Gelatin and Glue Research" (G. Stainsby, ed.), p. 92 Pergamon Press, New York, 1958.

128. A. Veis and J. Anesey, *J. Phys. Chem.* **63**, 1720 (1959).

129. P. J. Flory, "Principles of Polymer Chemistry," p. 432. Cornell Univ. Press, Ithaca, New York, 1953.

130. H. J. Poole, *Trans. Faraday Soc.* **21**, 114 (1925).

131. A. Leich, *Ann. Physik* [4] **14**, 139 (1904).

132. E. Hatschek, *J. Phys. Chem.* **36**, 2994 (1932).

133. S. E. Sheppard, S. S. Sweet, and J. W. Scott, *Ind. Eng. Chem.* **12**, 1007 (1920).,

134. E. Hatschek and R. S. Jane, *Kolloid-Z.* **39**, 300 (1926).

135. E. Kinkel and E. Sauer, *Z. Angew. Chem.* **38**, 413 (1925).

136. F. W. Schremp, J. D. Ferry, and W. W. Evans, *J. App . Phys.* **22**, 711 (1951).

137. M. Miller, J. D. Ferry, F. W. Schremp, and J. E. Eldridge, *J. Phys. Chem.* **55**, 1387 (1951).

138. C. W. N. Cumper and A. E. Alexander, *Australian J. Sci. Res.* **A5**, 153 (1952).

139. P. R. Saunders and A. G. Ward, *Proc. 2nd Intern. Congr. Rheol., Oxford, 1953* p. 284 (1954).

140. J. N. Ashworth and J. D. Ferry, *J. Am. Chem. Soc.* **71**, 622 (1949).

141. J. D. Ferry, *Rev. Sci. Instr.* **12**, 79 (1941).

142. J. D. Ferry, *J. Am. Chem. Soc.* **70**, 2344 (1948).

143. J. D. Ferry, W. M. Sawyer, and J. N. Ashworth, *J. Polymer Sci.* **2**, 593 (1947).

144. S. E. Sheppard and S. S. Sweet, *J. Am. Chem. Soc.* **43**, 539 (1921).

145. P. R. Saunders and A. G. Ward, *in* ."Recent Advances in Gelatin and Glue Research" (G. Stainsby, ed.), p. 197. Pergamon Press, New York, 1958.

146. A. Courts, *Biochem. J.* **73**, 596 (1959).

147. O. Gerngross, *Kolloid-Z.* **40**, 279 (1926).

148. A. Todd, *Nature* **191**, 567 (1961).

149. J. Pouradier, A. M. Venet, and L. Trigny, *Proc. 27th Intern. Congr. Chim. Ind., Bruxelles, 1954*, **3**, 709 (1955).

150. A. Courts, *Biochem. J.* **83**, 124 (1962).

151. J. W. Janus, *in* "Recent Advances in Gelatin and Glue Research" (G. Stainsby, ed.), p. 214. Pergamon Press, New York, 1958.

Author Index

Numbers in parentheses are reference numbers and are included to assist in locating references when the authors' names are not mentioned in the text. Numbers in italics refer to the page on which the reference is listed.

A

Abitz, W., 270, *412*

Abramson, H. A., 110 (66), *124*

Akabori, S., 200 (88), *220*

Alberty, R. A., 6, *44*, 112 (68), *125*

Alburn, H. E., 247 (36), *265*

Alexander, A. E., 391 (138), 393 (138), 404, 405, *416*

Almy, E. F., 240 (18), *264*

Altenschöpfer, T., 176 (50), 177 (50), 179 (50), 180 (50), 182 (50), 185 (50), 198 (50), *219*

Altgelt, K., 144, 147 (16), *218*, 330, 331, 332, 338 (72), 410 (72), *414*

Altman, K. I., 172, *219*, 243, *264*

Ambady, G. K., 11 (47), *45*

Ambrose, E. J., 18 (62), *45*, 119, *125*, 271, 273, *412*

Ames, W. M. 99, 100 (54, 55), 101, 102, 103, 104, 107, *124*, 147, 166, 187, 188, 194, 195 (23), 196, 197, 198 (23), 207, 211, 212 (22), *218*, *219*, 230, 232, 233, 234, 243, *264*

Anderson, R. A., 202, *220*

Andreeva, N. E., 307 (49), 310 (49), 311 (49), 337 (49), *413*

Anesey, J., 7 (20), *44*, 64 (20), 70, 77 (21), 78 (21), 85 (40), 109 (20), 110 (20), 111 (20), 112 (20), 113 (20), 114 (20), 115 (20), *123*, *124*, 144, 147 (14, 30, 32), 148 (32), 159 (30), 160 (14, 30, 32), 161 (14), 162 (32), 163 (32), 164 (14), 165 (14, 15), 191 (30), 192 (30), *218*, 326 (64, 67, 68, 69), 327, 328 (68), 329 (68), 339 (68), 361 (108), 364 (108), 388, 389, 390, *413*, *414*, *415*

Antonin, S., 256, *265*

Archibald, W. J., 85, *124*

Ashworth, J. N., 392 (140, 143), *416*

Astbury, W. T., 117 (71), *125*

B

Baldwin, R. L., 80 (37), 86, *124*

Bamford, C. H., 120, *125*, 277 (22), *412*

Bear, R. S., 2 (3), 11, 19, 23, 30, 31, *44*, *45*, 192, 206 (76), *220*, 306, 311, *413*

Beek, J. Jr., 7 (12, 13), *44*

Bello, H. R., 85 (42), *124*, 361, 362 (107), 363 (107), 364 (107), 365 (107, 116), 366 (116), 367 (116), 371, 373 (107), 374 (107), 378 (107), 381 (116), 382 (116), 384 (107), 404 (107), *415*

Bello, J., 85, 109, *124*, 173, 174, 176, 182, 192, 263, *219*, *220*, *265*, 361, 362, 363, 364, 365, 366, 367, 368, 369, 370, 371, 372, 373 (107), 374 (117), 376, 377, 378, 381 (117), 382, 383, 384, 404, *415*

Benoit, H., 79, *123*

Bensusan, H. B., 8, 28 (25), *44*, *219*, 183, 319, 340, 341, 342, 343 (88), 344 (88), 352 (87), 411, *413*, *414*

Berendsen, H. J. C., 310 (50), 311, 312, 319, 337 (50), *413*

Berger, A., 275, 276 (18), 277 (18), 281 (18), 284 (18, 30), 285 (30), 287 (18, 32, 33), 293 (33), 294 (33), 295 (33), 296 (33), 297 (33, 34, 40), 298 (33), 301 (33), 334 (33), 365, 366, 371 (33), 381, 388 (33), 389 (33), *412*, *413*, *415*

Beyer, G. L., 344, 346, 348, 351 (97), *414*

Bijvoet, J. M., 282 (26), *412*

Blout, E. R., 121 (82), *125*, 276, 280 (19), 281 (19), 283 (19), 286 (19), 287, 288, 289, 290, 297, 300, *412*

Blumenfeld, O. O., 183, 184, 185, *219*, 242, 243, *264*, 365 (109), *415*

417

Subject Index